POINTS OF VIEW

SELECTED PREFACES
AND INTRODUCTIONS

W. SOMERSET MAUGHAM

POINTS OF VIEW

—

SELECTED PREFACES AND INTRODUCTIONS

Published by arrangement with
William Heinemann Ltd.

The illustrations in this book were
reproduced by courtesy of
The Radio Times Hulton Picture Library: facing pp. 30, 162 and 214
The Mansell Collection: facing pp. 74 and 190
The National Portrait Gallery: facing p. 116

Edito-Service S.A., Geneva, Publishers

CONTENTS

POINTS OF VIEW

ACKNOWLEDGEMENTS

The author wishes to thank Messrs Routledge & Kegan
Paul Ltd for permission to quote from *Life and Works
of Goethe* by Professor J. G. Robertson and *Mercure de
France* for permission to quote from *Lettres à ma Mère*
by Paul Léautaud, as well as Messrs Jonathan Cape
Ltd for the quotation from *Between Two Worlds* by
J. Middleton Murry.

NOTE

Mr. Maugham has announced that this is the last book he will ever publish and since he seems to have a way of doing what he says he is going to do, we may safely assume that with this volume of essays he will take his leave of the reading public and so put an end to a relationship that with *Liza of Lambeth* began just over sixty years ago.

CONTENTS

The Three Novels of a Poet

I THINK IT ONLY FAIR to tell the reader of the following pages why, at this time of day, when surely everything that could be said about Goethe has long since been said, I should write an essay on his novels. It has given me pleasure to do so, and if there is a better reason for writing anything I have yet to hear of it. From my earliest years I could speak English and French; as a child, French better than English; and when still in my teens I spent a year in Germany and attended lectures at the University. I learnt German. I had read poetry at school, but as a task. Goethe's lyrics are the first poems I read for my pleasure and it may be that is why, when I read them now, I read them with the same rapture as I did more than half a century ago. I read not only with my eyes, but with the recollections of my youth, Heidelberg with its old streets, the ancient castle, the wooded walk to the top of the Königstuhl and the beautiful plain of the Neckar spread out before one, the skating in winter, the canoeing in summer, the interminable conversations about art and literature, free will and determinism; and first love, though, heaven knows, I never knew it for what it was.

It was during this period that I read the novels of Goethe. I did not read them again till a few years ago when, after a long interval, I began to pay visits to Germany. He wrote three. They are *The Sorrows of Werther*, *Wilhelm Meister's Apprenticeship*, with its sequel, and *The Elective Affinities*. Of these *Wilhelm Meister's Apprenticeship* is the most important and the most interesting. I suppose few people in England read it now, unless for scholastic reasons they are obliged to, and I don't know why anyone should—except that it is lively and amusing, both romantic and realistic; except that the characters are curious and unusual, very much alive and presented with vigour; except that there are scenes of great variety, vivid and admirably described, and at least two of high comedy, a rarity in Goethe's works; except that interspersed in it are lyrics as beautiful and touching as any that he ever wrote; except that there is a disquisition on Hamlet which many eminent critics have agreed is a subtle analysis of the Dane's ambiguous character; and above all, except that its theme is of singular interest. If, with all these merits, the novel on the whole is a failure, it is because Goethe, for all his genius, for all his intellectual powers, for all his knowledge of life, lacked the specific gift which would have made him a great novelist as well as a great poet.

If anyone were to ask me what this specific gift is, I should not know how to answer. It is evident that the novelist must be something of an extrovert, since otherwise he will not have the urge to express himself; but he can make do with no more intelligence than is needed for a man to be a good lawyer or a good doctor. He must be able to tell such story as he has to tell effectively so that he may hold his readers' attention. He need not love his fellow-creatures (that would be asking too much) but he must be profoundly interested in them; and he must have the gift of empathy which enables him to step into their shoes, think their thoughts and feel their feelings. Perhaps Goethe, terrific egoist as he was, failed as a novelist because he lacked just that.

In the following pages I do not propose to tell the story of Goethe's life; but since he said himself that pretty well everything he wrote, except the books devoted to his scientific interests, was in one way or another a revelation of himself, I shall be obliged to give some account of various events of his personal history. When just over twenty, he entered the university of Strasbourg to study law, the profession which, much against his own wishes, his father had decided he should follow. Goethe was then a very comely youth, so comely indeed, that those who saw him for the first time were lost in amazement. He was a little above the middle height, slender, and he held himself so well that he looked taller than he really was. He was of a darkish complexion and he had a fine head of hair, with a natural wave in it; his nose was straight, rather large, and his mouth full and well-shaped; but his magnificent brown eyes, with their unusually large pupils, were his most striking feature. He had immense vitality and a charm that was irresistible. Children doted on him, and he would play with them and tell them stories by the hour together.

After Goethe had been at Strasbourg for some months, a fellow-student suggested that they should ride over to Sesenheim, twenty miles away, to spend two or three nights with friends of his, a pastor, Brion by name, and his wife and daughters. Goethe agreed; they set out and were warmly welcomed. One of the daughters was called Friederike. Goethe fell in love with her at first sight and she with him. How could she fail to? She had never seen anyone so handsome, so charming, and so light on his feet. A new-fangled dance, the waltz. had come to Strasbourg only ten years before and, all the rage had ousted the old-fashioned minuet and gavotte. It was an added attraction that Goethe had learned it and was able to teach her. He loved everything about Friederike, her fair hair and blue eyes, her grace, her simplicity, her activity about the house, the peasant dress she so becomingly wore; and when, forty years later, he dictated an account of the romance in his auto-biography, they say that his emotion made his voice tremble. For some months the lovers were deliriously happy. Goethe wrote a number of poems to Friederike; many were lost, but those that remain attest the fervour of his passion. How far things went none can tell. It is asserted that the idea of marrying her never entered his head. That may be so. Even then, Goethe had that sense of class distinctions which in later life was markedly characteristic of him. He belonged to a well-to-do and respectable family, and he knew, of course, that his father, a stern and self-important man, on whom he was entirely dependent, would never consent to his marriage with the daughter of a penniless country parson. But he was young and in love. We all know that men under the influence of passion say things and make promises which in calmer moments they forget. They are taken aback to discover that the woman they have said them to has remembered and taken them seriously. It is surely not unlikely that Goethe at one time or another had said something to Friederike that led her to believe that he would marry her.

An incident eventually occurred which brought it home to him that, for all her charm and grace, she was little more than a peasant. The Brions had relations in Strasbourg, whom Goethe rather patronisingly describes as "of good position and reputa-tion, and in their circumstances comfortably off". Friederike and her sister, whom he calls Olivia, went to stay with them for a while. The two girls found it difficult to adapt themselves to a mode of life that was strange to them. They, like the servants, wore their peasant dress, whereas their cousins and the ladies who visited them were dressed in the French fashion. They could not but feel themselves out of place in these unaccustomed surroundings, and the cousins, perhaps none too pleased to produce to their friends these poor relations, did nothing to make things easy for them. Friederike bore the embarrassing situation with a certain placidity, but Olivia was deeply affronted. The visit was a dismal failure. "At last I saw them drive away," Goethe wrote, "and it seemed as though a stone fell from my heart, for my feelings had shared the feelings of Friederike and Olivia; certainly I was not passionately harassed like the latter, but I felt in no way comfortable like the former." It is not a pretty story, but it is understandable. If ever he had contemplated marrying Friederike, this experience proved to him that it was out of the question.

He made up his mind that they must part. Since at the time he was working for an examination, he had a decent excuse to go to Sesenheim less frequently. He took his degree and three weeks later left Strasbourg for home. He could not refrain from riding over to see Friederike once more. The parting was painful. "As I reached my hand from horseback, tears stood in her eyes, and I was heavy at heart." He left her, he says, when their parting almost cost her her life; but it looks as though even then he had not had the courage to tell her that it was for good. When at last he did, it was by letter. Friederike's answer, he tells us, rent his heart. "I now for the first time," he wrote, "felt the loss she suffered, and I saw no possibility of supplying it, or of alleviating the pain." He added, rather sourly, that the reasons of a girl who draws back in such a case always appear valid, but those of a man, never. "I had wounded the most beautiful heart in its depths, and so the period of a gloomy remorse, with the want of an animating love, to which

I had grown accustomed, was highly painful, indeed intolerable. But man wishes to live, and so I took a sincere interest in others." The young are able to bear the woes of others with a good deal of fortitude; Goethe was doubly fortunate in that, when his conscience told him that in his treatment of Friederike he had been sadly to blame, he could seek relief in poetry. "I pursued again the traditional poetic confession, so that by this self-tormenting penance I should become worthy of an inward absolution. The two Marys in *Götz von Berlichigen* and *Clavigo* [his first two plays] and the two sorry figures which their lovers cut may well have been the result of such penitent reflections." Had Goethe seduced her? We shall never know. One would think that if there had been no more between them than a violent flirtation his pangs of conscience would have been less persistent. It may well be that Goethe bore Friederike's anguish in mind when he wrote the beautiful and moving song of which the first line runs: *Meine Ruh ist hin, mein Herz ist schwer*; and perhaps, highly susceptible as he was and tremulously sensitive, it was the torture of his remorse that led him to give immortal expression to the tragic story of Gretchen.

But this is only one of the many conjectures that have been made to discover the origins of his greatest work. In no long while he was able to state that his heart was untouched and unoccupied.

2

The Sorrows of Werther was the outcome of another love affair. Six months or so after leaving Strasbourg and breaking with Friederike, Goethe, in order to complete his training as a lawyer, went to Wetzlar. There at a ball he danced with a girl called

Charlotte Buff. She was engaged to be married to a certain Johann Christian Kestner. Goethe fell in love with her there and then. Next day he called on her. Very soon he was seeing her every day. They took walks together, and Kestner, when his occupations left him free, accompanied them. He was a very decent fellow, somewhat matter-of-fact and uncommonly tolerant; but it is plain that, notwithstanding his good nature, Goethe's attention to his betrothed made him at times uneasy. He wrote in his diary, "When I've done with my work and go to see my girl, I find Dr. Goethe there. He's in love with her, and though he's a philosopher and a good friend of mine, he's not pleased when he sees me coming to have a pleasant time with my girl. And although I'm a good friend of his, I don't like it that he should be alone with my girl and entertain her."

A few weeks later he wrote, "Goethe got a good talking-to from Lottchen. She told him that he could not hope for anything more than friendship from her: he went pale and was very depressed. He went for a walk."

Goethe lingered on at Wetzlar through the summer, trying to make up his mind to leave Lotte, but unable to bring himself to do so; and it was not till the beginning of autumn that he at last summoned up the courage to go. He spent his last evening with Lotte and Kestner without disclosing his intention to them, and next morning was gone. He left a despairing letter to Lotte which brought tears to her eyes.

Goethe went back to Frankfort, and there, some weeks later, the news reached him that an acquaintance of his, a young man called Jerusalem, had committed suicide at Wetzlar owing to an unhappy love affair. He immediately wrote to Kestner for full details of the event and made a careful copy of the information thus supplied to him. "At this moment," he wrote in his autobiography, "the plan of *Werther* was found, the whole shot together from all sides and became a solid mass, as water in a vessel which is on the point of freezing is transformed into solid ice by the slightest agitation. To hold fast this strange prize, to keep before me and carry out in all its parts a work of such varied and significant contents was for me so much the more pressing, as I had already fallen into a painful situation, which permitted me less hope than those which had gone before, and foreboded nothing but depression, if not disgust." This refers to the fact that Goethe had again fallen in love. "It is a very pleasant sensation," he wrote, "when a new passion begins to stir within us, before the old one has quite passed away. Thus at sunset we like to see the moon rising on the opposite side, and one takes delight in the double splendour of the two heavenly luminaries." The young woman who occasioned this poetic simile was called Maximiliane de la Roche, and Goethe wrote to her mother: "Your Max I cannot do without as long as I live, and I shall always venture to love her." But a marriage had been arranged for her with a certain Peter Brentano, many years older than herself, a dealer in herrings, oil and cheese, who lived in Frankfort. The ill-suited pair were married and Goethe spent many hours a day in her company. But Peter Brentano was not so easy-going as Johann Kestner, and soon Goethe was forbidden the house.

It was, as his own words show, the news of Jerusalem's tragic death that served as the necessary spark so to kindle Goethe's imagination as to lead to the writing of *The Sorrows of Werther*. It cannot have been long before he saw that by making use of his unhappy love for Lotte Buff, and combining it with the suicide of Jerusalem, with all that had brought it about, he had to his hand the complete material for a novel. He had himself from time to time coquetted with the idea of suicide. Coquetted is the word George Henry Lewes used in his *Life of Goethe* (still readable after well over a hundred years) and I should say it was the right one. It is true that in the autobiography, written fifty years later, Goethe stated that his anguish was such that the temptation to do away with himself was deadly serious and no one could know how great an effort he had to make not to succumb to it. I venture to suggest that, as men, even the most eminent, are apt to do when they recall the past, he somewhat exaggerated. The young Goethe had high spirits, animation and a cheerful temper; but, like many another, he paid for it by periods of depression. At one time he went to bed with a dagger by his bedside and played with the notion of plunging it in his heart. But, of course, it was only a fantasy, such as, I suppose, many a young man has had in moments of dejection. His vitality was far too great for him ever really to determine to put an end to the life he enjoyed so much. But it is not unlikely that it occurred to him that the feelings which had now and then possessed him could be put to good use when he came to describe those of the hero of his novel. At last he began to write it. He used the form of letters, which was popular at the time owing to the novels of Richardson and Rousseau's *La Nouvelle Héloïse*. It is the easiest way for an inexperienced novelist to write a work of fiction. It is out of fashion now; but it has its merits, not the least of which is that it adds a convincing verisimilitude to the facts narrated.

The story of *The Sorrows of Werther* can be told in a few lines. A young man arrives at an unnamed town (Wetzlar, of course) and there meets an attractive girl at a country dance. He falls in love with her, discovers that she is engaged to be married, loves her to distraction and eventually tears himself away. After some time he returns, drawn back by love for her, to find her happily wedded. His passion undiminished, nay, aggravated, so absorbs him that nothing else in the world has meaning for him; and at last, since his love is hopeless, since life without her is intolerable, he shoots himself. The novel, short as it is (it can be read in a couple of hours) is divided into two books. The first ends with Werther's departure; the second begins with his return and ends with his death.

The first book, the reader will see from my account of Goethe's sojourn at Wetzlar, follows the facts very closely. In it Goethe has given his hero his own charm, his gaiety and good humour, his affectionateness, his ease in social intercourse, and his love of nature. In fact he has drawn a very engaging portrait of himself. Goethe wrote an idyll suffused with the poetry of the long summer days and the moonlit nights of that beautiful countryside. You get a pleasant feeling of the uprightness and decency of those simple and amiable people, and of the *Gemütlichkeit* of the life they led in Germany so long ago. You sympathise with Lotte (Goethe had given his heroine Lotte Buff's christian name), so good, so tender, so pretty and such an excellent housewife; you sympathise with her patient, sedate betrothed, whom Goethe called Albert; and you sympathise with Werther for the hopelessness of his love. The first book is a delight to read. It is clearly autobiographical. Now, the autobiographical novel, whether written in the first person or the third, is vitiated by a falsity which is irremediable. This does not consist in the author making himself more resourceful, more gallant and more attractive than he really is, abler and better-looking: that, if he chooses, is his right; he is writing fiction, not history. It consists in his omitting the one characteristic which determines his personality—his creative instinct. It is true that David Copperfield was an author, and a successful one; but it is not an essential element in the narrative; it is the accidental consequence of his circumstances. For all the effect it has on his life, and the story Dickens had to tell, he might just as well have been

16

a civil servant or a schoolmaster. We know that when Goethe found himself in a distressing situation, when he was unhappy and conscience-stricken, he turned to poetry for solace. He had a strong propensity to fall madly in love with any charming girl he ran across; but his mind seethed with the plays and poems he had in mind, and in his heart of hearts, I suggest, they meant more to him than his violent, but ephemeral, passions. Perhaps even, he slightly resented their interference with what was his main preoccupation—to create. There is in the Werther of the first book no such urge. He is a sociable, agreeable, but rather futile dilettante. When at last he brought himself to leave Wetzlar and Lotte, he would have consorted with his friends, consoled himself by writing poetry and fallen in love with somebody else. That, as the reader has seen, is exactly what Goethe himself did.

The second book is pure fiction. Werther is not the man we have come to know in the first. He is a very different one. When this occurred to me I thought I had made an interesting discovery and was rather pleased with myself. But by chance I came across an account of a visit Crabb Robinson had paid Frau Aja, Goethe's mother, and in course of conversation she remarked that the Werther of the first book was Goethe, whereas the Werther of the second was not. Since then so much has been written about this famous novel that the patent fact must have been noted over and over again. In truth, it stares one in the face. From the beginning Goethe had, of course, intended that Werther should commit suicide, and, to prepare the reader, he introduced early on a scene in which Werther, Lotte, and Albert discuss its justification. Lotte and Albert are horrified at the idea, but Werther argues that when a person finds life unbearable, it is his only refuge. He claims that in certain circumstances it is a necessary and courageous act, which should not be condemned, but applauded. Goethe's instinct must have told him that the character he had created in the first book, to whom he had given his own zest for life, would have been, whatever his anguish, no more likely to commit suicide than he himself; he had now to create one that would be irresistibly impelled to it. That is what Goethe did. It was inevitable that the Werther of the second book should turn out to be a very different man from the Werther of the first.

Some time after leaving Wetzlar, on the persuasion of his friends he accepts the post of secretary to a diplomatic representative at one of the German Courts. The Werther to whom we are now introduced is prickly, intolerant, disdainful and quick to take offence. His chief naturally wants letters to be written in his own way, and when Werther writes them in *his* way, he returns them and demands, to his secretary's indignation, that they should be re-written. There was at the time, it appears, a craze among the cultured young to make use of inversions. They thought it added elegance to their style. It was not unreasonable that the envoy, an experienced man of affairs, should regard this as out of place in official documents and prefer to have them written in the 'officialese' to which he was accustomed, rather than in what may be described as 'literatese'. Employer and employee were soon at loggerheads.

Presently an incident occurred which had unfortunate consequences. Werther had made friends with a high official of the Court to which his chief was accredited, and one evening dined with him. His host was giving a party to the nobility and gentry of the town and after dinner went to the drawing-room to receive his guests. Werther accompanied him. As a commoner of no position he had not been invited to the party. The guests arrived, Princes, Counts, Barons, with their ladies, and Werther immediately noticed that they were surprised to see him. He became aware that his presence in that exclusive gathering was creating unfavourable comment; but, with a singular lack of tact, he stayed on. After a while, one of the more important ladies went up to the host and protested; his host sent for him and politely enough asked him to leave. To us this must seem outrageous. One has to remember how great the gulf was at the time in Germany between the aristocracy and the middle class. The news spread quickly through the town that Werther had been guilty of a gross impertinence and had been turned out of the house. He was deeply mortified and a week later sent in his resignation.

A certain Prince, who has taken a fancy to the young man, perhaps out of pity for the humiliation he had suffered invites Werther to accompany him to his estates and spend the spring with him. This Werther does, but after a few weeks comes to the conclusion that the Prince and he have nothing in common. "He is a man of understanding," he writes, "but of quite ordinary understanding; his company entertains me no more than the reading of a well-written book." A supercilious youth! Werther decides to leave and drifts back to the town in which Lotte and Albert, now married, live. Albert appears to have been none too pleased to see him; his affairs obliged him to be absent now and then, and, though he does not openly object, he does not like the idea that Werther should be so much with his wife. Goethe has described Lotte's feelings with subtlety. She knows that Albert resents Werther's presence, and she wishes that he would go and leave them in peace, yet has not the heart to drive him away. She loves and respects her husband, but is more than a little in love with Werther. Christmas approaches. Albert is again absent. Lotte has made Werther promise that he will not attempt to see her while her husband is away, and when, nevertheless, he comes, she reproaches him bitterly for not keeping his promise. It is evening; and so that she should not be alone with him, she sends a message to some friends asking them to look in. They are engaged and unable to. Werther has brought books with him and Lotte suggests that he should read to her. He has made some translations of Ossian, and these he reads. What he reads moves them both, and she bursts into tears. Her tears shatter him and, weeping, he throws his arms round her and passionately kisses her. She is torn between love and anger. She pushes him away. "That's the last time!" she cries. "You shall never see me again." "And then," the author writes, "with a look of deep love at the wretched man, she hurried into the next room and shut herself in." Next day Werther writes a heart-stricken letter to Lotte in which he tells her that he is going to kill himself. He tells her that now at last he knows that she loves him. "You are mine, Lotte, to all eternity." Werther, learning from his servant that Albert has come home, sends him to ask for the loan of his pistols as he is going on a journey. Albert, we may presume relieved to know this, sends them, and early on the following morning Werther shoots himself. The letter to Lotte is found among his effects.

Such, baldly related, is the story of *The Sorrows of Werther*. The final pages, even today, are moving. The book was published and achieved a success that, perhaps, no other novel has had. It was widely read, widely discussed and widely imitated. It was translated into a dozen languages. The only persons who seem to have received the book somewhat coldly were Kestner and Lotte. That they had served as Goethe's models was immediately recognised. Kestner was justifiably annoyed to find himself portrayed as a dull, rather stupid fellow, unworthy of his charming wife, and to have it suggested that she had been in love with Goethe. Many wondered how much fiction there was in the novel, and how much fact. Kestner wrote to protest. Goethe's reply was high-handed. "Could you but realise," he wrote, "the thousandth part of what Werther is to a thousand hearts, you would not reckon the cost it is to you."

When one reads *The Sorrows of Werther* today one can hardly fail to ask oneself what there was in it to cause so great a sensation. I suppose the answer is that it exactly suited what we now call the climate of opinion. Romanticism was already in the air. The works of Rousseau were translated and eagerly read. Their influence was enormous. The young Germans of the day were impatient with the hard and cramping routine of the Age of Enlightenment, and the dryness of the orthodox religion offered nothing to hearts that were yearning for infinitude. Rousseau offered the young just what they craved for. They were only too ready to believe with him that emotion was more estimable than reason and the promptings of the heart nobler than the uncertainties of the mind. They cherished sensibility; it was the mark of a beautiful soul. They despised common sense; it showed want of feeling. Their emotions were uncontrollable; men and women on the smallest provocation burst into floods of tears. The letters they wrote, even of those old enough to know better, were extravagantly gushing. Wieland, a poet and a professor, in his forties, began a letter to Lavater by addressing him as Angel of God, and ended with the words, "If I could only spend three weeks with you! But I feel in advance that you would become too dear to me. I should in actual fact become ill with love; and die, when I had to leave you again." The German commentator of this effusion dryly adds that Wieland frequently visited his friends and left them without falling ill for love of them, and dying. If such was the climate of opinion, it is no wonder that *The Sorrows of Werther* captivated readers. They were touched by the hopelessness of the youth's passionate love; and that Werther, irked by the limitations of life on this earth, should have sought freedom in death aroused in their tender hearts awe and admiration. Werther made Goethe famous, and for many years, whatever else he wrote, he was universally known as the author of this book. Though he lived to old age he never again achieved such an astounding success.

3

The Sorrows of Werther was published in the autumn of 1774. Towards the end of that year a certain Major von Knebel, acting as bear-leader to the two young Princes of Weimar, knocked at the door of Goethe's house and asked to see him. He came with the message that his two charges desired to make the acquaintance of the distinguished author. The acquaintance was made, and the two boys, the elder of whom was not yet eighteen, were enchanted with him. Shortly after this, Goethe was taken by a friend to a party given by a certain Frau Schönemann, a rich banker's widow. She had an only child, a daughter, fair-haired and blue-eyed, who, when Goethe entered the room, was playing the piano. As was his way, he fell in love with her. Before long she loved him too. Their mutual attachment pleased neither her family nor his. Lili Schönemann's belonged to the upper class of Frankfort society and, as an heiress, was expected to make a good marriage. Goethe's grandfather was a tailor, who married the widow of an inn-keeper, and for the rest of his life followed his predecessor's lucrative profession. His son, Goethe's father, received a legal training and acquired the honorary rank of Imperial Councillor, which gave him a social status, but not such as to admit him into the higher ranks of Frankfort society. He was a harsh, austere man, and he was very much against his son's bringing into the house as his bride a young woman of fashion. Lili was sixteen and as was only natural took delight in the pleasures of her age. She loved dancing, parties and picnics. Goethe was not unaware that the gay life she led was not the life for him, but he was too much in love to care. He wrote poems to her, some of the most beautiful he ever wrote; but they have not quite the youthful abandon of those he wrote to Friederike; you feel in them some hint of uncertainty. He was not quite sure of himself, and not quite sure of Lili. Notwithstanding the opposition of their families, however, they became engaged. But no sooner had this happened than Goethe grew uneasy. He was twenty-six, conscious of his great powers, and his zest for life was intense. He had no wish to settle down.

So, after anxious consideration (we may surmise) and, if he gave a thought to Lili's distress, perhaps not without some qualms of conscience, he came to the conclusion that he must destroy his love for her. A happy chance enabled him, as he thought, to do something to effect this. Two young men of rank, the Counts Stolberg, fervent admirers of the poet, came to Frankfort and made friends with him. They were on their way to Switzerland and asked Goethe to join them. He consented. They started off in the costume which Werther had always worn and in which he had left instructions that he should be buried—blue coat, yellow hose and waistcoat, top boots and round grey hats. Goethe left without telling Lili he was going, without a word of farewell, and both she and her family very naturally resented it. It was, to say the least, unmannerly; but there was on occasion something of brutality in the way Goethe treated others. He was curiously insensitive to the pain he caused. The young men made a tour of Switzerland and admired the scenery; but Goethe did not succeed in forgetting Lili. From some touching lines he wrote we know how hungrily he hankered after her. So far as that went, the trip had been a failure.

He returned to Frankfort. From the accounts we have, it is not clear whether the young things still looked upon themselves as engaged. They continued to meet not infrequently. They were still in love. It was evident that something must be done, and Goethe's father, in order that relations between them should be definitely ended, proposed that he should go on a long journey to Italy. That was something that Goethe had long wished to do, and he willingly fell in with the suggestion. But while he was making his preparations, the young Duke of Weimar, who had just married a Princess of Hesse-Darmstadt, on his way home with his bride passed through Frankfort. In the most cordial way he pressed Goethe to come and spend a few weeks at Weimar. The invitation was tempting and, notwithstanding the opposition of his father, who did not approve of his son consorting with Princes, he accepted. A date was fixed. Whether this time Goethe had the grace to tell Lili that he was going, we do not know. We can only guess what *her* feelings were from an incident he has related in his autobiography. One night, a day or two before he was due to set out, he wandered about the streets of Frankfort and presently found himself under Lili's window. She was at the piano, and he heard her singing a song he had written for her not quite a year before. "I could not but think she sang it more expressively than ever," he wrote. "After she had finished singing, I saw by the shadow that fell on the blind that she had risen; she walked backwards and forwards; but in vain I tried, through the thick material of the blind, to catch a glimpse of the outline of her sweet self. Only my firm resolution to depart, not to trouble her with my presence, really to renounce her . . . made me decide to leave a proximity that was so dear to me." Eighteen months later Lili very properly married a wealthy banker.

When Goethe arrived at Weimar it was with the intention of staying no more than a month or two: with occasional absences he spent the rest of his life there. The young Duke was delighted with him and soon the pair were inseparable. They drank together, hunted together, and philandered with the peasant girls they came across on the countryside. The staid officials of the Duchy felt that the dissolute poet was leading their master astray and would have been glad to see him go; but the Duke could not bear to part with him and, to keep him, offered him a seat in the Cabinet, to which a salary was attached, and a cottage on the river to live in. He was well advised to persuade Goethe to settle in Weimar, for he was energetic, competent and resourceful. In time more and more duties were thrust upon him, and he performed them uncommonly well. It is the general opinion, I think, that when Goethe yielded to the Duke's wishes he made the tragic mistake of his life. He was a poet, and a great one, and he was set to work that a competent civil servant could have done just as well. That is true. But one must remember the circumstances. He was only twenty-six, he had an immense power of enjoyment and wanted to live life to the full. He was conscious of his modest place in society, and one need not be too hard on him if he was flattered to be made much of by persons of exalted rank. It was natural that he should welcome the chance of entering a world more various than the bourgeois world of Frankfort. His father had cut off his allowance. It was as impossible then as it is now for an author to make his living by writing poetry. Men of letters were forced to become tutors to young princelings or take ill-paid jobs at a university. Schiller, when the most popular dramatist in Germany, was forced to make translations from the French in order to earn money enough to live on.

I don't know that those who have bitterly blamed Goethe for throwing himself away by entering the service of a petty German Prince have suggested any other course he might have taken. As I have said over and over again and can get no one to believe: authors do not like to starve in garrets. In due course Goethe was promoted to one office after another, and by the time he was just over thirty, was virtually Prime Minister of the Duchy. At the Duke's request, the Emperor granted him a patent of nobility, and thenceforward his official name and title was Herr Geheimrath von Goethe. He had not been settled in Weimar for more than a few months when he again fell in love. This time the object of his affections was Charlotte von Stein, wife of the Baron von Stein, Master of the Horse. She was seven years older than Goethe and the mother of seven children, three of whom only, however, were living. She was not beautiful, but she had a slight and graceful figure, and she was intelligent. It was a joy to Goethe to find someone with whom he could talk of any subject that interested him and be sure of an attentive listener. He was, as usual, passionate and impatient, but Frau von Stein wanted a friend rather than a lover, and for four years she resisted his advances. Then Goethe persuaded the Duke to engage an actress, Corona Schröter, to come to Weimar to play in the ducal theatre. He had written a play, *Iphigenia*, and when it was acted for the entertainment of the Court, Corona Schröter played the name part and Goethe that of Orestes. The audience thought that no such beautiful pair had ever before been seen together on the stage. Frau von Stein, it appears, felt that she was in danger of losing Goethe to the clever and fascinating actress, and to hold him became his mistress. For the next four or five years their relations were completely happy.

4

From his early youth Goethe had taken an interest in the theatre. His grandmother had given him a puppet theatre; and he had written plays for it, and performed them to an admiring group of children and their elders. When he arrived at Weimar he found amateur theatricals all the rage. He was a welcome addition to the troupe. It consisted of members of the ducal house, such of the courtiers as could be made use of and, now and then, of a professional actress or two. They gave performances not only at Weimar, but also at the seats of neighbouring grandees. The scenery and properties were laden on mules, and the company rode on horseback. They would act their play in the open air, or in the great hall of the palace; and then, after supper, ride home again. It may be that the excitement of these activities, and the fun they were, brought back to Goethe's mind an idea for a novel he is said to have had while still in Frankfort. The first mention we have of it is a note he made in his diary in the year 1779. It was to be called *Wilhelm Meister's Theatrical Mission*. It was not till two years later, however, that he began to write. The plan he adopted, an old one, as old, I suppose, as the *Satyricon* of Petronius, was popular. The Spanish picaresque novelists had given it a vogue throughout Europe, and Le Sage in *Gil Blas*, Henry Fielding in *Tom Jones* and Smollett in *Humphrey Clinker* used it with success. Briefly, the scheme is to take the hero from his home, let him wander hither and thither, undergoing a variety of experiences, and finally bring about a happy ending through his marriage with a beautiful and well-dowered young woman. The advantage of this arrangement is that the author can introduce a number of different characters, narrate a series of more or less hazardous adventures, and thus, with so much diversity, gain and hold his reader's attention. Goethe's novel was to be in twelve books. He wrote the first book, paused for a couple of years, after which he wrote the second and third, then a book a year till he had completed the sixth.

That seems a very odd way to write a novel. Most authors, when engaged on a work of fiction, are so absorbed in it that they can think of nothing else, and when they give up for the day, exhausted, look upon the rest of it with impatience as so much time lost till next day they can set to work again. Goethe was apparently able, after an interval of a year, to take up the thread of his narrative as though he had left off the writing of it but a few hours before. It runs smoothly, chapter follows chapter in natural sequence, so that you can only suppose that he had in his mind from the beginning the story he had to tell and by a remarkable feat of memory was able exactly to recall it. Most of the theatres in Germany at the time were supported by the Princes; and the managers had to produce operas, farces and melodramas in order to satisfy an audience that wished only to be entertained. When Goethe began to write his novel it was with a definite idea, then very much in the air, that the theatre should serve as a means of education for the mass of the public and so have an important and valuable influence on German culture. So far as we can guess Goethe's plan, Wilhelm Meister, his hero, was, after sundry vicissitudes, to become manager of a playhouse and, both as actor and author, create a great national theatre and write plays which would place his country's drama on a level with that of France and England.

But for some time Goethe had been growing more and more restless. The Court ceremonies, the visits with the Duke to other Princes, had lost the glamour with which at first his imagination had invested them. Society at Weimar, which in the early years had seemed so brilliant and so full of intellectual stimulus, now appeared narrow and provincial. His official duties were burdensome. Goethe had fallen in love with Charlotte when she was thirty-three; she was now in her forties—forty-three, to be exact. It was no longer a romantic affair with a great lady; it was a habit, recognised and generally accepted, which bore a drab air of domesticity. There was something of the governess in Frau von Stein; she had polished Goethe's manners and guided him in his relations with a world new to him. She had made the poet into a courtier and a gentleman. The poems he wrote to her are tender and affectionate, but they suggest respect, esteem and admiration, rather than the turmoil of passion. The moment came when he felt that at all costs he must get away. At three o'clock one morning, with a servant, a knapsack and a portmanteau, under an assumed name—Johann Philipp Möller, merchant, of Leipzig—he started off for Italy. He left Charlotte without a word of farewell. He stayed away for nearly two years.

It has been suggested that Charlotte never became his mistress. Whether she did or not is today of small importance. That she did is proved to my mind by the fact that he kept it from her that he was going away for an indefinite period. Had she been no more than an intimate friend to whom for years he had read his poems, to whom he had written innumerable letters, whom he consulted when he was in a quandary, whose advice he valued, he would surely have discussed his plan with her. She might have been sorry to see him go, but she would have understood that for his spiritual welfare and for the work he had in mind, it was necessary that he should do so. If, however, Charlotte was his mistress, she could hardly be expected to take it in good part that her lover should leave her for his soul's good for at least some months. Goethe may well have dreaded the scene she might make him and so decided that it would be simpler to let her face the *fait accompli*. As I have mentioned before, he was always somewhat indifferent to the feelings of others. Moreover, if their relations had been merely platonic, there seems no reason why, on his return, she should have received him with marked coldness. She would not listen to his enthusiastic accounts of his experiences in Italy. She reproached him bitterly because he had left her for so long, and it was in vain that he told her that it was only on her account that he had come back. He received the impression that so far as she was concerned he might as well have stayed away for good. This was not the sort of treatment he was accustomed to, and he wrote to Charlotte, "I freely admit that I cannot endure the manner in which you have treated me up to now. When I was talkative you sealed my lips; when I was uncommunicative, you accused me of indifference; when I was active on behalf of my friends, of coldness and neglect. You watched my every look, you criticised my gestures, my manner, and constantly rendered me *mal à mon aise*. How could confidence and frankness thrive when you deliberately repulsed me?"

It was no use. Charlotte was not to be appeased and from then on they met only on formal occasions.

Before leaving Weimar, Goethe had started on the seventh book of his novel and, though it was often in his mind, both in Italy and after his return to Weimar, he did not go on with it. I hazard the suggestion that he did not know how to do so. He had written but just over half his novel and even then the end was in sight. Wilhelm was part manager of a theatre and

A silhouette of Johann Wolfgang von Goethe (1749-1832)

Goethe can hardly have failed to see that as such, until he reached the conventional end of a picaresque novel with a happy marriage, he had nothing much more to tell than he had already told. It may be that he would have left the work unfinished if he had not conceived an entirely new idea that might give his novel a depth and importance which his original plan had not allowed. Much had happened during the eight years that had passed since Goethe's flight to Italy. The French Revolution took place. Louis XVI and his lovely Queen met their deaths on the scaffold. The armies of the young Republic scattered the Austrian forces which had taken up arms against them and overran the Rhineland. It looks as though Goethe had some inkling that the man of the future would be very different from the man of the past. He would have to cope with a changed world. When, then, in 1794, he once more set to work on his novel it was with a different aim in view. It was to show the development of his hero's personality under the various influences to which he was subjected till at length, in full possession of such powers as nature had bestowed upon him, he could devote them to the service of his fellow-creatures. Goethe's theme was not, as it had been, the art of the theatre, but the art of life. I am not sure that there is such a thing as that, but the words seem to mean something, and it may be they do. In other arts, in painting for instance, the medium sets its own limitations; but in life the medium is limited only by death, and that puts an end to its practice. In other arts proficiency can be obtained, but in life little more can be done than to make the best of a bad job. Art is an effect of design: life is so largely controlled by chance that its conduct can be but a perpetual improvisation.

Goethe spent some time cutting, revising and transposing passages in his old manuscript, and finally published the completed novel under a new title. This was *Wilhelm Meister's Apprenticeship*.

5

The story is very complicated, and I can only give the reader its bare bones. Before I attempt to do this, I must warn him that the readers of the eighteenth century looked for lively action in a novel. They wanted to be surprised by unexpected incidents and, so long as they were, cared little if they were highly improbable. A coincidence had to be outrageous for them to cavil. Probability was introduced into fiction by the realistic novelists of the nineteenth century, and the idea they arrived at was that what happened should be not only likely, but inevitable. The reader of today, though he may not know it, is a determinist; the reader of the eighteenth century believed in the indiscriminations of chance.

Wilhelm Meister is the son of a merchant who is in partnership with a certain Werner, and the intention is that Wilhelm and Werner's son should follow their fathers' calling. When the novel begins, Wilhelm is having an affair with a pretty actress, Marianne by name, who has come to Frankfort with a travelling company. He hates the idea of entering his father's business. He is stage-struck and very much in love. He wishes to marry Marianne and go on the stage. But Wilhelm has little money, and she has a rich lover on whose generosity she is dependent. When Wilhelm discovers this he is deeply hurt, terribly unhappy, and has a breakdown in health. On his recovery, disgusted with the theatre, he decides to have nothing more to do with it. For three years he works industriously in the firm's office. Then his father and his father's partner send him on a journey to collect money that is owed them. He stays for a few days in a considerable town and comes across an actor and actress, Laertes and Philina, who are stranded there because their company, for want of money, has broken up. A troupe of acrobats arrive and give a performance. Among them is Mignon. It is to her that Goethe gave the most famous of his lyrics, *Kennst du das Land wo die Zitronen blühen*. Wilhelm, seeing her beaten by the manager of the troupe, rescues her and, after giving the brute a thrashing, buys her from him for thirty dollars. The acrobats move on, and shortly afterwards a couple of actors, man and wife, appear whom Wilhelm has known in the past. They have come to join the company to which Philina and Laertes belonged and are dismayed to learn that it has been disbanded. The association with these actors revives Wilhelm's passion for the stage and, so that they may form a company of their own, he is persuaded to provide the money to buy for them the properties and wardrobes left behind for sale by the former owners. Since this money was what he had collected on his firm's behalf, it seems somewhat unscrupulous on his part to make such use of it.

Other actors drift along and are engaged. A mysterious Harper appears, an old man with a long white beard, whose emaciated body is enveloped in a brown robe. Wilhelm is pleased with his playing and the songs he sings, and insists on his joining the company. Then an equerry comes riding to arrange accommodation at the inn at which Wilhelm and the actors are staying for a Count and his Countess who will be arriving next day. They are on their way to their castle, where they are to entertain a Prince, a famous general, who is advancing with his troops to take up his headquarters in the neighbourhood. The noble pair arrive and presently suggest engaging the strolling players so that they may offer theatrical entertainment to their distinguished guest. When Wilhelm is presented to the Countess he is struck by her beauty, grace and distinction. Arrangements are made, and Wilhelm decides to accompany the players to the castle, partly because he has a mind to see the delightful Countess once more and partly because he welcomes the chance of getting into touch with the nobility. He believed, as did Goethe, that it was only in its ranks that one could acquire manners, culture and breeding. Today, aristocracy, impoverished and bereft of power, is at pains to make no pretensions and when one or other of its members is foolish enough to put on airs of grandeur, he is an object of ridicule. I venture to remind the reader that in Goethe's day throughout Europe, and especially in Germany, there was an immense gulf between the gentry and the commonalty. They belonged to different species. The noble not only demanded a servile respect from his inferiors, but received it. In theory at least, he had polish and refinement, and in comparison the commoner was uncouth.

Of the characters to whom we have so far been introduced, Philina is the most engaging. She is a delightful creature—completely amoral, but generous, warm-hearted and sweet. She is a light o' love, prepared to give herself to any man who has taken her fancy or makes it worth her while. She is a trollop, and Goethe disapproves of her, but she is so winning, he cannot help liking her. He treats her throughout with tenderness and indulgence. I think he realised that, notwithstanding her loose morals, there was no vice in her. She loses her heart to Wilhelm the first time she sees him, but he, high-minded young man that he is, ignores her advances. She has enslaved a lad called Frederick, who runs errands for her and waits on her. They quarrel and she sends him packing, but after some days, unable to live without the charmer, he returns. By this time Wilhelm, after all not insensible to Philina's attractiveness, is about to

succumb to her blandishments when he is told that she has made
a conquest of the Count's equerry and they are to have supper
together. Wilhelm, jealous and angry because he has been fore-
stalled by another, decides thereupon to treat Philina with contempt. It is not without satisfaction, however, that he learns
that Frederick, when ordered by Philina to wait on her and the
equerry at supper, on bringing in the stew, instead of setting it
on the table, has thrown it at their heads.

The actors arrive at the castle in pouring rain to find that they
are to be quartered in a derelict building with not a stick of
furniture in it. Only Philina, through the equerry's good
offices, is given a room in the castle. She ingratiates herself with
the Countess, who soon cannot do without her, and it is through
Philina that Wilhelm is brought into contact with the high-
born lady. His good looks, his talent, his charm, captivate her.
He reads to her and recites his poems. As susceptible as Goethe
himself, Wilhelm begins to be in love with her, and he is
inclined to believe that she is not indifferent to him. When
Philina, with her sharp eyes, perceives this, though after her
fashion herself in love with him, she does whatever she can to
bring the two together. Truly, a remarkable young woman!
The Prince arrives with his staff, and various festivities are prepared for his amusement. These occurrences are described with
liveliness and humour. There is a charming description of the
Countess's levée, which Hofmannsthal has used with admirable
effect in the first act of *Der Rosenkavalier*. Wilhelm makes the
acquaintance of a certain Major Jarno, in the Prince's suite, who
is both a man of the world and an intellectual. He gives
Wilhelm a volume of Shakespeare's plays to read: it is a revelation. Then, seemingly on a sudden, war breaks out, and the
party at the castle is dispersed. The actors are rewarded and dismissed. On the night before they are to go, Philina brings

Wilhelm to say good-bye to the Countess and discreetly leaves them. The Countess gives him a ring in which there is a lock of her hair and, before either quite knows what is happening, they are clasped in one another's arms. She tears herself away and cries, "Fly from me if you love me." He flies.

The strolling players, hoping to find employment in the prosperous city of Hamburg, set out, but are attacked on the way by a band of armed men, overpowered and robbed of their belongings. Wilhelm makes a gallant fight, but is shot down. When he regains consciousness he finds himself lying in Philina's lap. Just then an elderly gentleman and a young woman, accompanied by a number of horsemen, ride up and, seeing the wounded man, stop. The young woman especially seems concerned and covers him with the elderly gentleman's greatcoat. Badly hurt as he is, Wilhelm is struck by her beauty and touched by her tenderness. He falls in love with her there and then, and thenceforward the Fair Amazon, as he poetically calls her, is constantly in his thoughts. He is taken to the inn of a neighbouring village and finds that the rest of the company have found refuge there. Philina has saved her luggage, with all the pretty things the Countess has given her, by having what is colloquially called a romp with the leader of the bandits. This, rather naturally, excites the indignation of the others, who have been left with nothing but what they stand up in. They blame Wilhelm because he had persuaded them to take a shorter, more dangerous route instead of a longer, safer one; and abandon him. He is left with the Harper, Mignon and Philina. Philina nurses him devotedly and he is soon well on the road to recovery. One morning, on waking, he finds her asleep at the foot of his bed. She wakes and he, pretending to be still asleep, closes his eyes. A day or two later, without a word, she decamps.

The attitude of an unattached young man who rejects the advances of a beautiful and charming woman of easy virtue is not one that, deplorable though it may be, is regarded by most people with unmixed admiration. Goethe said that Wilhelm was a beloved and dramatic portrait of himself, but he also said that he was a poor fish. Contemporary opinion and the opinion of posterity have agreed with him. Carlyle, who translated the *Apprenticeship*, called him a milksop. The term is unduly harsh. Wilhelm was kindly and charitable, and his heart was moved by others' distress. He took charge of the ill-used Mignon and the helpless, half-demented Harper. He did what he could to relieve the sufferings of the unfortunate and, it must be admitted, tiresome Aurelia, whom we shall meet later. Young and inexperienced as he was, he allowed himself to be duped by the worthless creatures to whom he gave money when they were in difficulties: that is a trait which is not unsympathetic. He was brave and, when the players were attacked, fought bravely till he was laid low. Many a hero of fiction has won the hearts of readers with virtues less striking. It little became Carlyle to be outraged by his continence.

Goethe, long before, had drawn a portrait of himself in the first book of *The Sorrows of Werther*, and again in his two plays, *Götz von Berlichingen* and *Clavigo*. All three have the same lack of character as we find in Wilhelm. They are weaklings and slaves of their emotions. One can only conclude that these were traits that Goethe found deeply rooted in himself. He ascribed to Wilhelm his own motives, thoughts, feelings and idiosyncrasies. Goethe was fond of reciting his own poetry, and so is Wilhelm; Goethe had a weakness for delivering long disquisitions on any subject that happened at the time to interest him, and so has Wilhelm. Goethe gave him his own temperament and his own ideals, his desire to cultivate himself, his own passion for art, his own poetic gift and his own susceptibility to the charm of women. He gave him also his own vacillation, his own want of perseverance and his own tendency to be influenced by all and sundry. One must admit that one has to be very tolerant not sometimes to be impatient with Wilhelm. And, as too often happens when the author is the hero of his novel, the hero is acted upon, rather than acts, with the result that he remains shadowy in comparison with the other persons, objectively seen, of the story.

6

When Wilhelm is restored to health, still determined to be an actor, he proceeds with the Harper and Mignon to Hamburg, where a friend of his, Serlo by name, is manager of the theatre. While there, he receives a letter from Werner, son of his father's partner, to tell him that his father (Wilhelm's) has died.

He then suggests that on the money Wilhelm has thus inherited, and with money of his own, they should buy an estate, which Wilhelm can manage. Wilhelm rejects the proposal and in answer writes a letter to Werner which one reads with something like dismay. I will quote, in Carlyle's translation, the salient points: "The cultivation of my individual self, here as I am, has from my youth upwards been constantly, though dimly, my wish and my purpose . . . I know not how it is in foreign countries; but in Germany, a universal, and if I may say so, personal cultivation is beyond the reach of anyone except a nobleman. A bourgeois may acquire merit; by excessive efforts he may even educate his mind; but his personal qualities are lost, or worse than lost, let him struggle as he will. Since the nobleman, frequenting the society of the most polished, is compelled to give himself a polished manner; since this manner, neither door nor gate being shut against him, grows at last an unconstrained one; since, in court or camp, his figure, his person, are a part of his possession, and it may be the most necessary part, he has reason enough to put some value on them, and to show that he puts some. A certain stately grace in common things, a sort of gay elegance in earnest and important ones, becomes him well; for it shows him to be everywhere in equilibrium. He is a public person, and the more cultivated his movements, the more sonorous his voice, the more staid and measured his whole being is, the more perfect is he. If to high and low, to friends and relations, he continues still the same, then nothing can be said against him, none may wish him otherwise. His coldness must be reckoned clearness of head, his dissimulation prudence. If he can rule himself externally at every moment of his life, no man has aught more to demand of him; and whatever else there may be in him or about him, capacities, talents, wealth, all seem gifts of supererogation."

I leave out three paragraphs. The letter goes on then as follows: "Now this harmonious cultivation of my nature, which has been denied me by birth, is exactly what I most long for. Since leaving you, I have gained much by voluntary practice;* I have laid aside much of my wonted embarrassment, and can bear myself in very tolerable style. My speech and voice I have likewise been attending to; and I may say, without much vanity, that in society I do not cause displeasure. But I will not conceal from you that my inclination to become a public person, and to please and influence in a larger circle, is daily growing more insuperable. With this, there is combined my love for poetry and all that is related to it; and the necessity I feel to cultivate my mental faculties and tastes, that so, in this

* Here Carlyle was not quite accurate. The word he has translated by voluntary practice is *Leibesübungen*, bodily exercises—which the flippant call physical jerks.

enjoyment henceforth indispensable, I may esteem as good the good alone, as beautiful the beautiful alone. You see well, that for me all this is nowhere to be met with except upon the stage; that in this element alone can I effect and cultivate myself according to my wishes. On the boards, a polished man appears in his splendour with personal accomplishments, just as he does in the upper classes of society; body and spirit must advance with equal steps in all his studies; and there I shall have it in my power at once to be and seem, as well as anywhere."

This appears to mean that by devoting himself to the stage the bourgeois, playing the parts of great and noble persons, may acquire the culture and breeding which is the natural heritage of the nobly born. But it might mean more than that; it might mean that since we live in a world that is merely an appearance of a reality for ever unknown to us, there is not much to choose between acting our parts on the stage of a theatre and acting them on the stage of what we absurdly call real life.

On the money Wilhelm now has at his disposal, he enters into partnership with Serlo to produce plays. Serlo agrees, somewhat against his will, to engage the strolling players whose fortunes Wilhelm has shared and who have now turned up. Philina is with them. It is then that she makes a remark to Wilhelm which has found a place in at least one dictionary of quotations: "If I love you, what business is that of yours?" To this, so far as we are told, Wilhelm has no come-back. Philina then becomes Serlo's mistress. The first play to be produced under the joint management is *Hamlet*, and Wilhelm is to take the part of the Prince. Goethe's humour was sarcastic rather than playful, and in his youth he had had a predilection for practical jokes: the production of *Hamlet* gave him the opportunity to write a scene of high comedy, though I am not too sure that he meant it to be that. The dress rehearsal takes place, and

Wilhelm retires to his room. He starts to undress when to his astonishment he notices a pair of slippers, obviously Philina's, by the side of his bed. Then he perceives that the curtains round the four-poster have been disturbed and jumps to the conclusion that Philina is hidden behind them.

"Come out, Philina," he cries angrily. "What do you mean by this? Where is your sense, your modesty? Are we to be the talk of the house tomorrow?"

Nothing happens.

"I'm not joking," he goes on, "these pranks are little to my taste."

Not a sound! Not a movement! He flings open the curtains and finds the bed—empty. He is none too pleased to find that the naughty girl has been making a fool of him. Next evening the first performance of the play takes place and Wilhelm has a great success. It is followed by a party, after which he again goes to his room. He strips and, putting out the light, gets into bed. He hears a slight rustling and sits up. Two soft arms clasp him and passionate kisses are showered on his mouth, a woman's breast presses against his, and he has not the courage to push it away. In the morning, on awakening, he finds his bed empty. Oddly enough, he is not quite sure who his bedfellow was; the reader, more astute, knows perfectly well that it was Philina. She must have found the experience less thrilling than she had expected, since very shortly afterwards she once more disappears. We never see her again, but towards the end of the book hear what has become of her.

A few pages back, I mentioned Aurelia. She was an actress, Serlo's sister, and played the part of Ophelia to Wilhelm's Hamlet. She had been seduced by a neighbouring nobleman, Lothario by name, who had deserted her and her child Felix. She is broken-hearted and stricken with a mortal illness. On her deathbed she writes a letter, which she makes Wilhelm promise to take to her betrayer. He, ever ready with his sympathy, is prepared to upbraid Lothario for his cruel conduct and bring home to him his responsibility for the poor girl's death. He sets out, leaving Mignon and the Harper behind, for Lothario's castle. The Harper has become quite crazy, and is put in charge of a friendly pastor. Relations between Wilhelm and Serlo have now become strained. Wilhelm has insisted that they should stage, not the plays the public wished to see, but those he felt for their souls' good they should see. Audiences fell off, and Serlo would have been relieved to be rid of his exacting partner.

On his way to the castle, Wilhelm rehearses the biting diatribe whereby, when he comes face to face with Lothario, he proposes to bring his infamy home to him. He arrives and after some difficulty is admitted to Lothario's presence. He hands him Aurelia's letter. Lothario takes it into an adjoining room and is seen reading it. He comes back and tells Wilhelm somewhat nonchalantly that he is too busy to discuss the matter with him just then. He hands him over to an Abbé with instructions that he should be given a room for the night.

From now on, the novel becomes more and more confused and less and less plausible. Goethe begins one of his chapters with the words: "In a play events follow one another with inevitableness and chance has no place in it, but in a novel chance may rightly play a part." There is some truth in that. But only some. In each case it depends on the sort of play and the sort of novel the author has in mind. In this part of *Wilhelm's Meister's Apprenticeship* Goethe has made unscrupulous use of it. The oddest things occur and the most unlikely coincidences. The novel, which on the whole had been realistic, now becomes wildly romantic. Of course Goethe had a difficult job to cope with. He wished to show that Wilhelm had got all possible cultivation, his aim from the beginning, out of his connection with the theatre, and thenceforward must enter a higher form of life. He chose an unfortunate means to effect this. There was at the time he wrote a great vogue in Germany for freemasonry, and both Goethe and the Duke, and many of the courtiers, were initiated. The men Wilhelm meets at the castle, Lothario, the Abbé and Jarno, whom he already knows, all of noble rank, have formed a secret society, whose ideal is the brotherhood of man. Wilhelm thus enters upon a new apprenticeship, an apprenticeship not as before to art, but to life; and life, he is to learn, has meaning only if it is devoted to practical activities useful to mankind. One cannot but admit that all this business of the secret society, with its mysterious tower, its ceremonies and mummeries, is somewhat childish; and the persons concerned carry no conviction: they talk endlessly; and their discourse, however edifying, is too often tedious. It appears that the brethren have long had their eye on Wilhelm, and have made themselves acquainted with his successive activities; but why these young noblemen should have selected to be one of their number the son of a Frankfort merchant of the middle class is never explained.

On the day after Wilhelm's arrival, Lothario fights a duel. He has broken off an affair with a married woman, and her husband, to avenge the affront thus put upon her, challenges him. Lothario is wounded, and so Wilhelm is prevented from broaching the subject which has brought him to the castle. He stays on. But when at length he can assail Lothario for his base betrayal of Aurelia, Lothario brushes him off with an unanswerable retort: "When she loved, she ceased to be lovable. That is the greatest misfortune that can befall a woman." Wilhelm is silenced, but then reproaches him for neglecting the child, Felix, she had borne him. To this Lothario replies that if Aurelia had a child, he is certainly not its father.

Wilhelm comes to realise that he has greatly misjudged his host. Lothario has spent part of his life in America, but, having arrived at the conclusion that he can exercise his gifts at home as well as abroad, he returns to Germany. "Here or nowhere is America," he cries in a phrase that has become famous. He is now occupied with the management of his estates. He has conceived the notion, wildly revolutionary at the time, that the labourer should receive his fair share of the wealth his work had created. He is admired, beloved and respected by all. He is affable with his equals, gracious with his inferiors, hospitable, cultured, intelligent, humane, and a natural leader of men. I think Goethe meant to draw the portrait of a great man and a perfect gentleman: in point of fact he has drawn a portrait of any rich man of high birth who has a reasonable sense of his responsibilities. I don't know that it is particularly to his credit that he should be a promiscuous womaniser.

Wilhelm is persuaded to go on an errand to place Lydia, a girl of humble origins who has been living at the castle as Lothario's mistress and whom he wants to be rid of, in charge of a certain Theresa. Theresa is a practical young woman, a good manager and a good housekeeper, economical and business-like. She is also comely, and Wilhelm, though still hankering after the Fair Amazon, is attracted. He spends several days with her, and she tells him at length the story of her life. All I need mention is that she had been about to marry Lothario when he discovered that a few years before he had been her mother's lover, whereupon in horror he breaks off the engagement. Why he should have done this is not clear, since such things happen in the very best society and have never been regarded as a bar to marriage. Wilhelm returns to the castle, and it is suggested that he should ride back to Hamburg to fetch Mignon and the little Felix. He goes and finally breaks with Serlo. He now discovers that Felix is not, as he had been led to believe, Aurelia's son, but his own. When he left Marianne she was pregnant and died in childbirth.

Back at the castle all sorts of unexpected things happen. Wilhelm, his education in the art of life being presumably complete, is accepted as a member of the brotherhood. Lothario inherits a fortune and prepares to buy an immense property in the neighbourhood, which will provide a handsome estate for each of the members. But a Frankfort merchant also wishes to buy the property, and Lothario, in order that they may come to an arrangement satisfactory to both sides, invites him to visit him. He arrives and, strangely enough, turns out to be Wilhelm's old friend, Werner. Wilhelm, deeply affected by his discovery that Felix is his son and acutely sensible of the responsibility thus thrust upon him, decides that the little boy must have a mother; so he writes to Theresa to ask her to be his wife. He does not love her, but respects and admires her, and is confident that she will love his son as though he were her own. While he is awaiting her answer, he goes on a visit to Lothario's sister, Natalie, who has been looking after the ailing Mignon. To his surprise (but not to ours) he finds that she is the Fair Amazon of his dreams. He has only to see her again to know that he deeply loves her. She hands him a letter which Theresa has asked her to give him. It is to tell him that she accepts his offer of marriage. The situation in which he thus finds himself might justly be described as a pretty kettle of fish. Fortunately, however, Lothario finds out that Theresa is not the daughter of his old mistress, but the illegitimate daughter of her husband, so that there is no obstacle to their union. This frees Wilhelm from his engagement, and he need no longer, as he was nobly prepared to do, suppress his passionate love for Natalie.

A new character arrives at the castle. This is an Italian Marquis who is making a tour of Germany. The Harper by now has recovered his wits, cut off his beard and wears the clothes suitable to a gentleman on his travels. The Marquis recognises him as his long-lost brother. Meanwhile, Mignon, who has been for some time in failing health, dies and is embalmed. When the Marquis is shown her body, he discovers by certain marks on her arm that she is his niece and the Harper's daughter, the result of an incestuous union of his brother, then a monk, with his sister. The Harper, learning by accident the unhappy facts, cuts his throat. The high-spirited scapegrace, Frederick, turns up and it appears that he is Lothario's younger brother. He has been living with Philina, but has not brought her with him, since, being pregnant, she is not fit to be seen. To complete the family, the Count and Countess, whom we have met before, arrive at the castle, and the Countess is another sister of Lothario's. Finally it is revealed that Natalie, the Fair Amazon, returns Wilhelm's love and they agree to marry. To tidy things up Jarno announces his approaching marriage to Lydia, Lothario's discarded mistress! While writing his novel, Goethe sent each book as it was finished to Schiller for his criticisms. Oddly enough the only improbability in the events narrated that Schiller objected to was that three persons of noble birth should marry three commoners!

Goethe must have thought that he had thus brought his novel to a satisfactory conclusion, for he makes Frederick, at the very end, say to Wilhelm, "You are like Saul, the son of Kish, who went out to seek his father's asses and found a kingdom." The commentators have found in this a profound significance. It puzzles me. I don't know what Wilhelm has found other than an aristocratic marriage and a fine estate. But what puzzles me still more is the assumption, which he blindly accepts, that the practical life, in Wilhelm's case that of the gentleman farmer, for he is apparently prepared to spend the rest of his life in the cultivation of his estate, is without question superior to that of the artist, the actor, the poet or the scholar. I should have thought it obvious that the best life is that which enables each to make good use of such qualities and aptitudes as nature has bestowed upon him.

To my mind it is a pity that Goethe was unable to finish his novel on the lines on which he had begun it. Not that it would have been a great book, but it would have been a good one and have stood comparison, not unfavourably, with the best of the picaresque tales. But if on the whole the novel which Goethe eventually sent to the press is a failure, it is of more consequence than many a novel which within its limits is completely successful. It is the prototype of a variety of fiction, the *Bildungsroman*, which a long line of German novelists have used with more or less felicity. The most notable example of it is, of course, Thomas Mann's *The Magic Mountain*. I know no satisfactory translation of the term, *Bildungsroman*; the common rendering, the novel of education, seems to me singularly uninviting. It is the novel that is concerned with a young man's apprenticeship to life. It is a mistake to think, as some appear to do, that it is a peculiarly German product: after all, *David Copperfield* and *Pendennis* are instances of the same sort of thing, and so is *L'Education Sentimentale*. It gives the author an opportunity to air his views on the various problems that confront man in the confusion and haphazards of life, and if, forgetting that philosophy had better be left to philosophers, who can deal with it better, he wishes to philosophise, he can do that too. It is a curious fact, which I do not know how to account for, and it may be that it is inevitable to the genre, that the protagonists of these novels, from Wilhelm Meister's *Apprenticeship* to *The Magic Mountain*, are creatures of no great force of character, and so we are more apt to be irritated by them than to sympathise.

7

Goethe had long intended to write a sequel to *Wilhelm Meister's Apprenticeship*, and Schiller unfortunately welcomed the idea. But it was not till years later that he set himself to the task. He gave it the title of *Wilhelm Meister's Wanderjahre*. When it was published, according to Eckermann, Goethe's secretary, no one knew what to make of it. It is a muddled, incoherent work, and horribly tedious. It is only fair to add that the reader will find in it a great number of sagacious remarks on such subjects as religion, education and social organisation, but they can more conveniently be read in the various collections that have been made of Goethe's wit and wisdom.

We have now reached the year 1808. On his return from Italy he had been relieved of his official functions, but remained the Duke's adviser. Besides the cottage by the river, the Duke had given him a large, handsome house in the town; and here he received his admirers and hospitably entertained his friends. He was no longer the slim, comely youth, with exuberant vitality and the overwhelming charm that fascinated everyone who came in contact with him. He was in his sixtieth year. He was corpulent; he had a double chin, and his fine features were somewhat blurred. There had always been a certain stiffness in his demeanour, as though he were instinctively protecting himself from anyone who might take a liberty with him, and this with age was greatly accentuated. He had become a formidable figure. Schiller, with whom Goethe after some hesitation became intimate, wrote of him in a letter to a friend, "To be often with Goethe would make me unhappy; even towards his nearest friends he has no moment of effusion; one cannot, as it were, seize hold of him. I believe, in fact, that he is an egoist to an extraordinary degree. He possesses the talent of captivating people and binding them to him by little attentions as well as by great ones, but he always keeps himself free; he makes his existence known by kindly actions, but only as a God, without giving anything of himself." Crabb Robinson, who was taken to see him, and who rightly regarded him as a genius, beheld a man of terrific dignity, with penetrating and unsupportable eyes and tightly closed lips. "My companion," he wrote, "talked about his youth of adversity and strange adventures. Goethe smiled, with, as I thought, the benignity of condescension. When we were dismissed, and I was in the open air, I felt as if a weight were removed from my breast, and exclaimed '*Gott sei Dank*'." Heine, no respecter of persons, when he was to pay Goethe a visit, prepared beforehand the profound and sublime things he proposed to say to him, but, on finding himself in his presence, was so overcome with awe that he could think of nothing to talk about but the savouriness of the plums that grew on the trees by the wayside on the road from Jena to Weimar.

All this gives one a somewhat chilling impression of the great man, and it is true that when he found himself in uncongenial company, he was cold and reserved; but when with people he liked, he could be easy, talkative and gay. For some time, owing to his increasing impatience with the provincial life of Weimar, Goethe had taken to spending long periods at the neighbouring university town of Jena. There he had come to know a cultured bookseller, Fromman by name, with whose family and friends he found it pleasant to discuss art and literature. Fromman and his wife had adopted when she was ten a little girl called Minna Herzlieb who became a great favourite with the poet. She grew up. At eighteen she was uncommonly attractive. Goethe fell in love with her and as usual his passion gave rise to poems. He wrote a short series of admirable sonnets. The Frommans, however, could not but regard Goethe's infatuation with dismay; for not only was he forty years older than Minna; he was married. Soon after his return from Italy, Goethe, while strolling in the park at Weimar, was approached by a girl who handed him a petition which entreated him to use his influence to get a post at Jena for her brother. Christiane Vulpius was the daughter of a minor employee of the state; he was dead, and she worked in a neighbouring factory. She was uneducated, but she had pretty hair, laughing eyes and a graceful figure. Goethe was fascinated by her and soon became her lover. After some months, since she was about to have a child, he took her to live with him, and in due course she was delivered of a son. He was called August after the Duke, who was his godfather, and was baptised by Herder, the ecclesiastical superintendent of the Duchy. In course of time Christiane bore three other children, one of which died in infancy and the other two in childbirth. Goethe married her in 1806. His secretary and his son, August von Goethe, seventeen years old by then, were the witnesses.

In view of Goethe's attachment, the Frommans had found it prudent to send Minna Herzlieb away for a while, and Goethe, at the cost of a severe inward struggle, decided that there was but one issue to the impossible situation: he went back to Weimar and Christiane. He had, as we have seen, been accustomed in moments of dejection to turn to poetry for relief; on this occasion he turned to prose, and wrote the novel called *The Elective Affinities*. He stated that there was not a line in it that he had not himself felt, and no work in which he had put so much of himself. When it was published, though the critics praised, the reading public, to Goethe's mortification, were cold. That is not surprising; its faults are glaring. Like many another author, he had a sharp eye for defects in the works of his fellow writers, but was obstinately blind to those in his own; and in his high and mighty way he stated that no one had the right to express a judgment on his novel who had not read it three times.

The idea on which the story is founded has been put very well by the late Professor Robertson in his *The Life and Work of Goethe*, and I cannot do better than quote his account of it. Early in the book, one of the characters explains that "substances have a natural affinity with themselves; drops of water unite to make a stream; but they also have affinities to other substances. They may mingle without difficulty, as wine mingles with water, or with the assistance of an alkali, as oil and water. This affinity may be so strong between different bodies that when they combine, the result is the creation of an entirely new body, as when sulphuric acid is poured upon chalk and produces two new products, carbonic acid and gypsum. There may even be a third degree of affinity, a double or cross one. Two pairs of elements, A and B, and C and D, may be closely united to each other, but when all four are brought together, A may prefer to dissociate itself from B and unite itself to D, while B and C are similarly affected. Thus early, Goethe makes his purpose with the novel plain; he will translate A, B, C and D into human terms."

It is well known that the great novelists of the nineteenth century founded the characters of their novels on persons they had themselves known. Some, indeed, Turgenev for instance, admitted that they could not create a character at all unless they had a living model to work on. They elaborated their models to suit their own purposes and in the end the characters they created often enough had very little in them of the models that had suggested them. But the models were there, indispensable and except for this or that trait of theirs, perhaps no more than a sullen smile, a crafty look or a boisterous laugh, the characters created would not have been just what they were. And it may be that it was just this trait that enabled them on occasion to fashion a character more lifelike than any creature of real life. I do not suppose that any novelist but Goethe ever conceived the fantastic notion of using as his models chemical substances.

The story of *The Elective Affinities* is simple. Edward, a rich Baron, is living in a castle on his estate with Charlotte, his wife. They had loved one another in early youth, but on pressure from their respective families both had made a marriage of convenience; their partners died and they married. We are not told how long ago this had happened, but at the beginning of the story they are in the prime of life. They are occupied with the improvement of the estate and the beautifying of the park. One day, Edward makes the suggestion to his wife that an old friend of his, who can be useful to them in this, and to whom he is under an obligation, should be invited to stay with them. The friend is not given a name, but is known only as the Captain. One would have expected Charlotte to say, "What a good idea! By all means ask him if you want to." In point of fact she replies, "That is to be well thought about and considered from more than one side." After a lot of argument, however, Charlotte agrees that the Captain should be invited, but at the same time proposes that her niece, Ottilie, should be invited too. Both arrive. Ottilie is eighteen, demure and beautiful; the Captain is a fine figure of a man. Edward and Ottilie are drawn together by mutual affinity and Charlotte and the Captain likewise. Then a very odd thing occurs: Edward has kept diaries of his youth in the army and conceives the idea of revising them and making them into a book. Ottilie is set to copy them. Edward reads her manuscript, and to his astonishment finds that, though the early part is written in Ottilie's schoolgirl hand, the later part is in what looks like his own handwriting. "You love me," he cries and clasps her in his arms. By this time Charlotte and the Captain have realised that they are deeply in love with one another, and the Captain decides that the only thing he can do is take himself off—which he does. Charlotte, well aware of her husband's passion for Ottilie, suggests that she should be sent back to school. This Edward will not hear of and proposes that he should go away, promising not to attempt to see Ottilie, nor write to her, so long as she is allowed to remain at the castle. He settles down in a house on another of his properties. By a common friend, he sends a message to Charlotte, asking her to consent to a divorce, which, it appears, was then in Protestant Germany easy to arrange, so that he can marry Ottilie and she can marry the Captain.

The messenger returns, bringing Edward the news that Charlotte is pregnant. Though so much in love with Ottilie, on a whim, almost by accident, he had spent a night with his wife. One would expect Edward to be thrilled by the announcement. After all, he possessed great estates one would have thought the possibility of an heir would delight him; he had loved Charlotte: the natural, the humane, the decent thing for him to do surely was to go back to the castle and behave as any man in these circumstances would. Not at all! For no apparent reason he decides that the only course open to him is to rejoin the army, engaged at the time in war, and get himself killed. The child is born, and to the surprise of all has the eyes of Ottilie and the features of the Captain. They might well be surprised. Goethe's idea presumably was that in the act of sexual congress Edward was obsessed by his passion for Ottilie and Charlotte by hers for the Captain, so that the infant conceived would be thus strangely conditioned. It is, of course, utter nonsense.

The war is won, and Edward returns to the house he had lived in before. He is joined by the Captain, whom presently he sends to Charlotte to get her to consent to a divorce. While he is waiting for her reply, he rides over to his estate and by chance comes across Ottilie, who was wandering by the lake with Charlotte's child. He tells her on what errand the Captain has gone and she promises to marry him if Charlotte will agree to the divorce. They part, and she steps into a boat to row on the lake. In her agitation she loses an oar and, while she reaches for it, the child falls into the water and is drowned. The four of them, Edward and Ottilie, Charlotte and the Captain, are once more gathered together at the castle. Charlotte, now that her child and Edward's is dead, consents to divorce him. It looks as if thus everything can be settled to the satisfaction of all parties. But Ottilie cannot get over the child's death, for which she holds herself responsible. She regards it as a judgment on her sinful love for Edward and refuses to marry him. She begins to act very strangely. She will not speak, she will not eat; finally she dies. Edward cannot survive her loss and he too dies. With Charlotte's consent he is buried beside Ottilie.

Such, in brief, is the story. Its improbabilities, both of events and conduct, are inordinate. It is marred by digressions. Goethe, early in life, had taken to dictating—a practice that has proved disastrous to more than one distinguished novelist—and when he had once begun to discourse on a matter that interested him, though it had nothing to do with his subject, he could not stop. He was much interested in what is now known as landscape gardening and in *The Elective Affinities* he describes the alterations Charlotte and the Captain make in Edward's park at intolerable length. But the worst of his digressions, to which he devotes page after page, is that which occupies the interval between Edward's going to the wars and his return. Charlotte has by her first marriage a daughter called Luciane. She has left school, and instead of coming to live with her mother, for a reason that is not given goes to live with a great-aunt. She becomes engaged to a young man, and the couple, with a host of relations and friends, come to visit Charlotte. It is mid-winter and the gay party skate and sleigh. They play a variety of instruments. They sing and dance and recite poetry. They get up *tableaux vivants*, and Goethe has described each one of them in tedious detail. From one point of view all this is not uninteresting, for it gives the reader a vivid enough picture of how in the last quarter of the eighteenth century the German aristocracy entertained themselves during their long visits, lasting several weeks, to the castles of their fellow nobles; but it has nothing to do with the story Goethe has to tell, and thus is merely tiresome. The characters who play their parts in it are not in themselves interesting and so we do not care what happens to them. They have no more personality than the letters of the alphabet. They are puppets the string of which the author manipulates to demonstrate an abstract theory. They lack the breath of life. Professor Robertson put the matter very neatly, "They owe such existence as they have not to intuition and imagination, but to ratiocination." A fatal error! But surely the great flaw of *The Elective Affinities* consists in the initial conception. That Edward and Ottilie should be attracted to one another, Charlotte and the Captain, though possible enough, is so neatly symmetrical that you cannot take it quite seriously. It is a subject for comedy rather than for drama. Marivaux might well have written a graceful play on the situation of these four persons and Shaw a witty and sardonic one. The tragic outcome arouses neither pity nor fear.

8

In this essay I have been led to say more about Goethe's life than I meant to. I cannot tell what impression the reader has gained of the sort of man he was, but I am sure it is an incomplete and, so, erroneous one. In one of Grimm's fairy tales there is a story of a youth who entered the Castle of the Golden Sun, where sat an enchanted Princess awaiting a deliverer. But when he saw her he had a shock. Her face was full of wrinkles, her eyes were sunk deep in her head and her hair was carroty. "Are you the King's daughter of whose beauty all the world talks?" he asked. "Alas," she replied, "this is not my true form; the eyes of mortal men can only see me in this hateful guise. But that you may know how beautiful is the reality, look in this mirror which cannot err. That will show you my face as it really is." She gave him the mirror, and he beheld in it the portrait of the most beautiful maiden the earth could contain. So it is with Goethe. As a man he was selfish and self-centred, stiff and unbending, impatient of criticism, with too servile a respect for rank, and somewhat indifferent to the pain he caused others. The witty and malicious Heine said that he was far from appreciative of such of his fellow writers as had talent, and reserved his commendation for the second-rate, so that praise from Goethe came to be regarded as a certificate of mediocrity. He was his true self only when he wrote poetry. The mirror of his lovely lyrics, of his great odes, shows you the man that he was in reality. Somewhere, Goethe has said that the great man is just like everyone else, except that he has greater virtues and greater defects. If he was thinking of himself, it was not without justification. But his defects, such as they were, with age were mitigated. We know a good deal about his last years through Eckermann's *Conversations with Goethe*. It is one of those agreeable books that you can take up on any page and find something well worth reading. It is true that Eckermann often gives you his own contributions to the conversation at undue length. So did Hazlitt, when he recorded his talks with Northcote, but Goethe's secretary was not the brilliant

posterously ill-assorted. Goethe was offended, unhappy and deeply mortified. He left Marienbad. In the carriage on the way home he wrote a poem, *Elegie*, in which he described the emotion to which his love for Ulrike had given rise and his passionate regret for what he had lost. It is a fine poem, but it lacks the spontaneity of one or other of those early lyrics, which is like a cry of the heart, as unpremeditated as the singing of a bird, and seems to be a poem only by a lucky accident. The emotion of *Elegie* is doubtless genuine, but it is recollected in a tranquillity sufficient to have enabled Goethe to achieve an elaborate technique. There is the same sort of difference between the early lyrics and *Elegie* as there is between the wild flowers that bloom in spring on the foothills of the Alps, gentian, daphne and aconite, and the cinerarias and cyclamen that grow under glass in our Northern climes. I find the two lines that introduce the poem deeply moving.

"Und wenn der Mensch in seiner qual verstummt,
Gab mir ein Gott, zu sagen was ich leide."

By the time he reached Jena, Goethe had sufficiently regained his composure to clinch the plan he had in mind to attach Eckermann to himself by inducing him to take up his residence at Weimar. Goethe drew an alluring picture of the advantage it would be to the young man to live in a cultured and intellectual society, by mixing with which he could develop his personality and so allow his poetic gifts to mature. Eckermann, dazzled and flattered, swallowed the bait, line, hook and sinker; and a fortnight later followed Goethe to Weimar. Goethe set him to work and for nine years kept him busy. Several times Eckermann tried to break away, but Goethe would not let him go. With the callousness which was characteristic of him, he thus prevented the poor fellow from cultivating such literary gifts as he had. It appears that they were small, so it was no matter; anyhow, Eckermann has achieved, though not in the way he wished, a modest immortality.

Eckermann used often to dine with Goethe, sometimes alone, sometimes in company, for as ever the old man entertained lavishly. August had married and Ottilie, his wife, acted as hostess at these parties. She was a sprightly young woman and Goethe liked her. He was devoted to his two grandsons. Eckermann noted all the interesting things Goethe said on the drives they took together, during the many hours they spent seated opposite one another in the work-room, and the remarks made when distinguished persons came to dinner. On one occasion he states that the conversation was gay and sparkling. One could wish that he had thought it worth while to record. He didn't. He was a serious young man and it was to Goethe's words of wisdom that he was chiefly attentive. Since Goethe had always had a fondness for moralising, this gave him ample material for his note-book. Meanwhile Goethe's friends had been dying. When Schiller died, he said that with him went half his existence. Friederike Brion died. When I was in Strasbourg I drove to Scsenheim to see what was left of the house in which the parson had lived with his happy family and the church in which he had preached. The immediate surroundings can have changed but little. The green fields in which Goethe and Friederike had walked were still there. Then I went to the cemetery to see if I could find her grave. I couldn't, but on my way out I came across twelve graves of airmen shot down during the war. On eleven of the neat, white grave stones the names and ages of the men were given. They were in their early twenties. But on the twelfth, I suppose because the remains had been so mangled that no identification was possible, they had inscribed the words, "A British Airman," and a little below, "Known to God." Heartrending.

Lotte Buff and Lili Schönemann died. Frau von Stein died. The Duke died. August von Goethe died. When they broke the news of this to his father, he is reputed to have said, "I did not think I had begotten an immortal." The stoical remark was characteristic. But no one can flout human nature with impunity: he felt the loss of his son more than he would have it appear, and a day or two afterwards he had a stroke. He recovered sufficiently to resume work, and it was not till two years later that he was stricken with the illness which was to end in his death. He took to his bed. On the morning of the twenty-second of March, 1832, feeling a little better, he got up and seated himself in an armchair. His mind began to wander, and his thoughts seemed to run on his memories of Schiller. The day wore on and the room grew dark. He said to his servant, "Open the shutters so that more light may come in." They were his last words. But posterity has been dissatisfied with that, and has decided that his last words, more characteristic in view of his long life of unceasing endeavour, were "More Light".

Once upon a time, when they were all young and wild and gay, the Duke had built a hunting lodge on the summit of a mountain peak, and on the wall Goethe had written a verse in pencil.

> *"Ueber allen Gipfeln*
> *Ist Ruh*
> *In allen Wipfeln*
> *Spürest du*
> *Kaum einen Hauch,*
> *Die Vögelein schweigen im Walde;*
> *Warte nur, balde*
> *Ruhest du Auch."*

During the last year of his life, he visited the spot again, and read the lines he had written hard on half a century before. He wept. What makes old age hard to bear is not the failing of one's faculties, mental and physical, but the burden of one's memories.

The Saint

I

WHEN I WENT TO INDIA, in 1936, it was with the intention of spending most of the time at my disposal in the native states. It was my good fortune to be given by an old friend, the Aga Khan, letters of introduction to various Maharajahs. They invited me to stay with them and sumptuously entertained me. When they discovered that I had not come to shoot a tiger, or to sell anything, nor especially to see the Taj Mahal, the Caves of Ajanta or the temple of Madura, but to meet scholars, writers and artists, religious teachers and devotees, they were surprised and pleased. I was something new in their experience. To what had been before merely a civil gesture was now added a desire to do what they could to satisfy a design that commended itself to them. I was thus able to make acquaintance with a number of persons who were to me of absorbing interest.

I have among my books the fifteen volumes of Baring-Gould's *Lives of the Saints*, and now and then I take down a volume and read the account he gives of one or other of them who for some reason has aroused my curiosity. I have read the autobiography of St. Theresa and the lives, written by those who knew them, of St. Francis of Assisi, of Catherine of Siena, and of Ignatius Loyola. But it never occurred to me that I might be so fortunate as to meet a saint in the flesh. But that is actually what

I did. In the course of my journey I went to Madras, and there met some people who seemed interested to know what I had been doing in India. I told them about the holy men who had suffered me to visit them, and they immediately proposed to take me to see a Swami who was the most celebrated and the most revered then in India. They called him The Maharshi. Pilgrims from far and near went to him for instruction, advice and consolation in their troubles. Swami is a Hindu word which means literally religious teacher, but it seems to be generally applied to any ascetic. This one lived, it appeared, only a few hours by car from Madras at a place called Tiruvannamalai, and his ashram, his hermitage, was at the foot of the holy mountain Arunachala, holy because the mountain was regarded as an emblem of the god Siva, and once a year great celebrations, attended by thousands of people, were held in his honour.

I did not hesitate to fall in with the suggestion and, a few days later, early one morning, we set out. After a dull, hot drive along a dusty, bumpy road, bumpy because the heavy wheels of ox-drawn wagons had left deep ruts in it, we reached the Ashram. We were told that the Maharshi would see us in a little while. We had brought a basket of fruit to present to him, as I was informed was the graceful custom, and sat down to the picnic luncheon we had been sensible enough to put in the car. Suddenly I fainted dead away. I was carried into a hut and laid on a pallet bed. I do not know how long I remained unconscious, but presently I recovered. I felt, however, too ill to move. The Maharshi was told what had happened, and that I was not well enough to come into the hall in which he ordinarily sat, so, after some time, followed by two or three disciples, he came into the hut into which I had been taken.

What follows is what I wrote in my note-book immediately on my return to Madras. The Maharshi was of average height for an Indian, of a dark honey colour, with close-cropped white hair and a close-cropped white beard. He was plump rather than stout. Though he wore nothing but an exiguous loin-cloth (what his biographer somewhat inelegantly calls a cod-piece) he looked neat, very clean and almost dapper. He had a slight limp, and he walked slowly, leaning on a stick. His mouth was somewhat large, with thickish lips, and the whites of his eyes were bloodshot. He bore himself with naturalness and at the same time with dignity. His mien was cheerful, smiling, polite; he did not give me the impression of a scholar, but rather of a sweet-natured old peasant. He uttered a few words of cordial greeting and sat down on the ground not far from the pallet on which I lay.

After the first few minutes, during which his eyes with a gentle benignity rested on my face, he ceased to look at me, but, with a sidelong stare of a peculiar fixity, gazed, as it were, over my shoulder. His body was absolutely still, but now and then one of his feet tapped lightly on the earthen floor. He remained thus, motionless, for perhaps a quarter of an hour; and they told me later that he was concentrating in meditation upon me. Then he came to, if I may so put it, and again looked at me. He asked me whether I wished to say anything to him, or to ask him any question. I was feeling weak and ill, and said so; whereupon he smiled and said, "Silence also is conversation". He turned his head away slightly and resumed his concentrated meditation, again looking, as it were, over my shoulder. No one said a word; the other persons in the hut, standing by the door, kept their eyes riveted upon him. After another quarter of an hour, he got up, bowed, smiled a farewell, and slowly, leaning on his stick, followed by his disciples, he limped out of the hut.

I do not know whether it was the consequence of the rest or of the Swami's meditation, but I certainly felt very much better, and in a little while I was well enough to go into the hall where he sat by day and slept by night. It was a long bare room, fifty feet long, it seemed to me, and about half as broad. There were windows all around it, but the overhanging roof dimmed the light. The Swami sat on a low dais, on which was a tiger skin, and in front of him was a small brazier in which incense burnt. Now and again a disciple stepped forward and lit another stick. The scent was agreeable to the nostrils. The faithful, inhabitants of the ashram or habitual visitors, sat cross-legged on the floor. Some read, others meditated. Presently two strangers, Hindus, came in with a basket of fruit, prostrated themselves and presented their offering. The Swami accepted it with a slight inclination of the head and motioned to a disciple to take it away. He spoke kindly to the strangers and then, with another inclination of the head, signified to them that they were to withdraw. They prostrated themselves once more and went to sit among the other devotees. The Swami entered that blissful state of meditation on the Infinite which is called Samadhi. A little shiver seemed to pass through those present. The silence was intense and impressive. You felt that something strange was taking place that made you inclined to hold your breath. After a time I tiptoed out of the hall.

Later, I heard that my fainting had given rise to fantastic rumours. The news of it was carried throughout India. It was ascribed to the awe that overcame me at the prospect of going into the presence of the holy man. Some said that his influence, acting upon me before ever I saw him, had caused me to be rapt for a while into the Infinite. When Hindus asked me about it, I was content to smile and shrug my shoulders. In point of fact that was neither the first nor the last time that I have fainted. Doctors tell me that it is owing to an irritability of the solar plexus, which presses my diaphragm against my heart, and that one day the pressure will last a little too long. I feel unwell, and know what to expect; I put my head between my legs as, many years ago, when a medical student at St. Thomas's Hospital, as a clerk in the outpatients' department I was taught to make nervous women do when they seemed about to faint; but it does not avail me: darkness descends upon me and I know nothing more till I regain consciousness. One day, I shall not. Since then, however, Indians come to see me now and then as the man who by the special grace of the Maharshi was rapt into the Infinite, as his neighbours went to see Herman Melville as the man who had lived among cannibals. I explain to them that this bad habit of mine is merely a physical idiosyncrasy of no consequence, except that it is a nuisance to other people; but they shake their heads incredulously. How do I know, they ask me, that I was *not* rapt into the Infinite? To that I do not know the answer, and the only thing I can say, but refrain from saying for fear it will offend them, is that if I was, the Infinite is an absolute blank. This idea of theirs is not so bizarre as at first glance it seems when one remembers their belief that in deep, dreamless sleep consciousness remains and the soul then is united with the Infinite Reality which is Brahman. But I shall have something to say later which will make this appear less strange.

The interest aroused by this incident, unimportant to me, but significant to the Maharshi's devotees, has caused them to send me a mass of material concerned with him, lives, accounts of his daily activities, conversations with him, answers to the questions put to him, expositions of his teaching, and what not. I have read a great deal of it. From it I have formed a vivid impression of the extraordinary man he was, and I propose in the following pages to tell the reader what I have learnt from the various publications that my kind, unknown friends in India have been good enough to send me. The story I wish to tell is strange and moving, and I should like to tell it as simply as I can, without comment or animadversion, without criticism of behaviour that to a Western reader must seem extravagant; as naïvely, in short, as those old monks wrote the lives of famous saints. But before setting about this, I must give the reader some account of the Maharshi's religious beliefs, for unless he knows something of them his motives and behaviour, his mode of life, will be hardly intelligible. I embark upon this undertaking with trepidation, since I am dealing with a matter with which my acquaintance is but superficial. What I know about it, I have read in books. The most important of these are Sir Charles Eliot's *Hinduism and Buddhism*; Radhakrishnan's *History of Indian Philosophy* and his translation of the Upanishads; Krisnaswami Iyer's *Vedanta, or the Science of Reality*; *Brahma-Knowledge* by Professor Barnett; and Sankara's *Vivekachudamani*. I have often used the very words of these authors and, except that it would have been tiresome, I might very well have put much of the next section of this essay in quotation marks. The religion of the Hindus is not only a religion, but also a philosophy; and not only a religion and a philosophy, but also a way of life. If you accept its first principles the rest follows necessarily, as the conclusion of a syllogism follows on the premise and the middle term. It is a very ancient religion, an amalgam of the religion of the Dravidians, the earliest inhabitants of India, with that of the Aryans, who invaded the country during the second millennium before Christ; and after a fashion it was systemised by the sages of the Upanishads, the first of whom flourished some thousand years later. That a religion is very old does not mean that it is true; but it does mean that for age after age it has satisfied the spiritual demands of those who believe in it.

2

On a previous page I had occasion to speak of Samadhi. Since I shall have to do so somewhat frequently and I may have readers who do not know precisely what it means, I think it may be well to tell them. Samadhi is usually, though not invariably, achieved through the prolonged practice of meditation. Meditation is an operation of the mind in which it is concentrated on an appropriate object. It differs from Samadhi in that there is not the complete unconsciousness of external objects which is characteristic of Samadhi. When the Maharshi's devotees at the ashram recited poems or read aloud, as they did at certain hours, if a word were mispronounced or a line of verse incorrectly quoted, the Maharshi, though rapt in meditation, would give the correct quotation and the proper pronunciation of the word. So, a skilled musician, entranced by a piece of great music, might on a sudden be distracted by a false note played, and in mind half unawarely correct it, while still continuing, unperturbed, to rejoice in the sounds that met his ear. Samadhi is a trancelike state of profound absorption in the Infinite Reality, which is Brahman, in which the adept is one with the Absolute, and in spirit enjoys existence, knowledge and bliss. The proficient is able to enter into this state at will, and is then insensible to the world about him. I will give an instance of this.

When I was in Calcutta I met an Indian biologist of some distinction, who had married an American woman. He was a deeply religious man and he spent an hour or two every day in meditation. We chanced to talk about Samadhi, and his wife told me that, a little while before, they had had to take a night's journey by train to some place where he was to attend a scientific conference. The carriage in which they found themselves was crowded and it was impossible to lie down. When the train started the biologist entered into Samadhi and did not emerge from it till next morning when they reached their destination. Their fellow travellers ate and talked throughout the night. The wooden seats were hard and uncomfortable, and the poor lady found it impossible to sleep. By morning she had a splitting headache and her every bone ached; her husband was fresh and rested. When they got to their hotel she could only go to bed; he went about his long day's work as though he had slept the night through in his own comfortable bed at home.

3

The Upanishads are a collection of dialogues in prose and verse composed during a long period of time by sages in search of truth. They are assumed to have been divinely inspired, and it is claimed that they are the highest and purest expression of the speculative thought of India. Their aim is not so much to reach philosophical truth as to bring peace and freedom to the anxious human spirit. They are often obscure and hard to understand. Various commentators have interpreted them, generally to substantiate their own doctrines, and of these, it is admitted, I think, that Sankara is the most notable. He is said to have been born in Southern India towards the eighth century of our era and to have died at the early age of thirty-two. He was a man of immense intelligence, a poet, a philosopher and a great religious teacher. His supreme achievement was to take the speculations of the Upanishads and in conjunction with them construct the religious philosophy which is known as Advaita. It is an absolute monism, or, as Indian scholars prefer to call it, a non-dualism. Its main principles, if I understand it aright, are two: they have the sort of connection that reminds one of the twin stars that astronomers tell us revolve about one another by the mysterious force of gravitation. These are Brahman and Reincarnation. Brahman is the only reality. Brahman is not personal as is the God of Christians and Muslims; it is neuter and is referred to as It. Brahman is being, consciousness and joy. It is without parts, without qualities, without action, without emotion; it knows no bonds, no suffering, no decay. It has neither beginning nor end. It is the universal spirit, the one without a second, infinite and immutable. It is unknowable, for it is the knowing subject and can be known only by itself. It is the omnipotent and omniscient cause of the origin, maintenance and dissolution of the universe. It is the sole source of life. Of all the gods that the fears and yearnings of men have devised, it is perhaps the most awe-inspiring as it is the most inscrutable.

The world is a manifestation of Brahman. It exists, potentially or actually, from eternity to eternity. But the question arises why Brahman, which is infinite, void of motive or desire, should thus manifest itself. Two theories seem to have been prevalent: one is that this manifestation is an expression of Brahman's joy and power. When one considers how full the world is of sorrow and suffering, one can hardly refrain from thinking that Brahman might have done better to leave well alone. A more engaging notion is that creation is the spontaneous overflow of the nature of Brahman. It can no more help creating than Newton's apple could help falling to the ground. The authors of the Upanishads knew nothing of the clusters of vast galaxies millions upon millions of light years away. They knew nothing of the myriad stars of the Milky Way, with their attendant planets on numbers of which it is only reasonable to suppose that life exists. The wit of man is hard put to it to conceive of a creator of such immensities. In comparison with these the universe of the Upanishads, with its fourteen worlds, all within time and space, inhabited by various kinds of beings, is a small one. When it came about that Brahman manifested itself in this world, it was by means of an aspect of itself to which the name of Isvara is given. Isvara is the personal God. He is the supreme spirit, omniscient, omnipotent and perfect. He is the first cause, the creator, preserver and destroyer of the world. The world issues from him and returns to him. He creates it by means of the power of Maya. Maya is a very difficult concept to explain. It is generally translated by the word *illusion*, and is used to denote the deceptive character of the phenomenal world. The world is neither real nor unreal. It is a reflection of Brahman, and its reality consists in the fact that it reflects Reality. The world is illusory, judged from the standpoint of Reality, but it is not an illusion. It is a fact of consciousness. The wise men of India are fond of using the following illustration: you see on a dark night what you take to be a snake and you run away from it; but when a light is brought, you see that what you took for a snake is in fact a rope. It was an illusion that what you saw was a snake, but it *was* a rope. And the rope has at least this reality, that you can tether an ox with it, tie up your boat with it—or hang yourself. The concept of Maya is intimately related with the concept of Avidya. This is translated as ignorance or false knowledge. It was through Avidya that you mistook the rope for a snake, and it is through Avidya that you ascribe the phantom world and your individual self to the reality of Brahman.

But why did an omnipotent and all good God create a world in which there is so much misery? Can God be the cause of the world in which some are treated well and some ill? God must be unjust and cruel when he inflicts such various lots upon his creatures. No one who has read *The Brothers Karamazov* can ever forget the horrible story Ivan tells his brother Alyosha when they are discussing the subject of evil. Ivan can believe in a God who punishes the wicked for their sins, but why should innocent children suffer? He tells Alyosha of a brutal land-owner who, when one of his serfs, a little boy, had thrown a stone at one of his dogs, and lamed it, has him stripped and, bidding him run, sets his dogs on him and sees him torn to death before his mother's eyes. Ivan says that if there is a God to permit such things, he is wicked, and he refuses to believe in him. The problem of evil, as we know, has always been a stumbling-block to monistic religions. The Hindus have coped with it by means of their belief in reincarnation and the con-ception of Karma. The body is destroyed at death, but some-thing, what the Hindus call the subtle body, passes on and migrates to another transitory tenement. No one seems to know how the idea of reincarnation entered the Indian con-sciousness. It has been suggested that it was designed to explain how it comes about that in a world created by an omnipotent deity there should be such inequalities in the lot of human beings, that some should have good fortune, others ill, that some should be born to happiness, others to affliction. This seems more like an explanation invented to justify a notion already accepted, rather than one to account for how it arose. It is more likely that it was taken over by the Aryan invaders from the animistic peoples they found in India who believed that after death their souls lived in trees and animals. To say that the Hindu believes in reincarnation is a gross understatement, it is an intimate conviction, bred in the bone, which he doubts as little as we should doubt that if we put our hand in the fire it would be burnt. Karma is the force that conditions the nature and circumstances of the human being as the result of his actions in previous existences. It is the events of past lives, and of the present life, which determine the character of succeeding lives. If we see our fellow-creatures suffering from misfortune that seems unmerited, if they are born with physical defects, if they meet with untoward accidents, if they are stricken with any of the ills that flesh is heir to, it is not to be ascribed to a malignant fate, but to the sins and errors they have committed in past lives. If Alyosha had been a Hindu, he would have answered Ivan by saying that there was nothing in his dreadful story to impugn the mercy of God. The child was suffering for deeds committed in previous births, so justice was done and, having thus atoned for them, he would be reborn in happier circumstances. So far as I know, this conception offers as plausible an explanation of the existence of evil in the world as has been devised by human wit.

When the Hindu dies, what is called his gross body—his limbs, lungs, heart and bowels—is burnt; but his subtle body—his mind, his senses, his ego—is immaterial and so cannot be destroyed by fire. The subtle body, like Christian in the *Pilgrim's Progress*, bears the burden of sins committed in the deceased's past lives and accompanies his soul when after an interval, short or long, it migrates into a new abode. Soul is the word translators use to signify the Sanskrit word Atman. But the Atman is more than soul, for the Christian soul is newly created with each birth, whereas the Atman has existed from all eternity. It is the real self and essence of every human being. It passes unchanged through innumerable births, unaffected by the accidents of life. It is the persistent identity of the human being which it inhabits. It does not change with his youth or age, nor knows its joys and sorrows. It is the unmoved witness. It is no bigger than a mustard seed and no smaller than the Infinite. The Atman is not part of Brahman, for Brahman is without parts; it *is* Brahman. How disturbing, how awful, how terrifying even, it is; how strangely must it affect our attitude towards our fellow creatures if we believe, nay, if we know for a certainty, that in all of us, not only in the good and the clever, but in murderers, thieves, cheats, in liars, hypocrites, humbugs, bores, fools—God dwells!

Isvara creates the world and after a period withdraws it within himself; after another period he re-creates it. During the interval, the souls that are still subject to the penalty of birth and rebirth remain dormant. It is natural to ask why Isvara should create the world again and again. The answer supplied is that opportunity must be given to those souls to atone for their past errors, and the process must be endless, for it had no beginning. The world exists from eternity to eternity. But if you ask why Isvara, omnipotent and all good, did not create human beings who were without sin, the only explanation that seems plausible is that, as the sparks fly upwards, man is born to sin. Just as he would not be man if he were without heart, lungs and bowels, so he would not be man if he were devoid of evil. Evil is a necessary component of him just as (if I may be permitted a flippant comparison) Noilly Prat is a necessary component of a dry martini. Without it you can make a side-car, a gimlet, a white lady, or a gin and bitters, but you cannot make a dry martini.

The aim of the pious Hindu is to achieve knowledge of Brahman. He must so conduct his life that he may overcome the evil which is in him and thus achieve release from this long, long series of birth and rebirth. He must suppress passion. His mind must be pure and he must be quit of lust. He must practise charity and renounce selfish desires. He must not give way to ill-temper, sloth, fretfulness or perplexity. It is well that he should pray to the God of his election, Siva or Vishnu, but he must not fail to remember that these Gods are merely aspects of

Brahman. (It is told of Sankara that on his death-bed he prayed to Brahman to forgive him for having worshipped in temples dedicated to other Gods.) He must make a practice of meditation on the One without a Second. When at last he attains the realisation that he is one with Brahman, and he attains it not by ratiocination, but by intuition and the grace of Brahman, saved, he is no longer subject to rebirth. For the remainder of his days, no longer under the sway of the errors, errors of deed, errors of thought, of his past lives, he lives on to atone for the deeds of his present life. It comes to an end, and his self is united for ever with the Eternal Self which is Brahman.

Does he retain his individuality? No. Why should he wish to since the ego is the source of suffering and sin, and to annihilate it has been the purpose of his life?

I have given this brief and inadequate outline of Sankara's doctrine so that the reader may the better be able to understand the following pages in which I propose to relate what I have been able to learn of the Maharshi's life. It has been written, under the title of *Self Realisation*, by Narasimha Swami.

4

The Maharshi was born in 1879, in a village of some five hundred houses about thirty miles from the important town of Madura. He was named Venkataraman. His father, Sundaram Ayyar, was an uncertified pleader in the local magistrate's court, something like a country solicitor in England, and he was a man of importance in the village. He was religious without being devout: "the priest in his house regularly worshipped a set of tiny images and offered the daily food to them before it was served to the family." Sundaram was kindly and hospitable, and it was said that every stranger found a ready seat at his table. There had been ascetics in the family. Once a sannyasin, a religious devotee, came to the house and was neither treated with respect, nor given anything to eat, whereupon he left with a curse that in each generation a member of the family should leave home and as an ascetic beg his food. Sundaram Ayyar's uncle and his elder brother had in fact donned the yellow robe and were seen no more. When Venkataraman was twelve, his father died. The widow, with her three sons and a daughter, went to live at Madura with her brother-in-law, and there the two elder boys went to school. Venkataraman seems to have been a very ordinary lad, fonder of playing games than of learning his lessons, and his idleness caused his family grave concern. When he was sixteen an odd thing happened. An elderly relation came to Madura, and when the boy asked him where he had come from, he replied, "From Arunachala." Venkataraman was suddenly filled with awe and joy at the name of the holy place, the hill which represents one of the eight forms of God, and he was strangely shaken. But the impression passed and to all appearance had no further effect on him. Not very long afterwards, however, he came upon a book that his uncle had borrowed. This was a collection of the lives of Tamil saints. They deeply moved him, but to no lasting consequence, and he continued to lead his usual life, playing football, running races, wrestling and boxing. He was a strong, active, handsome boy. The crisis came some months later. He was in his seventeenth year. His disciples have reported what happened then in his own words: "It was about six weeks before I left Madura for good that the great change in my life took place. One day I sat alone on the first floor of my uncle's house. I was in my normal health. . . . But a sudden and unmistakable fear of death seized me. I felt I was going to die. Why should I have so felt cannot now be

76

explained by anything felt in my body. Nor could I explain it to myself then. I did not, however, trouble myself to discover if the fear was well grounded. I felt I was going to die and at once set about thinking what I should do. I did not care to consult doctors or elders or even friends. I felt I had to solve the problem myself, then and there.

"The shock of fear of death made me at once introspective or introverted. I said to myself mentally, that is, without uttering the words, 'Now death is come. What does it mean? What is it that is dying? This body dies.' I at once dramatised the scene of death. I extended my limbs and held them rigid, as though *rigor mortis* had set in. I imitated a corpse to lend an air of reality to my further investigation. I held my breath and kept my mouth closed, pressing the lips tightly together so that no sound might escape. 'Let not the word "I", or any other word, be uttered!' 'Well then,' I said to myself, 'this body is dead. It will be carried stiff to the burning ground and there burnt and reduced to ashes. But with the death of the body, am "I" dead? Is the body "I"? This body is silent and inert. But I feel the full force of my personality, and even the sound "I" within myself apart from the body. So "I" is a spirit, a thing transcending the body. The material body dies, but the spirit transcending it cannot be touched by death. I am therefore the deathless spirit.' "

Though Venkataraman did not know it at the time, this condition was what the sages have called Illumination. He had read few books and, strange as it may seem, had never heard of Brahman, the One Real, underlying all phenomena, or of the endless succession of births and deaths. He knew nothing of life and had no idea that it was full of sorrow. The result of this crisis was that he lost any interest he had had in his studies and came to regard his friends and relations with indifference. He preferred to sit by himself in the posture proper for meditation and, closing his eyes, lose himself in concentration on the spirit which constituted himself. Almost every evening he went to the temple and, as he stood before the images, waves of emotion overcame him. He wept, not with any feeling of pleasure or pain, but from the overflow of his soul. Sometimes he prayed to Isvara, the controller of the universe and the destinies of mankind, that his grace might descend upon him and become perpetual. He did not know then that there was an Impersonal Real that underlay everything, and that Isvara, aspect of the Real, and himself were identical with it. Often he did not pray at all, but let the deep within himself flow on and into the deep without.

Naturally enough, this behaviour displeased his uncle and exasperated his brother. At school, his master grew impatient with him because he persistently neglected his work. He refused to listen to reason and was blandly indifferent to reproof. One morning, the date is given exactly, Saturday, 29th August 1896, when he had failed to prepare an English lesson, the master ordered him as an imposition to write out three times a passage from Bain's Grammar. He sat upstairs in his uncle's house and made two copies of the lesson; he started on the third and, suddenly, throwing the grammar and the copy aside, sat up in the fitting attitude, with his eyes closed, and lost himself in meditation. His brother, who was watching him, called out, "Why should one who behaves thus retain all this?" Why should one, this meant, who prefers meditation to his studies and to his domestic and social duties, continue to stay at home and pretend to study? It is stated that something like this had often been said to him before, but he had taken no notice of it. This time it went home, and he said to himself, "What my brother says is quite true. What business have I here any longer?" The thought of Arunachala, which some months before had so deeply moved him, recurred to him, and he was seized with a compelling desire to go there. Arunachala called him, and the call was the call of God.

He knew that he must go secretly and, so that his family should not know where he was and fetch him back, that his destination must be concealed. He rose to his feet and told his brother that he would go to school to attend a special class. His brother answered, "Well then, don't fail to take five rupees from the box below and pay my college fees." Venkataraman felt that this was manifestation of help from the Unseen; for with that money he would be able to buy himself a ticket to go by train to the town of Tiruvannamalai, near which was the temple of Arunachala. He looked at an old map and decided that this would not cost more than three rupees. His aunt gave him the five rupees he asked for. He left the balance of two rupees for his brother with the following note, "I have in search of my father and in obedience to his command started from here. This is embarking on a virtuous enterprise. Therefore none need grieve over this affair. To trace this one, no money need be spent.

Thus

— — — — —

As a postscript he added, "Your college fee has not been paid. Rupees two are enclosed herewith."

By referring to himself as *this*, by writing dashes instead of his name as a signature, he meant to indicate that he was no longer a person, but a spirit absorbed in the Infinite. From then on he never used the word *I*, but invariably, when speaking of himself, used the third person. He used it when he gave his devotees the account of his conversion from which I have quoted, and it is only for the convenience of the English reader that his biographer has made him speak in the first person.

Venkataraman went to the station and after taking his ticket was left with two rupees and thirteen annas. The train stopped at Trichinopoly at sunset, and by then he was hungry. He bought a couple of pears and began to eat, but when he had eaten a mouthful he was sated and could eat no more. He was surprised, since till then he had had a good appetite and eaten two full meals a day besides cold rice in the morning and a snack in the afternoon. He had to change at a place called Villupuram. It was three o'clock in the morning. He walked up and down the streets and when the day was somewhat advanced went to an inn and asked for food. The landlord told him he must wait till noon. The boy sat down and became immersed in Samadhi. At noon he was given a meal and in payment offered the inn-keeper two annas. "How much have you?" the inn-keeper asked him. "Only two annas and a half," he answered. "Keep it." He started off to the station and bought himself a ticket to a place called Mambalapattu, which was as far as his money would take him and, having arrived there, decided to walk the rest of the way. He walked on and on, and at last came to a temple. He waited till the door was opened and, going in, sat down to meditate. Suddenly he had a vision of dazzling light, which streamed forth and pervaded the pillared hall. It disappeared and he again entered into Samadhi. The priest roused him when it was time to close the temple. He asked for food, but the priest said there was none; then he asked if he might stay there, but was told that no one was allowed to do that. The priest, having a further service to hold, set out with his attendants to another temple at no great distance, and Venkataraman, told by one of them that after it was over he might get something to eat, followed. The priest performed his worship, but when it was over again refused to give the boy food. Then one of the attendants, the temple drummer, cried out, "Why, sir, give him my share." He was given a plate of boiled rice and led to a neighbouring house to get water to drink with it. But while he waited, he fell asleep and slept till morning.

At break of day, Venkataraman set out for the town of Tiru-vannamalai, on the outskirts of which, at the foot of the hill sacred to the god, was the great temple of Arunachala. But it was twenty miles away, and he was hungry and very, very tired. He had to get food and then enough money to go by train. He was wearing gold ear-rings, set with rubies, which were worth twenty rupees. He went to a house where a charit-able woman gave him a meal and her husband advanced him four rupees on the ear-rings and a receipt, so that, if he wished to, he could redeem them. They gave him another meal later in the day and sent him off with a packet of sweets to the station. On the way, as he had no intention of redeeming his ear-rings, he tore up the receipt. He slept the night at the station and next day caught the train for Tiruvannamalai. On arrival he beheld from afar the towers of the temple of Arunachala. He went there forthwith. He found the gates open and not a soul within; he made his way to the innermost shrine where there was a *linga*, the formless emblem of Siva, and there in ecstasy offered himself to the God. On his way back to the town, passing a tank, he threw into the water the parcel of sweets that the kind woman had given him the day before, saying to himself, "To this block why give sweetmeat?" By 'this block' he meant his body. While he was wandering about, a man asked him whether he did not want his hair cut off; he said he did, and the man led him to a barber's. He had been noted for the beauty of his long, jet-black locks: he came away with his head clean-shaven, which was the token of Sannyasa, asceticism, and a sign that he was parting with the vanities of the world. He tore his clothes to pieces, keeping only a thin strip to serve as a loin-cloth, and cast the rest away along with what was left of his money. He then removed the sacred thread from his body. This is a thin coil of three cotton threads worn over the left shoulder and allowed to hang diagonally across the body to the right hip. The Brahman is invested with it in his eighth year in a solemn ceremony, and it is the mark of his second birth. By thus ridding himself of it, Ventakaraman discarded his superiority of caste and every notion that the body was the self. He did not take the customary bath after having his head shaved—"Why should this block be accorded the comfort of a bath?" he asked himself; but, as though miraculously, a heavy shower of rain bathed him before he entered the hall of the temple with its thousand pillars, and sat down to meditate.

For some weeks, observing the rule of silence, he remained there, rapt for hours at a time in the bliss of Samadhi. A woman, touched by his youth and impressed by his piety, provided him with the little food he needed. But life was made difficult for him by the mischievous boys in the town who seem to have resented the behaviour of the stranger, no older than themselves, who had adopted the life of an ascetic. They amused themselves by throwing stones and broken pots at him. To escape them he moved into a large pit in the hall where the sacred images were kept. It was damp and dark and dirty, never lit and never swept. As the young Swami sat there, deep in meditation, vermin of all sorts, wasps, ants, mosquitoes, scorpions, attached themselves to his body and drank his blood. His legs were foul with purulent sores. He noticed nothing. One day a certain man, having chased away the boys who were still molesting him, went into the pit and, as his eyes grew used to the darkness he dimly saw the outline of a young face. Shocked, he went into the adjoining garden, where a religious was working with his disciples, told them what he had seen and brought the party back to the pit. They went down and carried the youth to the shrine of another temple and there deposited him. Ventakaraman, deep in Samadhi, with his eyes closed, was unconscious of what they did.

He remained where they had placed him for some weeks and was looked after by a Swami who lived there. The Swami fed him, but so rapt in meditation was the lad, often for eight or ten hours at a stretch, that the food had to be thrust into his mouth. Then he moved into a near-by garden and after a while settled himself at the foot of an illupai tree. He had by then attracted the attention of pilgrims, and numbers came to see him. A devotee, Nayinar by name, attached himself to the pious youth and attended to his bodily needs. Nayinar was a scholar, and would recite to him works expounding the Advaita doctrines, of which at the time Ventakaraman was ignorant. After all, he had till then no more than the elementary education he had been given at the school at Madura. But Nayinar could not be with him always, and during his absence the young Swami was much troubled by the curious and by the wretched boys, who thought he was crazy and constantly played foul practical jokes on him. It happened then that yet another Swami, deeply impressed by the youth's purity of heart and devotion, invited him to go to a shrine in a suburb of Tiruvannamalai where he could carry on his meditation undisturbed. He consented and remained there for eighteen months. During this time an ascetic, known as Palamiswamy, was induced to visit Ventakaraman, and at once, feeling that he had found his saviour, made up his mind to devote himself to his service. He kept the increasing crowds away from him and on his behalf received the offerings of food made by the devout. He gave a cupful to the Swami at noon, his only meal of the day, and returned what was over to those who had brought it.

Venkataraman continued to practise his austerities. He became fearfully thin. His body was smeared with unwashed dirt; his hair, grown again, was a clotted mass, and his nails were so long that he could not use his hands. He sat for weeks on the floor in deep Samadhi, unconscious of the thousands of ants that crawled over and bit him. In order to assume the proper posture of meditation he leant against a wall and for long after people saw with wonder the imprint on it of his back. The young Swami's fame increased and the swarm of pilgrims grew so intolerable that, with the faithful Palamiswamy, he moved to a mango grove, which no one was allowed to enter without the owner's leave. Here he stayed for six months. Palamiswamy had access to a library in the town and was able to bring Venkataraman Tamil books on Vedanta. The Swami read them and explained them to his devoted attendant. The biographer points out that the study of books was not necessary for the Swami's Realisation, since he had already attained it; he studied them in order to be able to answer the questions that were put to him by the seekers after truth who came to see him. It was presumably for this reason that he broke his rule of silence. He had maintained it for three years, and during the rest of his life resumed it from time to time for a period.

For some reason the Swami left the grove and moved to a neighbouring temple. He wished to see whether he could live entirely alone. He said to the good Palamiswamy, "You go one way, beg your food and get on. Let me go another way, beg my food and get on. Let us not live together." The poor man went away, but after a day came back. "Where can I go?" he asked. "You have the words of life." Venkataraman allowed him to stay and he remained in attendance on the Swami until he died twenty years later. The Swami, seeking to avoid the devotees who disturbed his meditations, tried place after place, and presently settled down on a spur of the hill Arunachala, where there was a spring, a cave and a temple to Isvara. His habit was to meditate in the temple and, when Palamiswamy happened to be away, go down to the town with his begging bowl and beg for food.

5

When Venkataraman ran away from home, his family, distressed, tried in vain to find him, and it was not till two years later that by chance they had news of him. A young man of their acquaintance happened to hear a pious man speak with great reverence of a young saint living at Tiruvannamalai, and on making further enquiries he grew certain that this was the fugitive. He told the family, whereupon Venkataraman's uncle decided to go to Tiruvannamalai. There he was told that the Swami was residing at the mango grove. He went there and sought to enter, but the owner refused to let him do so. He persuaded him, however, to take a note to the Swami. Venkataraman, having read it, agreed to see him. He besought the youth to come home, promising that the family would not interfere with his mode of life, but only wished him to settle near them, so that they might attend to his wants. Venkataraman listened, but answered neither by word nor gesture. His uncle could do nothing but leave him to his devotions.

On his return to Madura he told the boy's mother, whose name was Alagammal, how fruitless his errand had been. It seemed to her that if she could see Venkataraman herself she might induce him to change his mind, and that she resolved to do. She had to wait till her eldest son, a clerk in a government office, was able to get leave and then went with him to Tiruvannamalai.

Having arrived, they climbed the hill, for the Swami had left the mango grove by then, and found the lad, for he was still little more, lying on a rock. She was shocked by his matted hair, his filthy body, the long nails and the dirty loin-cloth. She begged him to go back with her. He remained silent. Day after day she went to see him, bringing him sweetmeats, and entreated him to have pity on her. He never said a word; he might have been of stone. At last she upbraided him for his callous indifference and burst into tears. Shaken, he got up and withdrew. She sought him again, and again with tears pleaded with him. He did not stir; she might have been speaking to the empty air. Then she addressed the devotees who were there and begged them to intercede for her. One of them, moved by her distress, thus spoke to the Swami:

"Your mother is weeping and praying. Why don't you at least give her a reply? Whether it is yes or no. Swami need not break his silence. Here are pencil and paper. Swami may at least write out what he has to say."

I have said on an earlier page that Venkataraman never used the word 'I' in speaking of himself. I should add here that no one ever addressed him as 'you'. He took the paper and wrote in Tamil:

"The Ordainer controls the fate of souls in accordance with their past deeds. Whatever is destined not to happen will not happen—try however hard you may. Whatever is destined to happen will happen—do what you will to stay it. This is certain. The best course, therefore, is to be silent."

The elder boy's leave came to an end, and he had to return to his office. The unhappy mother could not but go with him.

Shortly after this, Venkataraman once more changed his abode to go up the sacred hill, Arunachala, and for some years he dwelt in cave after cave. They are called caves, and doubtless they were, but from photographs you see that some work has been done on them to make them more fit for human habitation. His fame had by then so much increased that a stream of visitors brought him food—cakes, milk, fruit. But since the visitors had to be fed too, Palamiswamy and other devotees, who had gathered round, would go down to the town with their begging bowls and, blowing a conch, call the charitable to their aid. The Swami led his usual life of meditation. As the Sanskrit verse puts it, "For one who rejoices in and is contented with the Self, there is nothing to do." Sometimes offerings of money were made, but these he sternly refused to accept. Sometimes visitors brought books with them which they found hard to understand, and the Swami would read and expound them. What with the books he read and the recitations he heard, he grew versed in Indian thought; and his memory was such, so it was said, that after a single perusal of a book he could repeat it word for word. Ordinarily, however, he held to his rule of silence. We are not told when he began to give more attention to his body; somewhat later photographs show him very clean, with his loin-cloth washed, his hair short and his beard trimmed. In later years he had his hair cut and his beard shaved once a month. When I saw him he was, as I have said, neat and dapper.

His visitors were of all kinds. Some came for food, others for help in trouble, others again for the spiritual benefit they might get from one who had achieved liberation. Sometimes they had strange experiences. One, Pillai, employed in the Revenue Department, and so, one may presume, a responsible and intelligent man, when sitting near the Swami, had a vision in which he saw him surrounded by a halo. His body shone like the morning sun. Then there was Echammal. She was a woman who, while still in the early twenties, had lost her husband and children and could not get over her bitter grief.

With her father's permission, she went to a place in the Bombay Presidency to serve the holy sages who resided there in the hope that her terrible sorrow might be assuaged. But none of them could help her. She returned to the village and there was told that on the hill of Arunachala was a young and holy saint, who maintained silence and benefited many who approached him with faith. She went there and, climbing the hill, saw the Swami. He sat motionless and said never a word. She stood for an hour in his presence and suddenly felt that the load of grief was lifted from her heart. From that day on she prepared food for him and his followers, and so continued for many years. She had a house at Tiruvannamalai, where she made devotees and visitors welcome. One day, when she was going up the hill with food, she passed a cave and saw two persons standing near-by. One of them was the Swami and the other a stranger. As she went on, she heard a voice say, "When one is here (meaning, when I am here) why go farther up?" She turned to look at the Swami, but there was no one there. When she reached the cave she found him, seated cross-legged as usual, talking to the stranger.

The most noteworthy of the many who came under the magnetic spell of the Swami's personality was a certain Ganapati Sastri. He was a Sanskrit scholar, a man of learning and a poet. He had spent ten years wandering from one holy place to another, and performed penance under the most rigorous conditions. He had collected around him a band of disciples. At length, dissatisfied because he had not gained the peace he sought, he climbed the sacred hill and, prostrating himself, sought refuge at the Swami's feet. The instruction he received filled him with joy, and after this he frequently visited the Swami. At one time he spent seven years at Tiruvannamalai to be near him. The connection is a remarkable proof of the strange power which possessed the Swami; for Sastri was not a youth attracted to an older man; the two were of the same age; he was famous for his immense knowledge and he was a poet of distinction. Scholars and poets have a tendency to think very well of themselves, and Sastri was a masterful man, not apt to knuckle under to others. He caused his own disciples to become the Swami's and himself was the Swami's most ardent devotee. It was he who for the poems he wrote in praise of him contracted his name from Venkataraman to Ramana and instructed his own followers to style him Bhagavan Maharshi. It is as the Maharshi that I shall from now on refer to him.

The following story is told by the Maharshi's biographer. One year, Sastri went to a place called Tiruvottiyur near Madras to perform penance. There was a Ganesha temple there, and Sastri, observing a vow of silence for eighteen days, proceeded to practise meditation. On the eighteenth day, when he was lying down, wide awake, he saw the Maharshi come in and sit by his side. He was astonished, and tried to get up, but the Maharshi, taking hold of his head, pressed him down. This gave Sastri a strange feeling, which he regarded as the Maharshi's grace conferred by his hand. Now, the Maharshi had never left Tiruvannamalai since he first went there and had never in his life been to Tiruvottiyur. When, long afterwards, Sastri narrated the incident, the Maharshi, who was present, answered, "One day, some years ago, I lay down. But I was not in Samadhi. I suddenly felt my body carried up higher and higher, till all objects disappeared, and all around me was one vast mass of white light. Then suddenly the body descended and objects began to appear . . . The idea occurred to me that I was at Tiruvottiyur. I was on a high road and went along that road. On one side, and some distance away, was a Ganesha temple. I went in, and talked, but what I said or did, I do not recollect. Suddenly I awoke and found myself lying down in the cave. . . ."

Sastri found that the Maharshi's description of the place at Tiruvottiyur exactly tallied with the Ganesha temple at which he had carried out his penance.

Time passed. Alagammal, the Maharshi's mother, from time to time went to see him. Her eldest son and her brother-in-law died. The family was left very badly off. Alagammal thought she would be happier if she could live near her son, the Maharshi, so she went to Tiruvannamalai and for a while lived with Echammal. Then the Maharshi moved to what was called the Skandashram. Though he never accepted the money that well-to-do admirers pressed upon him, they were apt to leave it with his disciples so that it might be used for his benefit. When he went to the Skandashram it was thus possible to build a cottage and provide a garden. Alagammal installed herself and cooked for the community. Her youngest son, whose wife had also died, was sent for, so that for her remaining years he might live with his mother. He became a devotee of his brother and donned the yellow robe of the ascetic. Alagammal felt that she had a mother's claims on the Maharshi and that he should treat her with special consideration; but though he would talk with Echammal, he never spoke to her. When she complained of this, he told her that all women were mothers to him, and not she only. His aim was to rid her of worldly delusion and teach her detachment. They were hard lessons to learn, but gradually she learnt them; and when, in 1922, she died, to all appearance he felt no pain, but rather, relief, for he was assured that by a course of good works his mother had atoned for many of the errors of her past lives, so that her soul might rise to some higher region to dwell for a period with the gods and then again inhabit a human body to purge her remaining sins. When someone referred to her passing away, the Maharshi corrected him, "No, not passing away—absorbed." To him death was a triviality, a mere locution, a change to a new life which called for a new name. Alagammal was buried in the plain, a few yards from the road, masonry was built to cover the grave, and this later became a temple and a place of worship.

For six months the Maharshi went almost every day to visit his mother's grave, and one day he stayed there for good. At first, there was to house him no more than a little shed covering the *linga*, the symbol of Siva, but soon thatched huts were put up near-by. When it was seen that he meant to make this his permanent abode, money was offered by the faithful, and a hall was built where he could spend the day and pass the night. From then on, with his ever-increasing fame more and more visitors came. On ordinary days there would be as many as fifty, but on special occasions, such as the Maharshi's birthday, they came in hundreds. They brought gifts; but he would never accept anything that all present might not share. When eatables were offered, he would pick a little off the plate and distribute the rest. But his fame had drawbacks; the idea got about that he was rich, and one night thieves broke in. The Maharshi was resting as usual on the dais in the hall and four of his disciples were asleep by the windows. The Maharshi told the thieves that there was nothing for them to steal, but that they were welcome to take what they liked. The disciples were eager to make some attempt at resistance, but he would not let them. "Let the thieves play their role," he said. "We shall keep to ours. It is for us to bear and forbear. Let us not interfere with them." He offered to leave the hall with his companions so that the robbers might help themselves to whatever they wanted. The ruffians consented, but before they let them go, brutally beat them. The Maharshi received a blow on the leg. "If you are not satisfied with that," he said, "strike the other leg also." Left to themselves, the thieves broke open the bureaus, looking for money, but found none, for there was none to find, and eventually with a miserable booty left. In the confusion one of the disciples had managed to escape. He ran across the fields to the town for help and returned with the police. They found the Maharshi seated in the shed to which he had retired, discoursing, calm and composed, with his disciples on spiritual matters.

There is more than one account of the daily life at the Ashram. The Maharshi rose between three and four in the morning and, after performing his ablutions, sat on his dais. The disciples began the day with a chant in his honour or with the recitation of one of his own Tamil poems in praise of Arunachala. Then a period was devoted to meditation. By five or six, visitors came and, after prostrating themselves before the Maharshi, went about their own concerns. When they were gone a light meal was eaten of rice or semolina. Then the Maharshi resumed his seat in the hall. The disciples occupied themselves in various ways. Some picked flowers and made them into garlands; some worshipped at the tomb of the Maharshi's mother; others engaged in literary work; they composed, corrected, translated works by the Maharshi, who by then had produced a number of compositions, or by other holy personages; some busied themselves with the preparation of food for the inmates and for the visitors. The Maharshi often helped in these tasks and would cut the vegetables and mix the various ingredients that made up the meal. When he had no literary work on hand, he would polish walking-sticks, repair water bowls, stitch the leaf platters on which food was served, copy works in his own script, bind books and read letters.

Breakfast followed between eleven and twelve, and then

work, followed by a rest, was resumed. At about three another meal was eaten, after which visitors were received. As the day closed, meditation was resumed till it was time for the evening meal. All retired at nine. But sometimes the whole night was spent reading aloud, reciting verses or singing the hymns which the Maharshi had composed. At about this time he was commonly spoken of as Bhagavan and in talking of himself he habitually used it. This is translated as 'the blessed one' or 'the divine', and the pious used it in referring to or addressing God. When the devotees came into the Maharshi's presence they prostrated themselves before him. He listened graciously when they read to him the poems they had written in his praise. There seems in all this at first sight some lack of modesty; but it must be remembered that the Maharshi looked upon himself not as a person, but as pure spirit; his body was merely a sheath, there to enable him to work out the Karma of his present existence, and it was not to him that the devout prostrated themselves and chanted hymns of praise, but to Brahman, with which, on achieving realisation many years before, his Atman had become one.

The Maharshi loved animals and had a strange power over them. The Brahmins considered dogs unholy, polluting, and avoided their contact. The Maharshi regarded them as fellow-ascetics who had come to atone for the error of their past lives in his proximity. He saw that they were kept clean and comfortable, and lovingly called them the children of the Ashram. He talked to them and gave them instruction which they could understand and obey. There was a calf which had the run of the Ashram, and for which he had a great affection. He believed it to be the present incarnation of the Old Lady of the Greens, who, when the Maharshi first went up the sacred hill, would gather herbs and edible shrubs, which, after cooking, she would carry up to the young Swami. There were often serpents in the caves he lived in, but he would not allow them to be driven away. "We have come to their residence," he said, "and we have no right to disturb them." Squirrels and crows would come to the cave, bringing their young, and take food off the palm of his hand to feed them.

The hill swarmed with monkeys. The Maharshi came to understand their feelings and their cries. When there were quarrels between two groups, they would come to him and he composed their differences. On one occasion, he heard that one of their chieftains was dying and had it brought to the Ashram. It died, and the Maharshi buried it with the honours due to a dead sannyasin. Several times a year the Maharshi, accompanied by the inmates of the Ashram, made it a practice to walk round the sacred hill of Arunachala. There was a good road, shaded by handsome trees, with tanks, shrines and temples on one or the other side. Sometimes they would start after the evening meal and return at dawn. Sometimes they would set out at dawn and take a day or two to come back. The road was no more than eight miles long, and it could easily have been walked in a couple of hours; but the Maharshi, often in a state of Samadhi, walked at the rate of a mile an hour and rested at the end of each mile. One very hot day, when they were tired, hungry and thirsty, a group of monkeys, observing their condition, ran up a jambol tree, shook down a quantity of ripe fruit and ran away without taking any for themselves. The party ate it gladly. Thus the monkeys repaid their obligations to the Maharshi. On another occasion, however, he was less fortunate. He happened to brush against a nest of hornets and in a second the whole swarm was upon him. They dug their stings into the thigh that had disturbed them. "Yes, yes, this is the leg that is guilty," he said. "Let it suffer." He did not drive them away, nor move till they left him. He bore the excruciating pain as the working out of the law of Karma.

Year by year more and more visitors came to the Ashram. They were of all classes. One evening, after dark, he was sitting with a devotee in the hall when they heard someone calling from outside. The devotee went to see who it was and found a man with his family at the gate. The man asked him whether he and his wife and children could approach the Bhagavan and receive his grace. The devotee was surprised since the Maharshi was open to all comers. "Why do you ask?" he said. The man answered, "We are untouchables." The devotee knew that it would be an injustice to the Maharshi even to beg his permission, for caste signified nothing to him, and so told the man that they would be welcome. The party entered and prostrated themselves before the Maharshi. His look dwelt upon them for about ten minutes, and grace was vouchsafed them. The devotee said later that he had seen many rich and notable persons fall at the Maharshi's feet and receive no such favour. I venture to explain what is here meant by grace. The Tamil word which the biographers thus render might perhaps be better rendered with the word 'blessing'. It has something of the force of a magic spell which, once given, cannot be withdrawn; so, when Isaac found that he had given his blessing to Jacob under the impression that he was giving it to Esau he could do nothing but weep and rend his clothes. Grace is a boon, of efficacy to regenerate and sanctify men, "to inspire virtuous impulses, and to impart strength to endure trial and resist temptation."

The Maharshi seldom spoke. For the most part he remained lost in contemplation; but merely to be in his presence enabled visitors to shake off their troubles and find peace. Sometimes they saw him suffused in brilliant light, but when they told him of this he brushed it off as a matter of no importance. They asked him questions. When they were frivolous, he maintained silence; when, however, he saw that they were in earnest he gave the instruction suited to the enquirer's need. It seemed to many that he could read their minds, for he would on occasion answer questions that they had not ventured to put to him. Many, influenced by his example, left their homes and came to the Ashram, desiring to lead the life of austerity which would lead them to the blessed state of union with the Infinite which is termed illumination. When the Maharshi knew that they had duties, a wife and mother dependent upon them, for instance, he dissuaded them from taking the step. Often persons came to ask whether their avocations could not but interfere with their spiritual efforts. Here is what he told one such enquirer: "It is possible," he said, "to perform all the activities of life with detachment and regard only the Self as real. It is wrong to suppose that, if one is fixed in the Self, one's duties in life will not be properly performed. It is like an actor. He dresses and acts and even feels the part he is playing; but he knows that he is not that character, but someone else in real life. In the same way, why should the body-consciousness or the feeling 'I am the body' disturb you once you know that you are not the body, but the Self? Nothing that the body does should shake you from abidance in the Self. Such abidance will never interfere with the proper and effective discharge of whatever duties the body has, any more than the actor's being aware of his real status in life interferes with his acting a part on the stage."

I need touch but very briefly on the convictions which the Maharshi, as time passed, had come to entertain, and by which his life was regulated; for they were founded on the form of Vedanta promulgated by the great Sankara which I have described as best I could in the earlier part of this essay. The doctrine is pessimistic. That is not to condemn it. It is rash to decry a persuasion that since the beginning of recorded time has been held by sages, poets, and men of the world. The doctrine declares that the world, life and the state of man are evil. Man is destined to pass from birth to death, from death to life, hundreds, nay, thousands of times, until by the grace of Brahman he gains liberation and so is united with the Infinite. To the Maharshi the world was a place of suffering and sorrow. Such pleasures as it offers are negligible since they are transitory. What changes cannot be eternal, and only the eternal has value. But the cause of suffering is in ourselves alone. It is due to our ignorance. To those who came to the Maharshi to resolve their doubts, to pour out their troubles, he would tell to look into their own selves, their true selves, and so gain the happiness of salvation.

The Self he spoke of was situated in the heart, but not the heart that the anatomist dissects, the heart that the lover knows. It was Infinite Reality. So, when Mahatma Gandhi sent an emissary to see him who, on his departure, asked him, "What message may I take him?" the Maharshi answered, "What message is needed when heart speaks to heart?" Man, he taught, can only achieve freedom from bondage, the bondage of birth and rebirth, by disentangling the knot that binds the Atman to the ego. When men asked how it was possible to attain this blessed state, he told each one to ask himself, "Who am I?" He sought to impress upon the aspirant that he was not the body which he temporarily inhabited, but the Self which was eternal. It was on this that he must concentrate his mind. Many complained that when, with this object, they engaged in meditation, discordant thoughts crossed their minds. The Maharshi told them that this was no matter. They must discard them, and again fix the mind on the Self, and in course of time it would become easy. He was very tolerant of human weakness and taught that all methods of meditation were good. Each must choose for himself the way that suited his temperament and came more readily to him. Some might find that they could avoid distraction by such methods as fixing their attention on the space between the eyebrows or on the tip of the nose. These were Yoga practices, and the Maharshi regarded them with misgivings. The better way was to occupy the mind with such an object of devotion as Siva or Vishnu. But even this was no more than a device to help the aspirant to fix his mind on the real subject of the quest, the Self. Realisation is not gained by knowledge, but by inspiration. When the aspirant has made his own the knowledge that he is not the physical body (the sense organs) nor the mind (which is only the sum of his thoughts) and has discovered that the intellect is merely the instrument of the subject and not the subject itself, when, in short, he has destroyed the ego, so that only the Self remains, he will by the grace of Brahman achieve Realisation. But though the steps towards Realisation can be described, Realisation is indescribable. It can only be felt.

The Maharshi was a fatalist. Philosophers have discussed at length this matter of free will and determination, but, so far as I know, they have never come to a conclusion that is spiritually satisfactory. Unless I am mistaken, they appear to believe that we are able to choose whether we shall take one course rather than another, but having taken it, it was inevitable that we should do so. Suppose we come to a fork of the road when travelling and, uncertain whether to take the road on the right or the road on the left, toss up a coin, deciding that if it comes down heads we will take the road on the right and if tails, on the left—was it fated that the coin should come down heads and so lead us to take the road we actually took? When we look back on our lives, we, who are not philosophers, can hardly fail to recognise that much that has happened to change our life's course looks as though it had been due to mere chance. The Maharshi, I think, would have said that this is an illusion. People continually came to him for guidance. Some were concerned to know whether they would be justified in taking an active part in the struggle at long last to liberate their country from the foreign yoke; others, horrified at the appalling poverty of the masses of India, asked whether it would be right for them by engaging in social service to do what they could to alleviate their wretched lot. The Maharshi told them first of all to realise the Self in themselves, for that was the most important thing; after that they could do what they liked; but since nothing happens except by divine dispensation, nothing they might do could affect it. "If you are destined not to work, work cannot be got even if you hunt for it; if you are destined to work, you will not be able to avoid it; you will be forced to engage in it. So, leave it to the Higher Power; you cannot renounce or retain as you will." It was natural that the question should be put to him: If what is destined to happen will happen, is there any use in prayer or effort? It does not seem to me that he answered the question. "There are only two ways to conquer destiny and be independent of it," he replied. "One is to enquire for whom is this destiny and discover that only the ego is bound by destiny, and not the Self, and that the ego is non-existent. The other way is to kill the ego by completely surrendering to the Lord, by realising one's helplessness and saying all the time, 'Not I, but thou, O Lord,' and by giving up all sense of 'I' and 'Mine', and leaving it to the Lord to do what he likes with you. . . . True surrender is love of God for the sake of love and nothing else, not even for the sake of salvation."

6

The Maharshi was growing old. He was approaching the age of seventy. He had long been troubled with rheumatism, occasioned, it was thought, by the many years he had spent living in caves, and his eyes began to fail him. Towards the end of 1948 a small growth was noticed on his left elbow; it turned into a painful tumour and had to be operated on. The wound healed, but in a little while the growth, judged by then to be cancerous, returned, and a further operation was necessary. The surgeons decided that the only hope of saving the Maharshi's life was to amputate the arm, but this he refused. Smiling, he said, "There is no need for alarm. The body itself is a disease. Let it have its natural end. Why mutilate it?" He grew worse. Various methods were tried to stay the disease and for a while his general health improved. Then the tumour re-appeared and another operation was performed; a second tumour arose near the arm-pit and swelled rapidly. The doctors agreed that from then on they could do nothing but administer palliatives. The Maharshi suffered great pain, but seemed indifferent to it. Throughout, he remained unconcerned, and if he submitted to treatment it was only to please the devotees. "If I were asked," he said, "I should always say, as I have said from the beginning, that no treatment is necessary. Let things take their course." On one occasion he said to one of his faithful attendants, "When we have finished a meal, do we keep the leaf-plate on which we have eaten it?" On another, he told him that he who has right knowledge rejoices to be relieved of the body, as a servant rejoices to lay down his burden at the place of delivery.

During the two years his fatal illness lasted, the Maharshi continued as long as possible his daily routine. He took his morning bath an hour before sunrise, and sat up at fixed hours to grant the favour of his grace to the pilgrims who came to receive it. News of his condition spread throughout India and they came in hundreds. His seventy-first birthday was celebrated with the usual ceremonies, and he listened to the hymns that were chanted in his honour. The elephant of the temple of Arunachala came and, after bowing down to the Maharshi, stood for a while, and then took leave of him by touching his feet with his trunk. It was plain that he could not live much longer. Congestion of the lungs supervened, but when a doctor came, bringing medicine to relieve him, he waved him aside. He told him that it was not necessary and that everything would come right within a little while. He bade his attendants retire and leave him alone. That evening, reclining on his bed, he gave his last blessing to a great gathering of devotees. At sunset he asked to be raised to a sitting position, the ritual posture of meditation. A group of his disciples, seated on the temple ramp opposite the room in which he sat, began to chant the hymn to Arunachala which long ago he had composed. His eyes opened and tears of ecstasy rolled down his cheeks. His heart stopped beating. The Maharshi had entered the Reality of the One without a Second. At the moment he died, a comet moved slowly across the sky, reached the top of the sacred hill, Arunachala, and disappeared behind it. It was seen by vast numbers, and they ascribed the strange phenomenon to the passing of a great soul.

Prose and Dr. Tillotson

I LOOKED WITH MISGIVING at the thinnish parcel that lay on the hall table with the letters that had come by the morning's post. I guessed what it contained. Like all authors who have achieved a certain notoriety, I am sent manuscripts by strangers who ask me to tell them what I think of their productions and, not seldom, beg me to use such influence as I may have to get them published. Publishers send me novels, generally of inordinate length, with the request that I should offer an opinion that they can use in their advertisements. I am sent works of edification to convert me, something of a sceptic, to the particular variety of religion that the author holds; and long treatises, written often enough by superannuated civil servants or retired colonels, on abstruse subjects that only specialists are competent to deal with. Poets send me slim volumes of verse obviously published at their own expense. I regard them with a pang. With what high hopes of fame has each one launched on the world his elegantly printed, his austerely bound, little volume! If reviewed at all, it will be in two or three casual lines, and the friends to whom he has sent it will skim the pages in half an hour. It would be impossible to read all the books I receive, and the chances are that they are not worth reading. What can I do but write to one author after another a polite note of thanks and add, without strict regard to the truth, that I look forward to reading his work with interest when my own occupations allow me sufficient leisure? I did not open the parcel till after I had read my letters, and when I did so, it was, naturally enough, with composure. It contained, as I had surmised, a book, but not at all the sort of book I could possibly have expected. It was a slim volume, octavo, and the calf binding, though sadly battered, was handsomely tooled. The title was: *Maxims and Discourses, Moral and Divine: Taken from the works of Arch-Bishop Tillotson, and Methodized and Connected.* It was "printed for J. Tonson, at Shakespear's Head, over-against Katherine Street in the Strand", in the year 1719. The dedication ran as follows, "To the Most Excellent, Most Pious, and Beneficent Lady, Cassandra, Countess of Carnarvon: Illustrious in Her Family and Fortune, and more so in her Merits and Virtues, which are an Ornament to Her Station, and a Pattern to Her Sex: These Select Passages from Arch-Bishop Tillotson (Whose Writings are Entitled to the most Accomplish'd Persons) are with all Humility, Gratitude, and Veneration, Inscribed by Her Ladyship's Most Oblig'd, Humble, and Devoted Servant, Lawrence Echard."

At the end of the volume there is a list of the books printed by Jacob Tonson from which one learns that Lawrence Echard, Archdeacon of Stowe, was the author of an History of England in three volumes in folio and a general Ecclesiastical History from the Nativity of our Blessed Saviour to the first establishment of Christianity by Human Laws under the Emperor Constantine the Great. The list is imposing. It contains *Remarks on Several Parts of Italy, in the years* 1701, 1702, 1703. By Mr. Addison; the works of Mr. William Congreve, in three volumes; and the works of Mr. Francis Beaumont and Mr. John Fletcher in seven volumes, adorned with cuts. Jacob Tonson was an eminent member of his respectable profession. He was

Dryden's publisher and, as everyone knows, had bought from one Aylmer half his share of *Paradise Lost*, the copyright of which the said Aylmer had bought for five pounds. I don't know that I have ever seen a picture of a bookshop early in the eighteenth century, but I suppose it was small and dark and crowded with books. The printing press was at the back. Jacob Tonson, having prospered, bought himself a house in the village of Barnes, but it is likely enough that his nephew and partner, also called Jacob Tonson, lived with his family over the shop. Doubtless, as they do now at Bumpus's, bookish persons wandered from shelf to shelf glancing at one volume or another; and it amused me to think that among them may have been a young scholar from Oxford, recently ordained, who was passing through London on his way to the country, where he was to act as tutor to the scion of a noble house. It may be that he caught sight of the *Poetical Works* of Mr. John Milton in two volumes and, curiosity overcoming prejudice, took down one of them. As a Tory and an Oxford man, he held in execration the Usurper's former secretary, and it must have disconcerted him to be forced to admit that the lines he had come across by chance looked very like great poetry. He put the volume back quickly when a coach stopped at the door and a woman of quality, stylishly dressed, entered the shop and asked for *Ovid's Art of Love* in three books, together with his *Remedy of Love*. While I was allowing my fancy to run wild over Jacob Tonson's list of publications, I suddenly remembered why this particular book had been sent me. In something of mine I had had occasion to give a brief quotation from a piece that Dr. Tillotson had written. I must have come across it in some anthology of English prose and been taken by it.

2

In the preface which the Archdeacon of Stowe wrote to introduce the maxims and discourses which he had culled from the Archbishop's sermons, he remarks that works of this nature have been looked upon as both useful and entertaining in all ages, but admits that in productions of this kind no nation seems to have gone further than our neighbours the French. Among these writers "none have been more celebrated than the Duke of Rochefuocaut (for thus he spells his name) and Monsieur la Bruyere; Persons that have penetrated deep into Mankind and the secret Springs of Action, but have often brought up the Mud and the Dregs, as well as the Riches and Treasures of Human Nature." He expresses his regret that little of this amiable variety of literature has appeared in England, and that little, with the exception of what is to be found in the "works of the late famous Marquess of Halifax, who in Knowledge and Penetration has not been inferior to either Foreign or English writers," has never been highly esteemed. He proceeds as follows, "I have been long of opinion that out of the English writers many Apothegms, Wise Sentences and Contracted Arguments, as beneficial and agreeable as any in Foreign Authors, may be selected to excellent good purpose: And more particularly in Archbishop Tillotson's works may be found a number of Passages not inferior to the fore-mention'd Rochefuocaut and la Bruyere." In this, I am afraid, the Archdeacon was in error. True, he admits that they (La Rochefoucault and La Bruyère) "had sometimes a more artful turn, which the French Nation have study'd and practis'd almost to Affectation; his (Tillotson's) have a native Simplicity and Grandeur more agreeable to the English Taste." Echard's object was to make his selection "a most Useful and

Beneficent One, and such as will be Pleasant and Entertaining to all who have a true Taste for polite and correct Writing." He would, perhaps, have done better not to mention the two French writers, for it arouses in the reader an expectation that is not fulfilled. He divided his book into two parts. The first deals with the "Being and Nature of God and his Worship, and Religion both in Theory and Practice"; the second with "What most immediately concerns Man, and his natural Dispositions, together with the Social Virtues and contrary Vices." I confess that this is the part that I myself have found most interesting, and in the hope of interesting the reader I propose to make some quotations from it.

I think Lawrence Echard made a mistake when he entitled his work Maxims and Discourses Moral and Divine. Discourse indicates a discussion of some subject at length and a maxim is a proposition stating a truth in a pithy and sententious manner. The passages dealing with religion in general and the nature and being of God are for the most part less than a page long, and the moral maxims are far from pithy. They are sensible enough, the observations of a man of wide experience, but there is none which, once you have read, you can never forget, none that has the bitter truth of the French Duke's, *Entre deux amants il y a un qui aime et un qui se laisse aimer*. But what Tillotson had to say he put in an easy and telling manner. Here are some examples of it.

"Early habits of virtue, like new clothes upon a young and comely body, fit very gracefully upon a straight and well-shaped mind, and do mightily become it."

"By a general mistake ill-nature passes for wit, as cunning does for wisdom; though in truth they are nothing akin to one another, but as far distant as vice and virtue."

"Wit is a commendable quality, but then a wise man should always have the keeping of it. It is a sharp weapon, as apt for mischief as for good purposes, if it be not well managed. The proper use of it is to season conversation, to represent what is praiseworthy to the greatest advantage and to expose the vices and follies of men, such things as are themselves ridiculous."

"To praise anything well is an argument of much more wit than to abuse."

Dr. Tillotson knew very well that to commend does not come easily to men. "But in the way of invective, the invention of men is a plentiful and never failing spring; and this kind of wit is not more easy than it is acceptable. It is greedily entertained and greatly applauded, and every man is glad to hear others abused, not considering how soon it may come to his own turn to lie down and make sport of others."

Finally, "There is something of vanity mingled with all our earthly enjoyments. There is no sensual pleasure, but it is either purchased with some pain, or attended with it, or ends in it. A great estate is neither got without care, nor kept without fear, nor lost without trouble. Dignity and greatness is troublesome to almost all mankind; it is commonly uneasy to them that have it, and it is usually hated and envied by those that have it not."

I should like the reader to notice how modern these passages seem. The prose the Archbishop wrote is not very much different from that which an educated person would write today. Macaulay has described it as correct, lucid and workmanlike, but without brilliance. The word brilliance applied to prose makes me faintly uneasy. It suggests a flashy glitter that is not altogether agreeable. Half a century ago, I suppose one would have described Carlyle's prose as brilliant, and a generation or so later George Meredith's and Kipling's. Time has made their way of writing exasperating. It is possible that Macaulay looked upon his own style as brilliant, and not unjustly. The critics tell us that he founded it on that of Dr.

Johnson. Instead of the Doctor's long, elaborate periods, Macaulay used short, brisk sentences, and he made abundant use of the antithesis which had been all the rage in the late eighteenth century. He wrote a prose that was rapid, effective, dramatic, persuasive and eminently readable. If in the long run it is a trifle monotonous, so that it gives you the effect of an express train bumping at full speed over a slightly ill-laid track, it serves as a good example of Dr. Johnson's dictum that when once a man has developed a style he can seldom write in any other way.

During the last quarter of the seventeenth century a considerable change was effected in English prose—to see how great, you have only to compare Hobbes with John Locke and Milton with Addison. Rich and vivid as Hobbes's prose is, it is crowded and muddled: Locke's is orderly; it is not exciting, but it is compact and seemly. Milton's prose is rhetorical, splendid often and passionate, but cumbrous; Addison's is easy, graceful, and urbane. It is said, I do not know with what justification, that this change was occasioned in part by the fact that the royalist exiles who had fled to France, when they could no longer fight for their unhappy King, gained a taste for lucidity and concision from the French authors whom they read during their sojourn abroad; and later, after the Restoration, from their frequentation of coffee-houses, where the interminable conversations they indulged in led them, when they set pen to paper, to use the same sort of language as they had found effective in discussion. The fact remains that written English became more limpid, simpler and more natural. "The proprieties and delicacies of English are known to few," said Dryden, " 'tis impossible for even a good wit to understand and practice them without the help of a liberal education, long reading and digesting of those few good authors we have among us; the knowledge of men and manners; the freedom and habitude of conversations with the best company of both sexes; and, in short, without wearing off the rust he has acquired while laying in a stock of learning." These are wise words. The Life of John Tillotson, Archbishop of Canterbury, was written by Thomas Birch and in it he states that "Mr. Dryden frequently owned with pleasure, that if he had any talent for English prose, which must be allowed to have been a great one, it was owing to his having often read his Grace's writings. And Dr. Swift, whose judgment was not usually biassed by excess of civility, vouches (in a letter to a young gentleman lately entered into Holy Orders) the Archbishop the title of excellent." A little later, Thomas Birch adds, "Mr. Addison considered his writings as the chief standard of our language, and accordingly marked the particular phrases in the sermons published during his Grace's life-time, as the ground-work for an English dictionary, projected by that elegant writer, when he was out of all public employment after the change of ministry in the reign of Queen Anne." No one has written better English than these three distinguished authors, Dryden, Swift and Addison, and if it is true that they learnt and profited by the works of Tillotson, it gives him an importance that he would not otherwise have had. It may be that it is not too rash to suggest that if we write as we do now it is in part because the Archbishop wrote as he did.

There are two ways of writing English prose, the plain and the ornate. The greatest examples in our literature of the latter are, of course, Sir Thomas Browne and Jeremy Taylor in *Holy Dying*. No one would be so foolish as to deny the beauty of their respective styles. To describe that of either as brilliant would be to depreciate it. In a different class, you might add Dr. Johnson and Gibbon. Here opinions are divided. There are persons of discrimination who have nothing bad enough to say of them. The truth is, they are a drug, which, when you have once acquired a taste for it, you can hardly do without any more than the addict can do without his dope. Whatever their pomposity, their grandiloquence, you read with the same intense, increasing and amused delight. Of these two styles, the plain and ornate, you cannot say that one is better than the other. There is no right or wrong here. It is merely a matter of taste. I would suggest that the plain style is more suited to matters of practical interest than the ornate. If you are concerned with the subject of your discourse, the bread and butter of it, rather than the jam, you will be more persuasive if you eschew ornament. To substantiate this, I would ask the reader to compare Jeremy Taylor's *Liberty of Prophesying* with his *Holy Dying*. *Holy Dying*, is remarkable for its dazzling embroideries and the luxuriance of its images. The *Liberty of Prophesying* is written as plainly and straightforwardly, though of course in the idiom of the period, as if it were an official report on the condition of the navy. In this Jeremy Taylor was dealing with a matter in which he had a personal concern. His rich living had been sequestered, his estate seized, his house plundered and his family turned out of doors. After various hazards he found a refuge in South Wales, where the local grandee, the Earl of Carbery, welcomed him. His wife and children joined him. Lord Carbery made him his private chaplain, but the salary was small and, it is suggested, irregularly paid. It was in these untoward circumstances that he wrote *The Liberty of Prophesying*. He had suffered much, his future was dark, and he was dependent on the uncertain liberality of his patron; it is not strange that when he came to write this book, it should not have the "pomp of imagery", I am quoting Edmund Gosse, "which is characteristic of his finest writing." The style is pure and direct, though a trifle dry. The argument can be stated in a few words; and has been well put by the historian of the early Stuarts, "Reason is the ultimate judge of religion as of other matters; now, since reason is an individual attribute, there are likely to be different opinions. As no man can be certain that his opinion is right or better than another's, it is wrong to persecute unorthodox beliefs, for there is no demonstrable proof that they are erroneous." Could anything be more sensible?

The Liberty of Prophesying was written in 1646, *Holy Dying* in 1651. During the years Jeremy Taylor passed at Golden Grove, Lord Carbery's seat, his chief mainstay was the Earl's wife, who appears to have been a good, clever and courageous woman. After thirteen years of marriage, worn out by constant pregnancies, she died on giving birth to her tenth child. This was in 1650. A year later Jeremy Taylor's wife died. It is natural to suppose that it was these events which gave him the impulse to write *Holy Dying*. Everyone agrees that it is the greatest of his works. Critics have vied with one another to praise the sustained beauty and profusion of its style, its "limpid and continuous glory" and the amazing abundance of its images. It is written in a very different manner from that of *The Liberty of Prophesying*. In this he was concerned with his own private wrongs and he wrote, not to edify, but to persuade. In *Holy Dying* he gave free rein to his more precious gifts. There can be no doubt that his grief at the loss of the amiable Countess and of his affectionate wife was sincere. In *Holy Dying* he not only erected an imperishable monument to their memory, but it may well be found solace in the ingenious conceits that his fertile imagination presented to him and in the melodious sentences that his pen put to paper. For it is the inestimable privilege of the creative artist to win in creation release from the pains of life.

Of these two ways of writing English, I have a notion that the plain wears better than the ornate. The ornate demands a perfection which can only very rarely be achieved, and in all our literature, so far as I know, this has only been done by the two authors I have hitherto mentioned. Less gifted writers have practised it, but time has sorely maltreated it. Thomas de Quincey in the middle of last century was regarded by competent critics as supreme among the masters of English prose. They praised his power of dealing in unrivalled fashion with the subtleties and splendours of our language. I find his style affected and turgid. Some years ago Mr. Richard Aldington published an anthology of prose and verse by nineteenth century writers which he called *The Religion of Beauty*. The verse has maintained the charm it had when first written, but the stylists, George Meredith, Walter Pater, Max Beerbohm, are sadly dated. You can hardly read the delicious scene of the meeting of Ferdinand and Miranda in *The Ordeal of Richard Feverel* without embarrassment. The passage from Walter Pater's *Æsthetic Poetry* is dry and airless; you feel that it was imagined without inspiration and written with labour. The only pieces of prose in this interesting volume that can be read with pleasure are those, like Arthur Symons's piece on poor Ernest Dowson, in which the author has not tried to write finely, but in good plain English.

3

If one wanted an instance of the truth of Buffon's saying that *le style est l'homme même*, it would be difficult to do better than to adduce Dr. Tillotson. I propose now to give, as briefly as I can, an account of his life. Though he lived through stirring times, the Civil War, the Protectorate of Oliver Cromwell, the Restoration, the wars with the Dutch, the Plague, the Fire of London, the Glorious Revolution, his life was strangely uneventful. He was a good man and, as everyone knows, it is harder to write interestingly about a good man than about a bad one. There is a portrait of him in the National Portrait Gallery. It is that of an elderly, good-natured man, somewhat full in the face, but comely and of a pleasing appearance. Except for the canonicals you might take it for the portrait of a prosperous inn-keeper. Though with age he grew corpulent, he is said in youth to have been slender and good-looking with eyes full of ex-pression. He seems to have had to a considerable degree a quality which, so far as I know, the seventeenth century did not make the to-do about that we do now—charm. It is a dubious quality, for it is often an attribute of worthless creatures, and then you have to be on your guard against it; but when it is combined with talent, uprightness and high moral character, it makes its happy possessor irresistible.

Tillotson was born in 1630 at Sowerby in Yorkshire. His father was descended from an ancient county family and was by calling a clothier. It was then by no means unusual for gentle-men, the younger sons even of great noblemen, to go into trade. If we may judge from the novels of Jane Austen it was not till towards the end of the eighteenth century that this came to be considered degrading, an attitude which reached its culmination in the reign of Queen Victoria and needed two disastrous wars to be discarded. A clothier was a middleman who bought the newly sheared wool from the shearers and put it out among the local cottagers to spin the yarn and weave the cloth, which he then sold at a profit. Tillotson's father was a zealous Puritan and the boy's early education was austere. At the age of seventeen, having passed through the grammar schools with credit, he went to Cambridge. There he read "the immortal work of Mr. Chillingworth" and so became intimately acquainted with the Cambridge Platonists. His biographer, Thomas Birch, a member of the Established Church, states that he was thus freed from his early prejudices; yet, he adds, "he still adhered to the strictness of life to which he was bred, and retained a just value and due tenderness for the men of that persuasion" (the Puritans). In due course he took his degree and at the age of twenty-one was elected a Fellow of his college. His Tutor, Mr. Clarkson, transferred his own pupils to him. One of them, John Beardmore, has left an account of the way in which Tillotson performed his duties. "He was a very good scholar," he states, "an acute logician and philosopher, a quick disputant, of a solid judgment, and no way unqualified for the trust and charge incumbent upon him. . . . When we went to prayers in his chamber a-nights, he put us for some time at first upon construing or rendering into Latin a chapter in the Greek Testament, and afterwards, in process of time, he used to put some or other upon giving account of the day's reading. . . . This was ever done in Latin; for I know not that ever he spoke a word of English to us, whilst we were so together, or permitted any of us to do so." His prayers according to the use of Presbyterian style were what was called 'conceived', that is to say extemporary. On week-days, after prayers, as his pupils were leaving, he would retain one of them, talk to him kindly, encourage him to studiousness, seriousness and diligence, or tell him of "any fault he either observed or heard of in him and would reprove very sharply anyone who deserved it. He was careful of his pupils' behaviour and manner; had a love for those of us that he saw deport themselves well and was respectful to them, but very severe to those that did otherwise." John Beardmore adds that his Tutor was "a person of a very good wit, sharp and acute, pleasant in conversation, but with much decorum and gravity for his years." I may remind the reader that he was then in his early twenties.

In 1656, Tillotson left Cambridge to be tutor to the son of Edmund Prideaux, who was then Attorney-General. To occupy such a position in the household of a man of rank or of political importance was the surest way to preferment that any young man in orders could have, and after the Restoration it led almost certainly to prebends, deaneries and even bishoprics. Since Tillotson acted also as Mr. Prideaux's chaplain he must have been ordained, but when he was has remained obscure. As he could only have been ordained by a Presbyterian minister, it was doubtless better in later years not to refer to the matter. Oliver Cromwell died in 1658 and in 1660 Charles II began his disastrous reign. Tillotson submitted to the Act of Uniformity and so became a member of the Church by Law Established. He took Holy Orders from an old Scottish Bishop of Galloway, "who at that time had great recourse made to him on that account." In a note John Beardmore states that this bishop ordained all the English clergy who came to him, without demanding either oaths or subscriptions from them; and this he was presumed to have done merely for a subsistence from the fees for the letters of orders granted by him, for he was poor. The first office in the Church that Tillotson occupied was that of curate at Cheshunt in Hertfordshire; it was so near London that he was able frequently to visit his friends there and, having apparently already won some reputation as a preacher, he was often invited into the pulpits of the city. In 1663 he was presented to the rectory of Ketton in Suffolk, vacant by the ejection of the former rector for nonconformity. It was worth two hundred pounds a year. Thomas Birch, somewhat naïvely, says that the ejected minister had the satisfaction of being succeeded by a person of such eminent abilities, candour and moderation. While there, Tillotson was asked to preach before the Society of Lincoln's Inn in place of the usual lecturer, and it so happened that one of the benchers, Mr. Atkins by name, was present, and so pleased was he with the sermon "that he went to him in the vestry and offered his interest for the place of preacher at Lincoln's Inn, which would soon be vacant". Tillotson was accordingly elected to that office, "upon the terms allowed his predecessor, of one hundred pounds, payable at the end of every term by equal portions; the first payment to begin at the end of the next term, and twenty-five pounds more for vacation commons; with commons for himself and his servant in term time, and a chamber. And five of the masters of the bench were appointed to acquaint him with his election, and to inform him of the duty expected from him, that he should preach twice every Lord's day in term time, and next before and after term, and in reading time, and on every Lord's day in the vacation, and as other occasions should require; and administer the sacrament of the Lord's Supper, together with the chaplain of the house, every term and vacation; and reside constantly in the Society, without absenting himself thence, without leave of the masters of the bench in council."

It must be admitted that the benchers of Lincoln's Inn were demanding a good deal for their money. The arrangement, however, was so satisfactory to Tillotson that he determined to settle in London. He had recently married. His wife was Oliver Cromwell's niece. We know little about her except that she bore her husband two daughters and survived him. If we like to indulge in surmise we may suppose that he met her when he was chaplain to the Protector's Attorney-General, and it may be that there was an 'understanding' between them; but he was at the time in no position to marry. The connection then would doubtless have been advantageous; when he did marry her, which his salary at Ketton enabled him to do, it was honourable; the carcase of Cromwell had been drawn on a hurdle to Tyburn and hanged up in his coffin, and kinship with the usurper was regarded with suspicion. The salary Dr. Tillotson received from Lincoln's Inn was small and, with a wife to support, he

John Tillotson D. D. (1630-1694), a portrait after Kneller now in the National Portrait Gallery badly needed the additional income which his living at Ketton brought him. Though obliged to spend most of the year in London, he could very well have done what many beneficed clergymen, who did not care to live in their parish, did not scruple to do—engage a curate for as little as twenty pounds a year to do their duty for them; but this went against the grain with him, and he resigned his cure. It may be that he did so not without relief, for his parishioners, Puritans and Presbyterians, had not relished his sermons. Fortunately they were so successful at Lincoln's Inn that within a year Tillotson was appointed lecturer at St. Lawrence Jewry. There "he was commonly attended by a numerous audience, brought together from the remotest parts of the metropolis, and by a great concourse of the clergy, who came thither to form their minds". Many that heard him on Sunday at Lincoln's Inn went to St. Lawrence Jewry on the following Tuesday in the hope of hearing the same sermon over again.

There was at the time an enormous appetite for sermons. So great was their influence that the statesmen of the Restoration thought fit to exercise control over them. Preachers were bidden to dwell on the moral duties of the individual and to avoid the intricacies of theology. Free grace and predestination, which the Puritans had preached, were to be ignored. Sermons were long, often inordinately so, and it is told that the vergers of Westminster Abbey ordered the organ to strike up when they thought that Isaac Barrow, Master of Trinity, should bring his discourse to an end. On one occasion he preached on the subject of charity for three hours and a half. It may be that one reason for Tillotson's success was that "he retrenched both the luxuriance of style and the length of sermons". His biographer has described his as solid and yet lively, and grave as well as elegant. He laid aside all long and affected periods. His sentences were short and clear, and the whole thread was of a piece, plain and distinct. He very soon came to be considered the greatest preacher of his day.

When he had been settled in London for a couple of years the Great Plague broke out. Many of the clergy, both churchmen and nonconformists, fled the stricken city. Tillotson was not the man to follow their example. He remained throughout to tend the sick and minister to the dying.

His merits did not go unrewarded. In course of time he was presented to a prebend at Canterbury and to a prebend and a residentiaryship at St. Paul's. In case the reader does not know what that is, I may explain that it is an ecclesiastical term denoting an official abode, with an income attached, awarded to a canon of a cathedral. At the suggestion of Burnet, author of the history, he was appointed chaplain to Charles II. In 1672 he was advanced to the Deanery of Canterbury. One day he was called unexpectedly to preach before the King. At the end of his sermon, a certain nobleman stepped up to the monarch, who had slept soundly through it, and said to him, "Tis pity your Majesty slept, for we had the rarest piece of Hobbism that ever you heard in your life." "Ods fish, he shall print it then," answered the King, and immediately called the Lord Chamberlain and gave him his command to the Dean to print his sermon. The thesis of Hobbes, as perhaps not everyone remembers, is that the powers of the sovereign are unlimited. Unbounded power on the one side corresponds with unconditional obedience on the other. The sovereign may be despotic, but despotism is better than anarchy, and resistance to him is as futile as it is criminal. There is only one limitation to his power: the right of self-defence is absolute, and the subject has the right of self-defence even against the sovereign.

The King's command had unfortunate results. The sermon

gave offence to churchmen and dissenters alike. There was one passage which gave rise to virulent criticism: "I cannot think," said Tillotson, "till I am better informed, which I am always ready to be, that any pretence of conscience warrants any man . . . to affront the established religion of a nation, though it be false, and openly to draw men off from the profession of it, in contempt of the magistrate and the law. All that persons of a different religion can in such a case reasonably pretend to, is to enjoy the private liberty and exercise of their own conscience and religion, for which they might be very thankful, and to forbear the open making of proselytes to their own religion (though they be never so sure that they are in the right) till they have either an extraordinary commission from God to that purpose, or the providence of God makes way for it by the permission of the magistrate." To us, today, this may well seem reasonable, but passions were high, and the Dean of Canterbury was violently attacked. Dr. Patrick, afterwards Bishop of Ely, urged that he should give satisfaction by a retraction, and if he would not, should have no mercy, but be hounded out of the Christian Church. Mr. Howe, a learned nonconformist minister, in the course of a long conversation with the Dean, told him how much he was grieved that, in a sermon against popery, he should plead the popish cause against all the reformers. "The Dean at length fell to weeping freely, and said, that this was the most unhappy thing that had for a long time befallen him; and that he saw what he had offered was not to be maintained." It did not help. When this admission of his was made known, he was accused of having given satisfaction to the dissenters, without doing anything to remove the offence given to the brethren of his own Church.

What gave a certain plausibility to these charges was that Tillotson, whose early years had been spent in a Puritan atmosphere, had always remained on good terms with his nonconformist friends. But he had submitted to the Act of Uniformity with sincerity. The principles of the Established Church, which rejected the asperities of the dissenting sects on the one hand and the dogmas of what was somewhat incivilly called popery on the other, well suited his mild, pious and sensible temper, and there is no evidence that he took a very serious view of the differences that divided the Protestant parties. His earnest wish was that each side should make concessions so that the less rabid nonconformists should be drawn back to the Church. But his moderation was looked upon as a vice, rather than a virtue.

It is not to my purpose to deal with the religious dissensions that caused such grave troubles during the reign of Charles II. To us they may well seem trivial. Whether a clergyman should, or should not, wear a surplice does not seem so important as to be worth quarrelling about. That a communicant should receive the sacrament kneeling at the altar steps or seated in his pew one would have thought a matter of decorum rather than of religious principle. The Act of Uniformity deprived some two thousand ministers of their cures, and the Five Mile Act, which forbade them to go within five miles of a corporate body, made it hard for them to earn a living. Many, reduced to poverty, were forced to menial occupations. The Test Act rendered all who refused to take the oath of allegiance and supremacy, to receive the sacraments according to the Church of England, and who would not renounce belief in transubstantiation incapable of any employment, military or civil. This affected nonconformists and Roman Catholics alike. The oath of allegiance, I may add, demanded the recognition of the sovereign as lawful and rightful King and repudiated the papal claim that a heretic and excommunicated prince might be deposed and murdered.

The great mass of the English people looked upon Catholics as traitors, and many ascribed the Great Fire of London in 1666 to their malice. Even Milton felt that reasons of state justified their exclusion from toleration.

4

In 1683 an event occurred which for the remainder of his life gravely affected Dr. Tillotson. This was the discovery of what came to be known as the Rye House Plot. An anabaptist, Keeling by name, a salter and oil-man by calling, whose business was decaying, began to think, as Burnet puts it, that that of a witness would be a better trade. He went to Lord Dartmouth, who then held an office at Court, with a story of a scheme to kill the King and the Duke of York. Dartmouth sent him to Sir Leoline Jenkins, Secretary of State and an ardent royalist, who communicated the matter to the rest of the Ministry. News of this soon leaked out. Two men, Rumsey and West, whom Keeling had mentioned, were implicated. They had served in the parliamentary armies and, according to Burnet, had talked rashly of the fantastic schemes they had in mind, but "apprehending that they had trusted themselves to too many persons, who might discover them, they laid a story in which they resolved to agree so well together that they should not contradict one another". They formed a plan to come in of their own accord and make a confession which would not only save their lives, but might gain for them employment as informers "against the numerous emissaries of Satan then flourishing in England."

West declared that, on a day decided upon, the King and the Duke of York were to be killed on their way back to London from Newmarket, to which they went regularly for the races. The spot chosen was The Rye House, a farm belonging to a certain Rumbold, one of the alleged conspirators, which he offered for this purpose, since the royal coach had there to pass through a narrow road between high banks and could conveniently be stopped and the King's person seized. What seemed to confirm the story was that, owing to a fire that burnt out half the town, the King and his brother left Newmarket a week earlier than they had intended and so the plan miscarried. West charged Monmouth, Lord Russell, the Earl of Essex, Algernon Sydney and Lord Howard of Escrick with being parties to it. All, with the exception of Monmouth, were arrested. Lord Russell, son and heir of the Earl of Bedford, was the leader of the Country Party, later to be known as Whigs. He could have fled the country, but preferred to stay and face his accusers. He was committed to the Tower and brought to trial on a charge of high treason. Lord Howard, the dishonoured bearer of an honoured name, was found after a long search standing up within a chimney and, as soon as he was taken, fell a-crying. To save his life, he turned King's Evidence. He swore that there had been talk of a rising during the previous year. This was true. Shaftesbury, Dryden's Achitophel, "sagacious, bold, and turbulent of wit," disgraced, had been arrested and indicted for high treason, but was released on bail and, fearing for his life, had gone into hiding. A meeting was held at his lodgings at Wapping attended by the Duke of Monmouth, Lord Essex, Lord Russell and others of less consequence, at which the possibility of an insurrection was discussed; but for various reasons nothing came of it; and Shaftesbury, discouraged, in bad health and fearful, fled to Holland disguised as a Presbyterian minister and soon afterwards died. At the trial Rumsey swore that at a meeting at the house of a wine-merchant called

Shephard, in whom the conspirators had complete trust, at which Russell among others was present, there was a proposal to seize the King's guard, which the Lord Chief Justice in his summing up said could have no other end but to kill the King. Shephard in the witness-box confirmed this. Lord Russell admitted that he had been at Shephard's but said he had gone with the Duke of Monmouth, at his suggestion, to taste sherry. When there he had overheard some loose talk, but had not joined in it and soon left. It was a great deal to ask the jury to believe that the Duke would have made an appointment with Russell to go to a wine-merchant's merely to sample wine. Unfortunately for Russell, Lord Essex, who had been deeply depressed by his arrest, for reasons that seemed obvious committed suicide on the day the trial began. It looked like an admission of guilt and greatly prejudiced the defendant in the dock. The informers agreed fairly well in their stories, Lord Howard's evidence was damning, and the jury brought in a verdict of guilty of high treason. Lord Russell was condemned to death.

Efforts were made to save him. Lord Bedford offered first fifty thousand pounds, then a hundred thousand, if his son's life were spared. The offers were rejected. Russell well knew that there was no hope for him; yet, so that his wife, to whom he was devoted, should not be left with the feeling that he had omitted in do anything that might save his life, he consented, moved by her distress, to write petitions to the King and the Duke of York in which he offered to live abroad and never more concern himself with the affairs of England. Lady Russell, the daughter of the Earl of Southampton, was the widow of Lord Vaughan when Russell married her. She was a woman of a type not rare in English history, a loving wife and an affectionate mother, of strict moral principles, intelligent and cultured, courageous and unflinching in her devotion to duty, a noble woman, not only by birth, but in character. In that corrupt Court, where the greatest of the land accepted bribes and when woman to be chaste was to be ridiculous, she was respected, loved and admired. The petitions availed nothing. The King and the Duke of York were bitterly hostile to Russell because he had so strongly supported the Bill of Exclusion which sought to prevent the Duke, as a Roman Catholic, from succeeding to the throne on his brother's death.

After his condemnation, Russell sent for Tillotson, Dean of Canterbury, and Burnet. Tillotson, an old friend of the Russells, had attended the trial and given evidence on Russell's behalf. The two clergymen sought to persuade him to make a declaration against the lawfulness of resistance to the sovereign, in which case it might be possible to induce the King to pardon him. Burnet seems to have believed that he had persuaded Russell to do this and desired Tillotson to go to Lord Halifax, acquaint him with the fact and inform the King of it. This Halifax did and afterwards told the Dean that the King seemed more moved by it than by anything that had been said before. A day later, Tillotson, waiting on Russell, told him that he was very glad that he was satisfied on the point in question and hoped it would turn to his advantage. To his consternation, Russell told him that this was not the case. "He was still of opinion that the King was limited by law, and that when he broke through these limits, his subjects might defend themselves and restrain him." The Dean, much troubled, resolved the next day, the day before the execution, to bring Russell to change his mind. Thinking that his family might be with him, so that he would not have the opportunity to speak with him alone, he wrote a letter which he decided to give him with the request that he should read and consider it. It ran as follows:

"My Lord,

"I was heartily glad to see your Lordship this morning in that calm and devout temper at receiving the Sacrament. But peace of mind, unless it be well grounded, will avail little. And because transient discourse many times hath little effect for want of time to weigh and considerate, therefore, in tender compassion of your Lordship's case, and from all the good will that one man can bear to another, I do humbly offer to your Lordship's deliberate thoughts these following considerations concerning the points of resistance, if our religion and rights should be invaded, as your Lordship puts the case, concerning which, I understood by Dr. Burnet, that your Lordship had once received satisfaction, and am sorry to find a change.

"First, that the Christian religion doth plainly forbid the resistance of authority.

"Secondly, that though our religion be established by law (which your Lordship argues as a difference between our case and that of the primitive Christians) yet in the same law, which established our religion, it is declared, 'that it is not lawful upon any pretence whatsoever to take up arms, etc.' Besides that, there is a particular law declaring the power of the militia to be solely in the King. And this ties the hands of subjects, though the law of nature and the general rules of Scripture had left us at liberty, which I believe they do not, because the government and peace of human society could not well subsist upon these terms.

"Thirdly, your Lordship's opinion is contrary to the declared doctrine of all Protestant churches. And though some particular persons have thought otherwise, yet they have been contradicted herein, and condemned for it by the generality of Protestants. And I beg of your Lordship to consider how it will agree with an absurd asserting of the Protestant religion, to go contrary to the general doctrines of the Protestants.

"My end in this is to convince your Lordship, that you are in a very great and dangerous mistake; and, being so convinced, that, which before was a sort of ignorance, will appear of a much more heinous nature, as in truth it is, and calls for a very particular and deep repentance; which if your Lordship sincerely exercise upon the sight of your error by a penitent acknowledgment of it to God and man, you will not only obtain forgiveness of God, but prevent a mighty scandal to the reformed religion.

"I am very loth to give your Lordship any disquiet in the distress you are in, which I commiserate from my heart; but am much more concerned, that you do not leave the world in a delusion and false peace, to the hindrance of your eternal happiness.

"I heartily pray for you, and beseech your Lordship to believe that I am with the greatest sincerity and compassion in the world,

"My Lord,

"Your Lordship's most faithful and afflicted servant

JOHN TILLOTSON

It is the letter of a good and sincere man; but what a hideous brutality there may be in the goodness of the good!

When Tillotson was introduced into the presence of Lord Russell, he found him alone with his wife. He handed him the letter. Russell took it and with it went into an inner room. On returning, he said that "he had read the letter and was willing to be convinced, but could not say that he was so; and that it was not a time to trouble himself with politics; but that, though he

126

was in error, yet being willing to be convinced, he hoped that God would forgive him too!" He returned the letter to Tillotson, who, on leaving him, took it to Lord Halifax, so that his own position on the matter with which it dealt should be made plain.

I will here quote Burnet's account of Russell's last hours. "The day before his death, he received the Sacrament from Tillotson with much devotion; and I preached two short sermons to him, which he heard with great affection; and we were shut up till towards the evening. Then he suffered his children that were very young, and some few of his friends, to take leave of him; in which he maintained his constancy of temper, though he was a very fond father. He also parted with his lady with a composed silence; and, as soon as she was gone, he said to me, the bitterness of death is past; for he loved and esteemed her beyond expression, as she well deserved it in all respects. She had the command of herself so much, that at parting she gave him no disturbance. He went into his chamber about midnight, and I staid all night in the outward room, and was fast asleep till four, when, according to his order, we called him. He was quickly dressed, but would lose no time in shaving; for he said, he was not concerned in his good looks that day."

Russell was executed in Lincoln's Inn Fields in the presence of a great and silent crowd. Some, looking upon him as a martyr, dipped their handkerchiefs in his blood. Tillotson attended him to the scaffold, and in the course of the prayer he spoke to the people present uttered the following words, "Grant that all we, who survive, may learn our duty to God and to the King."

Russell was a man of no remarkable talents, but of conspicuous integrity. There is in the National Portrait Gallery a portrait of him as a young man. It is by an unknown painter.

He is wearing a full-bottomed wig and a lace jabot. With hi
fine eyes and handsome, strong nose, he has, notwithstanding
the beginnings of a double chin, a fine romantic look. I don'
know on what authority this is claimed to be a portrait of Lor
Russell: it does not at all resemble that, by Sir Peter Lely, which
is at Woburn. That one shows a much older man, with in
significant features, fat of face, with something of a smirk in the
eyes and on the lips. You would never guess that the man thu
portrayed had qualities of moral greatness which put him on
level with those old heroes of Roman history.

So great an outcry was raised at Court against Burnet and
Tillotson owing to their ministrations to Russell that Halifax, to
excuse them, felt constrained to show the Dean's letter to the
King. Tillotson was summoned to a Cabinet meeting and closely
examined. He was able to convince the King that there had been
nothing to blame in his conduct or in that of Burnet, and when
the Duke of York continued to badger him, "Brother," said the
King, "the Dean speaks like an honest man, press him no
farther." By the public at large, however, the two clerics were
viciously assailed for having urged Russell to save his life by
retracting an opinion of which his conscience was persuaded.
Burnet thought it well to go to Holland and did not return till
after the Revolution. Tillotson's biographer, writing long after
William of Orange had landed at Torbay and James the Second
fled the country, states that "it is not improbable that neither of
them (Burnet and Tillotson) had then sufficiently considered the
point, with so much attention and exactness, as the subsequent
manners of that reign, and the whole series of conduct of the
following one, necessarily led them to do." This means that
circumstances alter cases. With William and Mary King and
Queen of England it was only sensible to discard the opinion that
"faith and patience are the proper ways for the preservation of

religion, and the method of the Gospel is to suffer persecution rather than to use resistance."

During the next few years Tillotson seems to have lived as quietly as his position allowed. He bought himself a house at Edmonton, a country village later to be known in literary history, and he stayed there most of the year, only coming to London to deliver his lectures at Lincoln's Inn. In 1685 Charles II died and James II reigned in his stead. In 1687 the Dean had a stroke. He recovered, but to re-establish his health went to Tunbridge Wells to drink the waters. There he made the acquaintance of the Princess Anne, James the Second's younger daughter, who was spending the season at Tunbridge Wells with her husband, Prince George of Denmark. Tillotson had frequent conversations with her and preached before her in September 1688. Two months later the Prince of Orange landed. The events that followed are part of the History of England. I may mention that by gaining the confidence of Princess Anne, Tillotson was able to do a service which entitles him to a small place in that history. He persuaded the Princess to consent to William of Orange retaining his right to the crown after his wife's death, which till then, since it deprived her of the right to the succession, she had stubbornly refused to do.

5

William and Mary were proclaimed and crowned. Dr. Tillotson was admitted into a "high degree of favour and confidence with the King and Queen", and was appointed Clerk of the Closet to the King. This required his frequent attendance on their Majesties. The Deanery of St. Paul's fell vacant and, as it was more convenient for him to be within call of Whitehall, he exchanged his Deanery of Canterbury for that. It was a considerable loss of income to him, since, unwilling to hold two offices of profit at the same time, he felt constrained to resign his residentiaryship at St. Paul's.

William has had an indifferent press with posterity. On the whole, history has treated him as a hard, unsympathetic, on occasion ruthless, and cruel man, who used his position as King of England, not for the good of the country, but to further his own purposes on the continent; and it has only grudgingly admitted his greatness. Macaulay in his history has drawn a full-length portrait of him in a way that none could do better than he. It is a lively, effective piece of writing. There emerges from it a picture of a man, cold, sullen, devoid of ordinary human feelings, but of tenacity and courage, skilful in diplomacy and undismayed by failure. William was too good a judge of men not to become quickly conscious of John Tillotson's sincerity, disinterestedness and goodness; and it is possible that it was just his engaging sweetness that drew the stern, harsh King to him.

Throughout their connection William treated him with a kindness and consideration surprising in a man of his temper. It was to be expected that, since several bishoprics were vacant, he should wish that one of them should be filled by the Dean. Tillotson begged to be excused from accepting this preferment on the grounds of his age and infirmities. In a letter to the King's favourite and confidant, the newly created Earl of Portland, he wrote, "I thank God I have lived to have my last desire in this world, which was this happy Revolution; and now I care for no more but to see it established. And I have declared my sense of this great deliverance so openly, and I shall always do so, that I do not fear to be suspected of sullenness and discontent for my declining preferment."

Ten days after the Coronation, an Act of Parliament had been passed which enjoined certain oaths to be taken by all persons who were in any office, civil, military or ecclesiastical, in the Kingdom. "By the first of these, allegiance was sworn to their Majesties; by the second, the papal and foreign jurisdictions are renounced; and, by the statute which enjoins the taking of these oaths, it is enacted, that not only such as shall from that time be preferred to any ecclesiastical dignity or benefit, but all others, then in actual possession of any such preferments, should take the said oaths before the first of August following, on the penalty of suspension for six months following; and that at the end of the said six months, if they still persisted not to take the said oath, they were *ipso facto* to be deprived." Dr. Sancroft, Archbishop of Canterbury, refused to take the oath and was suspended. He had neither waited upon the King and Queen after their arrival nor obeyed the summons to attend the House of Lords. On the day of their Majesties' proclamation, the Queen sent two of her chaplains to Lambeth to crave the Archbishop's blessing. His own chaplain, Mr. Wharton, asked him what he should do. The Archbishop left it to his discretion, whereupon he resolved to obey the government which Providence established and prayed in express terms for King William and Queen Mary. But the same evening his Grace sent for him and in a great passion, *vehementer excandescens*, told him he must either omit naming the new King and Queen in his prayers, or pray no more in his chapel, since they could not be so (namely King and Queen) during the life of King James. At the end of the allotted period, since he still refused to take the required oaths, Dr. Sancroft was deprived of his great office. It was necessary to look for a successor, and the King fixed upon Dr. Tillotson. I will quote part of a letter he wrote to Lady Russell in connection with this:

"After I had kissed the King's hand for the Deanery of St.

Paul's, I gave his Majesty my most humble thanks, and told him that now he had set me at ease for the remainder of my life. He replied, 'No such matter, I assure you,' and spoke plainly about a great place, which I dread to think of, and said it was necessary for his service, and he must charge it upon my conscience. Just as he had said this, he was called to supper, and I had only time to say that when his Majesty was at leisure, I did believe I could satisfy him that it would be more for his service that I should continue in the station in which he had now placed me. This hath brought me into a real difficulty. For on the one hand it is hard to decline his Majesty's commands, and much harder yet to stand out against so much goodness as his Majesty is pleased to use towards me. On the other, I can neither bring my inclination nor my judgment to it. This I owe to the Bishop of Salisbury (Burnet), one of the worst and best friends I know. Best for his singular good opinion of me; and the worst for directing the King to this method, which I know he did; as if his Lordship and I had concerted the matter how to finish this foolish piece of dissimulation, in running away from a bishopric to catch at that of an archbishopric. This fine device hath thrown me so far into the briar that without his Majesty's great goodness I shall never get off without a scratched face. And now I will tell your Ladyship the bottom of my heart. I have for a long time, I thank God for it, devoted myself to the public service without any regard for myself, and to that end have done the best I could in the best manner I was able. Of late God hath been pleased by very severe ways, but in great goodness to me to wean me perfectly from the love of this world; so that worldly greatness is now not only undesirable, but distasteful to me. And I do verily believe that I shall be able to do as much or more good in my present station than in a higher, and shall not have one jot less interest or influence upon any others to any good purpose, for the people will naturally love a man that will take great pains and little preferment. But on the other hand if I could force my inclination to take this great place, I foresee that I should sink under it and grow melancholy and good for nothing, and after a little while die as a fool dies."

William III was not a man to be dissuaded from a course he had decided on, and for some months continued to press the Dean of St. Paul's to accept the office which he was determined he should occupy. Tillotson knew very well that his appointment would be violently resented by his fellow churchmen. They looked upon him "rather as an enemy of the Church, than fit to be a pillar of it; and when it was bruited abroad that he was to be made Archbishop of Canterbury, they said it was the end of the Established Church". To make their opinion more damning, they put it into Latin: *actum est de Ecclesia Anglicana.* He knew also that there were others who felt that their services, both before and after the Revolution, gave them claims to this eminent preferment. Bitter experience had taught him, as it teaches everyone in like case, that to have great success in life gives rise to the hatred, envy and malice of those who have not achieved it. Tillotson was a mild, gentle creature and it distressed him to make enemies. Honest man as he was, it went against the grain with him to step into the shoes of one who for reasons that he could not but respect had submitted to be deprived of a great office. The King brushed aside Tillotson's objections. As, in another letter to Lady Russell, the Dean put it, the King liked neither to importune nor to be denied. He had confidence in her judgment and, greatly troubled in spirit as he was, he wrote again, asking her to advise him. In her answer, she told him that she thought it was his duty to make the sacrifice, a noble sacrifice she called it, and no longer oppose the King's will. He gave in. He desired the King to give him an appointment, and then told him that he was prepared to accept the Primacy. The King "was graciously pleased to say that it was the best news that had come to him for a long while".

Tillotson requested that the appointment should be kept secret for the time, and the public declaration was not made till six months later. On the day this took place, Tillotson went to Lambeth with the purpose of seeing the deprived Archbishop. He sent in his name and waited for an answer, but received none and was obliged to go sadly away. Dr. Sancroft was warned by the Queen to leave the palace, but resolved not to stir till he was ejected by law. Proceedings were instituted and, after a legal squabble Dr. Sancroft, attended by his steward and the Master of the Faculties, took boat at Lambeth and went to a private house in the Temple. The Attorney-General sent a messenger to receive possession of the palace, but the steward left in charge, having orders to deliver it to none but the legal officer, refused to surrender it. The Under-Sheriff was then sent for and possession was delivered to him. Shortly afterwards, Dr. Sancroft left London and went to Fressingfield, in Suffolk, where he was born, and where two years later he died. Burnet described him as a man of learning and of solemn deportment, with a sullen gravity in his looks and a monastic strictness; dry, cold, reserved and peevish, so that none loved him and few esteemed him. That was unfair. Sancroft was a modest, retiring, contemplative man; and his mode of life was simple and frugal. Swift, in a note upon Burnet's accusation that he was avaricious, wrote, "False as Hell." Many years before the events I am dealing with, he went forth from Cambridge because he would not break his oath of allegiance to Charles I. He proved his courage when he refused to read in church King James's Declaration of Indulgence which suspended the penal laws against non-Anglicans. He was committed to the Tower with other bishops

134

who had refused to obey the King's order, was tried and triumphantly acquitted. Seven bishops, Heads and Fellows of certain
colleges and a number of beneficed clergymen refused to take
the oath of allegiance to the Prince of Orange and his Consort
and were duly suspended.

Macaulay had little but contempt for the non-jurors.
"Scarcely one can be named," he wrote, "who was qualified to
discuss any large question of morals or politics, scarcely one
whose writings do not indicate either extreme feebleness or
extreme flightiness of mind." That may be so. But after all,
the non-jurors passionately believed in the Divine Right of
Kings. The King was the Lord's Anointed and could do no
wrong. True, James had violated the laws of England. True,
he had persecuted the Established Church and sought to force
upon the country the Church of Rome. It was the duty of pious
churchmen to suffer persecution, and against the solemn pre-
cepts of their religion to offer resistance to the sovereign's will.
Lord Russell and Algernon Sidney had been sentenced to death
for just that, and many learned and pious men were of opinion
that they had been rightly sentenced. The non-jurors looked
upon it as a mere quibble to claim that when James left the
country, he had abrogated his rights to the crown. When
Charles I was beheaded, Charles II became King of England.
He too had fled the country. As long as James lived he was King
of England and William and Mary were usurpers. One would
have thought that Macaulay might have accorded something in
the nature of sympathy to men who for conscience' sake were
prepared to relinquish offices of dignity and profit, and go forth,
for all they knew without a roof over their heads, to earn their
bread in sorrow.

Tillotson had, of course, taken the oath of allegiance, and we
may be sure that he took it with a good conscience. It is true

that a few years before he had delivered a sermon on the Lawfulness and Obligation of Oaths in which he had asserted that "he is guilty of perjury who, having a real intention when he swears to perform what he promises, yet afterwards neglects to do it"; and, he added, perjury is a most heinous sin. But with his British common sense, that quality which foreigners too often mistake for hypocrisy, Tillotson doubtless believed that an oath could scarcely be binding when it entailed acquiescence in proceedings (the introduction of "popery and its inseparable companion, arbitrary power") which those who took it would never have assented to. In the *Thanksgiving Sermon for Our Deliverance by the Prince of Orange* which Tillotson preached before the Benchers of Lincoln's Inn he called attention to the ease with which the Revolution had been effected, "without a battle, and almost without blood", which proved that it was wrought by God. "And we may then say with the holy Psalmist: This is the Lord's doing, it is marvellous in our eyes." We may surmise that the learned Benchers thoroughly approved.

Dr. Sancroft left the palace in poor condition and while it was put in order Tillotson continued to live at the Deanery of St. Paul's. When everything was ready he moved to Lambeth. The non-juring party pursued him with unrelenting rage. The letter he had written to Lord Russell to persuade him to admit his errors had been printed at the time of the wretched man's execution and was now reprinted. In it Tillotson had declared in unmistakable terms that resistance to the Crown was a crime which deserved punishment both in this world and the next. The non-juring churchmen asked how he could reconcile the opinions he had held with his submission to the authority of one whom all right-thinking men regarded as an usurper. Cruel libels were published. When their authors were arrested, Tillotson went to see the Attorney-General and earnestly desired that no one should be punished on his account. On one occasion, while a gentleman was with him who had come to congratulate him on his preferment, a packet was brought to him. On opening it, he found a mask. "The Archbishop without any signs of emotion threw it carelessly among his papers on the table; and, on the gentleman expressing great surprise and indignation at the affront, his Grace only smiled and said that this was a gentle rebuke if compared with some others, that lay there in black and white—pointing to the papers on the table." A bundle of them was found among his effects after his death, on which he had written, "These are libels. I pray God forgive them. I do."

6

Not the least pertinacious of the Archbishop's enemies was an extraordinary man of whom, though it is something of a digression, I now propose to speak. This was Samuel Johnson. I was taken aback when I first came across the name, for to all bookish persons it seems naturally to belong to one particular man and out of the question that anyone else should venture to possess it. Of course, during the centuries there may well have been hundreds of Samuel Johnsons in England both before and after our cherished doctor. Him we know as we know hardly any character either in real life or in fiction. His true devotees love him not only for his personality, for his wit, his common sense and his kindness; they love him for his faults and would not have him less domineering in conversation, less voracious in his appetite, any more than they would have his prose less pompous, less ponderous and less orotund. Oddly enough, this earlier Samuel Johnson had somewhat of the lexicographer's character—his intolerance, his courage, his roughness in controversy, his doggedness, his intransigence. There is something in the English temper that produces now and then men of this stamp, men who refuse to see that there may be two sides to a question and who, fiercely convinced of the truth and importance of whatever opinions they may hold, will accept hardship, ruin, persecution, even imprisonment, rather than yield.

This Samuel Johnson was born in 1649 and, after being educated at St. Paul's School and Trinity College, Cambridge, was ordained. He left the living to which he had been presented, because he did not think the climate good for his health, and put it in charge of a curate. He settled in London and Lord Russell presently appointed him his domestic chaplain. In 1682 he published a work called *Julian the Apostate*, in which he fiercely attacked the doctrine of passive obedience and non-resistance. This was a dangerous thing to do at the time; the title he had given his book was an insulting reflection on the Duke of York, who had abandoned the faith of his fathers to join the Church of Rome. Johnson was prosecuted for what was claimed to be a scandalous and seditious libel. He was sentenced to pay a heavy fine and to be committed to prison till it was paid. The book was burnt by the common hangman. Since he could not pay the fine he remained in prison till, according to the Dictionary of National Biography, he regained his liberty before 1685. While still in jail he wrote a contumacious work to which he gave the formidable title: *"An humble and hearty address to all English Protestants in the Present Army."* Through the offices of a fellow prisoner who had connections with the outside world, he was able to smuggle the manuscript out of Newgate, and in 1686, James II having succeeded his charming, worthless brother, Johnson's book was printed and especially among the soldiers widely distributed. He must have known how dire the consequences would be, we must presume that such was his obdurate fanaticism, he was prepared to take them. Johnson was again tried and this time sentenced to stand in the pillory in Westminster, Charing Cross and the Royal Exchange, to pay a fine, and to be whipped from Newgate to Tyburn. He bore the whipping with rare fortitude. Before his punishment, he was degraded in the Chapter House of St. Paul's by three obsequious bishops and several divines of the City. He was not set free till after the Revolution, when the judgment against him was declared illegal and his degradation null.

Samuel Johnson had ability, learning and firmness of mind, but he was passionate, impatient of contradiction, dictatorial, arrogant, and apt not only to overrate his own merits, but to underrate those of others. He was immoderately ambitious. Lady Russell was interested in his welfare owing to his connection with her unfortunate husband, and she urged Tillotson, then still Dean of St. Paul's, to intercede with the King on his behalf. Through Tillotson's long and close friendship with the Russells, he and Johnson, their chaplain, must often have been thrown together. No two men could have been more unlike or less likely to be friends—one rough, violent and self-opinionated; the other tolerant, mild and kindly. Early during Johnson's imprisonment, Tillotson sent him a present of money. He received it with contempt, but his necessities forced him to accept it. Tillotson continued to assist the wretched man, but took care from then on that he should not know from whom the gifts came. Notwithstanding Johnson's attacks on the Dean, chiefly owing to his famous letter to Lord Russell, Tillotson was not the man to stand aside when he could alleviate another's distress. He spoke to the King. William seemed inclined to do something, but, owing to Johnson's difficult character, could not decide what it should be. Johnson was far from tactful, and even at Court was apt to deliver himself with sardonic wit: on one occasion he said that on the principle of kings being accountable only to God, the Rump Parliament had done right to send King Charles I to Him. Eventually he was offered the rich Deanery of Durham, but, prepared to accept nothing less than a bishopric, haughtily refused it. He then solicited the King to grant him a pension, and Tillotson sought to persuade William to do so. The King changed the conversation. Halifax, Lord Privy Seal, afterwards told the Dean that his Majesty thought it hard that, with Church preferments at his disposal, he should be expected to give pensions out of his own purse. He added that Johnson spoke very bitterly of the Dean. It was characteristic that he should vilify the only man who had the will and the interest to serve him. Halifax then suggested that the King might give him a good bishopric in Ireland, there being several vacant, and Tillotson thought well of the plan if it was acceptable to Johnson. It was not: Johnson would have an English bishopric or nothing. He was granted an adequate pension, and that is the last we hear of him. A man none could like, but few could fail to respect.

7

Tillotson did not live long to occupy the great office which he had accepted so unwillingly and which brought him little happiness. He continued to be scurrilously attacked. One sermon he preached caused a great clamour against him. It was delivered before the Queen and it concerned the eternity of hell torments. He argued that the endless miseries and torments of the wicked were well consistent with the justice and goodness of God, but, notwithstanding His threatenings, "if it be in any wise inconsistent with righteousness or goodness, which He knows much better than we do, to make sinners miserable for ever, that He will not do it". Tillotson's enemies angrily claimed that he denied the eternity of hell torments in order to console the Queen "then under the horrors of despair on account of her behaviour to her father". He bore his troubles with patience and resignation. It appears that it was customary for the dignitaries of the Church to keep open house, and Tillotson kept a splendid and plentiful table. As his old pupil, John Beardmore, put it, "he was of a very sweet nature, friendly and obliging, and ready to serve his friends in any way that he could by his interest and authority, when they applied to him." He adds that his common and familiar discourse was witty and facetious. The examples given of this are disappointing. A certain Sir John Trevor, who had been Speaker of the House of Commons and was expelled for bribery, passing by the Archbishop in the House of Lords, said in a loud voice, "I hate a fanatic in lawn sleeves," to which the Archbishop answered, "And I hate a knave in any sleeves." Dr. South had written a book in which he spoke disparagingly of the Archbishop and begged a friend to find out what he thought of the performance. The Primate, mildly enough, one would think, said that Dr. South wrote like a man, but bit like a dog. To this Dr. South, when it was repeated to him, replied that he would sooner bite like a dog than fawn like one. The Archbishop answered that for his part he would choose to be a spaniel rather than a cur. As repartees they are not brilliant.

One Sunday, in 1694, Tillotson was seized with a sudden illness while at the chapel in Whitehall, but thought it not decent to interrupt the service and so stayed till it ended. Four days later, in the sixty-fifth year of his age, he died. Owing to his generosity and manifold charities, he died penniless. He had nothing to leave his family, consisting of his wife, his son-in-law and his grandchildren, for his two daughters died before him, but the copyright of his unpublished sermons. They were sold for the then enormous sum of two thousand five hundred pounds. Tillotson was bitterly regretted by the Queen; and William III, that harsh, cold-blooded creature, said of him that he was the best man he ever knew and the best friend he had ever had. He granted the widow an annuity of four hundred pounds, which soon after was increased by another two hundred. So solicitous was the King that the pension should be paid regularly that he called for the money quarterly and sent it to her himself. Since the great ones of the earth are apt to look upon the services rendered them as their right, for which no thanks are needed, and seldom give a thought to those who can no longer be of use to them, this action of William's seems not only meritorious, but touching.

The sermons Tillotson had printed in his lifetime were translated into Dutch and French. On publication of the first volume, Monsieur Bernard in the course of a review in his *Nouvelles de la République des Lettres* remarked that the simplicity of the style "was no inconsiderable part of its merit among the English, so that many, who had no regard for religion, read these sermons merely for the beauty of the language". "It is to be observed," he added, "that the English do not love a pompous kind of eloquence, in which all the words are studied and placed with as much care as a statue of a saint in his niche. They are apprehensive of a design to surprise them, when they are approached with so much preparation; and they are zealous lest this elaborate dress should either conceal or disguise the truth. They prefer the simple beauty of nature to all this affected rhetoric, so oppressed, rather than adorned, by a thousand foreign ornaments." It is a pretty compliment that Monsieur Bernard has paid us, and I should like to think it deserved.

This is the place where by rights I should quote a passage from one of Tillotson's sermons so that the reader might see for himself what manner of writing it was that was so much admired. To do that is not easy. If one were writing, say, about Sir Thomas Browne or Burke, nothing would be easier. The paragraph in *Urn Burial* that begins with the words, "What song the Syrens sang," would give anyone a fair impression of Browne's rich and lovely style; or, with Burke, one would not have to seek far in the *Letter to a Noble Lord* to find a passage of noble rhetoric which would show him at his peerless best. I would not claim that Tillotson was a great artist. He was no genius. As I have repeatedly said, he was an honest, good, unselfish, pious and modest man. Unless the biographers have greatly deceived us, these are not qualities that are commonly attributes of genius. Tillotson's style was a workaday style; that of Sir Thomas Browne or of Jeremy Taylor in *Holy Dying* is not for daily use. It is like those crystal drinking cups, heavily engraved, with rich strands of gold or silver, that the craftsmen of Nuremberg made in the seventeenth century. They are so splendid, so elaborate, so rare, that they can only be put in a glass case. They are very good to look at, but if you are thirsty, a plain tumbler will serve your purpose better. Tillotson wrote his sermons to be delivered from the pulpit. He wrote simply and naturally, so that everyone should understand his meaning. He avoided rhetoric, high-sounding words, flowers of speech, the conceits that were fashionable at the time, similes and metaphors which might distract the listener from the purport of his address. It was like the conversation of a man of adequate learning, who knew what he wanted to say and was at pains to say it clearly and correctly. It is merely a matter of taste whether you like the conversational style or not; many distinguished writers, Flaubert for instance, have detested it: others have thought that it added to the dignity of letters to write in a formal manner, and have sought (often with success) by abundant use of balance, the triad and antithesis to give their productions a stately elegance. It is true that when you compare with these prose written in the conversational style, you may very well think that there is nothing much to it. It is not without hesitation, then, that I will quote some reflections which Tillotson wrote in shorthand in his commonplace book and which can never have been meant to be published. I will quote them not only for their manner, but for their matter. I do not think anyone can read them without sympathising with that maligned and amiable man.

"One would be apt to wonder that Nehemiah should reckon a huge bill of fare and a vast number of promiscuous guests among his virtues and good deeds, for which he desires God to remember him. But, upon better consideration, besides the bounty and sometimes charity, of a great table (provided there be nothing of vanity or ostentation in it) there may be exercised two very considerable virtues; one is temperance, and the other is self-denial, in a man's being contented, for the sake of the public, to deny himself so much as to sit down every day to a feast, and to eat continually in a crowd, and almost never alone, especially when, as it often happens, a great part of the company that a man may have is the company that a man would not have. I doubt it will prove but a melancholy business, when a man comes to die, to have made a great noise and bustle in the world and to have been known far and near, but all this while to have been hid and concealed from himself. It is a very odd and fantastical sort of life for a man to be continually from home and most of all a stranger in his own house.

"It is surely an uneasy thing to sit always in a frame and to be perpetually on a man's guard; not to be able to speak a careless word or to use a negligent posture without observation and censure.

"Men are apt to think that they who are in the highest places and have the most power, have more liberty to say and do what they please. But it is quite otherwise; for they have the least liberty because they are most observed. It is not mine own observation; a much wiser man (I mean Tully) says, '*In maxima quaque fortuna minimum licere.*' They that are in the highest and greatest condition have of all others the least liberty.

"In a moderate station it is sufficient for a man to be indifferently wise. Such a man has the privilege to commit little follies and mistakes without having any great notice taken of them. But he that lives in the light, i.e., in the view of all men, his actions are exposed to everybody's observation and censure.

"We ought to be glad when those that are fit for government, and called to it, are willing to take the burden of it upon them; yea, and to be very thankful to them too that they will be at the pains, and can have the patience, to govern and to live publicly. Therefore it is happy for the world that there are some who are born and bred up to it; and that custom has made it easy, or at least tolerable to them. Else who that is wise would undertake it, since it is certainly much easier of the two to obey a just and wise government (I had almost said any government) than to govern justly and wisely. Not that I find fault with those who apply themselves to public business and affairs. They do well and we are beholden to them. Some by their education, and being bred up to great things, and to be able to bear and manage great business with more ease than others, are peculiarly fitted to serve God and the public in this way; and they that do are worthy of double honour.

"The advantage which men have by a more devout and

retired and contemplative life is that they are not distracted about many things; their minds and affections are set upon one thing; and the whole stream and force of their affections run one way. All their thoughts and endeavours are united in one great end and design, which makes their life all of a piece, and to be consistent with itself throughout.

"Nothing but necessity or the hope of doing more good than a man is capable of doing in a private state (which a modest man will not easily presume concerning himself) can recompense the trouble and uneasiness of a more public and busy life."

In order not to tire the reader I leave out three or four paragraphs. The end of this piece is as follows:

"The capacity and opportunity of doing greater good is the specious pretence under which ambition is wont to cover the eager desire of power and greatness. If it be said (which is the most spiteful thing that can be said) that some ambition is necessary to vindicate a man from being a fool: to this I think it may be fairly answered, and without offence, that there may perhaps be as much ambition in declining greatness as in courting it; only it is of a more unusual kind, and the example of it is less dangerous because it is not like to be contagious."

This passage was evidently written *au courant de la plume*, and it is probable that if the harassed Archbishop had revised it, he would have altered a word and a construction here and there, and tightened it up; but for all that, I do not think it an inadequate sample of his simple and honest style. It is likely enough that on reading it you may say to yourself, "Well, there's nothing extraordinary about it; anyone might write like that." There is a picture in the Museum of Modern Art at New York by the Dutch painter, Mondrian, which consists of a few black lines and one red one which divide the white ground into oblongs and squares. For a reason that I have never discovered, when you have once seen it, you can never quite forget it. There is something about it that is strangely haunting. It means nothing, and why it so curiously disturbs, and at the same time satisfies you, you cannot tell. It looks as though you had only to take a ruler, a tube of black paint and a tube of red, and you could do the thing yourself. Try.

The Short Story

I

A GOOD MANY YEARS AGO the editor of a great new encyclopædia which was in preparation wrote to ask me if I would contribute the article on the short story. I was flattered by the compliment, but declined. Having been myself a writer of short stories, I did not think I could write such a piece with the impartiality it required. For a writer of short stories writes them in the way he thinks best; otherwise he would write them differently. There are several ways of writing them, and each writer uses the way that accords with his own idiosyncrasies. It seemed to me that the article on the subject would be much more adequately written by a man of letters who had never written stories himself. There would be nothing to prevent him from being an unbiased judge. Take, for instance, the stories of Henry James. He wrote many, and they are greatly admired by cultivated readers whose opinion one is bound to respect. It is impossible, I imagine, for anyone who knew Henry James in the flesh to read his stories dispassionately. He got the sound of his voice into every line he wrote, and you accept the convoluted style of so much of his work, his long-windedness and his mannerisms, because they are part and parcel of the charm, benignity and amusing pomposity of the man you remember. But, for all that, I find his stories highly unsatisfactory. I do not believe them. I do not believe that anyone who could visualise a child's agony when suffering from diphtheria could conceive that the child's mother would let him die sooner than allow him to grow up to read his father's books. That is what happens in a story called *The Author of Beltraffio*. I don't think Henry James ever knew how ordinary people behave. His characters have neither bowels nor sexual organs. He wrote a number of stories about men of letters, and it is told that when someone protested that literary men were not like that, he retorted, "So much the worse for them." Presumably, he did not look upon himself as a realist. Though I do not know that it is a fact, I surmise that he regarded *Madame Bovary* with horror. On one occasion Matisse was showing a lady a picture of his in which he had painted a naked woman, and the lady exclaimed, "But a woman isn't like that": to which he answered, "It isn't a woman, madam, it's a picture." I think, similarly, if someone had ventured to suggest that a story of James's was not like life, he would have replied, "It isn't life, it's a story."

Henry James stated his position on this matter in a preface he wrote to a collection of stories which he entitled *The Lesson of the Master*. It is a difficult piece and, though I have read it three times, I am not at all sure that I understand it. I *think* the gist is that, confronted with "the preponderant futilities and miseries of life" it is only natural that an author should seek "some fine example of the reaction, the opposition or the escape"; and since he cannot find models in real life to illustrate his intention, he must evolve them out of his inner consciousness. The difficulty, it seems to me, is that the author has to give these creatures of his invention *some* of the common traits of human beings, and they do not fit in with the traits he has arbitrarily ascribed to them, with the result that they fail to convince. But this is only an impression of my own, and I ask nobody to agree with me. Once, when Desmond MacCarthy was staying with me on the Riviera, we talked much of Henry James's stories. Memories are short nowadays and I may remind the reader that Desmond MacCarthy was not only a charming companion, but a very good critic. He was widely read, and he had the advantage, that not all critics have, of being a man of the world. His judgments within their limitations (he was somewhat in-different to the plastic arts and to music) were sound, for his erudition was combined with a shrewd knowledge of life. On this particular occasion we were sitting in the drawing-room after dinner and in the course of conversation I hazarded the remark that for all their elaboration many of Henry James's stories were uncommonly trivial. To this Desmond, who had a passionate admiration for him, violently protested; so, to tease him, I invented on the spur of the moment what I claimed was a typical Henry James story. As far as I remember, it ran some-what as follows:

Colonel and Mrs. Blimp lived in a fine house in Lowndes Square. They had spent part of the winter on the Riviera, where they had made friends with some rich Americans called—I hesitated for a name—called Bremerton Fisher. The Fishers had entertained them sumptuously, taken them on excursions to La Mortola, to Aix and Avignon, and had invariably insisted on paying the bill. When the Blimps left to return to England, they had pressed their generous hosts to let them know as soon as they came to London; and that morning Mrs. Blimp had read in the *Morning Post* that Mr. and Mrs. Bremerton Fisher had arrived at Brown's Hotel. It was evident that it was only decent for the Blimps to do something in return for the lavish hospitality they had received. While they were deciding what to do, a friend came in for a cup of tea. This was an expatriated

American, called Howard, who had long cherished a platonic passion for Mrs. Blimp. Of course she had never thought of yielding to his advances, which in fact were never pressing; but it was a beautiful relationship. Howard was the sort of American who, after living in England for twenty years, was more English than the English. He knew everybody of consequence and, as the phrase goes, went everywhere. Mrs. Blimp acquainted him with the situation. The Colonel proposed that they should give a dinner party for the strangers. Mrs. Blimp was doubtful. She knew that people with whom you have been intimate when abroad, and found charming, may seem very different when you see them again in London. If they asked the Fishers to meet their nice friends, and all their friends were nice, their friends would find them a crashing bore and the poor Fishers would be dreadfully 'out of it'. Howard agreed with her. He knew from bitter experience that such a party was almost always a disastrous flop. "Why not ask them to dinner by themselves?" said the Colonel. Mrs. Blimp objected that this would look as though they were ashamed of them or had no nice friends. Then he suggested that they should take the Fishers to a play and to supper at the Savoy afterwards. That didn't seem adequate. "We must do something," said the Colonel. "Of course we must do something," said Mrs. Blimp. She wished he wouldn't interfere. He had all the sterling qualities you expected from a colonel of the Guards, he hadn't got his D.S.O. for nothing, but when it came to social matters he was hopeless. She felt that this was a matter that she and Howard must decide for themselves; so next morning, nothing having been arranged, she telephoned to him and asked him to drop in for a drink at six o'clock when the Colonel would be playing bridge at his Club.

He came, and from then on came every evening. Week after

week Mrs. Blimp and he considered the pros and cons. They discussed the matter from every standpoint and from every angle. Every point was taken and examined with unparalleled subtlety. Who could have believed that it would be the Colonel who provided the solution? He happened to be present at one of the meetings between Mrs. Blimp and Howard while, almost desperate by now, they surveyed the difficult situation. "Why don't you leave cards?" he said. "Perfect," cried Howard. Mrs. Blimp gave a gasp of pleased surprise. She threw a proud glance at Howard. She knew that he thought the Colonel something of a pompous ass totally unworthy of her. Her glance said, "There, that's the true Englishman. He may not be very clever, he may be rather dull, but when it comes to a crisis you can depend upon him to do the right thing."

Mrs. Blimp was not the woman to hesitate when the course open to her was clear. She rang for the butler and told him to have the brougham brought round at once. To do the Fishers honour she put on her smartest dress and a new hat. With her card case in her hand, she drove to Brown's Hotel—only to be told that the Fishers had left that morning for Liverpool to take the Cunarder back to New York.

Desmond listened rather sourly to my mocking story; then he chuckled. "But what you forget, my poor Willie," he said, "is that Henry James would have given the story the classic dignity of St. Paul's Cathedral, the brooding horror of St. Pancras and—and the dusty splendour of Woburn."

At this we both burst out laughing, I gave him another whisky and soda, and in due course, well pleased with our-selves, we parted to go to our respective bedrooms.

Rather more than twenty years ago I wrote for American readers a long introduction to a selection I had made of short stories written during the nineteenth century. Some ten years later I used much of what I had said then in a lecture on the short story which I delivered before the members of the Royal Society of Literature. My anthology was never published in England and has been long out of print in America; and though my lecture was printed in the annual volume which the Royal Society of Literature issues of the lectures that have been delivered before it, it was available only to its members. On reading of late these two dissertations I found that on some points I had changed my mind and that certain predictions I had made had not been borne out by the event. In the following pages, though I am bound to repeat a good deal of what I have said before, more or less in the same words, since I do not know how to say what I have to say any better than I said it before, I propose to offer the reader my reflections, such as they are, on a variety of literary production which in the past I have myself somewhat assiduously practised.

It is natural for men to tell tales, and I suppose the short story was created in the night of time when the hunter, to beguile the leisure of his fellows when they had eaten and drunk their fill, narrated by the cavern fire some fantastic incident he had heard of. To this day in the cities of the East you can see the story-teller sitting in the market-place, surrounded by a circle of eager listeners, and hear him tell the tales that he has inherited from an immemorial past. But I suggest that it was not till the nineteenth century that the short story acquired a currency that made it an important feature of literary production. Of course short stories had been written before and widely read: there were the religious stories of Greek origin, there were the edifying narratives of the Middle Ages, and there were the immortal stories of *The Thousand and One Nights*. Throughout the Renaissance, in Italy and Spain, in France and England, there was a great vogue for brief tales. The *Decameron* of Boccaccio and the *Exemplary Tales* of Cervantes are its imperishable monuments. But with the rise of the novel the vogue dwindled. The booksellers would no longer pay good money for a collection of short stories, and the authors came to look askance on a form of fiction that brought them neither profit nor renown. When from time to time, conceiving a theme that they could adequately treat at no great length, they wrote a short story, they did not quite know what to do with it; and so, unwilling to waste it, they inserted it, sometimes, one must admit, very clumsily, into the body of their novels.

But at the beginning of the nineteenth century a new form of publication was put before the reading public which soon acquired an immense popularity. This was the annual. It seems to have originated in Germany. It was a miscellany of prose and verse, and in its native land provided its readers with substantial fare, for we are told that Schiller's *Maid of Orleans* and Goethe's *Hermann and Dorothea* first appeared in periodicals of this nature. But when their success led English publishers to imitate them, they relied chiefly on short stories to attract a sufficiency of readers to make the undertaking profitable.

It is fitting now that I should tell the reader something about literary composition of which, so far as I know, the critics, whose duty it doubtless is to guide and instruct him, have neglected to apprise him. The writer has in him the urge to create, but he has, besides, the desire to place before the reader the result of his labour and the desire (a harmless one with which the reader is

154

not concerned) to earn his bread and butter. On the whole he finds it possible to direct his creative faculty into the channels that will enable him to satisfy these modest aims. At the risk of shocking the reader who thinks the writer's inspiration should be uninfluenced by practical considerations, I must further tell him that writers quite naturally find themselves impelled to write the sort of things for which there is a demand. That is not surprising, for they are not only writers, they are also readers, and, as such, members of the public subject to the prevalent climate of opinion. When plays in verse might bring an author fame, if not fortune, it would probably have been difficult to find a young man of literary bent who had not among his papers a tragedy in five acts. I think it would occur to few young men to write one now. Today they write plays in prose, novels and short stories. It is true that of recent years a number of plays in verse have been successfully produced, but it has seemed to me, on witnessing such as I have had occasion to do, that audiences have accepted the verse as something they had to put up with rather than as something they relished; and actors, for the most part feeling this, have done what they could to allay their discomfort by speaking the verse as though it were in fact prose.

The possibility of publication, the exigences of editors, that is to say their notion of what their readers want, have a great influence on the kind of work that at a particular time is produced. So, when magazines flourish which have room for stories of considerable length, stories of that length are written; when, on the other hand, newspapers publish fiction, but can give it no more than a small space, stories to fill that space are supplied. There is nothing disgraceful in this. The competent author can write a story in fifteen hundred words as easily as he can write one in ten thousand. But he chooses a different story or treats it in a different way. Guy de Maupassant wrote one of his most celebrated tales, *L'Héritage*, twice over, once in a few hundred words for a newspaper and the second time in several thousand for a magazine. Both are published in a collected edition of his works, and I think no one can read the two versions without admitting that in the first there is not a word too little and in the second not a word too much. The point I want to make is this: the nature of the vehicle whereby the writer approaches his public is one of the conventions he has to accept, and on the whole he finds he can do this without any violence to his own inclinations.

Now, at the beginning of the nineteenth century the annuals and keepsakes offered writers a mean of introducing themselves to the public by way of the short story, and so short stories, serving a better purpose than merely to give a fillip to the reader's interest in the course of a long novel, began to be written in greater numbers than ever before. Many hard things have been said of the annual and the lady's book, and harder things still of the magazine which succeeded them in public favour; but it can scarcely be denied that the rich abundance of short stories during the nineteenth century was directly occasioned by the opportunity which these periodicals afforded. In America they gave rise to a school of writers so brilliant and so fertile that some persons, unacquainted with the history of literature, have claimed that the short story was an American invention. That, of course, is not so; but still, it may very well be admitted that in none of the countries of Europe has this form of fiction been so assiduously cultivated as it has been in the United States; nor have its methods, technique and possibilities been elsewhere so attentively studied.

In the course of reading for my anthology a vast number of stories written in the nineteenth century I learnt a good deal about the form. Now, I should warn the reader that the author, as I have suggested on an earlier page, treating of an art he pursues, is biased. He very naturally thinks his own practice best. He writes as he can, and as he must, because he is a certain sort of man; he has his own parts and his own temperament, so that he sees things in a manner peculiar to himself, and gives his vision the form that is forced upon him by his nature. He requires a singular vigour of mind to sympathise with work that is antagonistic to his instinctive prepossessions. One should be on one's guard when one reads a novelist's criticisms of other people's novels. He is apt to find that excellent which he is aiming at himself and likely to see little merit in qualities that he himself lacks. One of the best books I have read on the novel is by an admirable writer who has never in his life been able to devise a plausible story. I was not surprised to find that he held in small esteem the novelists whose great gift is that they can lend a thrilling verisimilitude to the events they relate. I do not blame him for this. Tolerance is a very good quality in a man; if it were commoner, the world of today would be a more agreeable place to live in than it is; but I am not so sure that it is so good in a writer. For what in the long run has he to give you? Himself. It is well that he should have breadth of vision, for life in all its extent is his province; but he can only see it with his own eyes, apprehend it with his own nerves, his own heart and his own bowels: his knowledge is partial, of course, but it is distinct, because he is himself and not somebody else. His attitude is definite and characteristic. If he really feels that any other point of view is as valid as his own, he will hardly hold his own with energy and is unlikely to present it with force. It is commend-able that a man should see that there are two sides to a question; but the writer, face to face with the art he practises (and his view of life is of course implicit in his art) can only attain this standpoint by an effort of ratiocination; and in his bones he feels that it is not six of one and half a dozen of the other, but twelve on his side and zero on the other. This unreasonableness would be unfortunate if writers were few, or if the influence of one were so great as to compel the rest to conformity; but there are thousands of us. Each one of us has his little communication to make, a restricted one, and from all these communications readers can choose, according to their own inclinations, what suits them.

I have said this in order to clear the ground. I like best the sort of story I can write myself. This is the sort of story that many people have written well, but no one more brilliantly than Maupassant; so, to show exactly what its nature is, I cannot do better than discuss one of his most famous productions, *La Parure*. One thing you will notice about it is that you can tell it over the dinner table or in a ship's smoking-room and hold the attention of your listeners. It relates a curious, but not improbable incident. The scene is set before you with brevity, as the medium requires, but with clearness; and the persons concerned, the kind of life they lead and their deterioration, are shown you with just the amount of detail that is needed to make the circumstances of the case plain. You are told everything that you need know about them. In case the reader does not remember the story, I will briefly relate it. Mathilde is the wife of a poor clerk in the Ministry of Education. The Minister asks them to an evening party and, having no jewellery of her own, she borrows a diamond necklace from a rich friend of her schooldays. She loses it. It has to be replaced and for thirty-four thousand francs, an immense sum for them, borrowed at usurious interest, the clerk and his wife buy a necklace exactly like the lost one. To pay their crushing debts they have to live in abject poverty, and when at last they have done so, at the end of ten miserable years, Mathilde tells her rich friend what had

158

happened. "But, my dear," says her friend, "the necklace was imitation. It wasn't worth more than five hundred francs."

A pernickety critic might object that from its own standpoint *La Parure* is not a perfect story, for this kind of narrative should have a beginning, a middle and an end; and when the end is reached the whole story should have been told and you should neither wish nor need to ask a further question. Your crossword is filled up. But in this case Maupassant satisfied himself with an end that was ironic and effective. The practised reader can hardly fail to ask himself, what next? It is true that the unfortunate couple had lost their youth and most of what makes life pleasant in the dreary years they had passed saving money to pay for the lost necklace; but when their mistake was discovered and the necklace they had bought returned to them, they would have found themselves in possession of a small fortune. In the aridity of spirit to which their sacrifice had brought them, it might well have seemed a not unsatisfactory compensation. Moreover, if the wretched woman had been sensible enough to go to the friend and tell her of the loss—and no valid reason is given why she shouldn't have done so—there would have been no story. It is a tribute to Maupassant's skill that few readers remain so self-possessed that these objections occur to them. Such an author as Maupassant does not copy life; he arranges it in order the better to interest, excite and surprise. He does not aim at a transcription of life, but at a dramatisation of it. He is willing to sacrifice plausibility to effect, and the test is whether he can get away with it; if he has so shaped the incidents he describes and the persons concerned in them that you are conscious of the violence he has put on them, he has failed. But that he sometimes fails is no argument against the method. At some periods readers exact a close adherence to the facts of life as they know them—it is then that realism is in fashion; at others,

indifferent to this, they ask for the strange, the unusual, th
marvellous; and then, so long as they are held, readers are pre
pared to exercise a willing suspension of disbelief. Probability i
not an entity that is settled once for all; it changes with the in
clinations of the time: it is what you can get your readers t
swallow. In fact, in all fiction certain improbabilities ar
accepted without question because they are usual and ofter
necessary to enable the author to get on with his story withou
delay.

No one has stated the canons of the kind of story which I an
now discussing with more precision than Edgar Allan Poe. Bu
for its length I would quote in full his review of Hawthorne'
Twice-Told Tales: it says everything that is to be said on the
matter. I will content myself with a short extract:

"A skilful artist has constructed a tale. If wise, he has no
fashioned his thoughts to accommodate his incidents; but having
conceived, with deliberate care, a certain unique or single effect
to be brought out, he then invents such incidents—he then
contrives such effects as may best aid him in establishing this pre-
conceived effect. If his very initial sentence tends not to the out-
bringing of this effect, then he has failed in his first step. In the
whole composition there should be no word written, of which
the tendency, direct or indirect, is not to the pre-established
design. And by such means, with such care and skill, a picture is
at length painted which leaves in the mind of him who contemplates it with a kindred art, a sense of the fullest satisfaction.
The idea of the tale has been presented unblemished, because
undisturbed . . . ."

3

It is not hard to state what Poe meant by a good short story: it is a piece of fiction, dealing with a single incident, material or spiritual, that can be read at a sitting; it is original, it must sparkle, excite or impress; and it must have unity of effect or impression. It should move in an even line from its exposition to its close. To write a story on the principles he laid down is not so easy as some think. It requires intelligence, not perhaps of a very high order, but of a special kind; it requires a sense of form and no small powers of invention. No one in England has written stories on these lines better than Rudyard Kipling. Among the English writers of short stories he alone can bear comparison with the masters of France and Russia. At present he is unduly depreciated. That is natural. When an author of renown dies, obituaries are published in the papers and everyone who has had commerce with him, even if no more than to have a cup of tea in his company, writes to *The Times* to give an account of the occurrence. In a fortnight he is no longer news, and is quite quietly consigned to oblivion. Then, if he is fortunate, after a certain number of years, perhaps few, perhaps many, depending often on circumstances having nothing to do with literature, he will be remembered and restored to public favour. The most notable example of this is, of course, Anthony Trollope. After a generation of neglect, with the change that had come over English life, his novels gained a nostalgic charm which attracted a multitude of readers.

Though Rudyard Kipling from very early in his career captured the favour of the great public, and held it, cultivated opinion was always somewhat condescending in its appraisal of him. Certain characteristics of his style were irksome to readers of fastidious taste. He was identified with an imperialism which was obnoxious to many sensible persons and which is now a source of mortification. He was a wonderful, varied and original teller of tales. He had a fertile invention and to a supreme degree the gift of narrating incident in a surprising and dramatic fashion. He had his faults, as every writer has; in him, I think, they were due to his environment and upbringing, to traits of character and to the time he lived in. His influence was great on his fellow writers, but perhaps greater on those of his fellow men who lived in one way or another the sort of life he dealt with. When one travelled in the East, it was astonishing how often one came across men who had modelled themselves on the creatures of his invention. They say that Balzac's characters were more true of the generation that followed him than of that which he purported to describe. I know from my own experience that twenty years after Kipling wrote his first important stories there were men scattered about the outlying parts of the Empire who would never have been just what they were except for him. He not only created characters; he moulded men. They were brave, decent men who performed the tasks set to them to the best of their ability according to their lights: it is a misfortune that, for reasons which I need not go into, they should have left behind them a legacy of hatred. Rudyard Kipling is generally supposed to have rendered the British people conscious of their Empire, but that is a political achievement with which I have not here to deal; what is significant to my present purpose is that in his discovery of what is called the exotic story he opened a new and fruitful field to writers. This is the story the scene of which is set in some country little known to the majority of readers. It deals with the re-actions upon the white man of his sojourn in an alien land and the effect which contact with peoples of another race and colour

162

Rudyard Kipling (1865-1936)

has upon him. Subsequent writers have treated this subject in their different ways, but Rudyard Kipling was the first to blaze the trail through this new-found region, and no one has invested it with a more romantic glamour, no one has presented it more vividly and with such a wealth of colour. The time will come when the occupation of India by the British will be ancient history and when the loss of that great dependency will arouse regret and bitter feelings no more than are aroused by the loss, centuries ago, of Normandy and Aquitaine. Then it will be realised that Rudyard Kipling in his Indian tales, in the *Jungle Books*, in *Kim*, wrote works that will honourably take a place in our great English literature.

People grow tired even of good things. They want change. To take an example from another art: domestic architecture during the Georgian era reached a rare perfection; the houses that were built then were good to look at and comfortable to live in. The rooms were spacious, airy and well-proportioned. You would have thought people would be content with such houses for ever. But no. The romantic era approached; they wanted the quaint, the fanciful, the picturesque; and architects, not un-willingly, built them what they wanted. It is hard to invent such a story as Poe wrote and, as we know, even he, in his small out-put, more than once repeated himself. There is a good deal of trickiness in a narrative of this kind and when, with the appear-ance and immediate popularity of the monthly magazine, the demand for such narratives became great, authors were not slow to learn the tricks. In order to make their stories effective they forced upon them a conventional design and presently deviated so far from plausibility in their delineation of life that their readers rebelled. They grew weary of stories written to a pattern they knew only too well. They protested that in real life things don't happen with this neatness; real life is an affair of broken

threads and loose ends; to arrange them into a pattern falsifies
They demanded a greater realism. Now, to copy life has neve
been the artist's business. Sir Kenneth Clark in his book *Th*
Nude has made this point abundantly clear. He has shown us tha
the great sculptors of ancient Greece were not concerned t
describe their models with exact realism, but used them as a
instrument to achieve their ideal of beauty. If you look at th
paintings and sculpture of the past you cannot but be surprised t
see how little the great artists have occupied themselves with a
exact rendering of what they saw before them. People are apt t
think that the distortions the plastic artists have imposed upo
their materials, best illustrated in the Cubists of yesterday, are a
invention of our own times. That is not so. They only thin
that because they have become so used to the distortions of th
past that they accept them as literal representations of fact. Fron
the beginnings of Western painting, artists have sacrifice
verisimilitude to the effects they wanted. It is the same wit
fiction. Not to go far back, take Poe; it is incredible that h
should have thought human beings spoke in the way he mad
his characters speak: if he put into their mouths dialogue tha
seems to us so unreal, it must be because he thought it suited th
kind of story he was telling and helped him to achieve th
deliberate purpose which we know he had in view. Artists have
only affected naturalism when it was borne in upon them tha
they had gone so far from life that a return was necessary, and
then they have set themselves to copy it as exactly as they could,
not as an end in itself, but, perhaps, as a salutary discipline.

In the short story naturalism in the nineteenth century came
into fashion in reaction to a romanticism that had become
tedious. One after the other, writers attempted to portray life
with unflinching veracity. "I have never truckled," said Frank
Norris. "I never took off the hat to fashion and held it out for

pennies. By God! I told them the Truth. They liked it or they didn't like it. What had that to do with me? I told them the Truth, I knew it for the Truth then, and I know it for the Truth now." (These are brave words, but it is hard to tell what the truth is; it is not necessarily the opposite of a lie.) Writers of this school looked upon life with less partial eyes than those of the generation that had preceded them; they were less sugary and less optimistic, more violent and more direct; their dialogue was more natural, and they chose their characters from a world that since the days of Defoe writers of fiction had somewhat neglected; but they made no innovations in technique. So far as the essentials of the short story are concerned they were content with the old models. The effects they pursued were still those pursued by Edgar Allan Poe; they used the formula he had laid down. Their merit proves its value; their artificiality expresses its weakness.

4

But there was a country in which the formula had little prevailed. In Russia they had been writing for a couple of generations stories of quite another order; and when the fact forced itself upon the attention both of readers and of authors that the kind of story that had so long found favour was grown tediously mechanical, it was discovered that in that country there was a body of writers who had made of the short story something new. It is singular that it took so long for this variety of the brief narrative to reach the Western World. It is true that the stories of Turgenev were read in French translations. He was accepted by the Goncourts, Flaubert and the intellectual circles in which they moved for his stately presence, his ample means and his aristocratic origins; and his works were appreciated with the modified rapture with which the French have always regarded the productions of foreign authors. Their attitude has been like that of Dr. Johnson with regard to a woman's preaching, "It is not done well, but you are surprised to find it done at all." It was not till Melchior de Vogué published his book *Le Roman Russe* in 1886 that Russian literature had any effect on the literary world of Paris. In due course, about 1905, I think, a number of Chekhov's stories were translated into French and were on the whole favourably received. He remained little known in England. When he died, in 1904, he was regarded by the Russians as the foremost writer of his generation: the *Encyclopædia Britannica* in the eleventh edition, published in 1911, had no more to say of him than, "But A. Chekhov showed considerable power in his short stories." Cold praise. It was not till Mrs. Garnett brought out in thirteen little volumes a selection from his enormous output that English readers took an interest in him. Since then the prestige of Russian writers in general, and of Chekhov in particular, has been enormous. It has to a large extent transformed the composition and the appreciation of short stories. Critical readers turn away with indifference from the story which is technically known as 'well made', and the writers who produce it still, for the delectation of the great mass of the public, are little considered.

Chekhov's life has been written by David Magarshack. It is a record of achievement effected notwithstanding terrific difficulties—poverty, onerous duties, harassing surroundings and wretched health. It is from this interesting and well-documented book that I have learnt the following facts. Chekhov was born in 1860. His grandfather was a serf who had saved enough money to buy his freedom and that of his three sons. One of them, Pavel by name, in due course opened a grocer's shop at Taganrog on the Sea of Azov, married and had five sons and one daughter. Anton Chekhov was his third son. Pavel was uneducated and foolish, vain, selfish, brutal and deeply religious. Many years later, Chekhov wrote of him, "I remember father began to teach me when I was five, or, to put it plainly, whip me when I was only five years old. He whipped me, boxed my ears, hit me over the head, and the first question I asked on waking in the morning was, shall I be whipped again today? I was forbidden to play games or romp. I had to attend the morning and evening church services, kiss the hands of priests and monks, read psalms at home. . . . When I was eight years old, I had to mind the shop, I worked as an ordinary errand boy, and that affected my health, for I was beaten almost every day. Afterwards, when I was sent to a secondary school, I studied till dinner, but from dinner till the evening I had to sit in the shop."

When Anton Chekhov was sixteen, his father, crippled with debts and fearful of arrest, fled to Moscow, where his two elder sons, Alexander and Nicholas, were at the university. Anton was left at Taganrog to continue his schooling and support himself as best he could by tutoring backward boys. When, after three years, he matriculated and was granted a scholarship of twenty-five roubles a month, he joined his parents in Moscow. Having decided to become a doctor, he entered the medical school. He was then a tall young man, just over six feet, with light brown hair, brown eyes and a full, firm mouth. He found his family living in a basement in a slum largely given over to brothels. Anton brought with him two school friends and fellow students to board with the family. They paid forty roubles a month, a third lodger paid another twenty and this, with Chekhov's twenty-five, came to eighty-five roubles on which to provide food for nine people and pay the rent. They soon moved to a larger flat in the same squalid street. Two of the boarders shared one room, the third had a small one to himself, Anton and two of his brothers occupied a third room, his mother and sister a fourth, and the fifth room, which served as dining- and sitting-room, was the bedroom of his brothers Alexander and Nicholas. Pavel, their father, had at last got a job at a ware-house for thirty roubles a month, and he had to live in, so for a while they were rid of the stupid, despotic man who had made their lives a burden.

Anton had the gift of improvising funny stories which, we are told, kept his friends in fits of laughter. In his family's desperate situation he thought he might try his hand at writing them. He wrote one and sent it to a Petersburg weekly called *The Dragon Fly*. One January afternoon, on his way back from the medical school, he bought a copy and found that his story was accepted. He was to be paid five copecks a line. I may remind the reader that the rouble was worth two shillings and there were a hundred copecks to the rouble, so the payment offered was about a penny a line. From then Chekhov sent *The Dragon Fly* a story almost every week, but few were accepted; he placed them, however, with the Moscow papers, but they could afford to pay little; they were run on a shoe-string, and sometimes contributors, to receive their pittance, had to wait at the office till the newsboys brought in the copecks they had collected from the sale of copies in the street. It was a Petersburg editor, Leykin by name, who gave Chekhov his first chance. He conducted a journal called *Fragments*, and he gave Chekhov a commission to write a weekly story of one hundred lines at eight copecks a line. It was a humorous paper, and when Chekhov now and then sent in a serious story, Leykin complained that this was not what his readers wanted. Though the stories he wrote were well-liked and gained him some reputation, the limitations imposed upon him, both with regard to the length and matter of his contributions, irked him, so, to satisfy him, Leykin, who seems to have been a reasonable and kindly man, got him an offer from the *Petersburg Gazette* to write a weekly story, longer and of a different kind, at the same price of eight copecks a line. From 1880 to 1885 Chekhov wrote three hundred stories!

They were potboilers. The Oxford Dictionary tells us that this is a word applied depreciatingly to a work of literature or art executed for the purpose of gaining a livelihood. It is a term that might well be dropped from the vocabulary of the literary journalists. I should say that the young author who discovers that he has a creative urge to write (and how he should have it is a mystery as impenetrable as the origin of sex) may think that it may bring him renown, but surely very seldom thinks that it may bring him money; and there he is well-advised, for in his beginnings it is most unlikely to do so. But when he decides to become a professional writer with the purpose of gaining his livelihood, he cannot be indifferent to the money his talent will procure him. The motive from which he writes is no business of his readers.

While Chekhov was writing this stupendous number of stories, he was working at the medical school to get his diploma. He could only write at night after his hard day's work at the hospital. The conditions under which he wrote were difficult. The lodgers had been got rid of and the Chekhovs moved into a smaller flat, but "In the next room", he wrote to Leykin, "the child of a relation of mine [his brother Alexander] is crying, in the other room father is reading aloud a Leskor story to mother, someone has wound up our musical box and I can hear Fair Helen. . . . My bed is occupied by my visiting relation, who comes up to me every minute and starts talking about medicine. . . The child is bawling! I have just made the resolution never to have children. I expect the French have so few children because they are a literary people . . ." A year later, in a letter to his young brother Ivan, he wrote, "I am earning more money than any of your army lieutenants, but I have no money, no decent food, no room of my own where I could do my work. . . . At this moment I haven't a penny, and I'm waiting anxiously for the first of the month when I shall receive sixty roubles from Petersburg, which I shall spend immediately."

In 1884 Chekhov had a hæmorrhage. Tuberculosis was in the family, and he could not but have known what this betokened, but from a fear that his suspicions would be confirmed he would not have himself examined by a specialist. To calm his anxious mother, he told her that the hæmorrhage was due only to a burst blood-vessel in the throat and had nothing to do with consumption. Towards the end of that year he passed his final examinations and became a qualified doctor. A few months later, he scraped together enough money to go for the first time to Petersburg. He had never attached any importance to his stories; they were written for money and he said that not one of them had taken him more than a day to write. On arriving in Petersburg he discovered to his amazement that he was famous. Slight as his stories were, intelligent persons in Petersburg, then the centre of culture in Russia, found in them freshness, liveliness and an original point of view. They made much of him. It was borne in upon him that he was looked upon as one of the most gifted writers of his day. Editors invited him to contribute to their journals at better prices than he had ever received before. One of Russia's most distinguished authors urged him to have done with the sort of stories he had been writing and set himself to write stories of serious interest.

Chekhov was impressed, but he had never intended to become a professional writer. "Medicine", he said, "is my lawful wife and literature only my mistress," and when he went back to Moscow it was with the intention of earning his living as a doctor. It must be admitted that he did little to establish a flourishing practice. He made a host of friends and they sent him patients, but they seldom paid him for his visits. He was gay and charming and, with his ringing, infectious laugh, an asset in the bohemian circles he frequented. He loved going to parties and giving parties. He drank freely, but, except at weddings, name days (the Russian equivalent of birthdays) and festivals of the Church, seldom got drunk. Women found him attractive, and he had a number of love affairs. But they were not important. As time went on he made frequent visits to Petersburg and went on journeys here and there in Russia. Every spring, leaving such patients as he had to look after themselves, he carted his whole family into the country and stayed there till autumn. As soon as it became known that he was a doctor, patients came in droves to consult him and, of course, paid him nothing. To make money he was obliged to write stories. They were more and more successful and he was well-paid for them, but he found it impossible to live within his means. In one of his letters to Leykin he wrote, "You ask me what I am doing with my money. I don't lead a dissipated life, I don't walk about dressed like a dandy, I have no debts, and I don't even have to keep a mistress (love I get gratis), but nevertheless I have only forty roubles left from the three hundred I received from you and Suvorin before Easter, out of which I shall have to pay forty tomorrow. Goodness only knows where my money goes." He moved into a new flat, where at last he had a room of his own, but he had to beg Leykin for an advance to pay the rent. In 1886 he had another hæmorrhage. He knew he should go to the Crimea, where at that time consumptives went for the warmer climate, as in Western Europe they went to the French Riviera

and to Portugal—and died like flies; but he hadn't a rouble to g
on. In 1889 his brother Nicholas, a painter of some talent, died
of tuberculosis. It was a shock and a warning. By 1892 his own
health was so bad that he was afraid to spend another winter in
Moscow. On borrowed money he bought a small estate near a
village called Melikhovo fifty miles from Moscow and as usual
took his family with him, his difficult father, his mother, hi
sister and his brother Michael. He brought a cartload o
medicaments and, as ever, patients flocked to see him. He treated
them as best he could and never charged them a copeck.

Off and on he spent five years at Melikhovo and on the whole
they were happy years. He wrote a number of his best storie
there and was handsomely paid for them, forty copecks a line
which was nearly a shilling. He concerned himself with local
affairs, got a new road made, and built schools for the peasantry
at his own expense. His brother Alexander, a confirmed
drunkard, came to stay, with his wife and children; friends cam
on visits that sometimes lasted for days, and though he com
plained that they interfered with his work, he could not live
without them. Though constantly ill, he remained gay
friendly, amusing and cheerful. Now and then he went on a
jaunt to Moscow. On one of these occasions, in 1897, he had so
severe a hæmorrhage that he had to be taken to a clinique, and
for some days he was at death's door. He had always refused to
believe that he had tuberculosis, but now the doctors told him
that the upper part of his lungs was affected and that, if he wanted
to live, he must change his mode of life. He returned to Melik
hovo, but knew that he could not spend another winter there
He realised that he must give up his medical practice. He went
abroad, to Biarritz and Nice, and finally settled at Yalta in th
Crimea. The doctors had advised him to live there permanently
and, on an advance from Suvorin, his friend and editor, he buil

himself a house there. He was as usual in dire financial difficulties.

That he could no longer practise medicine was a bitter blow to him. I don't know what sort of a doctor he was. After being qualified, he had never done more than three months, clinical work in a hospital and I surmise that his treatment of patients was somewhat rough and ready. But he had common sense and sympathy, and if he left nature to take its course, he probably did his patients as much good as a man with greater knowledge would have done. The varied experiences he thus gained served him well. I have reasons for believing that the training a medical student has to go through is to a writer's benefit. He acquires a knowledge of human nature which is invaluable. He sees it at its best and at its worst. When people are ill, when they are afraid, they discard the mask which they wear in health. The doctor sees them as they really are, selfish, hard, grasping, cowardly; but brave too, generous, kindly and good. He is tolerant of their frailties, awed by their virtues.

At Yalta, though he was bored there, Chekhov's health for a while improved. I have not had occasion till now to mention that, besides his vast number of stories, Chekhov by this time had written, without much success, two or three plays. Through them he came to know a young actress called Olga Knipper. He fell in love with her and in 1901, to the bitter resentment of his family, whom he had never ceased to support, he married her. It was arranged that she should continue to act and so they were together only when he went up to Moscow to see her or she, resting, as they say in theatrical circles, came down to Yalta. His letters to her have been preserved. They are tender and touching. The improvement in his health did not last and he became very ill. He coughed a great deal and could not sleep. To his great distress Olga Knipper had a miscarriage. She had long urged Chekhov to write a light comedy, which was what the

173

public wanted, and presently, chiefly, I think, to please her, he se
to work. It was to be called *The Cherry Orchard* and he promised
Olga to write a good part for her. "I am writing four lines
day," he wrote to a friend, "and even that gives me unbearable
pain." He finished it and it was produced in Moscow early in
1904. In the following June, on his doctor's advice, he went to
the German spa of Badenweiler. A young Russian man of letter
wrote an account of his meeting with Chekhov on the eve of his
departure. I quote the following lines from Magarshack's Life

"On a sofa, propped up by cushions, wearing an overcoat o
dressing-gown and with a rug over his legs, sat a very thin and
apparently small man, with narrow shoulders and a narrow
bloodless face—so emaciated and unrecognisable had Chekhov
become. I would never have thought a man could change so
much.

"He stretched out his weak, waxen hand, which I was afraid to
look at, and gazed at me with his gentle but no longer smiling
eyes.

" 'I'm leaving tomorrow,' he said. 'I'm going away to die.'

"He used a different word, a more cruel word than 'to die'
which I should not like to repeat now."

" 'I'm going away to die,' he repeated emphatically. 'Say
good-bye for me to your friends. . . . Tell them that I re
member them and that I am very fond of some of them. Wish
them success and happiness from me. We shall never meet
again.' "

At first he grew so much better at Badenweiler that he began
to make plans to go to Italy. One evening, when he had gone to
bed, as Olga had spent the whole day with him, he insisted that
she should go for a walk in the park. When she came back he
asked her to go down and have her dinner, but she told him the
gong had not yet sounded. To pass the time, he started to tell her

story of a holiday resort packed with fashionable visitors, fat bankers, Americans and healthy Britons. "One evening they all returned to their hotel to find that the cook had run off and there was no dinner waiting for them. Chekhov went on to describe how the blow affected each of these pampered people." He made a very funny story of it and Olga Knipper laughed uproariously. She rejoined him after dinner. Chekhov was resting quietly. But suddenly he took a turn for the worse and the doctor was sent for. He did what he could, but it was of no avail. Chekhov died. His last words were in German, *Ich sterbe*. He was forty-four.

Alexander Kuprin in his reminiscences of Chekhov wrote as follows, "I think he did not open or give his heart completely to anyone. But he regarded everybody kindly, indifferently so far as friendship is concerned—and at the same time with a great, perhaps unconscious interest." This is strangely revealing. It tells us more about Chekhov than any of the facts that in my brief account of his life I have had occasion to relate.

5

Chekhov's early stories were for the most part humorous. He wrote them very easily; he wrote, he said, as a bird sings, and attached no importance to them. It was not till after his first visit to Petersburg, when he discovered that he was accepted as a promising and talented author, that he began to take himself seriously. He set himself then to acquire proficiency in his craft. One day a friend found him copying a story of Tolstoy's and when asked what he was doing, he replied, "I'm re-writing it." His friend was shocked that he should take such a liberty with the master's work, whereupon Chekhov explained that he was

doing it as an exercise; he had conceived the idea (for all I know
a good one) that by doing this he could learn the methods of th
writers he admired and so evolve a manner of his own. It i
evident that his labour was not wasted. He learnt to compose hi
stories with consummate skill: *The Peasants*, for instance, is a
elegantly constructed as Flaubert's *Madame Bovary*. Chekho
trained himself to write simply, clearly and concisely, and w
are told that he achieved a style of great beauty. That, we wh
read him in translation must take on trust, for even in the mos
accurate translation the tang, the feeling, the euphony of th
author's words are lost.

Chekhov was very much concerned with the technique of th
short story and he had some uncommonly interesting things t
say about it. He claimed that a story should contain nothing tha
was superfluous. "Everything that has no relation to it must b
ruthlessly thrown away," he wrote. "If in the first chapter yo
say that a gun hung on a wall, in the second or third chapter i
must without fail be discharged." That seems sound enough
and sound too is his claim that descriptions of nature should b
brief and to the point. He was himself able in a word or two t
give the reader a vivid impression of a summer night when th
nightingales were singing their heads off or of the cold brilliance
of the boundless steppes under the snows of winter. It was :
priceless gift. I am more doubtful about his condemnation o
anthropomorphisms. "The sea laughs," he wrote in a letter
"you are of course in raptures over it. But it's crude and cheap
. . . The sea doesn't laugh or cry, it roars, flashes, glistens. Jus
look how Tolstoy does it: 'The sun rises and sets, the birds sing.
No one laughs or sobs. And that's the chief thing—simplicity.'
That is true enough, but, when all's said and done, we have beer
personifying nature since the beginning of time and it comes sc
naturally to us that it is only by an effort that we can avoid it

Chekhov himself did not always do so; and in his story, *The Duel*, he tells us that "a star peeped out and timidly blinked its one eye". I see nothing objectionable in that; in fact I like it. To his brother Alexander, also a short story writer, but a poor one, he said that an author must never describe emotions that he has not felt himself. That is a hard saying. Surely it is unnecessary to commit a murder in order to describe convincingly enough the emotions that a murderer may feel when he has done so. After all, the writer has imagination and if he is a good writer he has the power of empathy which enables him to feel the feelings of the characters of his invention. But the most drastic demand that Chekhov made was that an author should strike out both the beginning and the end of his stories. That was what he did himself, and so rigorously that his friends used to say that his manuscripts should be snatched away before he had a chance to mutilate them, "otherwise he will reduce his stories only to this, that they were young, fell in love, married and were unhappy." When this was told to Chekhov, he replied, "But look here, so it does happen in fact."

Chekhov took Maupassant as his model. If he had not told us that himself I would never have believed it, for their aims and methods seem to me entirely different. In general, Maupassant sought to make his stories dramatic and in order to do this, as I have before said, he was prepared if necessary to sacrifice probability. I am inclined to think that Chekhov deliberately eschewed the dramatic. He dealt with ordinary people leading ordinary lives: "People don't go to the North Pole to fall off icebergs," he wrote in one of his letters. "They go to offices, quarrel with their wives and eat cabbage soup." One may fairly object to this that people *do* go to the North Pole, and if they don't fall off icebergs they undergo adventures as perilous and there is no reason in the world why an author shouldn't write very good stories about them. Obviously it is not enough that people should go to their offices and eat cabbage soup, and I don't believe that Chekhov ever thought it was: in order to make a story, surely they must steal the petty cash at the office or accept bribes, beat or deceive their wives, and when they eat cabbage soup it must be with significance. It then becomes a symbol of a happy domestic life or of the anguish of a frustrated one.

Chekhov's medical practice, desultory though it was, brought him into contact with all manner of persons, the peasants and the factory workers, the owners of factories, the merchants and the more or less minor officials who played a devastating part in the lives of the people, the landowners who by the liberation of the serfs were reduced to penury. He does not seem ever to have been in touch with the aristocracy, and I know only one story, the bitter story called *The Princess*, in which he was concerned with it. He wrote with ruthless candour of the fecklessness of the landowners who let their properties go to rack and ruin; of the wretched lot of the factory workers who lived on the verge of starvation, toiling twelve hours a day so that their employers might add estate to estate; of the vulgarity and greed of the merchant class; of the filth, drunkenness, brutality, ignorance, laziness of the ill paid, ever hungry peasants and the stinking, verminous hovels in which they lived.

Chekhov could give an extraordinary reality to the events he described. You accept what is told you as you would the account of an event described by a trustworthy reporter. But, of course, Chekhov was not merely a reporter; he observed, selected, guessed and combined. As Koteliansky has put it, "In his wonderful objectivity, standing above personal sorrows and joys, Chekhov knew and saw everything. He could be kind and generous without loving; tender and sympathetic without attachment, a benefactor without expecting gratitude."

But this impassivity of Chekhov's was an outrage to many of his fellow writers and he was savagely attacked. The charge against him was his apparent indifference to the events and social conditions of the time. The demand of the intelligentsia was that a Russian writer was under an obligation to deal with them. Chekhov's reply was that the author's business was to narrate the facts and leave it to his readers to decide what should be done about them. He insisted that the artist should not be called upon to solve narrowly specialised problems. "For special problems," he said, "we have specialists; it is their business to judge the community, the fate of capitalism, the evil of drunkenness . . ." That seems reasonable. But since this is a point of view which just now appears to be somewhat widely discussed in the world of letters, I shall venture to quote some remarks I made several years ago in the course of a lecture I delivered to the National Book League. One day I read, as was my habit, the page which one of the best of our English weeklies devotes to the consideration of current literature. On this occasion the reviewer began his article on a work of fiction recently published with the words, "Mr. So and So is not a mere story teller." The word 'mere' stuck in my throat and on that day, like Paolo and Francesca on another occasion, I read no further. This particular reviewer is himself a well-known novelist and, though I have not been fortunate enough to have read any of his works, I have no doubt that they are admirable. But from this remark of his I can but conclude that in his opinion a novelist should be something more than a novelist. It is obvious that, though perhaps with some misgiving, he accepts the notion, prevalent among many writers today, that in the troubled state of the world we live in it is frivolous for an author to write novels designed only

179

to enable the reader to pass a few pleasant hours. Such works are, as we know, disparagingly dismissed as escapist. That, like 'potboiler', is a word that might well be discarded from the critic's vocabulary. All art is escapist, Mozart's symphonies as well as Constable's landscapes; and do we read Shakespeare's sonnets or the odes of Keats for anything but the delight they give us? Why should we ask more from the novelist than we ask of the poet, the composer, the painter? In point of fact there is no such thing as a 'mere' story. When he writes a story, the author, sometimes without any more intention than to make it readable, willy-nilly offers a criticism of life. When Rudyard Kipling in his *Plain Tales of the Hills* wrote of the Indian civilians, the polo-playing officers and their wives, he wrote with the naïve admiration of a young journalist of modest extraction dazzled by what he took for glamour. It is amazing that no one at the time saw what a damning indictment of the Paramount Power these stories were. You cannot read them now without realising how inevitable it was that the British sooner or later would be forced to surrender their hold on India. So with Chekhov. Objective as he tried to be, intent only on describing life with truth, you cannot read his stories without its being borne in upon you that the brutality and ignorance he wrote of, the corruption, the miserable poverty of the poor and the insouciance of the rich, must inevitably result in a bloody revolution.

I suppose most people read works of fiction because they have nothing much else to do. They read for pleasure, which is what they should do, but different people look in their reading for different kinds of pleasure. One is the pleasure of recognition. The contemporary readers of Trollope's *Barchester Chronicles* read them with an intimate satisfaction because he portrayed the sort of lives they led themselves. For the most part his readers belonged to the upper-middle class and they felt at home with the upper-middle class he dealt with. They felt the same pleasant glow of self complacency as they felt when dear Mr. Browning told them that "God's in his heaven—All's right with the world". Time has given these novels the attractiveness of *genre*. We find them amusing, and rather touching (how nice it was to live in a world in which life for the well-to-do was so easy and everything came out all right in the end!) and they have the same sort of charm as those anecdotic pictures of the mid-nineteenth century, with their bearded gentlemen in frock-coats and top-hats, and their pretty ladies in poke-bonnets and crinolines. Other readers seek in their novels strangeness and novelty. The exotic story has always had its votaries. Most people lead prodigiously dull lives, and it is a release from the monotony of existence to be absorbed for a while in a world of hazard and perilous adventure. I suspect that the Russian readers of Chekhov's stories found in them a very different pleasure from that found by readers of the Western World. They knew only too well the conditions of the people he so vividly described. English readers found in his stories something new and strange, horrible often and depressing, but presented with a truth that was impressive, fascinating and even romantic.

Only the very ingenuous can suppose that a work of fiction can give us reliable information on the topics which it is important to us for the conduct of our lives to be apprised of. By the very nature of his creative gifts the novelist is incompetent to deal with such matters; his not to reason why, but to feel, to imagine and to invent. He is biased. The subjects the writer chooses, the characters he creates and his attitude towards them are conditioned by his bias. What he writes is the expression of his personality and the manifestation of his instincts, his emotions, his intuitions and his experience. He loads his dice, sometimes

181

not knowing what he is up to, but sometimes knowing very well; and then he uses such skill as he has to prevent the reader from finding him out. Henry James insisted that the writer of fiction should dramatise. That is a telling, though perhaps not very lucid, way of saying that he must so arrange his facts as to capture and hold his reader's attention. This, as everyone knows, is what Henry James consistently did, but, of course, it is not the way a work of scientific or informative value is written. If readers are concerned with the pressing problems of the day, they will do well to read, as Chekhov advised them to do, not novels or short stories, but the works that specifically deal with them. The proper aim of the writer of fiction is not to instruct, but to please.

Authors lead obscure lives. They are not bidden to the Lord Mayor's Banquet. The freedom of great cities is not conferred upon them. Not for them is the honour of breaking a bottle of champagne against the hull of an ocean-going liner soon to set out on her maiden voyage. Crowds do not assemble, as they do with film stars, to see them emerge from their hotel to leap into a Rolls-Royce. They are not invited to open bazaars in aid of distressed gentlewomen, nor, in the presence of a cheering crowd, to hand a silver cup to the winner of the singles at Wimbledon. But they have their compensations. From prehistoric times men blessed with a creative gift have arisen who have by artistic production added adornment to the grim business of living. As anyone can see for himself by going to Crete, cups, bowls, pitchers have been decorated with patterns—not because it made them more serviceable, but because it made them more pleasing to the eye. Throughout the ages artists have found their complete satisfaction in producing works of art. If the writer of fiction can do that, he has done all that can reasonably be asked of him. It is an abuse to use the novel as a pulpit or a platform.

6

I think it would be an injustice to bring this desultory essay to an end without taking into consideration a talented author whose stories during the interval between the two wars were very much admired. This is Katherine Mansfield. If the technique of our English short-story writers of today differs from that of the masters of the nineteenth century it is, I believe, to some extent at least, owing to her influence. This is no place to tell the story of Miss Mansfield's life, but since her stories are for the most part intensely personal, I must give some slight account of it. She was born in 1888 in New Zealand. At an early age she had written a number of little pieces which showed promise and she had set her heart on being a writer. She found life in New Zealand dull and narrow, and she urged her father to let her go back to England, where, with her sisters, she had been at school for two years. Her respectable parents were shocked when they discovered that she had had a brief adventure with a young man she had met at a ball, and this apparently led them to agree to let her go. Her father made her an allowance of a hundred pounds a year, which at that time was enough, with economy, for a girl to live on. In London she renewed acquaintance with some New Zealand friends. One was Arnold Trowell, who had already made a name for himself as a cellist. In New Zealand she had been madly in love with him, but in London she transferred her affections to his younger brother, who was a violinist. They became lovers. Her board and lodging in a sort of home for unmarried women cost her twenty-five shillings a week and that left her only fifteen shillings for her clothes and her amusements. It irked her to live in these straitened circumstances and, when a teacher of singing, George Bowden by name, ten years older than herself, asked her to marry him, she accepted. She was married in a black dress with a girl friend as the only witness. They went to a hotel for the night. She refused to allow him to exercise what he looked upon as his marital rights, and left him next day. Later, she wrote a savage story about him called *Mr. Reginald Peacock's Day*. She joined her lover who was playing the fiddle at Liverpool in the orchestra of a travelling comic-opera company, and it is said that for a short period she joined it as a member of the chorus. She was pregnant, but whether she knew it before her marriage, or only a little later, is not known. Katherine had sent a cable to her parents in New Zealand to announce her approaching marriage and another to say that she had left her husband. Her mother came to England to see for herself what the situation was, and it must have been a shock to her to find her daughter was what in Victorian days they called 'in an interesting condition'. Arrangements were made for her to go to Wörishofen in Bavaria till her child was born. There she read Chekhov's stories, presumably in a German translation, and wrote the stories which were later published in a book called *In a German Pension*. Owing to an accident she was prematurely confined and the child was born dead. On her recovery she returned to England.

Her first stories were published in Orage's *New Age* and brought her some recognition. She came to know a number of her fellow writers. In 1911 she met Middleton Murry. While still an undergraduate he had founded a magazine called *Rhythm* and he accepted a story which, at his request, she had sent him. This was *The Woman in the Store*. Middleton Murry was born in the lower-middle class, but by a happy combination of intelligence and application he was able to go from a board school to a Higher Grade school, from there, on a scholarship, to Christ's Hospital and finally, again with a scholarship, to Oxford.

He had charm and looks. He was, indeed, so beautiful according to Francis Carco, a French man of letters whose acquaintance he had made on one of his vacations in Paris, that the whores of Montmartre vied with one another to have him go to bed with them free of charge. Murry fell in love with Katherine. This decided him to take a step which he had been contemplating; it was to leave Oxford without taking the First that was expected of him and, since he had no particular aptitude for anything but passing examinations, to earn his living as a writer. Oxford had disappointed him and he felt it had given him all that he could expect to get from it. Fox, his former tutor, introduced him to Spender, the editor of *The Westminster Gazette*, who agreed to give him a trial. He was looking for somewhere to live in London and, one day, when he was dining in company with Katherine, she offered him, for seven and sixpence a week, a room in a flat that had been lent her. He moved in. Since both of them were busy all day, she with her stories, he with his work for *The Westminster Gazette*, they met only in the evenings. Then they would talk to one another, chiefly as young things will, I suppose, about themselves till two in the morning. On one such evening, after a pause in the conversation, she asked him, "Why don't you make me your mistress?" "Oh, no," he answered, "that would spoil it all. Don't you think so?" "I do," she replied. He was surprised some time later to learn that his answer to her suggestion had bitterly affronted her. Shortly afterwards, however, they did have sexual relations and, according to Murry's autobiography, *Between Two Worlds*, they would have got married at once had she been free. George Bowden, possibly from pique, refused to give her a divorce. By way of a honeymoon they went to Paris, in part because Murry wanted her to know his great friend Francis Carco. On their return to England they lived sometimes in London, sometimes

185

in the country. No sooner were they settled in a place than Katherine took a dislike to it and they moved. In two years they moved thirteen times. Finally they decided to settle down for good in Paris. By this time Murry had made good as a journalist, and had been able to save part of his earnings; he now arranged with Spender and with Richmond, editor of *The Times Literary Supplement*, to write articles on current French literature. With his savings, with what he expected to earn in this way and with Katherine's allowance, they had no doubt that they would have enough to live on.

Once in Paris, they took a flat and at considerable expense brought over from England the furniture they had collected. They saw a great deal of Francis Carco. Katherine enjoyed his company; he was lively and amusing; and it may be that he made her what the French call *un petit brin de cour*. But Murry's articles were refused both by *The Westminster Gazette* and by *The Times Literary Supplement* and their money ran out. Carco could not help them: on the contrary he had been throughout something of an expense. They were at their wits' end. Then Murry received a letter from Spender to tell him that the post of art critic on *The Westminster Gazette* would shortly be vacant and if he came back he could have it. They returned unwillingly to England. This was in March 1914. As usual they lived here and there. In August war broke out and Murry's job as an art critic came to an end. They moved into a cottage at Cholesbury in Buckinghamshire, to be near D. H. Lawrence and his wife, with whom they had made friends. It was not a success. Katherine wanted city life, Murry disliked it. She was suffering from arthritis and could not write. They were hard up. She complained that Murry didn't want money and wouldn't earn money. He had little chance of doing so. They so got on one another's nerves that by Christmas it was understood that they

were about to part. Katherine and Francis had been correspond-
ing ever since Murry and she had left Paris. It may be that she
took his letters more seriously than he intended, for it looks as
though she thought he was in love with her. Whether she loved
him is anybody's guess. He was attractive and she wanted to get
away from Murry. She thought that Francis Carco could give
her the happiness that Murry no longer could. Murry, who
knew him better than she did, was certain that she was deceiving
herself, but made no attempt to disabuse her. Katherine's
brother, Leslie Heron Beauchamp, arrived in England to enlist
and gave her the money to go to France and join Francis Carco.
On Monday, 15th February, Murry went with her to London,
and two or three days later she left for Paris.

Carco had been called up and was stationed at a place called
Gray. It was in a zone forbidden to women, and Katherine had
difficulty in getting there. Carco met her at the station and took
her to the little house in which he was billeted. She stayed with
him for three days and then went back to Paris—bitterly dis-
illusioned. Why, one can only surmise. Suddenly Murry
received a telegram from her to say that she was returning and
would be at Victoria at 8 a.m. on the following day. On arrival
she told him (it must be admitted somewhat ungraciously) that
she was not returning to *him*, and had come simply because she
had nowhere else to go. They proceeded to live together once
more in what Murry called "a sort of weary truce". Katherine's
escapade gave her the material for a story called *Je ne Parle pas
Français*. In it she drew a scathing, but not quite fair, portrait of
Francis Carco and a vicious one of Murry. She gave it to him to
read in typescript, and he was deeply hurt—which, doubtless, is
what she intended him to be.

I can pass over the remaining years of Katherine's short life
very briefly. Some time in 1918, George Bowden having at last

divorced her, Katherine and Murry were able to marry. She was in very bad health. During the previous years she had had various illnesses and at least one serious operation. She was now suffering from tuberculosis of the lungs. After she had been treated by various doctors, Murry persuaded her to let herself be examined by a specialist. He came. Katherine was in bed and Murry waited downstairs to hear the result of the examination. The specialist, on joining him, told him that there was only one chance for her, to go into a sanatorium at once. If she didn't, she had no more than two or three years to live—four at the outside. I will quote now from Murry's autobiography: "I thanked him (the doctor), showed him out and went up to Katherine.

" 'He says I must go into a sanatorium,' she said. 'A sanatorium would *kill* me.' Then she darted a quick, fearful glance at me. 'Do *you* want me to go?'

" 'No,' I said dully. 'What's the good?'

" 'You do believe it would kill me?'

" 'Yes, I do,' I said.

" 'You do believe I shall get well?'

" 'Yes,' I said."

It seems strange that neither the doctor nor Murry had the sense to suggest that she might go to a sanatorium for a month and see how she liked it. There was a good one at Banchory in Scotland; I think she would have found life there pleasant enough, and I have no doubt that she would have got material for a story. The patients were of all kinds. There were some who had been there for years because they could only live if they lived there. Others were cured and left. Some died, and they died peacefully and, I think, without regret. I speak of what I know, for it so happened that I was at Banchory just at the time Katherine might have gone there. I should have met her. She would certainly have taken an immediate dislike to me, but that is neither here nor there.

From then on, in her desperate search for health, Katherine lived abroad with a friend, Ida Baker, to look after her. Ida Baker, a young woman of her own age, devoted years of her life to her service. Katherine treated her as she wouldn't have treated a dog, bullied her, railed at her, hated her, sometimes could have killed her, but made unscrupulous use of her; and Ida Baker remained her faithful, loving slave. Katherine was immensely self-centred, apt to have sudden fits of violent temper, fiercely intolerant, exacting, harsh, selfish, arrogant and domineering. That does not suggest a pleasing personality, but in fact she was extremely attractive. Clive Bell, who knew her, tells me that she was fascinating. She had a caustic wit and when she chose could be very amusing. Murry's work kept him in London and he could join her only at intervals. They wrote a vast number of letters to one another. After Katherine's death Murry published her letters to him, but naturally enough, I suppose, did not add his, so that you can only guess what their relations at this time were. For the most part her letters were very affectionate, but when he annoyed her they were virulent. Katherine's father had gradually increased her allowance, and it now amounted to two hundred and fifty pounds a year, but she was often in straits and when on one occasion she had written telling Murry that she had been put to unexpected expenses she wrote him a fiercely angry letter because he had not immediately sent her money, but had put her to the indignity of having to ask him for it. He had paid the doctors' bills and the expense of her illness. He was heavily in debt. "If money is tight," she asked him, "why did you buy yourself a mirror?" The poor brute had to shave. When Murry was appointed editor of *The Athenaeum* with a salary of eight hundred a year Katherine made a peremptory demand that he should send her ten pounds a month. It would have been graceful on his part if he had offered to do so. Perhaps he *was* rather mean with his money. It is significant that when Katherine sent him a story to be typed she told him expressly that it was to be at her expense. It was deliberately offensive.

The fact is that from the beginning they were ill suited to one another. Murry, though more considerate, was as self-centred as Katherine. He seems to have had little sense of humour, but he was kindly, placid, tolerant and wonderfully patient. Jealousy, as we know, may torture when love is dead, and though Murry was no longer in love with Katherine it must have been a humiliation when she left him for another man; and when, after her disappointing experience with Francis Carco, he took her back it was generous on his part and even magnanimous. There is no sign that she was grateful to him. She took whatever he did for her as her due. Though Murry was (in the current idiom) rather 'wet', he was not a negligible creature. He became a very good critic and his criticism of Katherine's stories was valuable to her. In later life he wrote a Life of Swift which, it is generally agreed, is the best that has ever been written on that sinister character but consummate stylist.

The English specialist's prognosis was correct. He had given Katherine four years at the outside to live. After spending some time on the Italian Riviera, then on the French, and later in Switzerland, she entered, as a last chance, the Gurdjieff Institute at Fontainebleau. She died there early in 1923. She was thirty-four.

It has been generally accepted that Katherine was greatly influenced by Chekhov. Middleton Murry denied this. He claimed that she would have written her stories exactly as she did if she had never read one of Chekhov's. There, I think, he

Anton Chekhov (1860-1904)

was wrong. Of course she would have written stories, to do so was in her blood; but I believe that save for Chekhov they would have been very different. Katherine Mansfield's stories are the outpourings of a lonely, sensitive, neurotic, sick woman who never felt quite at home in the Europe she had chosen to live in. This was their content. Their form she owed to Chekhov. The pattern of the short story as it was written in the past is simple. It consists of A, the setting, B, the introduction of the characters, C, what they do and what is done to them, and D, the outcome. This was a leisurely way of telling a story and the author could make it as long as he liked; but when newspapers began to publish stories their length was rigidly determined. In order to satisfy this requirement the author had to adopt a suitable technique; he had to leave out of his story everything that was not essential. The use of A, the setting, is to put the reader in a suitable state of mind to enjoy the story or to add verisimilitude to it; it can conveniently be omitted, and today generally is. To leave D, the outcome, to the imagination of the reader is a risk. He has been interested in the circumstances described, and if he is not told what they result in he may feel cheated, but when it is evident, to omit it is intriguing and effective. Chekhov's *The Lady with the Dog* is a perfect example. B and C *are* essential, for without them there is no story. It is obvious that a story which takes the reader at once into the midst of things gives it a dramatic quality which wins and holds the reader. Chekhov wrote several hundred stories on these lines and when, with increased popularity, he was able to write stories of some length to be published in magazines, he used, very often, the pattern he had become used to.

This pattern well suited the nature of Katherine Mansfield's temperament and capacity. She had a small but delicate talent. I think her extravagant admirers have done her a disservice in making claims for her which her work scarcely justifies. She had little power of invention. Invention is a curious faculty. It is an attribute of youth and with age is lost. That is natural, for it is an upshot of experience and with advancing years the events of life cease to have the novelty, the excitement, the stimulation that they had in youth and so no longer incite the author to expression. Katherine had no great experience of life. She knew she needed it. Murry, somewhat disapprovingly, says that "she wanted money, luxury, adventure, the life of cities"; of course she did, for only then could she get material for her stories. The writer of fiction, in order to tell the truth as he sees it, must play his part in the hurly-burly of life. If what the dictionary tells us is correct, that a story is a narrative of events that have happened or might have happened, it must be admitted that Katherine Mansfield had no outstanding gifts for telling one. Her gifts lay elsewhere. She could take a situation and wring from it all the irony, bitterness, pathos and unhappiness that were inherent in it. An example of this is the narrative which she called *Psychology*. She wrote a few stories which are objective, such stories as *The Daughters of the Late Colonel* and *Pictures*; they are good stories, but they might have been written by any competent writer; her most characteristic stories are those that are commonly known as stories of atmosphere. I have asked various of my literary friends what in this connection is the meaning of the word 'atmosphere'; but they either could not, or would not, give me an answer that quite satisfied me. The Oxford Dictionary does not help. After the obvious definition it gives, "figuratively, surrounding mental or moral element, environment." In practice it seems to mean the trimmings with which you decorate a story so thin that without them it would not exist. This, Katherine Mansfield was able to do with skill and charm. She had a truly remarkable gift of observation and could describe effects of nature, scents of the country, wind and rain, sea and sky, trees, fruit and flowers with rare delicacy. Not the least of her gifts was that which enabled her to give you the heartbreak that lay behind what to all appearances was a casual conversation over, say, a cup of tea; and heaven knows, that is not an easy thing to do. She wrote in a style that is pleasantly conversational and you can read even her slightest stories with pleasure. They do not stick in your memory as, for instance, does Maupassant's *Boule de Suif* or Chekhov's *Ward No.* 10; that is, perhaps, because it is easier to remember a fact than an emotion. You can remember falling down stairs and spraining your ankle, but not what it felt like to be in love. But whether it is a merit in a story that you should remember it after you have read it is something on which I would not venture to offer an opinion.

Katherine Mansfield found little to please her in New Zealand when she lived there, but later, when England had not given her what she expected, when her health failed, her thoughts went back to the early years she had spent there. There were moments when she wished she had never come away. In retrospect the life she had led then seemed full and varied and delightful. She could not but write about it. The first story she wrote was called *Prelude*. She wrote it when she and Murry were spending three months at Bandol on the French Riviera, and when they were happier together than they had ever been before or would ever be again. She intended to call it *The Aloe* and it was Murry who suggested that she should call it *Prelude*. I suppose he felt that rather than a story it was the setting for one. She began it, as we know, with the idea of writing a novel, and on that account, perhaps, it is somewhat shapeless. Later, she wrote, among other stories with the same background, *The Voyage*, *At the Bay* and *The Garden Party*. *The Voyage* describes a night's journey that a little girl, with her grandmother to take care of her, takes by sea from one port in New Zealand to another. It could not be more tender or more charming. The other stories are about her father, her mother, her brother, her sisters, her cousins and neighbours. They are fresh, lively and natural. We know that she put a lot of work into them, but they have an engaging air of spontaneity. They have none of the bitterness, the disillusionment, the pathos, of so many of her stories. They are to my mind the best things she ever wrote.

I am told that Katherine Mansfield's stories are not so highly thought of as they were during the 'twenties. It would be a pity if she were forgotten. I don't think she will be. After all, it is the personality of the author that gives his work its special interest. It does not matter if it is a slightly absurd one, as with Henry James, a somewhat vulgar one, as with Maupassant, a brash, tawdry one, as with Kipling—so long as the author can present it, distinct and idiosyncratic, his work has life. That surely is what Katherine Mansfield succeeded in doing.

Three Journalists

THE OXFORD DICTIONARY gives two meanings of the word 'journalist'. The first, and the more usual today, is 'one who earns his living by editing or writing for a public journal or journals'. The second is 'one who journalises or keeps a journal'. It is in the second sense that I here use the word. The three journalists with whom in the following pages I propose to deal are the Goncourt Brothers, treating them as one, which is what they themselves insisted on, Jules Renard and Paul Léautaud.

The journal is a form of literary production which, perhaps because we are by nature more reticent than our neighbours across the Straits of Dover, has been more practised by French writers than by ours in England. The Oxford Dictionary tells us that the journal is a record of events or matters of personal interest kept by anyone for his own use. Though, like the diary and the memoir, it is largely autobiographical, it differs from them to some extent in its matter and its method. The memoir, again according to the dictionary, is a person's written account of incidents in his own life, of the persons he has known, and the transactions in which he has been concerned. This precisely describes the memoirs of St. Simon. They are very personal, but at their best they deal with matters of state, such as the death

195

of the Dauphin and the degradation of the Duc de Maine, the bastard of Louis XIV. Greville wrote memoirs which are well worth reading if you are interested in the period, but he was too much of a gentleman (I use the word not in its present depreciatory sense, but in that which was held in the nineteenth century) to indulge in gossip and scandal, so that they somewhat lack spice. The diary, our authority tells us, is a daily record of matters affecting the writer personally or which come under his personal observation. It deals with facts rather than (as do the French Journalists) with reflections and emotions. I suppose everyone would agree that the greatest diary that has ever been written is that of Pepys. It is a lively record of the times and a telling portrait of the author. With its frankness and its intimacy it comes nearer than any other English work (the diary of John Evelyn for instance) to the Journals of the French.

When the first volumes of the Goncourts' Journal were published they created a sensation. It was inevitable that other writers should set about writing Journals of their own. I have mentioned Jules Renard and Paul Léautaud. André Gide began one. Charles du Bos wrote one. Maurice Barrès wrote his *Cahiers*. We have recently learnt that Paul Valéry's note-books are to be published in thirty-two volumes. And I daresay there are others that I do not happen to have come across. When you read such of these Journals as are easily obtainable, the most vivid impression you get of their writers is that they were terrific egoists. Of course, we are all egoists. It is natural for us to look upon all questions in relation to ourselves. But life has to be coped with; we come in contact with the egoism of our fellows and have to make the best of it. We may find it pays, if not to suppress, at least to conceal our egoism. A long time ago Prince Kropotkin wrote a book in which he gave instances to show that sympathy exists in many animals. It seems to be a quality that

exists in many men. Sympathy, and, above all, love, may make
it even a satisfaction to sacrifice oneself for others. Then, altruism
is the strange outcome of man's innate egoism. But we are not all
so happily constituted. The writers of these Journals were not.
Jules Renard once said to his wife, "You say I am an egoist. If I
weren't, I wouldn't be me." Paul Léautaud stated, "I am not
interested in anyone but myself." He said what others might
have said if they had been as frank. He added, "When I don't
think about myself, I don't think about anything."

The Journalists I am dealing with wrote novels, but they were
men of letters rather than novelists. I do not mean that a
novelist may not be a man of letters as well, but it is not essential.
He may write badly, he may not be particularly intelligent, he
may lack culture: if he has the specific gift he may yet write very
good novels. The Goncourts' novels are recitals of facts that
they had laboriously collected. Those of Jules Renard and Paul
Léautaud are purely autobiographical. When you read them in
connection with their Journals and, in Renard's case, with his
letters, you are surprised to discover how little use they made of
such power of invention as they had. Gide arranged his works
of fiction with more subtlety, but they too are narratives of his
personal experiences. One day Roger Martin du Gard came to
lunch with me and, knowing that he was an intimate friend of
Gide's, I led him to talk about him. I chanced to mention that
Gide had seldom written about anyone but himself. Martin du
Gard nodded and told me that he had once reproached Gide on
that score, whereupon Gide told him that he was engaged on a
novel in which he had taken the utmost pains to keep himself
out of it. It was to be called *Les Faux Monnayeurs*. He asked
Martin du Gard to stay with him in the country so that he might
read it to him when it was finished. In due course Martin du
Gard went and Gide read the first eighty pages. Suddenly he

saw that his guest was shaking with laughter. Somewhat disconcerted, Gide asked him what he was laughing at. "You told
me you were going to keep yourself out of your novel," he
answered. "You've never written anything in which you are
more flagrantly evident." That is true. *Les Faux Monnayeurs* is
not a very good novel, but it is more interesting than many a
better one, because Gide was a very intelligent and cultivated
man, and in it he has drawn an engaging portrait of himself at
his best.

His Journal is more consistently interesting than those of the
other Journalists whom I propose here to deal with. He had
more talent than they and a more catholic culture. For a
Frenchman he was widely travelled and well read in the literature of countries other than his own. He loved music and was
himself a fine pianist.

In an earlier essay in this volume I have hazarded the suggestion that egoism carried to an extravagant pitch may be
harmful to a novelist, and on a later page I have put forward the
idea that in the long run an author has nothing to give you but
himself. On the face of it the two statements seem hard to
reconcile. If the novelist is so supreme an egoist that his only
interest in others is in the effect he makes on them, he will never
know them sufficiently to create living creatures. If, on the
other hand, he is so constituted that he can interest himself in
people for their own sakes and then, his creative instinct coming
into action, feels that he can make literary use of them, he may
be fortunate enough to produce creatures who are more real
than their models. The obvious example of this is Mr. Micawber.
The author remains an egoist, but to a better purpose.

From the writer's standpoint the crab of egoism is that it
narrows his interests. Jules Renard and Paul Léautaud were indifferent to the arts; they cared only for literature. Léautaud,

though he spent his whole life in Paris, never troubled to go to the Louvre (when he mentions it, he hastens to explain that he means, not the picture gallery, but the shop) and when on one occasion he happened to go to the Luxembourg, where the early Impressionists were on view, he found there nothing but a collection of horrors. I cannot remember that Jules Renard in his Journal ever mentioned a picture. The Goncourts made no secret of the fact that music not only bored them, it irritated them, and the only music they could endure was that of a military band. They were, however, appreciative of the graphic arts. André Billy, their admirable biographer, states that their taste in painting was impeccable: it was peculiar. They considered Perugino a greater artist than Raphael, and of Michelangelo they said, "A sculptor, but no painter." One wonders whether they had ever glanced at the ceiling of the Sistine Chapel. It must be said in their favour that they were ravished by Turner and greatly admired Constable. They called Delacroix and Ingres painters who did not know how to paint. They had no patience with Courbet, "The ugly, always the ugly. And the ugly without its grand character, the ugly without the beauty of the ugly." They praised Théodore Rousseau, but never mentioned Manet, Degas or Monet without a sneer.

The Goncourts began their Journal in 1851. Léautaud began his in 1893, and the fourth volume that has been printed brings it down to 1924; but he did not die till many years later and, as he continued to write it, there must be further volumes to be issued from time to time. Jules Renard died in 1910. Gide kept his Journal till 1949. The four of them provide a record of literary life that covers nearly a hundred years. The last half-century of the eighteen-hundreds produced a group of authors in France with which no other nation could compare. The Gon-

courts knew Saint-Beuve, Taine, Renan, Michelet, Flaubert
Anatole France and Maupassant. They were contemporaries o
Baudelaire, Verlaine, Rimbaud and Mallarmé. It is an imposing
list.

2

Edmond de Goncourt was born in 1822, and Jules, his brother
in 1830. They were devoted to one another as brothers seldom
are. They shared their thoughts, their ambitions, their joys and
sorrows. Their great-grandfather, who bore the plebeian name
of Antoine Huot, was an attorney, a profession which in the
eighteenth century carried with it no social prestige. In way
that can only be surmised he made enough money to buy, three
years before the Revolution of 1789, something of an estate a
Goncourt and received under the seal of Louis XVI what in
England would be described as the lordship of the manor and
the right to call himself Huot de Goncourt. Thus ennobled, he
manufactured for himself a coat of arms. His grandson, father
of Edmond and Jules, served with distinction in Napoleon*
armies and was badly wounded in the Russian campaign.

Edmond and Jules de Goncourt set great store on their noble
birth. When they became sufficiently well-known to be
mentioned in a work of reference, it was as 'Edmond et Jule
Huot, dits de Goncourt' which indicated that it was a literary nom
de plume; they furiously protested and insisted on a rectification
being published in four important newspapers. Later, in 1860
when a certain Ambroise Jacobé was authorised by an imperia
decree to call himself Jacobé de Goncourt, they brought an
action against him. The legal authorities pointed out that M
Jacobé's ancestors had bought the lordship of the manor o

Goncourt in one department just as theirs had bought it in another. They were obliged to abandon their action.

Their father died and left his widow and sons none too well off. They lived in Paris. Jules, the younger brother, went to school. He had a rough time of it with his schoolfellows owing, according to Edmond, to the hatred of the vulgar for the aristocracy. The Goncourts were not so aristocratic as all that. When Edmond was nineteen he got a clerk's job in a lawyer's office, but a few years later changed for one in the Treasury with a salary of 1,200 francs a year. Their mother died in 1848. Her two sons were left with about four thousand francs in cash and the uncertain income from the farms they possessed. Edmond was twenty-six and Jules eighteen. In his leisure at the office Edmond had attended an art school and Jules showed some capacity as a painter, so they decided to become artists. They bought the necessary equipment and started off on foot for the south of France. They wandered from place to place, making drawings here and there, and painting in water-colour. Eventually they went to Algeria. They made notes, more and more copious, of all they saw, and Edmond afterwards claimed that it was this that made them writers. On their return to Paris they settled in an apartment in the rue Saint Georges. Since the house was mostly occupied by women of easy virtue the rent was low.

We are not told how it came about that the two brothers decided to abandon painting and become authors. They wrote three or four plays, but could get no manager to produce them. In 1851 they wrote their first novel. It was called *In 18 . . .*, and they published it at their own expense. A thousand copies were printed and sixty were sold. André Billy describes it as affected, obscure, pretentious and incoherent. It seems then to have occurred to them that they might write a semi-historical,

gossipy book about the eighteenth century. They were hard
workers and by 1854 had finished a work of nearly five hundred
pages which they entitled *History of French Society during the
Revolution*. They printed it, again at their own expense. It was
the practice of the time for authors to take steps to get reviews of
their productions and accordingly the two brothers called on the
critics or left cards on them and sent them their book. The
result was not unsatisfactory and they immediately set about
another work, of four hundred and fifty pages, on French
society during the Directory. The critics ignored it. Undeterred,
however, in 1856 they produced a work in two volumes called
Intimate Portraits of the Eighteenth Century. They sold it to a
publisher for three hundred francs. They were, apparently, the
first to write that bastard kind of history which is concerned with
back-stairs gossip and which in our own day finds favour
with the public. I cannot pretend that I have read all these
books, but I have read some of them. I found them dull. The
Goncourts seem to have had no sense of selection and you are
told the same sort of facts over and over again. They went into
intolerable detail. Their books would have been twice as
good if they had been half as long. In 1858 they wrote a life
of Marie Antoinette, and for the first time had something of a
success.

These productions of theirs earned them little money; that
they did not mind, for they were not mercenary and their farms
provided them with enough to live on; what they resented was
that they had not brought them the recognition which they
were convinced was their due. To get back on the critics who
had treated them somewhat scurvily, they wrote a novel called
Charles Demailly. It was an attack on the literary world and contained portraits, mostly virulent, of the journalists and men of
letters of the day. As was only natural, their victims damned it.

202

During the next few years they wrote three more. One of them was called *Germinie Lacerteux*. For twenty-five years they had had in the family a maid called Rose. She had tucked them up in bed when they were children and nursed their mother during her last illness. They were devoted to her and trusted her implicitly. She fell ill and died. Then they discovered that she had led a double life. She was crazy about men and to get them gave them the money, the wine and food of her masters. She had a lover, a young boxer, and she contracted the pleurisy from which she died by spending a night in the rain spying on him to see with what woman he was.

On this sordid story they wrote their novel. It shocked both the public and the critics. The Goncourts claimed that with this book they had created the realistic novel. They claimed, strangely enough, that only aristocrats could write such a book and, later, Edmond stated that he was attracted to the subject because "I am a well-born man of letters, and the common people, the mob, if you like, have for me the attractiveness of unknown and undiscovered races, something like the exotic that travellers at the cost of great suffering seek in far-off countries". The two brothers were industrious, but they had little imagination and no sense of form. They had conceived the idea that things are as important as people, and this led them to describe places, houses, furniture, objects of art, at dreary length. In *Manette Salomon*, their most readable novel, Coriolis, the painter, is never so vividly presented to the reader as the elaborately described studio in which he works. *Manette Salomon* is a picture of the way the painters of the time led their lives and, since the two brothers were always careful to document themselves, one may be sure that the picture was faithful. It is the story of a painter of talent who is destroyed by the Jewish model who is his mistress and whom he eventually marries; but before you come to this, you are asked to read a hundred and fifty pages relating the high jinks, the outings, the practical jokes of the art students of the day. I think the fault of the Goncourts as novelists was that they did not start a novel because they were absorbed by a theme and the characters which were needed to develop and expound it, but because its success would give them the literary status to which, they were firmly assured, they were by their talent and originality entitled. But though their novels were unsatisfactory, the Goncourts were intelligent and observant, and there are passages in them that in a book of sketches or brief essays would be very readable. They bore because they interrupt the flow of narrative. Palmerston is reputed to have said that dirt is matter in the wrong place. It is a remark that the writer does well to bear in mind.

But what the Goncourts chiefly set store by was the beauty and originality of their style. They invented what they called l'écriture artiste. Albert Thibaudet in his admirable history of French literature during the nineteenth century describes it as obscure, convoluted and affected. He says it is a language of its own that you have to learn—and life is short. Towards the end of his life Edmond had an uneasy feeling that the style he and his brother had laboriously cultivated was ill-advised. He came to the conclusion that the best style is a style that you don't notice—and a very sensible one too. But to my mind their greatest defect was that they could never bring themselves to say a thing once and leave it at that, but repeated it in other words two, three or even four times.

After their hard day's work the Goncourts very naturally liked to go out and amuse themselves. For all their noble birth, the company they kept was rather shoddy. It consisted of journalists, actors, popular dramatists and their hangers-on—all with their mistresses. They seem to have known no women who could be described as *femmes du monde*. Edmond was a handsome man, but stiff and unbending, and somewhat taciturn; Jules was smaller, with golden, wavy hair, fine eyes and a sensual mouth. He was gay, full of charm, high spirits and fun. Of the two he was the more gifted. He had a number of amorous affairs; they were of no consequence; Edmond appears to have been little interested in such things. Neither of them was ever in love. Indeed, they did not allow themselves to be so, since they were convinced that anything in the nature of an enduring passion could not but interfere with their literary activities. They were prepared to make any sacrifice to their ambition to be famous authors. They thus missed an interesting experience. They settled their sexual life, however, by means of an arrangement they made with a young woman called Maria. She had been seduced at the age of thirteen and after a certain amount of promiscuous fornication had become a midwife. They liked her because she was gay and loved to laugh. With her fair hair, her well covered body and her blue eyes, she reminded them of one of Rubens's women. She agreed to take them both on as lovers, if lovers is the right word to use in this connection; the arrangement is so reasonable (it saved bus fares) that I daresay it is only prudishness on my part if I think it rather disgusting. The two brothers were enchanted with her stories of her experiences as a midwife and made copious notes of them. In the Journal they wrote as follows: "Men like us need a woman with little culture and little education, a woman who has nothing but gaiety and natural high spirits, because so she will please and charm us like a nice animal that we can become attached to. But if our mistress has something of breeding, something of art, something of literature, and wants to deal with us *de plein pied*, with our thoughts and our sense of beauty, and has the ambition to be a companion of the work in progress and of our tastes she becomes as intolerable to us as a bad piano—and very soon an object of antipathy."

In 1862, Princess Mathilde, the great Napoleon's niece, who liked to surround herself with artists and men of letters, asked a friend of hers to bring the Goncourts to dine with her. She had read and liked their book on Marie Antoinette. She lived with her lover and a lady-in-waiting partly in Paris and partly at her 'place' at St. Gratien, which was within easy distance of the capital. The Princess was then a woman of forty-two, short of stature, but with the remains of good looks. On first acquaintance she made a poor impression on the Goncourts, but on dining with her a second time they liked her better. They found her gracious and charming, quick-tempered, but often witty. They would not have been the men they were if they had not made reservations. "There's nothing delicate about her," they wrote in their Journal, "nothing subtle, nothing tender; strength, intelligence, eloquence, all that attracts the masses, but nothing to attract the individual ... She doesn't thank you for being merely polite, attentive and amiable. She wants to imagine that you are attracted to her sexually and desire her."

From then on, the Goncourts dined with the Princess frequently and often stayed with her at St. Gratien. They gradually dropped the raffish friends with whom they had been in the habit of consorting.

It was during the first year of the Goncourts' acquaintance with the Princess that, on the suggestion of Gavarni, whom they liked and admired, and with the approval of Sainte-Beuve, they founded the celebrated dinners *chez Magny*. A small number of writers agreed to dine there twice a month. The early members of the group were Taine, Renan, Turgenev, Flaubert and Théophile Gautier. From time to time others were elected. Though at table the passion of love was discussed, often crudely, and religion, the conversation naturally enough dealt chiefly with art and literature. There were differences of opinion and arguments were heated. Quarrels were frequent, but the diners parted good enough friends. They did not know that when the Goncourts went home, Jules, partly at Edmond's dictation, wrote in their Journal an account of the conversations they had just listened to. Since they were as usual careful to be exact, we may be pretty sure that their report of the talk of these learned and brilliant men was faithful. It must be admitted that it is disappointing. It is true that when you are eating a good dinner and have drunk two or three glasses of wine, a commonplace uttered with assurance may look like an epigram, but when you see it in print it has sadly lost much of its lustre; and the fact is that you look in vain in these conversations for a clever repartee or a scintillating witticism.

The Goncourts found the early dinners gay, pleasant and amusing, but after no more than two or three years they were tired of them. They wrote in their Journal, "We are seized with contempt, with disgust, for these dinners at Magny's! To think that this is a gathering of the first minds in France! Certainly, for the most part, from Gautier to Sainte-Beuve, they are men of talent, but what a poverty of ideas they have, of opinions founded on their nerves and feelings! What a lack of personality and temperament!"

Sainte-Beuve was the oldest of the group, the most celebrated and the most influential. He liked the Goncourts and wrote about them with sympathy. He went so far as to say that they were the most charming people in the world and, when they talked of no longer attending the dinners at Magny's, he told them that if they ceased to go he would do so too. They detested him. They condemned the frigidity of his style, his ambiguous and hypocritical character, his cowardice, littleness of mind and his love of platitudes. On one occasion they went to see him. They asked themselves rhetorically how, artists and aristocrats as they were, they could be intimate with a man who was dressed like a porter and whose dwelling was like that of a country doctor. This did not prevent them from asking Sainte-Beuve to dinner in the most flattering and affectionate terms. Gautier and Flaubert were of the party, and they talked of lesbianism and transcendental homosexuality—whatever that may mean.

The Goncourts seem to have made the acquaintance of Flaubert in 1857, but did not come to know him well till some years later. It may seem strange that Flaubert, so open, frank and affectionate, did not captivate them. Though they wrote admiring letters to him, their attitude was vaguely hostile. When they were together, Flaubert, unaware that the brothers were watching him censoriously, would let himself go and talk, in his extravagant way, without reserve. They wrote, "We perceive what is lacking in Flaubert, *the defect we were long looking for*, his (Madame Bovary) lacks heart just as his descriptions lack soul." They found him vulgar and utterly devoid of taste or artistic feeling. Their final judgment was that he was a provincial genius and, as a man, much inferior to his books. (The above italics are mine.)

When *Manette Salomon* was published, they sent Taine a copy. In a letter of acknowledgment he praised warmly what he liked in it, but criticised their style. He told them that they wrote not for readers, but for men of letters like themselves, and ended by pointing out a number of errors. They had never cared for him: from then on they despised him. At first they disliked Renan because he was ugly; they deplored his bad taste and lack of frankness, but as they came to know him better they admitted that, notwithstanding his repellent appearance, he was pleasant and amiable. Later, they quarrelled with him.

In 1868 Jules was stricken with illness. His appetite left him, he could not sleep, and he was morbidly sensitive to noise. They still lived in the house they had settled in on establishing themselves in Paris. They decided to sell one of their farms and buy a house where they could be certain of quiet. They found one at Auteuil, which was but twenty minutes away from the centre of Paris. They moved in, only to find that there too the noise was intolerable. Jules grew worse. His mind began to fail. He was interested in nothing and would sit for hours, sunk in depression, in front of a tree, with his hat over his eyes. He no longer seemed to care for the brother whom he had so deeply loved. He could no longer even remember the names of the novels they had written together. There were certain letters he could no longer pronounce, or rather, he pronounced them as a child does. At one moment Edmond, distracted, had a mind to shoot his brother and shoot himself afterwards. He was haunted by the fear that he might die first and Jules, with no one to look after him, would be put in an asylum. The account of Jules's gradual disintegration which Edmond wrote in the Journal makes painful reading. One wonders how he could bring himself to set it down in black and white. Jules sank into the condition which doctors call infantilism. On one occasion, at a restaurant, when he upset a finger-bowl, "Do be careful," said Edmond, "or we shan't be able to go anywhere." Jules burst into tears. "It's not my fault," he sobbed, "it's not my fault." His trembling hand took Edmond's and they cried together. The end came at last. Edmond wrote in the Journal, "He's dying, he's dead. Praise be to God! He died after two or three gentle sighs like the breathing of a little child going to sleep."

Edmond persuaded himself that Jules's death was due to his passion for literature and his obstinate efforts to wring from the French language the perfection that was inherent in it. In fact,

Jules died of what in my medical-student days was called G.P.I., General Paralysis of the Insane, which is a dreadful resultant of syphilis. Jules had contracted it at Le Havre on one of their jaunts twenty years before. At the funeral Edmond, blinded with tears, stumbled as he walked and had to be supported by friends. He was consumed with grief. But fortunately human beings are so constituted that time assuages the bitterest sorrow. The Franco-Prussian War took place, which ended with the establishment of the Third Republic. Normal life began again. Princess Mathilde returned to Paris from her exile in Brussels. Meanwhile Edmond continued to write his Journal. He was lonely. He was in his early fifties and his friends thought he should marry. It appears that two young women were prepared to marry him. One, a maid of honour to the Princess, proposed to him. Though she was uncommonly attractive, and he liked her, he refused—for a reason which I shall now proceed to relate.

From boyhood Edmond had been a passionate collector. He passed all his spare time poking about in junk shops and attending sales. It was possible in those days to buy bits and pieces for a song, and one's mouth waters when one reads that one could buy Old Master drawings for a pittance. At one sale a number of La Tour's pastels fetched five francs apiece. Objects of Japanese art were brought to Paris and Edmond was ravished with them. He claimed that they were as great as Greek art. He bought the prints of Outamaro, kakemonas and makemonas, lacquer, armour, costumes. Little by little the collection increased. He bought cabinets ornamented with Buhl, consoles, tables, mirrors, tapestries, carpets. Edmond claimed later that for years he had spent eighty thousand francs a year on his collection. Since the Goncourts never had more than twelve thousand francs a year from their farms and their books brought them in next door to nothing, one wonders where he got the money. One can only suppose that he did a bit of dealing on the side. But wherever the money came from, by the 'seventies, owing to the fantastic rise in the value of the things he had bought, Goncourt was in possession of, for the time, a handsome fortune. The two brothers had long had it in mind to found an academy —later to be known as *L'Académie Goncourt*—not as a rival to the *Académie Française*, which they disliked and despised, but as a protest against the older establishment for its hide-bound prejudices, its lack of interest in new talent and its hatred of originality. The plan was to choose ten talented authors, who had not suffered the indignity of being widely read, and provide them with an income of six thousand francs a year so that they might devote themselves to the production of literature without having to take some employment in order to earn a living. They were to dine together once a month and every year award a prize of five thousand francs to the author of an outstanding work in prose. It was to carry out this scheme, which would need the whole of Edmond's fortune, that he abandoned all thought of marriage.

He survived his brother for twenty-seven years. I need not go into his literary activities during this time. They brought him neither cash nor credit. He continued assiduously to write his Journal. Because it came upon me as a surprise, I will quote a note he made on 22nd May 1892: "*Déjeuner chez Raffaelli, avec le beau Proust.*" He didn't know that one day his handsome fellow-guest would make quite a stir in the world and write a devastating, but vastly amusing, parody of the famous Journal. During this long period Edmond's most intimate friends were Alphonse and Julia Daudet. He dined or lunched with them two or three days a week and every summer went to stay with them at Champrosay, their house in the country. I suppose Alphonse

Daudet is little read today. He is still readable. His style is lively, natural and easy. His best book is *Sapho*. The theme is more or less the same as that of *Manette Salomon*, but it is a better novel than the Goncourts' and more plausible. Alphonse Daudet was popular and for the time made a great deal of money. He must have been a man of quite extraordinary charm and sweetness for Edmond, so difficult and so carping, to forgive him his success.

It was in July 1883, when the Daudets had been lunching with Edmond at Auteuil, that he read some passages of his Journal to them. They were interested enough to ask him for more, with the result that every summer on his visits to them at Champrosay he read them parts of it. Perhaps it was their approval that induced him to publish his Journal in volume form. He made two copies of the original manuscript. In that which he proposed to issue during his lifetime he deleted the passages which might offend persons still living; but he arranged that the work in its entirety should be published twenty years after his death, by which time he supposed that all the persons of whom he and his brother had spoken disparagingly would be dead. It is this which, after a number of lawsuits, the State of Monaco is now issuing. So far nineteen volumes have appeared, reaching to the year 1894, and I am told that more are to come.

The first volume appeared in 1887. During the following years eight more were published. The last was issued in 1896. They caused an enormous sensation in the literary world of Paris. They were attacked for their indiscretion, their lack of charity, their coarseness, their presumption. One critic described the first volume as a masterpiece of conceit and shallowness. Taine wrote to protest, "Let me beg you to leave out in your next volume all that may concern me. When I talked to you, or in your presence, it was *sub rosa*, as our poor Sainte-Beuve used to say . . . I will be responsible only for what I have written with reflection and with a view to publication." Goncourt did not much care. He was convinced that posterity would see in his Journal the truest and most vital description of the people and things of his time. The second volume had a better press, influenced, it seems, by an article that Alphonse Daudet wrote for the *Figaro*. But still, numbers of people expostulated. The Princess Mathilde came to see him and, though there was a good deal in it about her, never even mentioned it. "It doesn't matter," Edmond wrote, "princesses, even the most intelligent, are terribly stupid, and we are really great idiots to make them a present of immortality which they would never have had but for us."

In the fourth volume Edmond inserted his account of Renan's conversation at the bi-monthly dinners *chez Magny*. Renan was incensed. In a widely read article he wrote, "All these narratives of M. de Goncourt on the dinners of which he had no right to make himself the historian are complete transformations of the truth. He has not understood, and attributes to us what his mind, closed to any general ideas, made him believe he understood. So far as I am concerned, I protest with all my strength at this wretched reportage. It is a principle of mine that the rubbish of fools is of no consequence." In an interview Renan, among other remarks, stated that "M. de Goncourt is entirely devoid of intelligence and moral sense". To this Edmond loftily replied, "He seems jolly angry, the defrocked priest." The Daudets, alarmed by the enemies his Journal was making him, advised him, when he read to them the volume that dealt with 1877, not to publish it. Edmond seems to have thought they did so because they were dissatisfied with the praise he had accorded to the talent of Julia Daudet, Alphonse's wife, who was by way of being herself a writer. "Really," he wrote, "the dear woman is very charming, but very exacting." A critic of the fifth volume stated that of the élite of their day, Gautier, Sainte-Beuve, Renan, Taine, Flaubert, the two brothers had for the most part succeeded only in giving their readers grotesque and often repulsive portraits. That is true, and it is not to their credit. Almost the only intimate friends Edmond had left were the Daudets. One would have thought that prudence, if not affection and gratitude, would have led him to say nothing about them that would distress them. In extracts from his seventh volume, which were published in a daily paper, Edmond wrote of their mother in a way that deeply affronted them. Ernest Daudet, Alphonse's brother, wrote an angry letter of protest to the paper, but Alphonse persuaded him not to send it. He wrote to Edmond himself. He pointed out that there was not a word of truth in what Edmond had said and begged him to omit the passage from the forthcoming volume. This Edmond, one suspects with an impatient shrug of the shoulders, agreed to do.

Alphonse Daudet suffered from locomotor ataxy, a distressing sequela of syphilis, and was constantly in agonising pain. In order to sleep at night he had to take a heavy dose of chloral and on bad days was obliged to give himself as many as five or six injections of morphine. When Madame Daudet discovered that Edmond had disclosed these deplorable facts in his Journal, she besought him, both for her family's sake and for the effect they might have on her husband's vast public, to suppress all mention of them. He refused. He pointed out to her that his Journal was the most beautiful monument of a literary friendship that there had ever been. The Daudets did not take that view of it. It is no wonder that the friendship that had lasted for five and twenty years was imperilled. The Daudets no longer invited Edmond to dine with them, and when he paid them a visit made excuses to cut it short. Daudet told his friends that he had had enough of Goncourt. The last two volumes of the Journal were savagely

Edmond de Goncourt (1822-1896)

attacked. Edmond received dozens of anonymous and insulting letters. He was distressed, but scornful. He ascribed the venom of his critics to the probity and disinterestedness of his life, to his aristocratic birth and to the fact that owing to his private means he did not depend on literature for a living.

In 1897 Edmond de Goncourt was seventy-five. There had been a good deal of gossip in the papers in connection with the estrangement between Edmond de Goncourt and the Daudets, and Alphonse had thought it necessary to state publicly that there was no truth in the rumours. For years Edmond had gone to stay with them every summer, and if just then he did not come as usual, it would be proof that in fact the friendship was at an end. They invited him. The Daudets left Paris for Champrosay, and on the 11th of July Edmond joined them. For some time he had been in very poor health. He was taken ill and on the 17th of July died.

With the exception of a few legacies, Edmond left everything he possessed to found the academy which was designed to keep alive for ever his brother's name and his own.

The Goncourts claimed that with *Germinie Lacerteux* they had created the realistic novel and, moreover, had discovered the eighteenth century and Japanese art. "These," said Jules, "are the three great literary events of the second half of the nineteenth century, and we have led them, we, poor and obscure. Well, when one has done that, it is really difficult not to be somebody in the future." Though there is exaggeration in this, there *is* a grain of truth.

They never doubted that they were men of outstanding talent. They were, indeed, preposterously self-satisfied. "I feel a sort of intoxication on reading aloud to myself the first number of my Journal in the *Echo de Paris*," wrote Edmond. There is something almost touching in such self-complacency. Thinking of themselves as they did, it is natural that they should have held their contemporaries in small esteem. "In this century," Edmond said, "I shall perhaps have been the only one, and without resentment against the persons and solely for love of truth, the only one to put in their place the sham great men, Renan, Sainte-Beuve, etc., etc." We can guess that this etc. etc. would have included Taine, Michelet and Flaubert. The Goncourts were arrogant, vain and conceited, but it is only fair to admit that their passion for art, though often misguided, was genuine. They were disinterested and honest in a world in which corruption was rampant. (Janin, the important critic of the *Débats*, took six thousand francs from Princess Mathilde not to write a damaging article about one of her friends.) Their whole life was given up to the creation of literature. Their ambition—not an ignoble one—was to write a series of works that would render them famous to the end of time. They were well aware that a book produced is never a masterpiece; it becomes one; and they were convinced that, though they had had to put up with failure after failure, posterity would do them justice.

3

Jules Renard began to write his Journal in 1887. It is a singular document. He had no illusions about himself and described the man he was with a savage sincerity that at times gives the reader cold shivers. One can hardly believe that he ever intended it to be published. In one place he said that he wished his son to read it when he was worthy of it. What he meant by that is hard to say. One would have thought that when his son came to read it he would lose any respect and affection he may have had for his father. Renard, in the Journal shows himself unscrupulous, grossly selfish, ill-mannered, envious, hard and sometimes even cruel. He died in 1910 and there are few people still alive who knew him. The two or three I have met were agreed that, though brilliantly witty, he was detestable. It is at least to his credit that he never made an attempt to show himself better than he was.

It is easy to give some account of his life since one has as material not only the Journal, but the two novels he wrote, *Poil de Carotte* and *L'Écornifleur*, his three short plays, *Le Plaisir de Rompre*, *La Paix du Ménage*, *La Bigote*, and the narrative called *La Maîtresse*. All are autobiographical. Jules Renard was born of a family of peasants who had lived in Central France, in La Nièvre, for generations. His father, one of several children, was born in the one-roomed hovel in which his parents lived. Somehow or other, we are not told how, he managed to get some sort of education and became a contractor in the Department of Public Works. After building a bridge over the little river, La Viette, he had made enough money to retire and buy a house at Chitry. He spent the remaining years of his life there, fishing, shooting and farming the few acres of land he had acquired. He remained to his death a peasant at heart. Jules was the youngest of his three children. His mother hated him. She had never wanted him and his birth was due to an accident of sexual intercourse. He was an ugly little boy, with red hair, and dirty in his person. From an early age he was set to do the menial chores of the house. There is an incident described in *Poil de Carotte* that strikes one as in a way more revolting than even the beatings his mother gave him. Like not a few young children he was apt to wet his bed at night and next morning he would be soundly spanked. On one occasion, owing to the visit of a relation who had to be put up for the night, he was told to sleep in his mother's bed. He did everything he could to hold his water, but at last could do so no longer

.d urinated. As a punishment he was kept in bed next day. I
the evening, by way of supper, his mother brought him a bow
of soup. His brother and sister, trying hard not to giggle
watched while their mother thrust spoon after spoon down th
little boy's throat. When he had finished they clapped thei
hands and cried, "He's drunk it, he's drunk it." When hi
mother told him that it was the urine with which he had wette
the bed the night before, he merely said, "I had an idea it was."

Renard's father, whom in the novel he calls M. Lepic, was no
unkind to him, but would not interfere with his wife's treatmen
of the child. He was a silent, self-centred man who, though fron
necessity living in close quarters with his family, remained by hi
own wish apart. It was when once Poil de Carotte had tried t
enlist his father on his side, and failed, that he uttered th
despairing cry that so moved the reading public, "*Tout le mond*
ne peut pas être orphelin." When Jules was ten he was sent to
boarding school at Nevers. His father came to see him now an
again and they wrote letters to one another. In answer to one o
the boy's he wrote back to ask why in a letter he had just received
his son had begun each line with a capital letter. The boy
answered, "Dear Papa, you did not notice that my letter was i
verse." Jules Renard, Poil de Carotte, as he was called o
account of his red hair, was not a nice little boy. There wa
nothing in him of Little Lord Fauntleroy or even of Davi
Copperfield. He was in fact a horrid little beast. A story Renar
tells of his schooldays is shocking. One master, whose business i
was to inspect the dormitory when the boys were in bed, was i
the habit of sitting on the bed of one of them, talking to him and
when he got up to go, kissing him good night. Poil de Carotte
madly jealous, found an opportunity to tell the headmaster mucl
more than the truth of this harmless incident, with the result tha
the master was sent away. As the wretched man, ignominiously

discharged, was leaving, Poil de Carrote called out to him, "Why didn't you kiss me too?" Nasty, of course, but what pathos there is in that cry!

M. Renard sent Jules at seventeen, having done well at school, to Paris to continue his education. He allowed him a hundred and fifty francs a month, then equal to six pounds sterling. He took a room in a cheap hotel. He passed his *bachot* in 1883 and looked for a job. He could not find one. He had already begun to write and he sent some stories to a provincial paper, the *Journal de la Nièvre*; they were printed, but not paid for. Presently there were enough of them to make a book and he got a publisher to agree to publish them. The publisher decamped. He did his military service. When finished with that he returned to Paris and again looked for some means of earning his living. At last he got a job in a firm of real estate agents at a salary of a hundred francs a month. He seems to have made a good impression on the head of the firm, a M. Lion, and on his wife. After a time M. Lion engaged him as tutor to his three sons, at a somewhat higher, though still miserable, salary. I have learnt the above from the account of Jules Renard's early life which was written by Henri Bachelin as a preface to the edition of Renard's complete works published after his death. At this point M. Bachelin becomes strangely vague. Fortunately the piece called *La Maîtresse* and Jules's published letters to his father enable one to narrate facts which the author of the preface must have thought it indiscreet to allude to.

Through the Lions, who were persons of some culture, Renard came to know a number of their friends and was occasionally invited to parties. He was by then a tall young man, with a fine head of red hair, passable features, a good figure and an air of virility. After one of these parties he escorted back to her apartment an actress who had been one of the guests. Though a good deal older than he, she was an attractive woman and, on the way, he made proposals to her. She was somewhat startled at the suddenness of this, for they had never met before, but his audacity and persuasiveness did not displease her. She gave him to understand that she was handsomely kept by a rich man and could not afford to lose the handsome allowance he made her; she consented, however, to come to Renard's hotel room on his promise that he would never attempt to come to her apartment. Thus began an affair which, to their mutual satisfaction, lasted for a considerable time. The lady enabled him to get some verses of his printed and he recited them at various parties. His youth, his fine presence, even his provincial accent, which he never entirely lost, brought him a modest success. But such are the exigencies of youth, it caused him a certain uneasiness to share his mistress with another and, one day, knowing she was to receive his rival (if one may call him that) he stationed himself outside the house in which she lived till he saw entering it a stout, elderly business man. The sight of him profoundly disturbed Renard and he decided there and then to sever his connection with the kept woman. He could no longer bring himself to receive favours and accept presents from her which were in fact paid for by another and in a high frame of outraged delicacy he wrote a long and eloquent letter to her saying that she must choose between them. His pride, his honour, no longer permitted him to continue in this humiliating situation. She had arranged to come to his hotel on the very afternoon on which he composed the letter and as usual they hopped into bed together. He did not deliver the letter and the affair went on as before.

When the summer holidays came and Renard was no longer needed to teach M. Lion's three boys, he was invited to spend a few weeks at the seaside with some friends. Henri Bachelin does not tell us who they were, nor why they had thus asked him.

Renard's letters to his father explain it. A certain M. Morneau, a manufacturer of eighteenth century furniture, desired to write a book on the subject and, since he could not write, was in need of a ghost to provide a work which he could publish under his own name. It may be presumed that it was on M. Lion's suggestion that Jules Renard was engaged at a handsome remuneration. He was to live with the family, which consisted of M. Morneau, his wife and daughter. It was with the material thus acquired that Renard wrote his novel, *L'Écornifleur*. It has lately been chosen by a group of authors as the best novel that has been written in France during the last fifty years and was recently translated into English under the name, *The Sponger*. The story can be told in a few lines. The hero, young, impecunious and a poet, makes the acquaintance of a business man and his wife. The acquaintance ripens into friendship and they invite him to stay with them by the sea. They are joined there by their niece, an orphan with a fortune of her own. The young man looks upon it as his duty to attempt the seduction of his hostess. Though she is attracted by him, and presently more than a little in love with him, he does not succeed. He teaches the young girl to swim and she falls in love with him. Naturally enough, seeing the sort of man he is, he proceeds to seduce her. It is difficult in English to put in decorous terms how far the affair goes, and I can only say that it goes as far as possible without going all the way. With both aunt and niece in love with him, his situation is so embarrassing that he finds it prudent to return to Paris, and with his departure the story ends. Since Renard in the Journal remarks that his imagination consists of his memory and since he was immune to common decency, we may be pretty sure that his novel relates the actual facts with no greater divergence from the truth than is normal to the writer of fiction.

Back in Paris, Renard set to work to finish the book which

M. Morneau was to sign. He was hard up. Early in January 1884 he wrote to his father, "These last few days I have had to hesitate even to buy a stamp. I'm not exaggerating. December was especially hard." His friendship with the Morneaus was resumed on their return to Paris and he dined with them every night. He did not waste his time. On 18th February in a letter to his father he said, "I've spoken to you casually of a possible marriage. I've made my proposal." Unfortunately the letters in which he spoke of this have not been preserved and it comes upon the reader as a surprise. How could he in his circumstances think of marriage? His proposal was accepted and he wrote to his father asking him to let him have seven hundred and fifty francs to buy an engagement ring. The marriage between Jules Renard and Marinette, the daughter of M. and Madame Morneau, took place at the end of May and the happy couple went to Barfleur for their honeymoon. One wonders why a prosperous bourgeois family consented to their only daughter marrying a penniless and unknown writer. Renard's only income was the wretched salary he was still receiving from M. Lion. It is true that he wrote articles for the little reviews that led a short and hazardous life, but was paid little or nothing for them. The explanation that immediately occurs to one, namely that the marriage was necessary to save the girl's reputation, is without foundation. Their first child was not born till they had been married a year. One can only suppose that the Morneaus consented to the marriage on account of the odd French conception that to marry a daughter to a man of letters gives a bourgeois family a certain prestige.

It may be presumed that before his wedding Jules Renard went, as was only proper, to bid a final farewell to the mistress with whom for some months he had enjoyed the pleasures of sexual intercourse. Some nine years later he wrote a one-act play called *Le Plaisir de Rompre*. It is a dialogue between a young man and an older woman who has been his mistress. He is going to marry on the following morning a young girl who has money, and she, his mistress, on her side has arranged to make a marriage of convenience which will ensure her future. They are still more than a little in love with one another and, now that the bridegroom of next day sees the charming woman for the last time, in a moment of passion he says that she has only to say the word and he will jilt his fiancée and they will resume their relations for keeps. Her common sense prevails—love is all very well and very beautiful, but one can't live on it—and they part for ever. It is a charming, witty, moving little piece and, when acted, was a great success. After the first performance, Jules Renard asked himself in his Journal what the real Blanche, the model of his little play, would think of it.

After the honeymoon the Renards went to stay with his parents at Chitry. His mother took a dislike to Marinette and was very satirical about the 'fine lady' that her son had married. She did everything she could to make life intolerable to her daughter-in-law; but they stayed on, presumably for economy's sake, till their first child, a boy, was born. They then took a flat in Paris. A sardonic note in the Journal suggests how this was possible. "Did M.M. (M. Morneau, Renard's father-in-law) become a fortunate and clever tradesman so that his rich daughter should marry a poor man of letters?" During the next few years, during which Marinette had another child, a daughter, Jules Renard wrote a good deal of journalism, but it was badly paid and one can only suppose that they were more or less supported by the fortunate and clever tradesman. Since this is the last we hear of him, we may presume that in due course he died. In 1888 Jules published his first book, *Crime de Village*, a collection of stories most of which he had written long before.

Jules Renard genuinely loved Marinette. In his Journal he seldom has a good word to say of the persons he mentions, but of her he speaks always with deep affection. "Marinette appears," he writes, "and the earth is sweeter (*plus douce*) under one's feet." In the literary circles in which, as his reputation increased, he moved, the men were flagrantly unfaithful to their wives. Renard was flagrantly faithful to his. He was one of the founders of the *Mercure de France*, which, as every one knows, became the most distinguished and most advanced magazine of the time. Renard wrote for it regularly. It was not till 1892 that he published *L'Écornifleur* and not till 1895 that he published *Poil de Carotte*. These books established him as an original and talented writer. His nervous, alert and very personal style was highly praised by the critics. *L'Écornifleur* was thought well of by his fellow authors, but its cynical humour was not to the liking of the general public. *Poil de Carotte*, on the other hand, was a great success and the critics were unanimous in praising its pathos, its irony and its humour. In course of time Renard dramatised these narratives: *L'Écornifleur*, which for the stage he names *Monsieur Vernet*, was a disappointment, but *Poil de Carotte* was a winner. The public were delighted with it and it has since then been often revived.

In 1895, Renard's circumstances were so much easier, perhaps on account of the money that Marinette had inherited on her father's death, that he was able to rent, and then buy, at Chaumont, which was close to Chitry, where his parents lived, a house with sufficient land attached to enable him to keep chickens, ducks, geese, a horse, a donkey, sheep, pigs, a cow and a bull. To tend the livestock he engaged a peasant called Philippe and, as a maid of all work, his wife Ragotte. Marinette looked after the children and, with Ragotte to help, did the cooking. From then on, Renard, with his wife and children, spent from May to October at Chaumont and only the winter in Paris. He was nowhere so happy as in the country, for he was at heart still, as his enemies said, the peasant that his forebears had been. His enemies were many, since he seems to have taken a malign pleasure in antagonising people. They admitted his talent, but were incensed by his rudeness, his indifference to the feelings of others and his arrogance. In the country he could shoot and fish, pastimes which he shared with his father, and was at his ease with the peasants as he never quite was with his friends in Paris.

In 1897 his father fell ill. A few weeks later he wrote to Tristan Bernard, "My dear friend. Despairing of getting well, my father killed himself yesterday by shooting himself through the heart. I assure you that I am filled with respect and admiration for the manner of his death. Your very sad friend." He told another acquaintance that his father had died like the great sportsman he was and like a sage. To another he wrote, "As for me, I hope to show, in those solemn hours of my life, such strength of soul and such clear intelligence."

After the death of her husband Renard's mother continued to live at Chitry. She remained as she had always been, hard, domineering and narrow-minded. We are not told whether she had ever read *Poil de Carotte* and, if she had, what she thought of the portrait her son had drawn of her. She was little impressed by his literary success, but after he took to village politics and was elected a member of the council and, later, mayor, so that the people of his native province, who till then had ignored him, began to look upon him as a person of importance, she was, not unnaturally, pleased—with herself. She did not survive her husband long. Two years after his death, in a letter to a correspondent Jules wrote, "My dear friend, I have just read your nice letter. I was going to write to you that my mother, by accident,

I believe, fell and was drowned in the well. I am a little shocked. Marinette is as she was. The children are in good health. I embrace you and will write to you later."

Did he really believe it was an accident? He made up his mind to sell the house at Chaumont and move into the house at Chitry which, though he was not actually born there, he regarded as his native place.

To Antoine, the actor and manager, he wrote, "I thank you for your cordial note about my mother's death. As you can imagine, the burlesque side of this business hasn't escaped me. For the last fortnight I've been rather upset. I'll tell you all about it. Meanwhile I'm restoring the house a bit, where, doubtless, I shall die too. When you like for *La Bigote*. The theatre still goes on." *La Bigote* was a play Renard had written in which he showed how the peace and happiness of a family were ruined by the subserviency of the mother to the village priest. The mother, of course, was a vicious portrait of his own parent. The play was produced a few months after her death. The critics on the whole praised it and Renard thought it would have a run; but the public disliked it and it was withdrawn after a few performances.

By then, through the success of his one-act plays, Renard had come to know a number of persons connected with the theatre, such as Tristan Bernard, Capus, both dramatists, and Lucien Guitry, the actor. But his chief friends were Edmond Rostand and his wife. Rostand, after eighteen months of negotiation, managed to get the Legion of Honour granted to Renard. There is something rather engaging in the childish pleasure this harsh, intolerant man took in his decoration. He tells us in the Journal that when he went to a tobacconist to buy a packet of cigarettes he could not help unbuttoning his greatcoat so that the salesman should see his red ribbon. Renard was not a man who made friends easily and, when he did, didn't keep them long. He said himself that he should never make friends because he was bound to quarrel with them. Rostand was the great literary figure of the day; he was sought after and made much of. Renard was conscious that though Rostand thought him a good writer, he thought himself a better one. Of Rostand he wrote, "He is the only man I'm capable of admiring even though I detest him." "It's cracking, it's cracking," and a line later, "Sad as a dead friendship." It must be admitted that if Renard lost Rostand's friendship, he was to blame. He wrote a one-act play called *La Paix du Ménage*. A couple, husband and wife, are staying in the country with another couple; Pierre, the host, is attracted by his friend's pretty wife and is confident that if he makes advances to her she will not reject them. They discuss the situation with frankness. Pierre tells the young woman that he is very happy with his wife and would not cause her pain for anything in the world. She, on her side, has exactly the same feelings with regard to her husband, and they come to the conclusion that it isn't really worth while to enter upon a love affair. It is a charming little piece, and if you feel that it is rather cynical, well, common sense often has an air of cynicism.

Rostand and his wife had stayed with the Renards at Chaumont. He was no fool and when he read the little play he could hardly fail to realise that it narrated a scene that had taken place between Jules and his own wife. It is true that she had not been unfaithful to him, but it was not very nice to know that the two of them had discussed the possibility of it. Nor could he look upon it as a friendly act on Renard's part, in view of what he, Rostand, had done for him, even to consider the seduction of his wife. When Renard asked him to come to the first performance, and, somewhat obtusely, without his wife, his suspicion was confirmed and he refused to go. He called the little play a piece of malevolent reportage. Renard swore that it was nothing of the sort, but he had never made a secret of the fact that he was entirely devoid of any power of invention, and Rostand knew he was lying. The time came when Renard could write, "Rostand is the poet of the masses and thinks he is the poet of the chosen few."

With the exception of Capus and Tristan Bernard, he despised his fellow writers, but that did not prevent him from writing them effusive letters when they sent him their productions, for, said he, authors are so sensitive that you have to praise them a good deal more than they deserve. Of critics, amusingly enough, he wrote, "One should be indulgent with critics; they spend their lives talking about other people and nobody talks about them."

In 1908 he published a novel called *Ragotte*. It is written partly in stage dialogue, with the name of the speaker preceding the words in the way a play is printed, and partly in narrative. It is the life story of the Renards' maid-of-all-work, sixty years old by then, her husband, Philippe, and their children. Ragotte had gone into service when she was twelve. She had a daughter, who married, a son, Paul, with whom she had quarrelled, and a younger son, Joseph, whom the Renards took to Paris to find him a job. He fell ill, was taken to the hospital and died. It was this book that brought about a break between Renard and the *Mercure de France*, to which he had for years been a constant contributor. It is a sympathetic and, in parts, touching story of the poverty-stricken peasants of the Nivernais—the sort of book that a reviewer would skim through in an hour and, feeling that it was the kind of thing many people would read with pleasure, write a good review of. Fiction in the *Mercure de France* was reviewed by Rachilde, herself a novelist of some repute, the wife of Alfred Vallette, the founder and editor-in-chief of the magazine. She dealt with Renard's novel very cursorily. He was deeply affronted that not only as a contributor, but as a shareholder of the company and an editor, a book of his should be thus treated. He resigned from the editorial board, but in a few days withdrew his resignation; he seems to have thought that amends would be made to him, perhaps by another, more substantial review, but when he was disappointed in this, he again resigned and then sold his shares in the company. It was Alfred Vallette's pride that his contributors should be free to say whatever they liked, however provocative, without giving a thought to the indignant response that might ensue. It was, indeed, this principle which was largely the cause of the magazine's success. I have had the curiosity to look out in an old number of the *Mercure de France* what Rachilde had said thus to affront Jules Renard. She gave his book eight lines at the very end of her article. She mentioned the title, but neither praised nor blamed it. In fact she said nothing about it at all. No review could have been more scathing. She said that now that Renard was mayor of Chitry and a member of the *Académie Goncourt* he could get commissions to write whatever he liked and, when people wrote articles about him, it was to praise him; she added that she had recently read one such an article and it seemed to her complete nonsense. One can only suppose that Renard had at some time offended Rachilde, as he offended so many of his friends, and she took this opportunity to get back on him.

Ragotte was, I believe, the last book he wrote. "What do I owe my family?" he asked himself. "How ungrateful! They have provided me with my works ready made." By this time, in fact, he had made all the use he could of them, and he found himself in the unfortunate situation of a professional writer who ash nothing to write about. He took refuge in his Journal. "I've

229

acquired the habit of writing everything that occurs to me. I make a note of a thought just as it comes, even if it's unhealthy or criminal. It is obvious that these notes will not always show the man I am." No doubt he made some of them because their ferocity or their humour amused him. Here are a few instances: "It isn't enough to be happy; others mustn't be happy too." "You don't know what courage it needs to prevent oneself from making others suffer." "When someone tells me that a woman has been saying nasty things of me, I answer, 'I don't understand. After all, I've never done her a good turn'." He had a shyness which he never managed to surmount; it was perhaps on that account that when someone said a flattering thing to him, he could never bring himself to say an amiable one in return. He said himself that he preferred to be rude rather than obvious. Early on in the Journal he had written that it should not be just prattle as was so much of the Goncourts', but should serve to form his character and amend it. Somewhat unexpectedly he wrote, "There is no heaven, but one must try so to behave that there should be one." He felt that the Journal 'emptied' him, it was not a literary work; but for all that he was sure that it was the best thing and the most useful that he had done in his life. Perhaps he was right. I do not know that any writer, except perhaps Pepys, and he without intention, has drawn such a brutally honest portrait of himself as did Jules Renard. He was devoured with envy. "Envy is not a noble sentiment," he wrote, "but neither is hypocrisy, and I wonder what one gains by replacing one with the other." He would not read his friends' books in case he found in them something he was forced to admire. "The success of others irks me, but less than if it were deserved". He was even envious of Marinette's happiness and almost angry with her because she found it possible to be happy with a man whose character made him

230

intolerable to everybody. Yet, after seventeen years of marriage, he could say that the best thing in his life was Marinette's devotion. "Woman, what is it," he asked somewhat rhetorically, "that attaches you to him?" He gave the answer himself, "The need he has of me." Elsewhere he wrote, "I want nothing of the past. I don't count on the future. I am a happy man because I have renounced happiness." Perhaps the most tragic note he ever made was this: "Life without its bitterness would be intolerable."

There is a passage in the Journal which one cannot read without pain. One evening, after Renard had been shooting with his man Philippe, the man timidly asked him for a rise for his son Paul, who was also working for him. Renard flew into a rage and, going to his wife, sent for the two men. "Succeeding in not getting angry, I told Philippe that he had wounded me, that I no longer had confidence in him, that he had put a wall between us, and to Paul that he could find himself another place. They were downcast, they ate only a spoonful of soup, didn't sleep that night, and next day Ragotte was in tears." Ragotte apologised humbly and begged Marinette to forgive them. "From pity, from egoism also (always, always) I was touched: it was only the second time that I'd seen Ragotte crying. 'We've been so mortified,' she said. Philippe spent the day shelling peas, sheepish and sad. An old servant with white hair, wretched for having said a stupid thing, who doesn't know how to go about it to make amends—what could be sweeter to the miserable pride of an employer?"

If the reader, who has read so far, has come to the conclusion that Jules Renard was an odious man, he would be right. No one was more aware of it than himself. But human beings are not all of a piece. If they were, the novelist's task would be simpler—and his novels duller. The strange thing about them is that the most discordant qualities may possess them so that they seem a mass of contradictions and you cannot understand how they can exist together and somehow combine to form a consistent personality. Grossly selfish as Renard was, ill-tempered and quick to take offence, he was capable of infinite tenderness. When he was parted from Marinette, he wrote to her every day. He began his letters with "My dear, dear one". He ended one with the words, "Good-bye and till soon, my sweet. At bottom you see, there's nothing for me but you, and when you're not there nothing goes right with me." He adored his two children. The boy was called Fantec and the girl Baïe. When on one occasion he had to go to Bourges to do a short spell of military service, he wrote the day after his arrival to Marinette, "I was much pleased by the funny little face you made as I was leaving. Perhaps you cried afterwards, but you were grand at that last moment. Poor dear! I behaved well also, and Fantec too, who was playing in the sand, and, without disturbing himself, said 'You're going to Corbigny, Daddie?' 'No, to Bourges.' 'All right. Good-bye,' said Fantec, already deep in the sand. I kissed him with all my heart for his sweet unconcern, and I have still on my cheek your kiss and Baïe's."

The children began to grow up. Baïe remained at home, but Fantec went to school. Renard's letters to him are charming. They are not the letters of a father to a son, but of a friend to a friend. He consoles the boy when he hasn't got the prize he expected and praises a dissertation he has had to write, "What particularly pleases me is that your language has improved. It is strong, solid and clear. You now say what you want to say, and if you knew how rare that quality is! And one loses it as soon as one wants to have style above everything else." Surely one can forgive him his envy, his jealousy of others' success, his churlishness, when one remembers his devoted love for his dear

Marinette and his two children; he was a man warped by the un-happiness of his childhood, the hardship of his early life and a shyness that was almost pathological; he had rare qualities of heart.

I have little more to say about Jules Renard. In 1907 he was elected a member of the *Académie Goncourt*. This gave him a regular income of four thousand francs a year. It was less than the Goncourts had intended their academicians to receive but, notwithstanding, was welcome, for his journalism was wretchedly paid. The only way then in which an author could make a reasonable income was by writing plays. Renard's one-act plays earned him little. The managers wanted plays in three acts. That was something Renard could never manage to do. Perhaps through Léon Blum, still only a man of letters, he had come to know Jean Jaurès, who was to be assassinated by a fanatic in 1914, and through his influence he became a socialist. With his usual bitter knowledge of himself he made this note in his Journal: "Should I be a socialist if I could write a play in three acts?" Though he did not write much, he occupied himself in other ways. As mayor of his village he performed the necessary duties with zeal. He made political speeches in the department and presided at political banquets. He delivered well-attended lectures at the Odéon. He had always been passionately fond of shooting, but on a sudden he found that to kill birds no longer gave him pleasure. One day, out with his gun, a lark rose. He fired, not to kill, but to see what would happen. The little bird was lying on its stomach, its beak opening and shutting. "Lark," he wrote in the Journal, "may you become the most delicate of my thoughts, the most dear of my feelings of remorse. You died for others. I tore up my licence and hung up my gun on a nail."

I have not had occasion to do more than mention that Renard

had a brother and a sister. They went their different ways. He treated them with kindness and, when need arose, helped them with good advice and money. Towards the end of 1909, in a letter to his sister he told her that of late he had not been well, "But Marinette is there, and I too, and we'll look after ourselves." In the following year, he told her that the doctors said he was suffering from arteriosclerosis and he was threatened— "Oh, much later, in thirty years or so, with internal hæmorrhages, senile decay and partial paralysis." In March, presumably to reassure her, he wrote again to say that he was in no danger. "The mysterious malady arteriosclerosis always gives me a certain anxiety, which I'll have to watch, but there's no immediate menace. I'll try to live with it. Perhaps one has to be slightly ill to live fully and reasonably." On 6th April 1910, Renard wrote to Lugné Poë, the actor and manager, that he wanted his play *Poil de Carotte* to enter the repertory of the Comédie Française. He died next day. He was only forty-six. When one considers the long torture of his life, one cannot resist the impression that his misfortune was to have been born with a talent, even a remarkable talent, but without the creative faculty. He would have been a happier man if he had never written a line.

4

Now I come to the last of my three journalists. Paul Léautaud was the oddest, the most disreputable, the most outrageous, but to my mind the most sympathetic of the three. Though he produced little, two short autobiographical novels, two volumes of theatrical criticism and a number of articles that appeared for the most part in the *Mercure de France*, I am inclined to think that he had a remarkable and individual talent. He had traits that shock one and traits that extort one's admiration. He was an egoist, but devoid of vanity, a lecher without passion, cynical and conscientious, desperately poor, but indifferent to money, harsh in his dealings with his fellows, but to animals compassionate, savagely independent, indifferent to what others thought of him, a brilliant talker with a caustic wit, truthful, honest, but cheerfully tolerant of the dishonesty of others—altogether a very strange man, as will appear when I narrate as best I can something about him. The sources are the two novels I have mentioned, *Le Petit Ami* and *In Memoriam*, the four volumes of his Journal dating from 1893 to 1924, and the talks on the radio with Robert Mallet that he gave from November 1950 to July 1951. It is they, by their frankness, their spice, and their revelation of an unusual creature, that brought him at the age of seventy-eight, after the long obscurity of his life, what I would not venture to call fame, but notoriety.

Paul was born in 1872. His father, Firmin Léautaud, the son of a peasant in the Basses Alpes, did not come to Paris till he was twenty, at which age he was apprenticed to an uncle, a working jeweller and watchmaker, who had a shop in Montmartre. On his uncle's death he entered the Conservatoire and eventually became an actor. He was apparently not a good one, for after some years he abandoned the profession to become prompter at the Comédie Française, a job which he held for something like thirty years. Besides acting as prompter, he trained the younger members of the company in elocution and diction. He was a handsome man—so fascinating that he only had to look at a woman with his fine eyes for her to fall. At the time I am now dealing with he had an actress, called Fanny, living with him in Montmartre. One evening Fanny's younger sister, Jeanne, seventeen years old, came to see them. It grew late and they did not like her

to go home by herself to Montparnasse, where her parents lived
so Léautaud suggested that she should spend the night with them
As there was only one bed in the apartment the three of them
slept together, with Léautaud in the middle. I don't quite know
how to put what happened in terms that will not seem coarse
after some amorous dalliance with Fanny, Léautaud transferred
his attentions to her sister. Next day her parents turned her out
for her misconduct and she went back, having nowhere else to
go, to Fanny and Léautaud. A few days later Fanny left the
apartment in a huff and Jeanne stayed on. In due course she had
a baby. Since father and mother were on the stage, acting
separately, it was farmed out. Such were the origins of Paul
Léautaud. He did not go back to his father till he was over two
by which time Firmin and Jeanne had separated. Firmin
engaged a nurse to look after him. She was called Marie Pezé
and he loved her as a mother. He did not sleep in the apartment
in the rue des Martyrs, but with his nurse, partly because he
could not be left alone at night and partly because his father
seldom came home without a new mistress. When Paul was five
his mother, on her way to Berlin to fill an engagement or to
meet a lover, came with her mother, Madame Forestier, to see
him in his nurse's attic room. He was lying in bed ill, and very
sulky, with his back turned to the two women. Marie Pezé had
to force him to say good morning to them. He never forgot the
remark his mother made, "My God, how disagreeable that
child is!" They stayed five minutes and it was three years before
he saw her again. One day she appeared at the apartment in the
rue des Martyrs and Paul was brought in. He was shy, hardly
daring to look at her, and timidly called her *Madame*. She
arranged that next morning he should come to the house where
she had taken a room so that they could spend the day together
after which she would leave him at the tavern which his father

frequented on getting back from the theatre. He went as planned. He found his mother in bed, sitting up, her hair in some disorder, her arms bare and, her night-dress having slipped, her breast uncovered. She took him in her arms, drew him to her bosom and kissed him. She was very pretty, supple, lively and graceful. She dressed and they went to have luncheon with his father. After that they took a cab and went to the zoo. Paul was allowed to ride a pony. Then they went to the restaurant at the Palais Royal and dined there. After that Jeanne took him to see a play at the Châtelet. They left a little before the end and went on to the Folies Bergère. His mother went straight to the promenade to gossip with old friends. He couldn't get over all the people she knew. They greeted her like a long-lost sister. From time to time she pointed to him and told them who he was. "Oh, it's your son. He's sweet." At closing time they went with a group to have supper at a neighbouring inn. Then Jeanne took him back to the tavern where his father was waiting for him. She kissed him and left. He didn't see her again for two or three years and then only for half an hour. After that he heard nothing of her for twenty years. He was told that she had got married. The day he spent with his mother was his most cherished recollection.

When Paul was eight his father picked up a girl, Louise by name, who lived in the quarter. She was fifteen and he was forty-eight. She spent several nights with him. Marie Pezé, outraged, protested that he was giving the little boy a shocking example, whereupon Firmin lost his temper and, to Paul's bitter grief, discharged her. He took the girl to live with him. Paul was given a tiny room in the apartment. Until then he had been happy enough, but he did not get on with the new mistress, and one day he threw a bottle of ink at her, for which he was severely beaten. His father as ever remained brutal,

negligent and dissolute. Every night after dinner Paul wa
locked up in his room and, notwithstanding his tears, left alone
terrified, in the dark.

A year or two later Firmin Léautaud decided to live out or
town and took a house in the neighbouring suburb of Courbevoie. Paul went to school there. At fifteen he went to work
in Paris. He earned twenty-five francs, which his father took
for his board. I can pass over the next years of Léautaud'
life very briefly. He entered the army to do his military service,
but was myopic and after seven months was discharged. He
got a job at a wholesale glover's and began to write verse. After
throwing up this job, he got one as third clerk in an attorney's
office. He liked the work and stayed for ten years. Then he
entered the office of a certain Lemarquis, who was a trustee in
bankruptcy. He was evidently competent, for he was given
important assignments. Among others he had to administer the
estate of a man who on his death had left two million francs, then
eighty thousand pounds, and enormous debts. Lemarquis told
him to manage the affair so as to have as much as possible left
over for the widow. He did this so satisfactorily (and somewhat
unscrupulously) that when the negotiations with creditors came
to an end he received a handsome gratuity.

During this long time, after his day's work he was in the habit
of going to a *crèmerie*, near the Folies Bergère, where prostitutes had their mid-day and evening meals before dressing and
going to the cafés and music halls in the hope of finding
customers. He soon became very friendly with them. They
would consult him about a new hat or a dress. They would
show him their letters and he would write a draft of the answer
they should send. Sometimes he accompanied them to a café.
They knew he had no money and gave him cigarettes and
chocolates. At the evening's end, if one of them hadn't done any

business, she would ask him to come back with her, not always to make love, but to go quietly to bed. Sometimes one or other would ask him to come to see her in the afternoon and they would gossip by the hour. They talked of their early years and Léautaud talked to them of his mother. He claimed that these friends of his taught him a great deal. It may be they did.

Owing to a disagreement with Lemarquis, which resulted in his discharge, Paul, in his late twenties by this time, found himself out of a job, with nothing to live on but the gratuity his employer had given him. He shared a room with Van Bever, a minor man of letters with whom he had been at school. Both were miserably poor. Paul's father would give him nothing, but Fanny, his aunt, had never ceased to take an interest in him and did her best to see him once or twice a year. She gave him a few francs now and then and sent him clothes; they were cheap and nasty, but he was grateful for them. He continued to write verses. In the hope of getting them published, he asked Van Bever if he could get Lugné Poë, whose secretary Van Bever was at the time, to give him a letter of introduction to Alfred Vallette, the editor of the *Mercure de France*. When Léautaud went to see him with the letter, Vallette said to him, "One doesn't need an introduction to come here. The only introduction is your verse, good or bad." A few weeks later Léautaud saw himself in print.

He had made a good impression on Vallette. Léautaud was a brilliant talker. Acid, but witty. His repartees were prompt, often cruel, but always amusing. Many years later he published a very short book, called *Propos d'un Jour*, which was a collection of epigrams, aphorisms and wisecracks. When the critics remarked that there were too many of his own, he retorted that most people were so dull, he seldom came across witticisms as good as his own. Vallette, who enjoyed his conversation, very

sensibly advised him to write in prose and during the next three
or four years he produced a number of essays which appeared in
the magazine. They are stylishly written in a manner presumably well liked at the time, but which Léautaud soon abandoned
for one of a more pleasing simplicity. He became a regular
contributor to the *Mercure*; he reviewed books and, in collaboration with Van Bever, published an anthology of the poetry
of the day which had a considerable success. It is not my
intention to describe the two or three more or less serious love
affairs, if that is the proper name for them, that Léautaud had.
They are uninteresting. He himself said, "Love interests me too
little." Van Bever got married and at the beginning of the
century we find Léautaud living in a tiny apartment with a
young woman called Blanche. Léautaud liked her; she gave him
peace and did not interfere with his work. Presently he started
on a novel which, at Vallette's suggestion, was to be named *Le
Petit Ami*. It was on the whole an accurate account of Léautaud's
early life; but when he had finished with his reminiscences of the
prostitutes with whom he had consorted, ending up with the
charming and pathetic description of the death of one called La
Perruche, he found himself at a dead end. Then something
happened which, as he said afterwards, was a bit of luck. He
received a telegram from his grandmother, Madame Forestier, to
tell him that his Aunt Fanny was desperately ill and if he wanted
to see her once more he must come at once. The old lady and
her daughter had been living for a good many years at Calais,
where Fanny, an actress, had been a member of the stock company which played there. Paul supposed that Jeanne, his mother,
would have been sent for. He had not seen her for twenty years,
but he still remembered the charming, graceful creature with
whom so long ago he had spent a day. He wondered how he
would find her. He feared he would find a rather battered,

serious lady and he was in half a mind not to go. He went. When he got to Calais, his grandmother, whom he had seen but once in his life and then only for five minutes, began at once to talk to him of his mother. Paul knew that she was married, but he learned then that she lived in Geneva with her husband and her two children. Her husband, a man of some importance, had fallen in love with her while she was a member of the company at Geneva, and she became his mistress. She bore him a boy and a girl and then he married her. Madame Forestier told Léautaud that his mother had never once spoken of him. He suggested that it would be embarrassing for her to find him installed there without having been warned. His grandmother told him it was no matter: she wouldn't recognise him.

Paul was thirty. He was a little man, with a heavy brown beard and a moustache. He wore steel-rimmed spectacles. Though his linen was clean, as always, he was so shabby that his grandmother gave him ten francs to go there and then to buy a pair of trousers. His mother arrived at half-past one in the afternoon. Léautaud had just accompanied to the door someone who had come to have news of Fanny when he heard steps on the stairs. He looked over the banister and saw a woman coming up, in a black dress, with a small valise in her hand. He recognised her at once. He told his grandmother she was on the way and shut himself up in his room. Jeanne entered the apartment, kissed her mother and, after taking off her hat and coat, went in to see her sister. Then she asked for luncheon. They were to eat in the kitchen and to get to it the two women, mother and daughter, had to pass through the room in which Léautaud was seated. His mother bowed slightly and said, "*Bonjour, Monsieur.*" He answered, "*Bonjour, Madame.*" When they got into the kitchen, he heard his mother ask who he was. Since he did not want to hear the answer he made a noise in his room. Later his grandmother told him. "I preferred not to say who you were. It might have been awkward for her. I said you were a friend, someone from the theatre, who had come to help us." Léautaud did not believe a word of it. His mother knew very well who he was, but wanted to act as though she didn't. It was not till she had gone back to Geneva that his grandmother told him the truth. When Jeanne had asked, "Who is that?" she had answered, "It's Paul." "Who is Paul?" "Why, your son."

Anyhow, after a while, Jeanne joined them and the two women began to gossip. She talked of her children with affection. Then his grandmother told Léautaud that, since her daughter would be using his bed, he would have to take a room in a near-by hotel. "I must apologise, *Monsieur*, for making you turn out," his mother said to him then. "Not at all, *Madame*," he replied. "It's the least I can do."

The ice was broken and, while the old lady went to see about one thing and another, Jeanne asked him to tell her the Paris news, spoke of the Comédie Française and enquired of friends whom she had once known. He told her all he could. As I have said, he was a clever talker and he amused her.

When they had dined, Léautaud sat with his mother in Fanny's room. After some time, she said, "Listen, Paul, I know who you are." She began to talk in undertones of her early youth, her first love affairs when she was fifteen or sixteen, of her husband and children. Then she explained her long silence. She had often asked Fanny and her mother about him, but had learnt nothing. She had read his name two or three years before in connection with something he had written in the *Mercure*. Oh, if she had only known where to write to him! In 1900 she went to Paris for the Exhibition with her husband and children. How she would have hurried to him if she had only known where to find him! Léautaud knew there wasn't a word of truth in anything she said. After all, she only had to write to him at the office of the *Mercure*. He did not speak. When she had done talking he took her to her room. She kissed him. In his eyes she was still young and desirable. He put his arm round her waist and took her in his arms, and kissed her neck, her eyes, her breast. "You mustn't mind," he said. "What?" "I don't know, but I don't kiss you like a mother." While she was turning down the sheets, he said to her, "I'll go into the sitting-room. I'll come back when you're in bed and sit by you." Though he insisted, she wouldn't let him do that, and he went to his hotel. When he returned next morning he was told that Fanny was dead.

Léautaud had a lot of things to see to, but he and Jeanne were able to pass the afternoon and evening together. They talked. She cross-questioned him about his love life. When they were alone she would put her arm round his neck and say, "Kiss me quick. What would people say if they saw us kissing like this in secret?" And once, "You see, we look like two lovers. What would have happened ten years ago?" He could not but think what he would have felt to kiss her as he would have kissed a mistress—his mother, but, after all, a woman like another. For her he was just a man, and a young man at that. He thought of her slim, graceful body and wondered what her thoughts were when she looked at him. When he left her for the night, as she kissed him again, "You'll never know how much I love you," he said. He asked himself if she had the same passionate feeling for him as he had for her. Who could tell—loose as she had been and as, from the questions she had put to him, still seemed to be?

While Léautaud was undergoing these shattering emotions he did not forget the unfinished book he had left in Paris. From the moment of his mother's arrival, he made notes whenever he had the opportunity. Once she noticed him at it and asked him what he was about. He told her that he was jotting down his expenses. Alone in his hotel room at night, he thought of all that had passed. He told himself that his mother's tenderness did not mean much. But after all, he said to himself, one mustn't ask too much of the poor woman; she did what she could. He took up his note-book and put down all that had happened during the day. He ends the paragraph of *Le Petit Ami* in which he has described this with the words, "Grandeur of the man of letters! One may be a son, one may have found one's mother again after twenty years of separation, the moment one has a book on the stocks, that goes before everything. There are no things that one has felt, heard or seen that one doesn't intend to put in it, however sacred they may be. It may be that these things were not very sacred."

Next day there was a funeral service for Fanny, who was to be buried in Paris. When it was over the two women and Léautaud went home. It had been arranged that he should take the coffin to Paris that evening. Jeanne was to leave next day. Since she would have to wait for three hours in Paris before her train started for Geneva, they agreed that Léautaud should meet her at the station so that he might show her his apartment, after which they could dine together. He arrived in Paris at five in the morning and by ten o'clock everything was finished and Fanny buried. He got Blanche to make herself scarce for a few hours so that his mother should not know that he lived with a woman. The day seemed very long and at five, with an hour still to wait, he was at the station. On the way he had bought a bunch of violets. The train came in. His mother was not on it. He waited till eight, watching one train come in after another. Nobody. Then it occurred to him that she might have changed her mind and had sent a telegram to tell him that she was detained in Calais.

He took a cab, a fearful extravagance for him, and went to his apartment. Nothing. He hurried back to the Gare de Lyon and got there at eight-thirty-five. The train for Geneva was to start at eight-fifty. He ran on to the platform and along the train.

Jeanne was sitting in the corner of a carriage, quite quietly, looking at the people who passed. He jumped in. "Well, my boy, what is it?" she said. He burst into tears. She reasoned with him. After all, it was only a date that had gone wrong. "Poor boy," she said. "We'll arrange all that. We'll meet again. We'll make up for it." She kissed him. She was surrounded by parcels and it was obvious that she had never intended to meet him, but had got out of the train at a previous station and gone shopping. It may well be that she did not want to spend two or three hours alone with the unknown son whose demonstrative affection somewhat embarrassed her. The porters were shutting the carriage doors. She offered him a five-franc piece which, bitterly hurt, Paul refused. He put the bunch of violets, somewhat crushed by then, on the seat beside her, said good-bye and left. He cried all night in the arms of Blanche. On arrival at Geneva, Jeanne sent a post-card to Madame Forestier. It ran as follows, "The train got to Paris an hour and a quarter late. I didn't see Paul. Did he get tired of waiting? That grieved me and I don't know what to think."

On the day after these events Paul wrote a ten-page letter to his mother, reproaching her for having treated him so cruelly, but telling her that he loved her with all his heart. On the same day she wrote to him from Geneva. "Only a word in haste," she began, "to assure you of my affection, why had there to be that wretched mishap to deprive me of the sweet hours that I was rejoicing to spend with you, I'd longed to see your room, so that I could follow you in my thoughts, and what a night I passed in that horrid train that was taking me away from you." And she finished, "Good-bye, my dear one, take the tender kisses of your mother who has never forgotten you and to whom your presence has put a ray of sunshine in her heart." Léautaud, when he read this phrase, remarked, "She must read some very poor books."

From then on for a while they wrote to one another almost every day. Jeanne's letters were affectionate, Paul's passionate. In one of hers she wrote, "I must tell you that I am often hurt and worried by the sort of affection that you show me, until now I've ascribed many things to your sentimentality, but your letters, which it was a joy to me to keep, are sometimes so equivocal as to be possibly dangerous, and I think I shall destroy them; what pains me also is to see you interpreting my letters as you do and however flattered I am by the admiration you show me, I find it excessive and embarrassing." Oddly enough, in one letter she advised Paul to write a novel founded on his early life. It never occurred to her that he had already written a great part of it and was even then busy with the copious notes he had made during the three days they had spent together in Calais. Financial matters arose which further strained their relations. Léautaud's grandmother had taken a fancy to Paul and gave him such stocks as she possessed on the understanding that he should send her the dividends during her lifetime and after her death inherit them. She told the plan to her daughter, who was indignant. "You're not going to give everything you have to this man whom we don't know!" Considering that her husband was well-to-do, whereas her son was penniless, it was not generous on her part.

It would be tedious to describe at length the correspondence between Léautaud and his mother. Her letters grew colder. She complained that he read into them more than she meant. She got it into her head that he was reproachful for her long neglect of him. She was afraid that he might come to Geneva and begged him not to do so without her consent. Finally she asked him to return her letters. He did not send them and she asked for them again; then she wrote, "Until you have sent me back my letters, without leaving out a single one, I shall not write to you." He refused to do so. In a further letter she wrote to him she said, "There's only one thing I regret and that is to have given you in my letters, from a sense of duty, the illusion of an affection that I couldn't feel, as I didn't know you, which all the same I might have had if you had shown yourself worthy of it. I can only congratulate myself on not having brought you up, for I should feel profoundly humiliated. Now whether you come to Geneva or not, doesn't matter to me; we shall be two to receive you; my husband and I . . ." In return he wrote a stinging letter. She answered with one which ended with the words, "I tell you again that I am so indifferent to you, you are so little my son, that I don't feel myself concerned or humiliated by your shameful conduct; it would certainly have been better if I had always ignored you, but what then? You will have passed in my life like a bad dream, which, believe me and notwithstanding everything, will fade quickly from my memory." After that, though he continued to write, she did not reply. She did not even write when he told her in two lines that his father, her old lover, had died.

When *Le Petit Ami* was published it was much talked about, much praised and much abused. Owing to the closeness of the tie that unites mother and son in France, a tie that, though sometimes merely conventional, is for the most part genuine, many readers were frankly horrified. That Paul should have made it clear that he had incestuous desires for his mother, that she should, if not encourage them, at least not discourage them, was shocking. It didn't make it any better that he said they were strangers to one another. She did not repel his passionate embraces; whenever they were alone she kissed him fondly, and it was she who said that they were more like two lovers than mother and son. She even went so far as to hint that if they had met ten years before, when he was twenty, things might have gone differently. One gets the impression that she was far from displeased with his passion and, if she did not yield, it was not for the immorality of the matter, but from her prudence as a respectably married woman. His feelings were unequivocal. Perhaps such feelings are not so rare as is generally believed. An intelligent psychiatrist of my acquaintance, whose work is chiefly with juvenile delinquents, has told me they often tell him, with something like shame, that they would like to go to bed with their mothers. I think he would ascribe it to the promiscuity in which the boys of that class live, the lack of privacy and the fact that the only love they have known is that which their mother gave them when they were children, so that when the sexual instinct became active it was directed towards her. Paul Léautaud was not a juvenile delinquent, but he had been a neglected child, he had longed for his mother's love, he had idolised her and had never forgotten that day when he had found her, half naked, in bed and she had covered his face with kisses; it may be abominable that he should have had the desire to have sexual connection with her when after twenty years he saw her again, so graceful, so charming, so tender, but it was not unnatural. I do not condone, I merely state the facts. You may say he should never have written an account of those three wanton days at Calais: to write was his passion and, devoid of imagination as he was, he could only write about himself and what happened to him.

In 1903 Firmin Léautaud died. After having a son by Louise, the little harlot he had taken to live with him, he married her. Paul detested her, but went to see his father, still living at

Courbevoie, every other Sunday. For six years Firmin had been partly paralysed and could only go from one room to another with the help of his wife and his young son. One Sunday, going as usual to Courbevoie, Paul found that his father had grown worse. He spent a couple of days there and returned to Paris. The following morning he received a telegram bidding him come at once. He found his father dying. Four days later he died. Paul Léautaud had always been interested in death and during these four days he stored in his memory every step of his father's disintegration, the conversation of the friends who came to see the dying man, who, after a few minutes during which they expressed their sympathy, began to chatter about their own affairs; the impatience of the man's wife and son, and his own too, because the agony lasted so long. Though they would not admit it, they felt that if he had to die, the sooner the better.

Paul Léautaud wrote a long account of his father's death and published it in the *Mercure*. It was called *In Memoriam*. Some subscribers were so outraged that they refused to renew their subscriptions to the magazine, but in literary circles it was much admired for its ruthless sincerity and its strange mixture of cynicism and emotion. Some members of the *Académie Goncourt* were anxious to give it the yearly prize. Unfortunately it was too short. It ran to a little over thirty pages. But there was a dearth of candidates for the prize, and members of the academy assured Léautaud that if he could so spin it out as to make something of a book there was no doubt that it would receive the award. Vallette was eager that he should do this, since it would be a good advertisement for the firm. Léautaud was tempted. In theory he did not approve of such prizes, but this one would not only bring him five thousand francs, two hundred pounds, an immense sum for him, but, with the publicity that the choice brought, would ensure a sale of four or five thousand copies. In the Journal Léautaud has described at tedious length the discussions that took place. At last it was arranged that he should re-write two articles that had appeared under the name of *Amours* in the *Mercure*. They dealt with his early love affairs, but it is hard to see how they could possibly have been incorporated in an account of his father's death. Nothing came of it and the prize was given to someone else.

Vallette had for some time been dissatisfied with his dramatic critic and he pressed Léautaud to take his place. The *Mercure* was a fortnightly and he was to be paid seven francs a page, but not more than twenty-eight francs a number. This looks like wretched payment, but the *Mercure* had a circulation of only three thousand and Vallette could not afford to be lavish. After some hesitation Léautaud accepted the offer. For his theatrical criticism he used the pseudonym of Maurice Boissard. This was supposed to be an elderly gentleman of modest means, who was not a man of letters, but who liked the theatre. Léautaud wrote dramatic criticism for seventeen years. At the end of this time he collected his articles and published them in two volumes. Although most of the plays he dealt with have long been forgotten, his articles can still be read with pleasure. They are caustic, lively, humorous and prejudiced. Léautaud had no patience with the plays that sought to instruct, to preach or to moralise. He hated the pompous, the verbose and the artificial. He asked of a play that it should amuse or move. He insisted that people should talk as they talked in real life and was scathing in his condemnation of dialogue that no human being could dream of speaking. He greatly liked the plays of Sacha Guitry. He admitted that he was a light-weight, but in his plays people did speak as they spoke in ordinary life and behaved as it was natural for them to behave. When Léautaud found a play worthless he wrote of anything that occurred to him, and only just mentioned the piece he was supposed to deal with. His victims were incensed, but readers enjoyed his articles and some bought the magazine solely to read them. Eventually it was learnt that Maurice Boissard, the old gentleman living on his savings, was none other than the author of the scandalous *Le Petit Ami* and the hardly less scandalous *In Memoriam*. Rachilde, Vallette's wife, had never liked him. She was in the habit of receiving on Tuesday evenings the literary persons and their wives who cared to come. Some might be authors, or the friends of authors, whom Léautaud, as Maurice Boissard, had made bitter fun of. They did not fail to complain of their ill-treatment. She told her husband, but he answered that Léautaud was read and the *Mercure* had never been more prosperous. She persisted, others backed her up, and finally Vallette yielded. He took the dramatic criticism in the *Mercure* away from Léautaud. Fortunately for him, however, André Gide offered him, at a much higher rate, the position of dramatic critic on the *Nouvelle Revue Française*, of which he was the mainstay. Léautaud was glad to take it. But that only lasted for two years. It came to an end when he wrote a mocking criticism of a play by Jules Romains and refused to alter a word of it. The editors of the *Nouvelle Revue Française* were in an awkward position. They were publishers as well and they published Jules Romains's novels. Romains was furious at being so cruelly ridiculed in the magazine and they were afraid he would leave them for another publisher. They did not want to lose a valuable property and Léautaud was dismissed. Then he wrote for the *Nouvelles Littéraires*, but, owing to his obstinacy to have every word he had written printed, only for a few months. Thus ended, in 1923, his career as a dramatic critic.

Now I must return briefly to 1907. Léautaud was miserably poor. At one time he was forced to pawn his father's watch and his cuff-links. They brought him thirty-five francs. He was still living with Blanche. The money he had received from Lemarquis was coming to an end and their situation was desperate. In the hope of improving it, she started a boarding-house on funds provided by a former lover. They reckoned that after paying expenses it would give a profit of two hundred francs a month and with this, and the pittance Léautaud earned at the *Mercure*, they could just scrape along. Léautaud had always felt that an author should not live by his pen, but should provide for his board and lodging by some other occupation. It was only thus that he could be certain of retaining his literary independence. He looked about now for a job, but found it impossible to get one that suited him. Then Vallette offered him the post of secretary to the *Mercure de France*. His working hours were to be from nine-thirty till six and he would be paid 125 francs a month. This sum Vallette unwillingly increased to 150 francs, but made it plain that there would be no further rise. Blanche advised him to refuse and keep his liberty. It seemed shocking that at the age of thirty-five, and with the reputation he had acquired, he should accept such a paltry salary; but he was afraid that if he refused the offer Vallette would be angry with him and perhaps no longer want him to write for the magazine. Finally he accepted and on the first of January 1908 entered upon his duties. They were to remind subscribers that their subscriptions were due, see visitors and keep them from disturbing Vallette if he thought fit, receive manuscripts and consider them, correct proofs and in short do any odd jobs that needed doing. He held the post for thirty-three years and on the whole enjoyed it. The life suited him. He met the literary men of the day, and had plenty of time for gossip, which was the great pleasure of his life.

A thousand copies of *Le Petit Ami* had been printed. It took twenty years to sell them. Vallette then wanted to re-issue it. Léautaud refused to let him. He was dissatisfied with it and wanted to re-write it. There were parts that he thought too literary. Léautaud used the word *littérature* in two ways. When he spoke of *ma littérature* he only meant his writings; when he cried, "*La littérature avant tout*," it was to affirm his right to write of his mother without respect and of his father without affection. It is true that his mother had no claim to his respect nor his father to his affection. Léautaud took the craft of writing very seriously, and there are numerous passages of the Journal concerned with it. He conceived the notion that he wrote his best when he wrote what had occurred to him on the spur of the moment. I suppose he means by that when he wrote with what we call inspiration. When he laboured to put down on paper what he wanted to say the result, to his own mind, was dull and lifeless. Above all, he aimed at being natural. When he came across in *Le Petit Ami* a grammatical mistake he left it because it had come naturally. He thought that the word that first occurs to one is the best one to use and he would not own a dictionary. In this, oddly enough, Chekhov agreed with him. Léautaud thought that all writers used too many words and that what they wrote would be all the better if they wrote fewer. He had no patience with words put in to balance a phrase; he believed that if one said just what was needed, the phrase *had* balance. He liked poetic prose as little as he liked prosy poetry. He had no use for the flowery and the ornate. He eschewed metaphors and similes. His desire was to be brief, vivid and succinct. All this is reasonable enough and without doubt we should all write better if we bore his principles in mind.

Of course Léautaud had his prejudices. He detested Flaubert for the artificiality and the monotony of his style and claimed, rashly, that anyone could write like him who cared to take the trouble. One of Léautaud's cherished notions was that a writer's style should be so individual that you have only to read a page to name him. That is all very well, but from this Léautaud seems to infer that the style is good. It does not follow. No one who had ever read the novels of George Meredith, and in the later years of the nineteenth century all young men who fancied themselves cultured idolised him, no one who read a page from one of his novels could fail to know who had written it. It is just that fantastic, tortured, acrobatic style that now makes him, notwithstanding his great merits, difficultly readable.

Léautaud had never been out of France. He seldom left Paris. He loved its streets, he loved its shops; he had associations with every corner of Montmartre and the quarter of the left bank which had its centre in St. Sulpice and the Panthéon. In 1911 he left Paris to live in a suburb. This harsh, selfish, bitter man had a passion for animals. The sight of a broken-down nag pulling a heavy cart shattered him so that he could think of nothing else all day. His heart was wrung when he saw in the streets dogs and cats that their owners, going away for a holiday, had left to fend for themselves. When he came upon a lost dog he would go to a shop and buy four sous' worth of cooked meat and give it to him, then try to find someone who would give it a home. Every evening he bought minced meat at the butcher's and took it to the stray cats that wandered about the gardens of the Luxembourg. And remember, he was desperately poor; he had to scrape and save to have enough to eat. On one occasion he came across a dog that was obviously starving. He had only a franc in his pocket for his day's food and that only because he had been thrifty the day before. He went and bought meat for the lost brute. That day, as on many others, he ate only bread and cheese. Léautaud had a cat of his own whom (or which) both he and Blanche doted on. From their constant squabbles it looks as though their passion for Boule, that was the cat's name, was the only thing that kept them together. Boule eventually died and Léautaud found and adopted a strange dog whom he called Amis and to whom he soon grew devoted. The time came when he had to make one of his numerous changes of habitation and for the dog's sake he looked for an apartment on the ground floor so that it could easily be let out. The various *concierges* of the houses he applied at told him that dogs were not allowed, so he decided to live out of town. He found a small house with a garden in the suburb called Fontenay aux Roses and settled there. There he remained for the rest of his life.

It is not clear whether Blanche went with him. From remarks he made in one of his dramatic criticisms, in which, as I have said, he was apt to talk of everything except of the play upon which he was called to deliver judgment, he tells of a woman, presumably Blanche, who lived with him, abandoned him for a rich lover, returned and abandoned him again, and when she once more returned, he would have nothing more to do with her. He said, characteristically enough, that though you no longer love your mistress, when she leaves you for another, you can't help being angry and jealous. He was able now to house all the stray cats and lost dogs that he came across. He often had as many as thirty. It complicated his life. He had to take the train in the morning to be at the offices of the *Mercure* by nine-thirty and when they were closed at six he had to take the train back to Fontenay to feed his animals; then, two or three times a week at least, he had to return to Paris to see a play and did not get home till after midnight. Sometimes he had a woman of mature age to clean up and cook for him, but it was not a success, since sooner or later she made advances to him and, when he rejected them, left in a huff. He was on the whole better off alone. He managed well enough. His tastes were simple. He did not mind what he ate, he never drank spirits, and wine but seldom. His only luxury was tea.

The years went by. The First World War was waged. The Second World War broke out. Most of Léautaud's friends, Van Bever, his oldest friend, died; Remy de Gourmont, with whom he was more intimate than with any other man of letters of his day, died; Alfred Vallette died. Vallette had published his first poems, had encouraged him to write and had printed in the *Mercure* everything he wrote. Though he scolded him sometimes for his unpunctuality in arriving at the office in the morning and for the unconscionable time he stayed away when he went out to lunch, he defended him from the attacks of his enemies and when he was penniless cheerfully lent him money. He was a curious editor. He never read the contributions to his magazine until they were in print and then only if for some reason he was obliged to. He chose his staff with care and gave them freedom to do what they thought fit. The only thing he asked of them was that they should not bore. He made the *Mercure* an influential magazine with, comparatively, a wide circulation. One day someone asked him if he had read a certain book. "Good God, no," he answered. "Isn't it enough that I published it?" Vallette's successor as head of the firm was a certain Jacques Bernard. One morning when Léautaud arrived at the office, the *concierge* told him that Bernard wished to see him at once. On going to his room Jacques Bernard said to him, "Léautaud, I have decided to part with you for the pleasure of not seeing you any more." He added, "If I have to take money from my own pocket, I'll take it." Léautaud, never at a loss for a repartee, answered, "When one gets such a pleasure, it's worth a certain sacrifice." He took his bits and pieces out of the room he had occupied for three and thirty years, and departed. Thus brutally fired after so long a period, he was destitute. He was sixty-nine. He applied for an old age pension and was granted it. When the war came to an end Jacques Bernard was tried on the charge of collaboration with the enemy. He must have been nervous when he heard that Léautaud was one of the witnesses for the prosecution. The evidence he gave was so temperate that Bernard was acquitted. Some months before this Léautaud had an experience that few of us authors have the luck to enjoy. The Vichy radio announced that he was dead. The news occasioned a great number of articles, and Léautaud was astounded to find that they were laudatory. That was the last thing he expected.

During the German Occupation Léautaud lived quietly at Fontenay aux Roses. He suffered from the cold. Since coal was unobtainable, he cut down the trees in his garden for firewood. Food was scarce and he was reduced to eating four potatoes a day. He cooked them himself. To his sorrow he could no longer provide for the large number of cats and dogs that he had cared for so tenderly. He was forced to get rid of them. The war ended. He made a little money by journalism, but remained desperately poor: it was a stroke of luck for him when someone had the idea, in 1950, of getting him to have a series of conversations on the radio with a writer called Robert Mallet. They were later published and one edition after another was issued. Mine is the sixteenth. Léautaud was seventy-eight. In these talks he proved himself as pig-headed and pugnacious, as vivacious, witty and prejudiced, as scornful of sentimentality, as sensible and unreasonable as he had always been. They delighted listeners. We may hope that the money he received from them enabled him to live in some comfort for the rest of his life. He died in the eighty-fourth year of his age.

I don't know what the reader of these pages will make of the sketch, necessarily inadequate, of the strange man whom I have done my best to describe. He was a card. He cannot

be judged by ordinary standards. He was a mixture of hetero-
geneous traits. He was callous and emotional, ruthlessly
independent, passionately interested in literature and indignant
with those who made it a business and a source of advance-
ment, irascible and impatient with those who did not think
as he did, faithful to those he liked and merciless to those he
despised. He prided himself on never having done anyone
harm. It is odd that it never occurred to him that a word
might be more hurtful than a blow. When people asked him
how he could be so kindly to animals and to his fellow creatures
so brutal, he answered that animals were defenceless, dependent
on people, but human beings could defend themselves. I have
said little about his love life. He was interested in women only if
he could have with them what the papers nowadays delicately
call intimacy. He thought them deceitful, malicious, exacting,
mercenary and stupid. From his own accounts he was an unsatisfactory lover—for reasons which the reader, if he thinks it
worth the trouble, can find out for himself in the Journal. Love,
of course, is not the right word in this connection, but the right
word is unprintable. He was incapable of love, for he was
interested only in himself. He was surely right when he said that
love is rooted in sexual attraction and cannot arise without it, but
seems not to have seen that it only becomes love when it gives
rise to feelings, bitter pains and ecstatic joys, more commendable.

Paul Léautaud looked upon his Journal as his only work of any
importance. He attached very little to *Le Petit Ami* and *In
Memoriam*. Four volumes of the Journal have been published.
They deal with his life from 1903 to 1924, but as he went
on writing it till the end of it there must be a good many
volumes to come. When it is complete it will provide an
interesting account of the literary world of his day. It will deal
with no such figures as the Goncourts had the advantage of

dealing with. Sainte-Beuve, Taine, Renan, Michelet, Flaubert were long since dead. So were the poets Victor Hugo, Baudelaire, Verlaine, Rimbaud, and Mallarmé. These were the great figures that had given distinction to their era and made France the proud centre of culture and civilisation. Even the popular novelists, Alphonse Daudet and Émile Zola, were dead. Who were the authors that Léautaud found to write about? It would be unfair to say that they were trivial. They were gifted, but their gifts were on a smaller scale than those of their predecessors. There was Henri de Régnier, a delicate poet and a graceful novelist; there was Barrès, who intoxicated the young with his *Culte du Moi*, but turned to politics and propaganda; there was the talented and cultivated André Gide. There was Anatole France, much admired in his own day and unjustly despised in ours. There was Moréas, a Greek, whose *Stances* Léautaud admired and whom he liked as a man for his modesty, good nature and bohemian ways; there was Apollinaire, a Pole, who was killed in the First World War; there was Paul Valéry. The writers who held the stage during the first thirty or forty years of this century were talented in their different ways, but they had neither the significance for their contemporaries, nor the authority and influence which their predecessors of the nineteenth century had had for theirs.

The volumes of Léautaud's Journal that have so far been published make curious reading. There is a good deal that can be skipped. Léautaud loved a bit of scandal: you cannot at this time of day be interested in the long recital of a sordid love affair between persons you have never heard of. But as a picture of the literary life in Paris during the period of which Léautaud wrote, the book is remarkable. The phrase tells us that dog don't eat dog. That was not the case with these authors. They seldom had a good word to say for one another. There was a certain amount of corruption. An author who had money was not above paying the editor of a newspaper to insert the eulogistic review of his book that he had himself written. Authors were not ashamed to bring all the influence they could bring to bear in order to get favourable notices. Intrigue was general, to get published, to get publicity, to get a decoration; and nowhere was it more rampant than when it was a matter of getting one of the literary prizes, like the *Prix Goncourt*, of which there were already several. It is not a pretty picture and, though Léautaud was an acid observer who preferred to blame rather than to praise, to say a disagreeable thing rather than a pleasant one, you get the impression that it was on the whole a true one. In extenuation it is only fair to add that at the bottom of the corruption, envy, jealousy, backbiting and the rest was the need for money. Writers were wretchedly paid, and if they wanted to make a living, they could not afford to be over scrupulous. Léautaud spent thirty years as an employee, doing work that any clerk could have done, in order to maintain his independence so that he could write, as he claimed every author should, purely for his pleasure. It is greatly to his credit.

I don't know what the reader will think of these three journalists whom I have to the best of my ability described to him. Not much, I suppose. They had few redeeming traits. Their egoism was ferocious. They were riddled with prejudices. They were monstrously touchy. Though they had little good to say of others, they fiercely resented criticism of themselves. They had no morals. They were indifferent to the arts, with exception of the art of letters, and when, as they sometimes did, they offered an opinion on music, painting or sculpture, it was (at all events to our present judgment) absurd. They were callous to the feelings of others. They were malicious and unkind.

But if they had these traits, we know them only because they have told us of them themselves. If I were asked whether on the whole they were any worse than other men, I should be at a loss for an answer. On one occasion Léautaud was presented to the Abbé Mugnier. The Abbé Mugnier was one of those priests who are now and then produced by the Catholic Church. He was a wit and a scintillating talker. He was a welcome guest at the dinner tables of the Boulevard St. Germain; he would hold the company entranced by his eloquent and amusing conversation. But though (to the scandal of some of his fellow priests) he much frequented the rich and noble, he never forgot his sacred office. The rich and noble too had souls to save. He persuaded the dissolute to mend their ways and won back not a few free-thinkers to the Church. When the party which he had graced with his presence broke up he returned to his very modest dwelling. There he was always to be seen by the poor and humble who came to him in their troubles for advice or aid. He helped them with his money, little though he had, and with his heartfelt sympathy. He was a man of a shining virtue. He knew that Léautaud was an aggressive sceptic—there were few people of his day about whom the Abbé Mugnier didn't know whatever was to be known—and he said to him, "God will forgive you, Monsieur Léautaud, because you have loved animals."

SELECTED PREFACES
AND INTRODUCTIONS

ACKNOWLEDGEMENT

The Introduction to *A Choice of Kipling's Prose* is reprinted by permission of Messrs Macmillan & Co. Ltd

PUBLISHER'S NOTE

The Prefaces and Introductions collected in this volume provide a conspectus of Mr Maugham's views of a writer's craft, and of his own work in particular.

By Mr Maugham's direction a few passages from the originals have been deleted, to avoid either repetition or references which might be confusing unless the reader had at hand the works to which the Prefaces and Introductions applied.

CONTENTS

Part I

CONCERNING MR MAUGHAM'S OWN WORKS

Part II

CONCERNING THE WORKS OF OTHER WRITERS

PART I

Concerning Mr Maugham's Own Works

Ten Novels and their Authors

'THE ART OF FICTION'*

(1954)

I should like to tell the reader of this book how the essays in it first came to be written. One day, while I was in the United States, the Editor of *Redbook* asked me to make a list of what in my opinion were the ten best novels in the world. I did so, and thought no more about it. Of course my list was arbitrary. I could have made one of ten other novels, just as good in their different ways as those I chose, and given just as sound reasons for selecting them. If a hundred persons, well read and of adequate culture, were asked to produce such a list, in all probability at least two or three hundred novels would be mentioned, but I think that in all the lists most of those I have chosen would find a place. That there should be a diversity of opinion in this matter is understandable. There are various reasons that make a particular novel so much appeal to a person, even of sound judgment, that he is led to ascribe outstanding merit to it. It may be that he has read it at a time of life when, or in circumstances in which, he was peculiarly liable to be moved by it; or it may be that its theme, or its setting, has a more than ordinary significance for him owing to his own predilections or personal associations. I can imagine that a passionate lover of music

---

* Though this essay appeared in the book as Chapter One it is essentially an Introduction and so is here included.

might place Henry Handel Richardson's *Maurice Guest* among the ten best novels, and a native of the Five Towns, delighted with the fidelity with which Arnold Bennett described their character and their inhabitants, might in his list place *The Old Wives' Tale*. Both are good novels, but I do not think an unbiassed judgment would put either of them among the best ten. The nationality of a reader lends to certain works an interest that inclines him to attribute a greater excellence to them than would generally be admitted. During the eighteenth century, English literature was widely read in France, but since then, till fairly recently, the French have not taken much interest in anything that was written beyond their own frontiers, and I don't suppose it would occur to a Frenchman to mention *Moby Dick* in such a list as I myself made, and *Pride and Prejudice* only if he were of quite unusual culture; he would certainly, however, include Madame de Lafayette's *La Princesse de Clèves;* and rightly, for it has outstanding merits. It is a novel of sentiment, a psychological novel, perhaps the first that was ever written: the story is touching; the characters are soundly drawn; it is written with distinction, and it is commendably brief. It deals with a state of society which is well known to every schoolboy in France; its moral atmosphere is familiar to him from his reading of Corneille and Racine; it has the glamour of association with the most splendid period of French history, and it is a worthy contribution to the golden age of French literature. But the English reader may think the magnanimity of the protagonists inhuman, their discourse with one another stilted, and their behaviour incredible. I do not say he is right to think this; but thinking it, he will never class this admirable novel among the ten best in the world.

In a brief commentary to accompany the list of books I made for *Redbook*, I wrote: 'The wise reader will get the greatest enjoyment out of reading them if he learns the useful art of skipping.' A sensible person does not read a novel as a task. He reads it as a diversion. He is prepared to interest himself in the characters and is concerned to see how they act in given circumstances, and what happens to them; he sympathizes with their troubles and is gladdened by their joys; he puts himself in their place and, to an extent, lives their lives. Their view of life, their attitude to the great subjects of human speculation, whether stated in words or shown in action, call forth in him a reaction of surprise, of pleasure or of indignation. But he knows instinctively where his interest lies and he follows it as surely as a hound follows the scent of a fox. Sometimes, through the author's failure, he loses the scent. Then he flounders about till he finds it again. He skips.

Everybody skips, but to skip without loss is not easy. It may be, for all I know, a gift of nature, or it may be something that has to be acquired by experience. Dr Johnson skipped ferociously, and Boswell tells us that 'he had a peculiar facility in seizing at once what was valuable in any book without submitting to the labour of perusing it from beginning to end.' Boswell was doubtless referring to books of information or of edification; if it is a labour to read a novel it is better not to read it at all. Unfortunately, for reasons I shall go into presently, there are few novels which it is possible to read from beginning to end with unfailing interest. Though skipping may be a bad habit, it is one that is forced upon the reader. But when the reader once begins to skip, he finds it hard to stop, and so may miss much that it would have been to his advantage to read.

Now it so happened that some time after the list I had made for *Redbook* appeared, an American publisher put before me the suggestion of reissuing the ten novels I had mentioned in an abridged form, with a preface to each one written by me. His idea was to omit everything but what told the story the author had to tell, expose his relevant ideas and display the characters he had created so that readers might read these fine novels, which they would not have done unless what might not unfairly be described as a lot of dead wood had been cut away from them; and thus, since nothing but what was valuable was left in them, enjoy to the full a great intellectual pleasure. I was at first taken aback; but then I reflected that though some of us have acquired the knack of skipping to our profit, most people have not, and it would surely be a good thing if they could have their skipping done for them by a person of tact and discrimination. I welcomed the notion of writing the prefaces to the novels in question, and presently set to work. Some students of literature, some professors and critics, will exclaim that it is a shocking thing to mutilate a masterpiece, and that it should be read as the author wrote it. That depends on the masterpiece. I cannot think that a single page could be omitted from so enchanting a novel as *Pride and Prejudice*, or from one so tightly constructed as *Madame Bovary*; but that very sensible critic George Saintsbury wrote that 'there is very little fiction that will stand concentration and condensation as well as that of Dickens.' There is nothing reprehensible in cutting. Few plays have ever been produced that were not to their advantage more or less drastically cut in rehearsal. One day, many years ago, when we were lunching together, Bernard Shaw told me that his plays were much more successful in Germany than they were in England. He ascribed this to the stupidity of the British public and to the greater intelligence of the German. He was wrong. In England he insisted that every word he had written should be spoken. I had seen his plays in Germany; there the directors had ruthlessly pruned them of verbiage unnecessary to the dramatic action, and so provided the public with an entertainment that was thoroughly enjoyable. I did not, however, think it well to tell him this. I know no reason why a novel should not be subjected to a similar process.

Coleridge said of *Don Quixote* that it is a book to read through once and then only to dip into, by which he may well have meant that parts of it are so tedious, and even absurd, that it is time ill-spent, when you have once discovered this, to read them again. It is

274

a great and important book, and a professed student of literature should certainly read it once through (I have myself read it from cover to cover twice in English and three times in Spanish), yet I cannot but think that the ordinary reader, the reader who reads for delight, would lose nothing if he did not read the dull parts at all. He would surely enjoy all the more the passages in which the narrative is directly concerned with the adventures and conversations, so amusing and so touching, of the gentle knight and his earthy squire. A Spanish publisher has, in point of fact, collected these in a single volume. It makes very good reading. There is another novel, certainly, important, but to be called great only with hesitation. Samuel Richardson's *Clarissa*, which is of a length to defeat all but the most obstinate of novel readers. I do not believe I could ever have brought myself to read it if I had not come across a copy in an abridged form. The abridgment had been so well done that I had no feeling that anything was lost.

I suppose most people would admit that Marcel Proust's *À la Recherche du Temps Perdu* is the greatest novel that has been produced in this century. Proust's fanatical admirers, of whom I am one, can read every word of it with interest; in a moment of extravagance, I stated once that I would sooner be bored by Proust than amused by any other writer; but I am prepared now, after a third reading, to admit that the various parts of his book are of unequal merit. I suspect that the future will cease to be interested in those long sections of desultory reflection which Proust wrote under the influence of ideas current in his day, but now in part discarded and in part commonplace. I think then it will be more evident than it is now that he was a great humourist and that his power to create characters, original, various and lifelike, places him on an equality with Balzac, Dickens and Tolstoy. It may be that some day an abridged version of his immense work will be issued from which will be omitted those passages that time has stripped of their value and only those retained which, because they are of the essence of a novel, remain of enduring interest. *À la Recherche du Temps Perdu* will still be a very long novel, but it will be a superb one. So far as I can make out from the somewhat complicated account in André Maurois' admirable book, *À la Recherche de Marcel Proust*, the author's intention was to publish his novel in three volumes of about four hundred pages each. The second and third volumes were in print when the First World War broke out, and publication was postponed. Proust's health was too poor to allow him to serve in the war and he used the ample leisure thus at his disposal to add to the third volume an immense amount of material. 'Many of the additions,' says Maurois, 'are psychological and philosophical dissertations, in which the intelligence' (by which I take him to mean the author in person) 'comments on the actions of the characters.' And he adds: 'One could compile from them a series of essays after the manner of Montaigne; on the role of music, novelty in the arts, beauty of style, on the small number of human types, on flair in medicine, etc.' That is true, but whether they add to the value of the novel as a novel depends, I suppose, on what opinions you hold on the essential function of the form.

On this different people have different opinions. H. G. Wells wrote an interesting essay which he called *The Contemporary Novel*: 'So far as I can see,' he says, 'it is the only medium through which we can discuss the great majority of the problems which are being raised in such a bristling multitude by our contemporary social development.' The novel of the future 'is to be the social mediator, the vehicle of understanding, the instrument of self-examination, the parade of morals and the exchange of manners, the factory of customs, the criticism of laws and institutions and of social dogmas and ideas.' 'We are going to deal with political questions and religious questions.' Wells had little patience with the idea that it was merely a means of relaxation, and he stated categorically that he could not bring himself to look upon it as an art-form. Strangely enough, he resented having his own novels described as propaganda,

'because it seems to me that the word propaganda should be confined to the definite service of some organized party, church or
doctrine.' The word, at all events now, has a larger meaning than
that; it indicates the method through which by word of mouth,
through the written word, by advertisement, by constant repetition, you seek to persuade others that your views of what is
right and proper, good and bad, just and unjust, are the correct
views, and should be accepted and acted upon by all and sundry.
Wells's principal novels were designed to diffuse certain doctrines
and principles; and that is propaganda.

What it all comes down to is the question whether the novel is a
form of art or not. Is its aim to instruct or to please? If its aim is to
instruct, then it is not a form of art. For the aim of art is to please.
On this poets, painters and philosophers are agreed. But it is a truth
that shocks a good many people, since Christianity has taught
them to look upon pleasure with misgiving as a snare to entangle
the immortal soul. It seems more reasonable to look upon pleasure
as a good, but to remember that certain pleasures have mischievous
consequence and so may more wisely be eschewed. There is a
general disposition to look upon pleasure as merely sensual, and
that is natural since the sensual pleasures are more vivid than the
intellectual; but that is surely an error, for there are pleasures of the
mind as well as of the body, and if they are not so keen, they are
more enduring. The Oxford Dictionary gives as one of the
meanings of art: 'The application of skill to subjects of taste, as
poetry, music, dancing, the drama, oratory, literary composition,
and the like.' That is very well, but then it adds: 'Especially in
modern use skill displaying itself in perfection of workmanship,
perfection of execution as an object in itself.' I suppose that is what
every novelist aims at, but as we know, he never achieves it. I think
we may claim that the novel is a form of art, perhaps not a very
exalted one, but a form of art nevertheless. It is, however, an
essentially imperfect form. Since I have dealt with this subject in

lectures which I have delivered here and there, and can put what I have to say now no better than I did in them, I am going to permit myself briefly to quote from them.

I think it an abuse to use the novel as a pulpit or a platform, and I believe readers are misguided when they suppose they can thus easily acquire knowledge. It is a great nuisance that knowledge can only be acquired by hard work. It would be fine if we could swallow the powder of profitable information made palatable by the jam of fiction. But the truth is that, so made palatable, we can't be sure that the powder will be profitable, for the knowledge the novelist imparts is biassed and thus unreliable; and it is better not to know a thing at all than to know it in a distorted fashion. There is no reason why a novelist should be anything but a novelist. It is enough if he is a good novelist. He should know a little about a great many things, but it is unnecessary, and sometimes even harmful, for him to be a specialist in any particular subject. He need not eat a whole sheep to know what mutton tastes like; it is enough if he eats a chop. Then, by applying his imagination and his creative faculty to the chop he has eaten, he can give you a pretty good idea of an Irish Stew; but when he goes on from this to broach his views on sheepraising, the wool industry and the political situation in Australia, it is wise to accept them with reserve.

The novelist is at the mercy of his bias. The subjects he chooses, the characters he invents and his attitude towards them, are conditioned by it. Whatever he writes is the expression of his personality and it is the manifestation of his innate instincts, his feelings and his experience. However hard he tries to be objective, he remains the slave of his idiosyncrasies. However hard he tries to be impartial, he cannot help taking sides. He loads his dice. By the mere fact of introducing a character to your notice early in his novel, he enlists your interest and your sympathy in that character. Henry James insisted again and again that the novelist must dramatize. That is a telling, though perhaps not very lucid, way of saying that he must arrange his facts in such a manner as to capture and hold your attention. So, if need be, he will sacrifice verisimilitude and credibility to the effect he wants to get. That, as we know, is not the way a work of scientific or informative value is written. The aim of the writer of fiction is not to instruct, but to please.

There are two main ways in which a novel may be written. Each has its advantages, and each its disadvantages. One way is to write it in the first person, and the other is to write it from the standpoint of omniscience. In the latter, the author can tell you all that he thinks is needful to enable you to follow his story and understand his characters. He can describe their emotions and motives from the inside. If one of them crosses the street, he can tell you why he does so and what will come of it. He can concern himself with one set of persons and series of events, and then, putting them aside for a period, can concern himself with another set of events and another set of persons, so reviving a flagging interest and, by complicating his story, give an impression of the multifariousness, complexity and diversity of life. The danger of this is that one set of characters may be so much more interesting than the other, as, to take a famous example, happens in *Middlemarch*, that the reader may find it irksome when he is asked to occupy himself with the fortunes of persons he doesn't in the least care about. The novel written from the standpoint of omniscience runs the risk of being unwieldy, verbose and diffuse. No one has written it better than Tolstoy, but even he is not free from these imperfections. The method makes demands on the author which he cannot always meet. He has to get into the skin of every one of his characters, feel his feelings, think his thoughts; but he has his limitations and he can only do this when there is in himself something of the character he has created. When there isn't, he can only see him from the outside, and then the character lacks the persuasiveness which causes the reader to believe in him.

I suppose it was because Henry James, with his solicitude for form in the novel, became conscious of these disadvantages that he devised what may be described as a sub-variety of the method of omniscience. In this the author is still omniscient, but his omniscience is concentrated in a single character, and since the character is fallible the omniscience is not complete. The author wraps himself in omniscience when he writes: 'He saw her smile'; but not when he writes: 'He saw the irony of her smile'; for irony is something he ascribes to her smile, and it may be, without justification. The usefulness of the device, as Henry James without doubt very well saw, is that since this particular character, in *The Ambassadors*, Strether, is all important, and it is through what he sees, hears, feels, thinks, surmises that the story is told, and the characters of the other persons concerned in it are unfolded, the author finds it easy to resist the irrelevant. The construction of his novel is necessarily compact. The device, besides, gives an air of verisimilitude to what he writes. Because you are asked to concern yourself primarily with one person, you are insensibly led to believe what he tells you. The facts that the reader should know are imparted to him as the person through whom the story is told gradually learns them; and so the reader enjoys the pleasure of the elucidation, step by step, of what was puzzling, obscure and uncertain. The method thus gives the novel something of the mystery of a detective story, and so the dramatic quality which Henry James was always eager to obtain. The danger, however, of divulging little by little a string of facts is that the reader may be more quick-witted than the character through whom the revelations are made and so guess the answers long before the author wishes him to. I don't suppose anyone can read *The Ambassadors* without growing impatient with Strether's obtuseness. He does not see what is staring him in the face, and what everyone he comes in contact with is fully aware of. It was a *secret de Polichinelle* and that Strether should not have guessed it points to some defect in the method. It is unsafe to take your reader for more of a fool than he is.

Since novels have for the most part been written from the standpoint of omniscience, it must be supposed that novelists have found it on the whole the most satisfactory way of dealing with their difficulties; but to tell a story in the first person has also certain advantages. Like the method adopted by Henry James, it lends verisimilitude to the narrative and obliges the author to stick to his point; for he can tell you only what he has himself seen, heard or done. To use this method more often would have served the great English novelists of the nineteenth century well, since, partly owing to methods of publication, partly owing to a national idiosyncrasy, their novels have tended to be shapeless and discursive. Another advantage of using the first person is that it enlists your sympathy with the narrator. You may disapprove of him, but he concentrates your attention on himself and so compels your sympathy. A disadvantage of the method, however, is that the narrator, when, as in *David Copperfield*, he is also the hero, cannot without impropriety tell you that he is handsome and attractive; he is apt to seem vainglorious when he relates his doughty deeds and stupid when he fails to see, what is obvious to the reader, that the heroine loves him. But a greater disadvantage still, and one that no authors of this kind of novel have managed entirely to surmount, is that the hero-narrator, the central character, is likely to appear pallid in comparison with the persons he is concerned with. I have asked myself why this should be, and the only explanation I can suggest is that the author, since he sees himself in the hero, sees him from the inside, subjectively, and telling what he sees, gives him the confusions, the weaknesses, the indecisions he feels in himself; whereas he sees the other characters from the outside, objectively, through his imagination and his intuition; and if he is an author with say, Dickens's brilliant gifts, he sees them with a dramatic intensity, with a boisterous sense of fun, with a keen delight in their oddity, and so makes them stand out with a vividness that overshadows his portrait of himself.

There is a variety of the novel written on these lines which for a time had an immense vogue. This is the novel written in letters; each letter, of course, is written in the first person, but the letters are by different hands. The method had the advantage of extreme verisimilitude. The reader might easily believe that they were real letters, written by the persons they purported to have been written by, and come into his hands by a betrayal of confidence. Now, verisimilitude is what the novelist strives to achieve above all else; he wants you to believe that what he tells you actually happened, even if it is as improbable as the tales of Baron Munchausen or as horrifying as Kafka's *The Castle*. But the genre had grave defects. It was a roundabout, complicated way of telling a story, and it told it with intolerable deliberation. The letters were too often verbose and contained irrelevant matter. Readers grew bored with the method and it died out. It produced three books which may be accounted among the masterpieces of fiction: *Clarissa*, *La Nouvelle Héloise* and *Les Liaisons Dangereuses*.

There is, however, a variety of the novel written in the first person which, to my mind, avoids the defects of the method and yet makes handsome use of its merits. It is, perhaps, the most convenient and effective way in which a novel can be written. To what good use it can be put may be seen in Herman Melville's *Moby Dick*. In this variety, the author tells the story himself, but he is not the hero and it is not his story that he tells. He is a character in it, and is more or less closely connected with the persons who take part in it. His role is not to determine the action, but to be the confidant, the mediator, the observer of those who do take part in it. Like the chorus in a Greek tragedy, he reflects on the circumstances which he witnesses; he may lament, he may advise, he has no power to influence the course of events. He takes the reader into his confidence, tells him what he knows, hopes or fears, and when he is non-plussed frankly tells him so. There is no need to make him stupid, so that he should not divulge to the reader what the author wishes to hold back, as happens when the story is told through such a character as Henry James's Strether. On the contrary, he can be as keen-witted and clear-sighted as the author can make him. The narrator and the reader are united in their common interest in the persons of the story, their characters, motives and conduct; and the narrator begets in the reader the same sort of familiarity with the creatures of his invention as he has himself. He gets an effect of verisimilitude as persuasive as that which the author obtains who is himself the hero of his novel. He can so build up his protagonist as to arouse your sympathy and show him in an heroic light, which the hero-narrator cannot do without somewhat exciting your antagonism. A method of writing a novel which conduces to the reader's intimacy with the characters, and adds to its verisimilitude, has obviously much to recommend it.

I will venture now to state what in my opinion are the qualities that a good novel should have. It should have a widely interesting theme, by which I mean a theme interesting not only to a clique, whether of critics, professors, highbrows, bus-conductors, or bartenders, but so broadly human that its appeal is to men and women in general; and the theme should be of enduring interest: the novelist is rash who elects to write on subjects whose interest is merely topical. When they cease to be so, his novel will be as unreadable as last week's newspaper. The story the author has to tell should be coherent and persuasive; it should have a beginning, a middle and an end, and the end should be the natural consequence of the beginning. The episodes should have probability and should not only develop the theme, but grow out of the story. The creatures of the novelist's invention should be observed with individuality, and their actions should proceed from their characters; the reader must never be allowed to say: 'So and so would never behave like that'; on the contrary, he should be obliged to say: 'That's exactly how I should have expected so and so to behave.' I think it is all the better if the characters are in themselves interesting. In Flaubert's *L'Éducation Sentimentale* he wrote a novel which has a great reputation among many excellent critics, but he chose for his hero a man so null, so featureless, so vapid that it is impossible to care what he does or what happens to him; and in consequence, for all its merits, the book is hard to read. I think I should explain why I say that characters should be observed with individuality; it is too much to expect the novelist to create characters that are quite new; his material is human nature, and although there are all sorts and conditions of men, the sorts are not infinite, and novels, stories, plays, epics have been written for so many hundreds of years that the chance is small that an author will create an entirely new character. Casting my mind's eye over the whole of fiction, the only absolutely original creation I can think of is Don Quixote, and I should not be surprised to learn that some learned critic had found a remote ancestry for him also. The author is fortunate if he can see his characters through his own individuality, and if his individuality is sufficiently out of the common to give them an illusive air of originality.

And just as behaviour should proceed from character, so should speech. A woman of fashion should talk like a woman of fashion, a street-walker like a street-walker, a racing tout like a racing tout and an attorney like an attorney. (It is surely a fault in Meredith and Henry James that their characters invariably talk like Henry James and Meredith respectively.) The dialogue should be neither desultory nor should it be an occasion for the author to air his views; it should serve to characterize the speakers and advance the story. The narrative passages should be vivid, to the point, and no longer than is necessary to make the motives of the persons concerned, and the situations in which they are placed, clear and convincing. The writing should be simple enough for anyone of fair education to read with ease, and the manner should fit the matter as a well-cut shoe fits a shapely foot. Finally, a novel should be entertaining. I have put this last, but it is the essential quality, without which no other quality avails. And the more intelligent the entertainment a novel offers, the better it is. Entertainment is a word that has a good many meanings. One item is that which affords interest or amusement. It is a common error to suppose that in this sense amusement is the only one of importance. There is as much entertainment to be obtained from *Wuthering Heights* or *The Brothers Karamazov* as from *Tristram Shandy* or *Candide*. The appeal is different, but equally legitimate. Of course, the novelist has the right to deal with those great topics which are of concern to every human being, the existence of God, the immortality of the soul, the meaning and value of life; though he is prudent to remember that wise saying of Dr Johnson's that of these topics one can no longer say anything new about them that is true, or anything true about them that is new. The novelist can only hope to interest his reader in what he has to say about them if they are an integral element of the story he has to tell, essential to the characterization of the persons of his novel and affect their conduct—that is, if they result in action which otherwise would not have taken place.

But even if the novel has all the qualities that I have mentioned, and that is asking a lot, there is, like a flaw in a precious stone, a faultiness in the form that renders perfection impossible to attain. That is why no novel is perfect. A short story is a piece of fiction that can be read, according to its length, in anything between ten minutes and an hour, and it deals with a single, well-defined subject, an incident or a closely related series of incidents, spiritual or material, which is complete. It should be impossible to add to it or to take away from it. Here, I believe, perfection can be reached, and I do not think it would be difficult to collect a number of short stories in which this has in fact been done. But a novel is a narrative of indefinite length; it may be as long as *War and Peace*, in which a succession of events is related and a vast number of characters are displayed through a period of time, or as short as *Carmen*. Now, in order to give probability to his story, the author has to narrate a series of facts that are relevant to it, but that are not in themselves interesting. Events often require to be separated by a lapse of time, and the author for the balance of his work has to insert, as best he can, matter that will fill up this lapse. These passages are known as bridges. Most writers resign themselves to crossing them, and they cross them with more or less skill, but it is only too likely that in the process they will be tedious. The novelist is human and it is inevitable that he should be susceptible to the fashions of his day, since after all he has an unusual affectivity, and so is often led to write what, as the fashion passes, loses its attractiveness. Let me give an instance: until the nineteenth century novelists paid little attention to scenery, a word or two sufficed to enable them to say all they wanted to about it; but when the romantic school, and the example of Chateaubriand, captivated the public fancy, it grew modish to write descriptions for their own sake. A man could not go down a street to buy a toothbrush at the chemist's without the author telling you what the houses he passed looked like and what articles were for sale in the shops. Dawn and the setting sun, the starry night, the cloudless sky, the snow-capped mountains, the dark forests—all gave occasion to interminable descriptions. Many were in themselves beautiful; but they were irrelevant: it took writers a long time to discover that a description of scenery, however poetically observed and admirably expressed, was futile unless it was necessary—that is, unless it helped the author to get on with his story or told the reader something it behoved him to know about the persons who take part in it. This is an adventitious imperfection in the novel, but there is yet another that seems inherent. Since it is a work of considerable length, it must take some time to write, weeks at least, generally months and occasionally even years. It is only too likely that the author's inventiveness will sometimes fail him. Then he can only fall back on dogged industry and his general competence. It will be a marvel if by these means he can hold his readers' attention.

In the past, readers, preferring quantity to quality, to get their money's worth wanted their novels long, and the author was often hard put to it to provide more matter for the printer than the story he had to tell required. He hit upon an easy way to do this. He inserted into his novel stories, sometimes long enough to be called novelettes, which had nothing to do with his theme or, at best, were tacked on to it with little plausibility. No writer did this with greater nonchalance than Cervantes in *Don Quixote*. These interpolations have always been regarded as a blot on an immortal work, and can only be read now with impatience. Contemporary criticism attacked him on this account, and in the second part of the book we know he eschewed the bad practice, so producing what is generally thought to be impossible, a sequel that was better than its forerunner; but this did not prevent succeeding writers (who doubtless had not read the criticisms) from using so convenient a device to enable them to deliver to the booksellers a quantity of copy sufficient to make a saleable volume. In the nineteenth century new methods of publication exposed novelists to new temptations. Monthly magazines that devoted much of their space to what is somewhat depreciatingly known as light literature achieved great success, and so provided authors with the opportunity to bring their work before the public in serial form with profit to themselves. At about the same time, the publishers found it to their advantage to issue the novels of popular authors in monthly numbers. The authors contracted to provide a certain amount of material to fill a certain number of pages. The system encouraged them to be leisurely and long-winded. We know from their own admissions how from time to time the authors of these serials, even the best of them, Dickens, Thackeray, Trollope, found it a hateful burden to be obliged to deliver an instalment by a given date. No wonder they padded! No wonder they burdened their stories with irrelevant episodes! When I consider how many obstacles the novelist has to contend with, how many pitfalls to avoid, I am not surprised that even the greatest novels are imperfect; I am only surprised that they are not more imperfect than they are.

I have in my time, hoping to improve myself, read several books on the novel. Their writers are, on the whole, as disinclined as was H. G. Wells to look upon it as a means of relaxation. One point they are pretty unanimous on is that the story is of little consequence. Indeed, they are inclined to regard it as a hindrance to the reader's capacity to occupy himself with what in their opinion are the novel's significant elements. It does not seem to have occurred to them that the story, the plot, is as it were a lifeline which the author throws to the reader in order to hold his interest. They consider the telling of a story for its own sake as a debased form of fiction. That seems strange to me, since the desire to listen to stories appears to be as deeply rooted in the human animal as the sense of property. From the beginning of history men have gathered round the camp-fire, or in a group in the market place, to listen to the telling of a story. That the desire is as strong as ever is shown by the amazing popularity of detective stories in our own day. The fact remains that to describe a novelist as a mere story-teller is to dismiss him with contumely. I venture to suggest that there is no such creature. By the incidents he chooses to relate, the characters he selects and his attitude towards them, the author offers you a criticism of life. It may not be a very original one, or very profound, but it is there; and consequently, though he may not know it, he is in his own modest way a moralist. But morals, unlike mathematics, are not a precise science. Morals cannot be inflexible for they deal with the behaviour of human beings, and human beings, as we know, are vain, changeable and vacillating.

We live in a troubled world, and it is doubtless the novelist's business to deal with it. The future is uncertain. Our freedom is menaced. We are in the grip of anxieties, fears and frustrations. Values that were long unquestioned now seem dubious. But these are serious matters, and it has not escaped the writers of fiction that the reader may find a novel that is concerned with them somewhat heavy going. Now, owing to the invention of contraceptives, the high value that was once placed on chastity no longer obtains. Novelists have not been slow to notice the difference this has made in the relations of the sexes and so, whenever they feel that something must be done to sustain the reader's flagging interest, they cause their characters to indulge in copulation. I am not sure they are well-advised. Of sexual intercourse Lord Chesterfield said that the pleasure was momentary, the position ridiculous and the expense damnable: if he had lived to read modern fiction he might have added that there is a monotony about the act which renders the reiterated narration of it excessively tedious.

At present there is a tendency to dwell on characterization rather than on incident and, of course, characterization is important; for unless you come to know intimately the persons of a novel, and so can sympathize with them, you are unlikely to care what happens to them. But to concentrate on your characters, rather than on what happens to them, is merely one way of writing a novel like another. The tale of pure incident, in which the characterization is perfunctory or commonplace, has just as much right to exist as the other. Indeed, some very good novels of this kind have been written, *Gil Blas*, for instance, and *Monte Cristo*. Scheherazade would have lost her head very soon if she had dwelt on the characters of the persons she was dealing with, rather than on the adventures that befell them.

I have given in each case some account of the life and character of the author I am writing about. This I have done partly to please myself, but also for the reader's sake, since I think that to know what sort of a person the author is adds to one's understanding and appreciation of his work. To know something about Flaubert explains a good deal that would otherwise be disturbing in *Madame Bovary*, and to know the little there is to know about Emily Brontë gives a greater poignancy to her strange and wonderful book. A novelist myself, I have written these essays from my own standpoint. The danger of this is that the novelist is very apt to like best the sort of thing he himself does, and he will judge the work of others by how nearly they approach his own practice. In order to do full justice to works with which he has no natural sympathy, he needs a dispassionate integrity, a liberality of spirit, of which the members of an irritable race are seldom possessed. On the other hand, the critic who is not himself a creator is likely to know little about the technique of the novel, and so in his criticism he gives you either his personal impressions, which may well be of no great value, unless like Desmond MacCarthy he is not only a man of letters, but also a man of the world; or else he proffers a judgment founded on hard and fast rules which must be followed to gain his approbation. It is as though a shoemaker made shoes only in two sizes and if neither of them fitted your foot, you could for all he cared go shoeless.

The essays which are contained in this volume were written in the first place to induce readers to read the novels with which they are concerned, but in order not to spoil their pleasure it seemed to me that I had to take care not to reveal more of the story than I could help. That made it difficult to discuss the book adequately. In re-writing these pieces I have taken it for granted that the reader already knows the novels I treat of, and so it cannot matter to him if I divulge facts which the author has for obvious reasons delayed to the end to tell him. I have not hesitated to point out the defects as well as the merits that I see in these various novels, for nothing is of greater disservice to the general reader than the indiscriminate praise that is sometimes bestowed on certain works that are rightly accepted as classics. He reads and finds that such and such a motive is unconvincing, a certain character unreal, such and such an episode irrelevant and a certain description tedious. If he is of an impatient temper, he will cry that the critics who tell him that the novel he is reading is a masterpiece are a set of fools, and if he is of a modest one, he will blame himself and think that it is above his head and not for the likes of him; if, on the other hand, he is by nature dogged and persistent he will read on conscientiously, though without enjoyment. But a novel is to be read *with* enjoyment. If it doesn't give the reader that, it is, so far as he is concerned, valueless. In this respect every reader is his own best critic, for he alone knows what he enjoys and what he doesn't. I think, however, that the novelist may claim that you do not do him justice unless you admit that he has the right to demand something of his readers. He has the right to demand that they should possess the small amount of application that is needed to read a book of three or four hundred pages. He has the right to demand that they should have sufficient imagination to be able to interest themselves in the lives, joys and sorrows, tribulations, dangers and adventures of the characters of his invention. Unless a reader is able to give something of himself, he cannot get from a novel the best it has to give. And if he isn't able to do that, he had better not read it at all. There is no obligation to read a work of fiction.

Maugham's Selection of Ten Novels and their Authors

Henry Fielding and *Tom Jones*

Jane Austen and *Pride and Prejudice*

Stendhal and *Le Rouge et le Noir*

Balzac and *Le Père Goriot*

Charles Dickens and *David Copperfield*

Flaubert and *Madame Bovary*

Herman Melville and *Moby Dick*

Emily Brontë and *Wuthering Heights*

Dostoevsky and *The Brothers Karamazov*

Tolstoy and *War and Peace*

A Writer's Notebook

'PREFACE'

(1949)

THE *Journal* of Jules Renard is one of the minor masterpieces of French literature. He wrote three or four one-act plays, which were neither very good nor very bad; they neither amuse you much nor move you much, but when well acted they can be sat through without ennui. He wrote several novels, of which one, *Poil de Carotte*, was very successful. It is the story of his own child-hood, the story of a little uncouth boy whose harsh and unnatural mother leads him a wretched life. Renard's method of writing, without ornament, without emphasis, heightens the pathos of the dreadful tale, and the poor lad's sufferings, mitigated by no pale ray of hope, are heartrending. You laugh wryly at his clumsy efforts to ingratiate himself with that demon of a woman and you feel his humiliations, you resent his unmerited punishments, as though they were your own. It would be an ill-conditioned person who did not feel his blood boil at the infliction of such malignant cruelty. It is not a book that you can easily forget.

Jules Renard's other novels are of no great consequence. They are either fragments of autobiography or are compiled from the careful notes he took of people with whom he was thrown into close contact, and can hardly be counted as novels at all. He was so devoid of the creative power that one wonders why he ever became a writer. He had no invention to heighten the point of an incident or even to give a pattern to his acute observations. He collected facts; but a novel cannot be made of facts alone; in themselves they are dead things. Their use is to develop an idea or illustrate a theme, and the novelist not only has the right to change them to suit his purpose, to stress them or leave them in shadow, but is under the necessity of doing so. It is true that Jules Renard had his theories; he asserted that his object was merely to state, leaving the reader to write his own novel, as it were, on the data presented to him, and that to attempt to do anything else was literary fudge. But I am always suspicious of a novelist's theories; I have never known them to be anything other than a justification of his own shortcomings. So a writer who has no gift for the contrivance of a plausible story will tell you that story-telling is the least important part of the novelist's equipment, and if he is devoid of humour he will moan that humour is the death of fiction. In order to give the glow of life to brute fact it must be transmuted by passion, and so the only good novel Jules Renard wrote was when the passion of self-pity and the hatred he felt for his mother charged his recollections of his unhappy childhood with venom.

I surmise that he would be already forgotten but for the publication after his death of the diary that he kept assiduously for twenty years. It is a remarkable work. He knew a number of persons who were important in the literary and theatrical world of his day, actors like Sarah Bernhardt and Lucien Guitry, authors like Rostand and Capus, and he relates his various encounters with an admirable but caustic vivacity. Here his keen powers of observation were of service to him. But though his portraits have verisimilitude, and the lively conversation of these clever people has an authentic ring, you must have, perhaps, some knowledge of the world of Paris in the last few years of the nineteenth century and the first few years of the twentieth, either personal knowledge or knowledge by hearsay, really to appreciate these parts of the journal. His fellow writers were indignant when the work was issued and they discovered with what acrimony he had written of them. The picture he paints of the literary life of his day is savage. They say dog does not bite dog. That is not true of men of letters in France. In England, I think, men of letters bother but little with one another. They do not live in one another's pockets as French authors do; they meet, indeed, infrequently, and then as likely as not by chance. I remember one author saying to me years ago: 'I prefer to live with my raw material.' They do not even read one another very much. On one occasion, an American critic came to England to interview a number of distinguished writers on the state of English literature, and gave up his project when he discovered that a very eminent novelist, the first one he saw, had never read a single book of Kipling's. English writers judge their fellow craftsmen; one they will tell you is pretty good, another they will say is no great shakes, but their enthusiasm for the former seldom reaches fever-heat, and their disesteem for the latter is manifested rather by indifference than by detraction. They do not particularly envy someone else's success, and when it is obviously unmerited, it moves them to laughter rather than to wrath. I think English authors are self centred. They are, perhaps, as vain as any others, but their vanity is satisfied by the appreciation of a private circle. They are not inordinately affected by adverse criticism, and with one or two exceptions do not go out of their way to ingratiate themselves with the reviewers. They live and let live.

Things are very different in France. There the literary life is a merciless conflict in which one gives violent battle to another, in which one clique attacks another clique, in which you must be always on your guard against the gins and snares of your enemies, and in which, indeed, you can never be quite sure that a friend will not knife you in the back. It is all against all, and, as in some forms of wrestling, anything is allowed. It is a life of bitterness, envy and treachery, of malice and hatred. I think there are reasons for this. One, of course, is that the French take literature much more seriously than we do, a book matters to them as it never matters to us, and they are prepared to wrangle over general principles with a vehemence that leaves us amazed—and tickled, for we cannot get it out of our heads that there is something comic in taking art so seriously. Then, political and religious matters have a way of getting themselves entangled with literature in France, and an author will see his book furiously assailed, not because it is a bad book, but because he is a Protestant, a nationalist, a communist or what not. Much of this is praiseworthy. It is well that a writer should think not only that the book he himself is writing is important, but that the books other people are writing are important too. It is well that authors, at least, should think that books really mean something, and that their influence is salutary, in which case they must be defended, or harmful, in which case they must be attacked. Books can't matter much if their authors themselves don't think they matter. It is because in France they think they matter so much that they take sides so fiercely.

There is one practice common to French authors that has always caused me astonishment, and that is their practice of reading their works to one another, either when they are in process of writing them, or when they have finished them. In England writers sometimes send their unpublished works to fellow craftsmen for criticism, by which they mean praise, for rash is the author who makes any serious objections to another's manuscript; he will only offend, and his criticism will not be listened to; but I cannot believe that any English author would submit himself to the excruciating boredom of sitting for hours while a fellow novelist reads him his latest work. In France it seems to be an understood thing that he should, and what is stranger, even eminent writers will often rewrite much of their work on the strength of the criticism they may have thus received. No less a person than Flaubert acknowledges that he did so as a result of Turgenev's remarks, and you can gather from André Gide's *Journal* that he has often profited in the same way. It has puzzled me; and the explanation that I have offered to myself is that the French, because writing is an honourable profession (which it has never been in England), often adopt it without having any marked creative power; their keen intelligence, their sound education and their background of an agelong culture enable them to produce work of a high standard, but it is the result of resolution, industry and a well-stored, clever brain rather than of an urge to create, and so criticism, the opinions of well-intentioned persons, can be of considerable use. But I should be surprised to learn that the great producers, of whom Balzac is the most eminent example, put themselves to this trouble. They wrote because they had to, and having written, thought only of what they were going to write next. The practice proves, of course, that French authors are prepared to take an immense deal of trouble to make their works as perfect as may be, and that, sensitive as they are, they have less self-complacency than many of their English fellow craftsmen.

There is another reason why the antagonisms of authors in France are more envenomed than in England; their public is too small to support their great number: we have a public of two hundred millions; they have one of forty. There is plenty of room for every English writer; you may never have heard of him, but if he has any gift at all, in any direction, he can earn an adequate income. He is not very rich, but then he would never have adopted the profession of letters if riches had been his object. He acquires in time his body of faithful readers, and since in order to get the publishers' advertisements the papers are obliged to give a good deal of space to reviews, he is accorded a sufficient amount of attention in the public Press. He can afford to look upon other writers without envy. But in France few writers can make a living by writing novels; unless they have private means or some other occupation that enables them to provide for their needs, they are forced to resort to journalism. There are not enough book-buyers to go round, and the success of one author can greatly attenuate the success of another. It is a struggle to get known; it is a struggle to hold one's place in the public esteem. This results in frantic efforts to attract the benevolent attention of critics, and it is to the effect their reviews may have that must be ascribed the anxiety felt even by authors of reputation when they know that a notice is to appear in such and such a paper, and their fury when it is not a good one. It is true that criticism carries greater weight in France than it does in England. Certain critics are so influential that they can make or mar a book. Though every person of culture in the world reads French, and French books are read not only in Paris, it is only the opinion of Paris, of its writers, its critics, its intelligent public, that the French author really cares about. It is because literary ambition is centred in that one place that it is the scene of so much strife and heart-burning. And it is because the financial rewards of authorship are so small that there is so much eagerness, so much scheming to win the prizes that are every year awarded to certain books, or to enter into one or other of the academies which not only set an honourable seal on a career but increase an author's market value. But there are few prizes for the aspiring writer, few vacancies in the academies for the established one. Not many people know how much bitterness, how much bargaining, how much intrigue goes to the awarding of a prize or the election of a candidate.

But, of course, there are authors in France who are indifferent to money and scornful of honours, and since the French are a generous people, these authors are rewarded with the unqualified respect of all. That is why, indeed, certain writers who, judged by any reasonable standards, are evidently of no great consequence enjoy, especially among the young, a reputation that is incomprehensible to the foreigner. For unfortunately talent and originality do not always attend nobility of character.

Jules Renard was very honest, and he does not draw a pretty picture of himself in his *Journal*. He was malignant, cold, selfish, narrow, envious and ungrateful. His only redeeming feature was his love for his wife; she is the only person in all these volumes of whom he consistently speaks with kindness. He was immensely susceptible to any fancied affront, and his vanity was outrageous. He had neither charity nor good will. He splashes with his angry contempt everything he doesn't understand, and the possibility never occurs to him that if he doesn't the fault may lie in himself. He was odious, incapable of a generous gesture, and almost incapable of a generous emotion. But for all that the *Journal* is wonderfully good reading. It is extremely amusing. It is witty and subtle and often wise. It is a notebook kept for the purposes of his calling by a professional writer who passionately sought truth, purity of style and perfection of language. As a writer no one could have been more conscientious. Jules Renard jotted down neat retorts and clever phrases, epigrams, things seen, the sayings of people and the look of them, descriptions of scenery, effects of sunshine and shadow, everything, in short, that could be of use to him when he sat down to write for publication; and in several cases, as we know, when he had collected sufficient data he strung them together into a more or less connected narrative and made a book of them. To a writer this is the most interesting part of these volumes; you are taken into an author's workshop and shown what materials he thought worth gathering, and how he gathered them. It is not to the point that he lacked the capacity to make better use of them.

I forget who it was who said that every author should keep a notebook, but should take care never to refer to it. If you understand this properly. I think there is truth in it. By making a note of something that strikes you, you separate it from the incessant stream of impressions that crowd across the mental eye, and perhaps fix it in your memory. All of us have had good ideas or vivid sensations that we thought would one day come in useful, but which, because we were too lazy to write them down, have entirely escaped us. When you know you are going to make a note of something, you look at it more attentively than you otherwise would, and in the process of doing so the words are borne in upon you that will give it its private place in reality. The danger of using notes is that you find yourself inclined to rely on them, and so lose the even and natural flow of your writing which is somewhat pompously known as inspiration. You are also inclined to drag in your jottings whether they fit in or not. I have heard that Walter Pater used to make abundant notes on his reading and reflections and put them into appropriate pigeonholes, and when he had enough on a certain subject, fit them together and write an essay. If this is true, it may account for the rather cramped feeling one has when one reads him. This may be why his style has neither swing nor vigour. For my part, I think to keep copious notes is an excellent practice, and I can only regret that a natural indolence has prevented me from exercising it more diligently. They cannot fail to be of service if they are used with intelligence and discretion.

It is because Jules Renard's *Journal* in this respect so pleasantly engaged my attention that I have ventured to collect my own notes and offer them to the perusal of my fellow writers. I hasten to state that mine are not nearly so interesting as his. They are much more interrupted. There were many years in which I never kept notes at all. They do not pretend to be a journal; I never wrote anything about my meetings with interesting or famous people. I am sorry that I didn't. It would doubtless have made the following pages more amusing if I had recorded my conversations with the many and distinguished writers, painters, actors and politicians I have known more or less intimately. It never occurred to me to do so. I never made a note of anything that I did not think would be useful to me at one time or another in my work, and though, especially in the early notebooks, I jotted down all kinds of thoughts and emotions of a personal nature, it was only with the intention of ascribing them sooner or later to the creatures of my invention. I meant my notebooks to be a storehouse of materials for future use and nothing else.

As I grew older and more aware of my intentions, I used my notebooks less to record my private opinions, and more to put down while still fresh my impressions of such persons and places as seemed likely to be of service to me for the particular purpose I had in view at the moment. Indeed, on one occasion, when I went to China, vaguely thinking that I might write a book upon my travels, my notes were so copious that I abandoned the project and published them as they were. These, of course, I have omitted from this volume. I have likewise omitted everything I have elsewhere made use of, and if I have left in a phrase or two here and there that a diligent reader of my works recalls, it is not because I am so pleased with it that I want to repeat it, but from inadvertence. On one or two occasions, however, I have deliberately left in the facts that I noted down at the time and that gave me the idea for a story or a novel, thinking it might entertain the reader who chanced to remember one or the other, to see on what materials I devised a more elaborate piece. I have never claimed to create anything out of nothing; I have always needed an incident or a character as a starting point, but I have exercised imagination, invention and a sense of the dramatic to make it something of my own.

My early notebooks were largely filled with pages of dialogue for plays that I never wrote, and these, because I thought they could interest no one, I have also left out, but I have not left out a considerable number of remarks and reflections that seem to me now exaggerated and foolish. They are the expression of a very young man's reaction to real life, or what he thought was such, and to liberty, after the sheltered and confined existence, perverted by fond fancies and the reading of novels, which was natural to a boy in the class in which I was born; and they are the expression of his revolt from the ideas and conventions of the environment in which he had been brought up. I think I should have been dishonest with the reader if I had suppressed them. My first notebook is dated 1892; I was then eighteen. I have no wish to make myself out more sensible than I was. I was ignorant, ingenuous, enthusiastic and callow.

My notebooks amounted to fifteen stoutish volumes, but by omitting so much, as I have above described, I have reduced them to one no longer than many a novel. I hope the reader will accept this as a sufficient excuse for its publication. I do not publish it because I am so arrogant as to suppose that my every word deserves to be perpetuated. I publish it because I am interested in the technique of literary production and in the process of creation, and if such a volume as this by some other author came into my hands I should turn to it with avidity. By some happy chance what interests me seems to interest a great many other people; I could never have expected it, and I have never ceased to be surprised at it; but it may be that what has happened so often before will happen again, and some persons may be found who will discover here and there in the following pages something to interest them. I should have looked upon it as an impertinence to publish such a book when I was in the full flow of my literary activity; it would have seemed to claim an importance for myself which would have been offensive to my fellow writers; but now I am an old man, I can be no one's rival, for I have retired from the hurly-burly and ensconced myself not uncomfortably on the shelf. Any ambition I may have had has long since been satisfied. I contend with none, not because none is worth my strife, but because I have said my say and I am well pleased to let others occupy my small place in the world of letters. I have done what I wanted to do and now silence becomes me. I am told that in these days you are quickly forgotten if you do not by some new work keep your name before the public, and I have little doubt that it is true. Well, I am prepared for that. When my obituary notice at last appears in *The Times*, and they say: 'What, I thought he died years ago,' my ghost will gently chuckle.

Of Human Bondage

'FOREWORD'

(1915)

THIS is a very long novel and I am ashamed to make it longer by writing a preface to it. An author is probably the last person who can write fitly about his own work. In this connection an instructive story is told by Roger Martin du Gard, a distinguished French novelist, about Marcel Proust. Proust wanted a certain French periodical to publish an important article on his great novel and thinking that no one could write it better than he, sat down and wrote it himself. Then he asked a young friend of his, a man of letters, to put his name to it and take it to the editor. This the young man did, but after a few days the editor sent for him. 'I must refuse your article,' he told him. 'Marcel Proust would never forgive me if I printed a criticism of his work that was so perfunctory and so unsympathetic.' Though authors are touchy about their productions and inclined to resent unfavourable criticism they are seldom self-satisfied. They are miserably conscious how far the work on which they have spent much time and trouble comes short of their conception and when they consider it they are much more vexed with their failure to express this in its completeness than pleased with the passages here and there that they can regard with complacency. Their aim is perfection and they are wretchedly aware that they have not attained it.

I will say nothing then about my book itself, but will content

302

myself with telling the reader of these lines how a novel that has now had a fairly long life, as novels go, came to be written; and if it does not interest him I ask him to forgive me. I wrote it first when, at the age of twenty-three, having taken my medical degrees after five years at St Thomas's Hospital, I went to Seville determined to earn my living as a writer. The manuscript of the book I wrote then still exists, but I have not looked at it since I corrected the typescript and I have no doubt that it is very immature. I sent it to Fisher Unwin, who had published my first book (while still a medical student I had published a novel called *Liza of Lambeth*, which had had something of a success), but he refused to give me the hundred pounds I wanted for it and none of the other publishers to whom I afterwards submitted it would have it at any price. This distressed me at the time, but now I know that I was very fortunate; for if one of them had taken my book (it was called *The Artistic Temperament of Stephen Carey*) I should have lost a subject which I was too young to make proper use of. I was not far enough away from the events I described to use them properly and I had not had a number of experiences which later went to enrich the book I finally wrote. Nor had I learnt that it is easier to write of what you know than of what you don't. For instance, I sent my hero to Rouen (which I knew only as an occasional visitor) to learn French, instead of to Heidelberg (where I had been myself) to learn German.

Thus rebuffed I put the manuscript away. I wrote other novels, which were published, and I wrote plays. I became a very successful playwright and determined to devote the rest of my life to the drama. But I reckoned without a force within me that made my resolutions vain. I was happy, I was prosperous, I was busy. My head was full of the plays I wanted to write. I do not know whether it was that success did not bring me all I had expected or whether it was a natural reaction from it, but I was but just firmly established as the most popular dramatist of the day when I began once more to be obsessed by the teeming memories of my past life. They came back to me so pressingly, in my sleep, on my walks, at rehearsals, at parties, they became such a burden to me, that I made up my mind there was only one way to be free of them and that was to write them all down in a book. After submitting myself for some years to the exigencies of the drama I hankered after the wide liberty of the novel. I knew the book I had in mind would be a long one and I wanted to be undisturbed, so I refused the contracts that managers were eagerly offering me and temporarily retired from the stage. I was then thirty-seven.

For long after I became a writer by profession I spent much time on learning how to write and subjected myself to very tiresome training in the endeavour to improve my style. But these efforts I abandoned when my plays began to be produced and when I started to write again it was with different aims. I no longer sought a jewelled prose and a rich texture, on unavailing attempts to achieve which I had formerly wasted much labour; I sought on the contrary plainness and simplicity. With so much that I wanted to say within reasonable limits I felt that I could not afford to waste words and I set out now with the notion of using only such as were necessary to make my meaning clear. I had no space for ornament. My experience in the theatre had taught me the value of succinctness and the danger of beating about the bush. I worked unremittingly for two years. I did not know what to call my book and after looking about a great deal hit upon *Beauty from Ashes*, a quotation from Isaiah which seemed to me apposite; but learning that this title had been recently used was obliged to search for another. I chose finally the name of one of the books in Spinoza's *Ethics* and called it *Of Human Bondage*. I have a notion I was once more lucky in finding that I could not use the first title I had thought of.

Of Human Bondage is not an autobiography, but an autobiographical novel; fact and fiction are inextricably mingled; the emotions are my own, but not all the incidents are related as they

304

happened and some of them are transferred to my hero not from my own life but from that of persons with whom I was intimate. The book did for me what I wanted and when it was issued to the world (a world in the throes of a dreadful war and too much concerned with its own sufferings and fears to bother with the adventures of a creature of fiction) I found myself free for ever from the pains and unhappy recollections that had tormented me. It was very well reviewed; Theodore Dreiser wrote for *The New Republic* a long criticism in which he dealt with it with the intelligence and sympathy which distinguish everything he has ever written; but it looked very much as though it would go the way of the vast majority of novels and be forgotten for ever a few months after its appearance. But, I do not know through what accident it happened after some years that it attracted the attention of a number of distinguished writers in the United States and the references they continued to make to it in the press gradually brought it to the notice of the public. To these writers is due the new lease of life that the book was thus given and them must I thank for the success it has continued increasingly to have as the years go by.

FROM:

The Collected Plays

I hope the reader will not accuse me of stupid egotism if I hazard the suggestion that the form of drama that I knew is destined to end very soon, and of course I do not mean for any such foolish reason as that I ceased to write. Realistic drama in prose is a form of art, though a minor one, and a minor art, responding to a particular state in civilization, is likely to perish with a change in that state. The history of prose drama is short. It seems to have sprung into life here and there, during the sixteenth century, in rude farces like those played by Tabarin in a booth to attract customers for his quack medicines. In Spain it quickly achieved uncommon merit in the racy plays of Lope de Rueda, but was killed by the greater attractiveness to the public of verse. It was raised to a form of art by Molière, flourished with his reflected light in the comedies of the Restoration, and was practised with elegance by Marivaux and Beaumarchais in the France of the eighteenth century; it throve with increasing luxuriance in France during the next hundred years, and was cultivated by a long series of men of talent. It reached its utmost height in the solid work of Ibsen. It seems to me that Ibsen brought the realistic prose drama to such perfection as it is capable of, and in the process killed it. His plays seem stagy enough now; *When We Dead Awaken*, which many good judges think an important work, is a piece of theatrical clap-trap that you cannot believe in for a moment; but it was his influence that finally stripped the drama of those elements of recreation which, in my opinion, are essential to it. The dramatists have wilfully cast aside the ornaments that made their plays an entertainment for the eye and ear. The desire for verisimilitude has resulted in an intolerable dullness. Realism, where realism is out of place, has forced the dramatists in order to hold the attention of their audience to resort to themes outside the normal run of life, and so is responsible for the plays of murder and detection that give, with all their absurdities, the opportunity for thrilling incident.

The great dramatists of the past sacrificed truth of characterization and probability of incident to situation, which (to my mind, rightly) they considered the essence of drama. But the interest of the present day is in the analysis of character. I think this is something new, and points to a change of civilization, and this, as I suggested just now, entails the death of a form of art that was sustained by it. The characters of the older fiction were static; Balzac and Dickens told you all about their persons when they first brought them before your notice, and they remained unaltered, whatever happened to them and however long a period elapsed, till their authors had finished with them. This view of human nature evidently suited the prepossessions of the time, and it was perfectly convenient to the playwright. It enabled him to make his characters consistent and distinct. But the characters of fiction now are diverse and unstable. It has been found that the novelist can get all the excitement of a tale of adventure by the gradual disclosure of a person's character; in other cases he is concerned to show the changes in it that are occasioned by lapse of time and the circumstances of life. He examines, sometimes naively, sometimes subtly, the contradictions of human nature, and his readers are ready to take an interest in the complexity of the man in the street. All this is very difficult for the dramatist to deal with, and he has discarded the two devices, the soliloquy and the aside, by which he might have achieved at least some success. The burden is thrown upon the actors to translate into flesh and blood the conventional hieroglyphs which are all the dramatist can provide them with. It is too great a burden. The spectator no longer believes in the persons that are set before him.

But my melancholic prognosis applies only to the modern realistic prose drama. I do not mean of course that the drama can die. Its long history shows that like music, painting, architecture and poetry it responds to a permanent need of the human race. But when a form of art has reached what perfection it is capable of and then decays there is nothing to do but return to its origins. You have an example in sculpture at the present day which is finding a new inspiration in the wood-carving of the negroes and in the stone work of the Mayan and Peruvian craftsmen. The early drama amused the eye with spectacle and dancing and the ear with verse and music. I think the modern playwright would do well to call in these allied arts to his help. I do not suppose blank verse can profitably be used again, but a quick, running metre like that used by the old Spanish dramatists, though with less frequent rhymes, may well be acceptable, not only to the 'chosen few', but to the public at large. A long tirade in verse, as everyone knows who has seen a play of Racine, has apart from the sense, by its volume of rhythmical sound, a very high dramatic value. I do not see why music should not be used, as in the old melodramas, to prepare a mood or emphasize an emotion. There is no need to remark on the diverting effect of beautiful scenes and gay costumes or on the agreeableness of good dancing. An ingenious dramatist should be able to make all these an integral part of his play. With such pleasant means of recreation he may render attractive that drama of the soul which, as I have suggested, seems the natural development forced upon him by the success of the cinema.

But I would not condemn the dramatist to occupy himself only with high and serious matters. Comedy also has its claims. It has been greatly hampered by the demand for verisimilitude. My good fortune has brought me in contact with most of the celebrated wits of my day; and I have noticed that they sparkle but intermittently; no one in private life shines so continuously as a witty character should in a play, he is never so pointed, finished and apt; the conversation of a comedy is artificial in its essence, and to take pains to make it resemble the conversation of real life is absurd. The aim of comedy is not to represent life, but amusingly to comment on it. There is no valid reason why farce should not enter into it. In practice it is almost impossible to hold the attention of an audience for two hours and a half with pure comedy. But when the humours grow broad the critics shake their heads and, mildly or acrimoniously, regret the introduction of horse-play. I think they make a mistake. Comedy, depending as it does on wit, appeals only to the intellect; that is not enough: farce appeals to the belly. The great comic writers of the past felt no fear of it, and I would have the comic writers of the future feel no fear of it either, but use it, as freely as Aristophanes and Molière, whenever it suits their purpose. They must not mind if the very superior look down their noses. They can always console themselves with the recollection that Walter Pater laughed consumedly at *The Magistrate*.

FROM:

The Complete Short Stories

Volume I—East and West*

'PREFACE'

(1921–1952)

THIS book contains thirty stories. They are all about the same length and on the same scale. The first was written in 1919 and the last in 1931. Though in early youth I had written a number of short stories, for a long time, twelve or fifteen years at least,

* This essay and the one page 330 form the Prefaces to the American edition of *The Complete Short Stories of W. Somerset Maugham.* The English edition is published in three volumes; the figure preceding each title indicates in which volume the story may be found.

occupied with the drama, I had ceased to do so; and when a journey to the South Seas unexpectedly provided me with themes that seemed to suit this medium, it was as a beginner of over forty that I wrote the story which is now called *Rain*. Since it caused some little stir the reader of this preface will perhaps have patience with me if I transcribe the working notes, made at the time, on which it was constructed. They are written in hackneyed and slipshod phrases, without grace; for nature has not endowed me with the happy gift of hitting instinctively upon the perfect word to indicate an object and the unusual but apt adjective to describe it. I was travelling from Honolulu to Pago Pago and, hoping they might at some time be of service, I jotted down as usual my impressions of such of my fellow-passengers as attracted my attention. This is what I said of Miss Thompson: 'Plump, pretty in a coarse fashion, perhaps not more than twenty-seven. She wore a white dress and a large white hat, long white boots from which the calves bulged in cotton stockings.' There had been a raid on the Red Light district in Honolulu just before we sailed and the gossip of the ship spread the report that she was making the journey to escape arrest. My notes go on: '*W. The Missionary*. He was a tall thin man, with long limbs loosely jointed, he had hollow cheeks and high cheek bones, his fine, large, dark eyes were deep in their sockets, he had full sensual lips, he wore his hair rather long. He had a cadaverous air and a look of suppressed fire. His hands were large, with long fingers, rather finely shaped. His naturally pale skin was deeply burned by the tropical sun.' *Mrs W. His Wife*. 'She was a little woman with her hair very elaborately done, New England; not prominent blue eyes behind gold-rimmed pince-nez, her face was long like a sheep's, but she gave no impression of foolishness, rather of extreme alertness. She had the quick movements of a bird. The most noticeable thing about her was her voice, high, metallic, and without inflection; it fell on the ear with a hard monotony, irritating to the nerves like the ceaseless clamour of a pneumatic drill. She was dressed in black and wore round her neck a gold chain from which hung a small cross.' She told me that W. was a missionary on the Gilberts and his district consisting of widely separated islands he frequently had to go distances by canoe. During this time she remained at headquarters and managed the mission. Often the seas were very rough and the journeys were not without peril. He was a medical missionary. She spoke of the depravity of the natives in a voice which nothing could hush, but with a vehement, unctuous horror, telling me of their marriage customs which were obscene beyond description. She said, when first they went it was impossible to find a single good girl in any of the villages. She inveighed against dancing. I talked with the missionary and his wife but once, and with Miss Thompson not at all. Here is the note for the story: 'A prostitute, flying from Honolulu after a raid, lands at Pago Pago. There lands there also a missionary and his wife. Also the narrator. All are obliged to stay there owing to an outbreak of measles. The missionary finding out her profession persecutes her. He reduces her to misery, shame, and repentance, he has no mercy on her. He induces the governor to order her return to Honolulu. One morning he is found with his throat cut by his own hand and she is once more radiant and self-possessed. She looks at men and scornfully exclaims: "dirty pigs". '

An intelligent critic, who combines wide reading and a sensitive taste with a knowledge of the world rare among those who follow his calling, has found in my stories the influence of Guy de Maupassant. That is not strange. When I was a boy he was considered the best short story writer in France and I read his works with avidity. From the age of fifteen whenever I went to Paris I spent most of my afternoons poring over the books in the galleries of the Odéon. I have never passed more enchanted hours. The attendants in their long smocks were indifferent to the people who sauntered about looking at the books and they would let you read for hours without bothering. There was a shelf filled with the works of Guy de Maupassant, but they cost three francs fifty a volume and that was not a sum I was prepared to spend. I had to read as best I could standing up and peering between the uncut pages. Sometimes when no attendant was looking I would hastily cut a page and thus read more conveniently. Fortunately some of them were issued in a cheap edition at seventy-five centimes and I seldom came away without one of these. In this manner, before I was eighteen, I had read all the best stories. It is natural enough that when at that age I began writing stories myself I should unconsciously have chosen those little masterpieces as a model. I might very well have hit upon a worse.

Maupassant's reputation does not stand as high as it did, and it is evident now that there is much in his work to repel. He was a Frenchman of his period in violent reaction against the romantic age which was finishing in the saccharine sentimentality of Octave Feuillet (admired by Matthew Arnold) and in the impetuous slop of George Sand. He was a naturalist, aiming at truth at all costs, but the truth he achieved looks to us now a trifle superficial. He does not analyse his characters. He takes little interest in the reason why. They act, but wherefore he does not know. 'For me,' he says, 'psychology in a novel or in a story consists in this: to show the inner man by his life.' That is very well, that is what we all try to do, but the gesture will not by itself always indicate the motive. The result with Maupassant was a simplification of character which is effective enough in a short story, but on reflection leaves you unconvinced. There is more in men than that, you say. Again, he was obsessed by the tiresome notion, common then to his countrymen, that it was a duty a man owed himself to hop into bed with every woman under forty that he met. His characters indulge their sexual desire to gratify their self-esteem. They are like the people who eat caviar when they are not hungry because it is expensive. Perhaps the only human emotion that affects his characters with passion is avarice. This he can understand; it fills him with horror, but notwithstanding he has a sneaking sympathy with it. He was slightly common. But for all this it would be foolish to deny his excellence. An author has the right to be judged by his best work. No author is perfect. You must accept his defects; they are often the necessary complement of his merits; and this may be said in gratitude to posterity that it is very willing to do this. It takes what is good in a writer and is not troubled by what is bad. It goes so far sometimes, to the confusion of the candid reader, as to claim a profound significance for obvious faults. So you will see the critics (the awe-inspiring voice of posterity) find subtle reasons to explain to his credit something in a play of Shakespeare's that any dramatist could tell them needed no other explanation than haste, indifference or wilfulness. Maupassant's stories are good stories. The anecdote is interesting apart from the narration so that it would secure attention if it were told over the dinner-table; and that seems to me a very great merit indeed. However halting your words and insipid your rendering, you could not fail to interest your listeners if you told them the bare story of *Boule de Suif*, *L'Héritage* or *La Parure*. These stories have a beginning, a middle and an end. They do not wander along an uncertain line so that you cannot see whither they are leading, but follow without hesitation, from exposition to climax, a bold and vigorous curve. It may be that they have no great spiritual significance. Maupassant did not aim at that. He looked upon himself as a plain man; no good writer was ever less a man of letters. He did not pretend to be a philosopher, and here he was well-advised, for when he indulges in reflection he is commonplace. But within his limits he is admirable. He has an astonishing capacity for creating living people. He can afford little space, but in a few pages can set before you half a dozen persons so sharply seen and vividly described that you know all about them that you need. Their outline is clear; they are distinguishable from one another; and they breathe the breath of life. They have no complexity, they lack strangely the indecision, the unexpectedness

314

the mystery that we see in human beings; they are in fact simplified for the purposes of the story. But they are not deliberately simplified: those keen eyes of his saw clearly, but they did not see profoundly; it is a happy chance that they saw all that was necessary for him to achieve the aim he had in view. He treats the surroundings in the same way, he sets his scene accurately, briefly and effectively; but whether he is describing the charming landscape of Normandy or the stuffy, overcrowded drawing-rooms of the eighties his object is the same, to get on with the story. On his own lines I do not think that Maupassant is likely to be surpassed. If his excellence is not at the moment so apparent it is because what he wrote must now stand comparison with the very different, more subtle and moving work of Chekhov.

His stories are the models that young writers naturally take. This is understandable. On the face of it it is easier to write stories like Chekhov's than stories like Maupassant's. To invent a story interesting in itself apart from the telling is a difficult thing, the power to do it is a gift of nature, it cannot be acquired by taking thought, and it is a gift that very few people have. Chekhov had many gifts, but not this one. If you try to tell one of his stories you will find that there is nothing to tell. The anecdote, stripped of its trimmings, is insignificant and often inane. It was grand for people who wanted to write a story and couldn't think of a plot to discover that you could very well manage without one. If you could take two or three persons, describe their mutual relations and leave it at that, why then it wasn't so hard to write a story; and if you could flatter yourself that this really was art, what could be more charming?

But I am not quite sure that it is wise to found a technique on a writer's defects. I have little doubt that Chekhov would have written stories with an ingenious, original and striking plot if he had been able to think of them. It was not in his temperament. Like all good writers he made a merit of his limitations. Was it not

Goethe who said that an artist only achieves greatness when he recognizes them? If a short story is a piece of prose dealing with more or less imaginary persons no one wrote better short stories than Chekhov. If, however, as some think, it should be the representation of an action, complete in itself and of a certain limited length, he leaves something to be desired. He put his own idea clearly enough in these words: 'Why write about a man getting into a submarine and going to the North Pole to reconcile himself to the world, while his beloved at that moment throws herself with a hysterical shriek from the belfry? All this is untrue and does not happen in real life. One must write about simple things: how Peter Semionovitch married Maria Ivanovna. That is all.' But there is no reason why a writer should not make a story of an unusual incident. The fact that something happens every day does not make it more important. The pleasure of recognition, which is the pleasure thus aimed at, is the lowest of the aesthetic pleasures. It is not a merit in a story that it is undramatic. Maupassant chose very ordinary people and sought to show what there was of drama in the common happenings of their lives. He chose the significant incident and extracted from it all the drama possible. It is a method as praiseworthy as another; it tends to make a story more absorbing. Probability is not the only test; and probability is a constantly changing thing. At one time it was accepted that the 'call of the blood' should enable long-lost children to recognize their parents and that a woman only had to get into men's clothes to pass as a man. Probability is what you can get the readers of your time to swallow. Nor did Chekhov, notwithstanding his principles, adhere to his canon unless it suited him. Take one of the most beautiful and touching of his stories, *The Bishop*. It describes the approach of death with great tenderness, but there is no reason for the Bishop to die, and a better technician would have made the cause of death an integral part of the story. 'Everything that has no relation to the story must be ruthlessly thrown away,' he says in his advice to Schoukin. 'If in the first chapter you say that a gun hung on the wall, in the second or third chapter it must without fail be discharged.' So when the Bishop eats some tainted fish and a few days later dies of typhoid we may suppose that it was the tainted fish that killed him. If that is so he did not die of typhoid, but of ptomaine poisoning, and the symptoms were not as described. But of course Chekhov did not care. He was determined that his good and gentle bishop should die and for his own purposes he wanted him to die in a particular way. I do not understand the people who say of Chekhov's stories that they are slices of life. I do not understand, that is, if they mean that they offer a true and typical picture of life. I do not believe they do that, nor do I believe they ever did. I think they are marvellously lifelike, owing to the writer's peculiar talent, but I think they are deliberately chosen to square with the prepossessions of a sick, sad and overworked, grey-minded man. I do not blame them for that. Every writer sees the world in his own way and gives you his own picture of it. The imitation of life is not a reasonable aim of art; it is a discipline to which the artist from time to time subjects himself when the stylization of life has reached an extravagance that outrages common sense. For Chekhov life is like a game of billiards in which you never pot the red, bring off a losing hazard or make a cannon, and should you by a miraculous chance get a fluke you will almost certainly cut the cloth. He sighs sadly because the futile do not succeed, the idle do not work, liars do not speak the truth, drunkards are not sober and the ignorant have no culture. I suppose that it is this attitude that makes his chief characters somewhat indistinct. He can give you a striking portrait of a man in two lines, as much as can be said of anyone in two lines to set before you a living person, but with elaboration he seems to lose his grasp of the individual. His men are shadowy creatures, with vague impulses to good, but without will-power, shiftless, untruthful, fond of fine words, often with great ideals, but with no power of action. His women are lachrymose, slatternly and feeble-minded. Though they think it a sin they will commit fornication with anyone who asks them, because they have passion, not even because they want to, but not because it is too much trouble to refuse. It is only in his description of young girls that he seems touched with a tender indulgence. 'Alas! regardless of their doom, the little victims play.' He is moved by their charm, the gaiety of their laughter, their ingenuousness and their vitality; but it all leads to nothing. They make no effort to conquer their happiness, but yield passively to the first obstacle in the way.

But if I have ventured to make these observations I beg the reader not to think that I have anything but a very great admiration for Chekhov. No writer, I repeat, is faultless. It is well to admire him for his merits. Not to recognize his imperfections, but rather to insist that they are excellencies, can in the long run only hurt his reputation. Chekhov is extremely readable. That is a writer's supreme virtue and one upon which sufficient stress is often not laid. He shared it with Maupassant. Both of them were professional writers who turned out stories at more or less regular intervals to earn their living. They wrote as a doctor visits his patients or a solicitor sees his clients. It was part of the day's work. They had to please their readers. They were not always inspired, it was only now and then that they produced a masterpiece, but it is very seldom that they wrote anything that did not hold the reader's attention to the last line. They both wrote for papers and magazines. Sometimes a critic will describe a book of short stories as magazine stories and thus in his own mind damn them. That is foolish. No form of art is produced unless there is a demand for it and if newspapers and magazines did not publish short stories they would not be written. All stories are magazine stories or newspaper stories. The writers must accept certain (but constantly changing) conditions; it has never been shown yet that a good writer was unable to write his best owing to the conditions under which alone he could gain a public for his work. That has never been anything but an excuse of the second-rate. I suspect that Chekhov's great merit of concision is due to the fact that the newspapers for which he habitually wrote could only give him a certain amount of space. He said that stories should have neither a beginning nor an end. He could not have meant that literally. You might as well ask of a fish that it should have neither head nor tail. It would not be a fish if it hadn't. The way Chekhov in reality begins a story is wonderfully good. He gives the facts at once, in a few lines; he has an unerring feeling for the essential statements, and he sets them down baldly, but with great precision, so that you know at once whom you have to deal with and what the circumstances are. Maupassant often started his stories with an introduction designed to put the reader in a certain frame of mind. It is a dangerous method only justified by success. It may be dull. It may throw the reader off the scent; you have won his interest in certain characters and then instead of being told what you would like to know about them, your interest is claimed for other people in other circumstances. Chekhov preached compactness. In his longer stories he did not always achieve it. He was distressed by the charge brought against him that he was indifferent to moral and sociological questions and when he had ample space at his command he seized the opportunity to show that they meant as much to him as to any other right-thinking person. Then in long and somewhat tedious conversations he would make his characters express his own conviction that, whatever the conditions of things might be then, at some not far distant date (say 1934) the Russians would be free, tyranny would exist no longer, the poor would hunger no more and happiness, peace and brotherly love rule in the vast empire. But these were aberrations forced upon him by the pressure of opinion (common in all countries) that the writer of fiction should be a prophet, a social reformer and a philosopher. In his shorter stories Chekhov attained the concision he aimed at in a manner that is almost miraculous.

319

And no one had a greater gift than he for giving you the intimate feeling of a place, a landscape, a conversation or (within his limited range) a character. I suppose this is what people mean by the vague word atmosphere. Chekhov seems to have achieved it very simply, without elaborate explanation or long description, by a precise narration of facts; and I think it was due with him to a power of seeing things with amazing naïvety. The Russians are a semi-barbarous people and they seem to have retained the power of seeing things naturally, as though they existed in a vacuum; while we in the West, with our complicated culture behind us, see things with the associations they have gathered during long centuries of civilization. They almost seem to see the thing in itself. Most writers, especially those living abroad, have in the last few years been shown numbers of stories by Russian refugees who vainly hope to earn a few guineas by placing them somewhere. Though dealing with the present day they might very well be stories by Chekhov not at his best; they all have that direct, sincere vision. It is a national gift. In no one was it more acutely developed than in Chekhov.

But I have not yet pointed out what to my mind is Chekhov's greatest merit. Since I am not a critic and do not know the proper critical expressions I am obliged to describe this as best I can in terms of my own feeling. Chekhov had an amazing power of surrounding people with air so that, though he does not put them before you in the round and they lack the coarse, often brutal vitality of Maupassant's figures, they live with a strange and unearthly life. They are not lit by the hard light of common day but suffused in a mysterious greyness. They move in this as though they were disembodied spirits. It is their souls that you seem to see. The subconscious seems to come to the surface and they communicate with one another directly without the impediment of speech. Strange, futile creatures, with descriptions of their outward seeming tacked on them like a card on an exhibit in a museum, they move as mysteriously as the tortured souls who crowded about Dante when he walked in Hell. You have the feeling of a vast, grey, lost throng wandering aimless in some dim underworld. It fills you with awe and with uneasiness. I have hinted that Chekhov had no great talent for inventing a multiplicity of persons. Under different names, with different environment, the same characters recur. It is as though, when you looked at the soul, the superficial difference vanishes and everyone is more or less the same. His people seem strangely to slip into one another as though they were not distinct individuals, but temporary fictions, and as though in truth they were all part of one another. The importance of a writer in the long run rests on his uniqueness. I do not know that anyone but Chekhov has so poignantly been able to represent spirit communing with spirit. It is this that makes one feel that Maupassant in comparison is obvious and vulgar. The strange, the terrible thing is that, looking at man in their different ways, these two great writers, Maupassant and Chekhov, saw eye to eye. One was content to look upon the flesh, the other, more nobly and subtly, surveyed the spirit; but they agreed that life was tedious and insignificant and that men were base, unintelligent and pitiful.

I hope the reader will not be impatient with me because in an introduction to my own stories I have dwelt at length on these remarkable writers. Maupassant and Chekhov are the two authors of short stories whose influence survives to the present day and all of us who cultivate the medium must in the end be judged by the standards they have set.

So far as I could remember it I have placed the stories in this volume in the order in which they were written. I thought it might possibly interest the reader to see how I had progressed from the tentativeness of the first ones, when I was very much at the mercy of my anecdote, to the relative certainty of the later ones when I had learnt so to arrange my material as to attain the result I wanted. Though all but two have been published in a magazine these stories were not written with that end in view. When I began to write them I was fortunately in a position of decent independence and I wrote them as a relief from work which I thought I had been too long concerned with. It is often said that stories are no better than they are because the editors of magazines insist on their being written to a certain pattern. This has not been my experience. All but *Rain* and *The Book-Bag* were published in the *Cosmopolitan Magazine* and Ray Long, the Editor, never put pressure on me to write other than as I wished. Sometimes the stories were cut and this is reasonable since no editor can afford one contributor more than a certain amount of space; but I was never asked to make the smallest alteration to suit what might be supposed to be the taste of the readers. Ray Long paid me for them not only with good money, but with generous appreciation. I did not value this less. We authors are simple, childish creatures and we treasure a word of praise from those who buy our wares. Most of them were written in groups from notes made as they occurred to me, and in each group I left naturally enough to the last those that seemed most difficult to write. A story is difficult to write when you do not know *all* about it from the beginning, but for part of it must trust to your imagination and experience. Sometimes the curve does not intuitively present itself and you have to resort to this method and that to get the appropriate line.

I beg the reader not to be deceived by the fact that a good many of these stories are told in the first person into thinking that they are experiences of my own. This is merely a device to gain verisimilitude. It is one that has its defects, for it may strike the reader that the narrator could not know all the events he sets forth; and when he tells a story in the first person at one remove, when he reports, I mean, a story that someone tells him, it may very well seem that the speaker, a police officer, for example, or a sea-captain, could never have expressed himself with such facility and with such elaboration. Every convention has its disadvantages. These must be as far as possible disguised and what cannot be disguised must be accepted. The advantage of this one is its directness. It makes it possible for the writer to tell no more than he knows. Making no claim to omniscience, he can frankly say when a motive or an occurrence is unknown to him, and thus often give his story a plausibility that it might otherwise lack. It tends also to put the reader on intimate terms with the author. Since Maupassant and Chekhov, who tried so hard to be objective, nevertheless are so nakedly personal, it has sometimes seemed to me that if the author can in no way keep himself out of his work it might be better if he put in as much of himself as possible. The danger is that he may put in too much and thus be as boring as a talker who insists on monopolizing the conversation. Like all conventions this one must be used with discretion. The reader may have observed that in the original note of *Rain* the narrator was introduced, but in the story as written omitted.

Three of the stories in this volume were told me and I had nothing to do but make them probable, coherent and dramatic. They are *The Letter*, *Footprints in the Jungle* and *The Book-Bag*. The rest were invented, as I have shown *Rain* was, by the accident of my happening upon persons here and there, who in themselves or from something I heard about them suggested a theme that seemed suitable for a short story. This brings me to a topic that has always concerned writers and that has at times given the public, the writer's raw material, some uneasiness. There are authors who state that they never have a living model in mind when they create a character. I think they are mistaken. They are of this opinion because they have not scrutinized with sufficient care the re-collections and impressions upon which they have constructed the person who, they fondly imagine, is of their invention. If they did they would discover that, unless he was taken from some book they had read, a practice by no means uncommon, he was suggested by one or more persons they had at one time known or seen. The great writers of the past made no secret of the fact that their characters were founded on living people. We know that the good Sir Walter Scott, a man of the highest principles, portrayed his father, with sharpness first and then, when the passage of years had changed his temper, with tolerance; Henri Beyle, in the manuscript of at least one of his novels, has written in at the side the names of the real persons who were his models; and this is what Turgenev himself says: 'For my part, I ought to confess that I never attempted to create a type without having, not an idea, but a living person, in whom the various elements were harmonized together, to work from. I have always needed some groundwork on which I could tread firmly.' With Flaubert it is the same story; that Dickens used his friends and relations freely is notorious; and if you read the *Journal* of Jules Renard, a most instructive book to anyone who wishes to know how a writer works, you will see the care with which he set down every little detail about the habits, ways of speech and appearance of the persons he knew. When he came to write a novel he made use of this storehouse of carefully collected information. In Chekhov's diary you will find notes which were obviously made for use at some future time, and in the recollections of his friends there are frequent references to the persons who were the originals of certain of his characters. It looks as though the practice were very common. I should have said it was necessary and inevitable. Its convenience is obvious. You are much more likely to depict a character who is a recognizable human being, with his own individuality, if you have a living model. The imagination can create nothing out of the void. It needs the stimulus of sensation. The writer whose creative faculty has been moved by something peculiar in a person (peculiar perhaps only to the writer) falsifies his idea if he attempts to describe that person other than as he sees him. Character hangs together and if you try to throw people off the scent, by making a short man tall for example (as though stature had no effect on character) or by making him choleric when he has the concomitant traits of an equable temper, you will destroy the plausible harmony (to use the beautiful phrase of Baltasar Gracian) of which it consists. The whole affair would be plain sailing if it were not for the feelings of the persons concerned. The writer has to consider the vanity of the human race and the Schadenfreude which is one of its commonest and most detestable failings. A man's friends will find pleasure in recognizing him in a book and though the author may never even have seen him will point out to him, especially if it is unflattering, what they consider his living image. Often someone will recognize a trait he knows in himself or a description of the place he lives in and in his conceit jumps to the conclusion that the character described is a portrait of himself. Thus in the story called *The Outstation* the Resident was suggested by a British Consul I had once known in Spain and it was written ten years after his death, but I have heard that the Resident of a district in Sarawak, which I described in the story, was much affronted because he thought I had had him in mind. The two men had not a trait in common. I do not suppose any writer attempts to draw an exact portrait. Nothing, indeed, is so unwise as to put into a work of fiction a person drawn line by line from life. His values are all wrong, and, strangely enough, he does not make the other characters in the story seem false, but himself. He never convinces. That is why the many writers who have been attracted by the singular and powerful figure of the late Lord Northcliffe have never succeeded in presenting a credible personage. The model a writer chooses is seen through his own temperament and if he is a writer of any originality what he sees need have little relation with the facts. He may see a tall man short or a generous one avaricious; but, I repeat, if he sees him tall, tall he must remain. He takes only what he wants of the living man. He uses him as a peg on which to hang his own fancies. To achieve his end (the plausible harmony that nature so seldom provides) he gives him traits that the model does not possess. He makes him coherent and substantial. The created character, the result of imagination founded on fact, is art, and life in the raw, as we know, is of this only the material. The odd thing is that when the charge is made that an author has copied this person or the other from life, emphasis is laid only on his less praise-worthy characteristics. If you say of a character that he is kind to his mother, but beats his wife, everyone will cry: Ah, that's Brown, how beastly to say he beats his wife; and no one thinks for a moment of Jones and Robinson who are notoriously kind to their mothers. I draw from this the somewhat surprising conclusion that we know our friends by their vices and not by their virtues. I have stated that I never even spoke to Miss Thompson in *Rain*. This is a character that the world has not found wanting in vividness. Though but one of a multitude of writers my practice is doubtless common to most, so that I may be permitted to give another instance of it. I was once asked to meet at dinner two persons, a husband and wife, of whom I was told only what the reader will shortly read. I think I never knew their names. I should certainly not recognize them if I met them in the street. Here are the notes I made at the time. 'A stout, rather pompous man of fifty, with pince-nez, grey-haired, a florid complexion, blue eyes, a neat grey moustache. He talks with assurance. He is resident of an outlying district and is somewhat impressed with the importance of his position. He despises the men who have let themselves go under the influence of the climate and the surroundings. He has travelled extensively during his short leaves in the East and knows Java, the Philippines, the coast of China and the Malay Peninsula. He is very British, very patriotic; he takes a great deal of exercise. He has been a very heavy drinker and always took a bottle of whisky to bed with him. His wife has entirely cured him and now he drinks nothing but water. She is a little insignificant woman, with sharp features, thin, with a sallow skin and a flat chest. She is very badly dressed. She has all the prejudices of an Englishwoman. All her family for generations have been in second-rate regiments. Except that you know that she has caused her husband to cease drinking entirely you would think her quite colourless and unimportant.' On these materials, I invented the story which is called *Before the Party*. I do not believe that any candid person could think that these two people had cause for complaint because they had been made use of. It is true that I should never have thought of the story if I had not met them, but anyone who takes the trouble to read it will see how insignificant was the incident (the taking of the bottle to bed) that suggested it and how differently the two chief characters have in the course of writing developed from the brief sketch which was their foundation.

'Critics are like horse-flies which prevent the horse from ploughing,' said Chekhov. 'For over twenty years I have read criticisms of my stories, and I do not remember a single remark of any value or one word of valuable advice. Only once Skabichevsky wrote something which made an impression on me. He said I would die in a ditch, drunk.' He was writing for twenty-five years and during that time his writing was constantly attacked. I do not know whether the critics of the present day are naturally of a less ferocious temper; I must allow that on the whole the judgment that has been passed on the stories in this volume when from time to time a collection has been published in book form has been favourable. One epithet, however, has been much applied to them, which has puzzled me; they have been described with disconcerting frequency as 'competent'. Now on the face of it I might have thought this laudatory, for to do a thing competently is certainly more deserving of praise than to do it incompetently, but the adjective has been used in a disparaging sense and, anxious to learn and if possible to improve, I have asked myself what was in the mind of the critics who thus employed it. Of course none of us is liked by everybody and it is necessary that a man's writing, which is so intimate a revelation of himself, should be repulsive to persons who are naturally antagonistic to the creature he is. This should leave him unperturbed. But when an author's work is somewhat commonly found to have a quality that is unattractive to many it is sensible of him to give the matter his attention. There is evidently something that a number of people do not like in my stories and it is this they try to express when they damn them with the faint praise of competence. I have a notion that it is the definiteness of their form. I hazard the suggestion (perhaps unduly flattering to myself) because this particular criticism has never been made in France where my stories have had with the critics and the public much greater success than they have had in England. The French, with their classical sense and their orderly minds, demand a precise form and are exasperated by a work in which the ends are left lying about, themes are propounded and not resolved and a climax is foreseen and then eluded. This precision on the other hand has always been slightly antipathetic to the English. Our great novels have been shapeless and this, far from disconcerting their readers, has given them a sense of security. This is the life we know, they have thought, with its arbitrariness and inconsequence; we can put out of our minds the irritating thought that two and two make four. If I am right in this surmise I can do nothing about it and I must resign myself to being called competent for the rest of my days. My prepossessions in the arts are on the side of law and order. I like a story that fits. I did not take to writing stories seriously till I had had much experience as a dramatist, and this experience taught me to leave out everything that did not serve the dramatic value of my story. It taught me to make incident follow incident in such a manner as to lead up to the climax I had in mind. I am not unaware of the disadvantages of this method. It gives a tightness of effect that is sometimes disconcerting. You feel that life does not dovetail into its various parts with such neatness. In life stories straggle, they begin nowhere and tail off without a point. That is probably what Chekhov meant when he said that stories should have neither a beginning nor an end. It is certain that sometimes it gives you a sensation of airlessness when you see persons who behave so exactly according to character, and incidents that fall into place with such perfect convenience. The story-teller of this kind aims not only at giving his own feelings about life, but at a formal decoration. He arranges life to suit his purposes. He follows a design in his mind, leaving out this and changing that; he distorts facts to his advantage, according to his plan; and when he attains his object produces a work of art. It may be that life slips through his fingers; then he has failed; it may be that he seems sometimes so artificial that you cannot believe him, and when you do not believe a story-teller he is done. When he succeeds he has forced you for a time to accept his view of the universe and has given you the pleasure of following out the pattern he has drawn on the surface of chaos. But he seeks to prove nothing. He paints a picture and sets it before you. You can take it or leave it.

FROM:

The Complete Short Stories

Volume II—The World Over

330

'PREFACE'

(1922–1952)

THIS book contains all the stories I have written that are not included in *East and West*. The tales in that collection were of about the same length and written on the same scale and so it seemed convenient to publish them together in a single volume. Most of the stories which I have now gathered together are very much shorter. Some were written many years ago, others more recently. They appeared in magazines and were afterwards issued in book form. To the first lot I gave the title of *Cosmopolitans*, because they were offered to the public in the *Cosmopolitan Magazine*, and except for Ray Long, who was then its editor, would never have been written.

When I was in China in 1920 I took notes of whatever I saw that excited my interest, with the intention of making a connected narrative out of them; but when I came home and read them it seemed to me that they had a vividness which I might easily lose if I tried to elaborate them. So I changed my mind and decided to publish them as they stood under the title: *On a Chinese Screen*. Ray Long chanced to read this and it occurred to him that some of my notes might well be taken for short stories. I have included two of them, 'The Taipan' and 'the Consul,' in this volume. The fact is that if you are a story-teller any curious person you meet has a way of suggesting a story, and incidents that to others will seem quite haphazard have a way of presenting themselves to you with the pattern your natural instinct has impressed on them.

Magazine readers do not like starting a story and, after reading for a while, being told to turn to page one hundred and something. Writers do not like it either, for they think the interruption disturbs the reader and they have besides an uneasy fear that sometimes he will not take the trouble and so leave their story unfinished. There is no help for it. Everyone should know that a magazine costs more to produce than it is sold for, and could not exist but for the advertisements. The advertisers think that their announcements are more likely to be read if they are on the same page as matter which they modestly, but often mistakenly, think of greater interest. So in the illustrated periodicals it has been found advisable to put the beginning of a story or an article, with the picture that purports to illustrate it, at the beginning and the continuation with the advertisements later on.

Neither readers nor writers should complain. Readers get something for far less than cost price and writers are paid sums for their productions which only the advertisements render possible. They should remember that they are only there as bait. Their office is to fill blank spaces and indirectly induce their readers to buy motor accessories, aids to beauty and join correspondence courses. Fortunately this need not affect them. The best story from the advertisers' standpoint (and they make their views felt on this question) is the story that gives readers most entertainment. Ray Long conceived the notion that the readers of the *Cosmopolitan* would like it if they were given at least one story that they could read without having to hunt for the continuation among the advertisements, and he commissioned me to write half a dozen sketches of the same sort as those in *On a Chinese Screen*. They were to be short enough to print on opposite pages of the magazine and leave plenty of room for illustration.

The sketches I wrote pleased and the commission was renewed. I went on writing them until my natural verbosity got the better of me and I found myself no longer able to keep my stories within the limits imposed upon me. Then I had to stop. I think I learned a good deal from the writing of them and I am glad that I did. My difficulty was to compress what I had to tell into a number of words which must not be exceeded and yet leave the reader with the impression that I had told all there was to tell. It was this that made the enterprise amusing. It was also salutary. I could not afford to waste a word. I had to be succinct. I was surprised to find how many adverbs and adjectives I could leave out without any harm to the matter or the manner. One often writes needless words because they give the phrase balance. It was very good practice to try to get it into a sentence without using a word that was not necessary to the sense.

The matter, of course, had to be chosen with discretion; it would have been futile to take a theme that demanded elaborate development. I have a natural predilection for completeness, so that even in the little space at my disposal I wanted my story to have a certain structure. I do not care for the shapeless story. To my mind it is not enough when the writer gives you the plain facts seen through his own eyes (which means of course that they are not plain facts, but facts coloured by his own idiosyncrasy); I think he should impose a pattern on them. Naturally these stories are anecdotes. If stories are interesting and well told they are none the worse for that. The anecdote is the basis of fiction. The restlessness of writers forces upon fiction from time to time forms that are foreign to it, but when it has been oppressed for a period by obscurity, propaganda or affectation, it reverts, and returns inevitably to the proper function of fiction, which is to tell an interesting story.

In the preface to *East and West* I said pretty well all I had to say about the short story in general. I have nothing to add to that. I have written now nearly a hundred stories and one thing I have discovered is that whether you hit upon a story or not, whether it comes off or not, is very much a matter of luck. Stories are lying about at every street corner, but the writer may not be there at the moment they are waiting to be picked up or he may be looking at a shop window and pass them unnoticed. He may write them before he has seen all there is to see in them or he may turn them over in his mind so long that they have lost their freshness. He may not have seen them from the exact standpoint at which they can be written to their best advantage. It is a rare and happy event when he conceives the idea of a story, writes it at the precise moment when it is ripe, and treats it in such a way as to get out of it all that it implicitly contains. Then it will be within its limitations perfect. But perfection is seldom achieved. I think a volume of modest dimensions would contain all the short stories which even closely approach it. The reader should be satisfied if in any collection of these short pieces of fiction he finds a general level of competence and on closing the book feels that he has been amused, interested and moved.

With one exception all the stories I have written have been published in magazines. The exception is a story called 'The Book-Bag.' When I sent it to Ray Long he wrote to me, in sorrow rather than in anger, that he had gone further with me than with any other author, but when it came to incest he had to draw the line. I could not blame him. He published the tale later in a collection of what he thought in his long career as editor of the Cosmopolitan were the best short stories that had ever been offered him. I know that in admitting that my stories have been published in magazines I lay myself open to critical depreciation, for to describe a tale as a magazine story is to condemn it. But when the critics do this they show less acumen than may reasonably be expected of them. Nor do they show much knowledge of literary history. For ever since magazines became a popular form of publication authors have found them a useful medium to put their work before readers. All the greatest short-story writers have published their stories in magazines, Balzac, Flaubert and Maupassant; Chekhov, Henry James, Rudyard Kipling. I do not think it rash to say that the only short stories that have not been published in a magazine are the stories that no editor would accept. So to damn a story because it is a magazine story is absurd. The magazines doubtless publish a great many bad stories, but then more bad stories are written than good ones, and an editor, even of a magazine with literary pretensions, is often obliged to print a story of which he doesn't think highly because he can get nothing better. Some editors of popular magazines think their readers demand a certain type of story and will take nothing else; and they manage to find writers who can turn out the sort of thing they want and often make a very good job of it. This is the machine-made article that has given the magazine story a bad name. But after all, no one is obliged to read it. It gives satisfaction to many people since it allows them for a brief period to experience in fancy the romance and adventure which in the monotony of their lives they crave for.

But if I may judge from the reviews I have read of the volumes of short stories that are frequently published, where the critics to my mind err is when they dismiss stories as magazine stories because they are well constructed, dramatic and have a surprise ending. There is nothing to be condemned in a surprise ending if it is the natural end of a story. On the contrary it is an excellence. It is only bad when, as in some of O. Henry's stories, it is dragged in without reason to give the reader a kick. Nor is a story any the worse for being neatly built, with a beginning, a middle and an end. All good story writers have done their best to achieve this. It is the fashion of today for writers, under the influence of an inadequate acquaintance with Chekhov, to write stories that begin anywhere and end inconclusively. They think it enough if they have described a mood, or given an impression, or drawn a character. That is all very well, but it is not a story, and I do not think it satisfies the reader. He does not like to be left wondering. He wants to have his questions answered. That is what I have tried to do, and when a story was suggested to me of which I didn't know the answer I forbore to write it. One such story I wrote about in *A Writer's Notebook*, and since I don't expect everyone to have read everything I have written I think it may amuse the reader if I here repeat it. When I was in India I received a letter from a man unknown to me in which he told me the following incident in the belief that I might be able to make use of it:

Two young fellows were working on a tea plantation in the hills and the mail had to be fetched from a long way off so that they only got it at rather long intervals. One of the young fellows, let us call him A, got a lot of letters by every mail, ten or twelve and sometimes more, but the other, B, never got one. He used to watch A enviously as he took his bundle and started to read; he hankered to have a letter, just one letter; and one day, when they were expecting the mail, he said to A: 'Look here, you always have a packet of letters and I never get any. I'll give you five pounds if you'll let me have one of yours.' 'Right-ho,' said A, and when the mail came in he handed B his letters and said to him: 'Take whichever you like.' B gave him a five-pound note, looked over the letters, chose one and returned the rest. In the evening when they were having whisky and soda before dinner, A asked casually: 'By the way, what was that letter about?' 'I'm not going to tell you,' said B. A, somewhat taken aback, said: 'Well, who was it from?' 'That's my business,' answered B. They had a bit of an argument, but B stood on his rights and refused to say anything about the letter he had bought. A began to fret, and as the weeks went by he did all he could to persuade B to let him see the letter. B continued to refuse. At length A, anxious, worried, and curious, felt he couldn't bear it any longer, so he went to B and said: 'Look here, here's your five pounds, let me have my letter back again.' 'Not on your life,' said B. 'I bought it and paid for it, it's my letter and I'm not going to give it up.'

In *A Writer's Notebook* I added: 'I suppose if I belonged to the modern school of story writers I should write it just as it is and leave it. It goes against the grain with me. I want a story to have form, and I don't see how you can give it that unless you can bring it to a conclusion that leaves no legitimate room for questioning. But even if you could bring yourself to leave the reader up in the air you don't want to leave yourself up in the air with him.' The facts as my correspondent gave them to me intrigued a good many people, and a magazine in Canada and *The New Statesman* in England, independently of one another, offered prizes to their readers for the best conclusion to the story. I don't know that the results were particularly successful.

I read once an article on how to write a short story. Certain points the author made were useful, but to my mind the central thesis was wrong. She stated that the 'focal point' of a short story should be the building of character and that the incidents should be invented solely to 'liven' personality. Oddly enough she remarked earlier in her article that the parables are the best short stories that have ever been written. I think it would be difficult to describe the characters of the Prodigal Son and his brother or of the Good Samaritan and the Man who fell among thieves. They are in fact not characterized and we have to guess what sort of people they were, for we are only told about them the essential facts necessary for the pointing of the moral. And that, whether he has a moral to point or not, is about all the short-story writer can do. He has no room to describe and develop a character; at best he can only give the salient traits that bring the character to life and so make the story he has to tell plausible. Since the beginning of history men have gathered around the campfire or in a group in the market place to listen to the telling of stories. The desire to listen to them appears to be as deeply rooted in the human animal as the sense of property. I have never pretended to be anything but a story-teller. It has amused me to tell stories and I have told a great many.

I have been writing stories for fifty years. In that long period I have seen a number of bright stars creep shyly over the horizon, travel across the sky to burn with a more or less gem-like flame for a while in mid-heaven, and then dwindle into an obscurity from which there is little likelihood that they will ever emerge. The writer has his special communication to make, which, when you come to analyse it, is the personality with which he is endowed by nature, and during the early years of his activity he is groping in the dark to express it; then, if he is fortunate, he succeeds in doing this and if there is in his personality a certain abundance he may contrive for a long time to produce work which is varied and characteristic; but the time comes at last (if he is so imprudent as to live to a ripe age) when, having given what he has to give, his powers fail. He has fashioned all the stories he himself is capable of digging out of the inexhaustible mine which is human nature and he has created all the characters which can possibly be constituted out of the various sides of his own personality. For no one, I believe, can create a character from pure observation; if it is to have life it must be at least in some degree a representation of himself. A generation has arisen which is strange to him and it is only by an effort of will that he can understand the interests of a world of which he can now be only an observer. But to understand is not enough; the writer of fiction must feel, and he must not only feel with, he must feel in. It is well then if he can bring himself to cease writing stories which might just as well have remained unwritten. He is wise to watch warily for the signs which will indicate to him that having said his say, it behoves him to resign himself to silence.

I have written my last story.

PART II

Concerning the Works of Other Writers

FROM:

Traveller's Library

'GENERAL INTRODUCTION'*

(1933)

THERE are people who have no head for cards. It is impossible
not to be sorry for them, for what, one asks oneself, can the
future have to offer them when the glow of youth has departed and
advancing years force them, as they force all of us, to be spectators
rather than actors in the comedy of life? Love is for the young and
affection is but a frigid solace to a pining heart. Sport demands
physical vigour and affairs a strenuous activity. To have learnt to
play a good game of bridge is the safest insurance against the
tedium of old age. Throughout life one may find in cards endless
entertainment and an occupation for idle hours that rests the mind
from care and pleasantly exercises the intelligence. For the people
who say that only the stupid can play cards err; they do not know
what decision, what quickness of apprehension, what judgment,
what knowledge of character, are required to play a difficult hand
perfectly. The good card-player trusts his intuition as implicitly as
Monsieur Bergson, but he calls it a hunch; the brilliant card-player
has a gift as specific as the poet's: he too is born not made. The
student of human nature can find endless matter for observation in
the behaviour of his fellow card-players. Meanness and generosity,
prudence and audacity, courage and timidity, weakness and

* This Introduction was written for a volume of selections from the Traveller's
Library. A full list of works which appeared in this series is printed in the Appendix.

strength; all these men show at the card-table according to their natures, and because they are intent upon the game drop the mask they wear in the ordinary affairs of life. Few are so deep that you do not know the essential facts about them after a few rubbers of bridge. The card-table is a very good school for the study of mankind. The unhappy persons who have no card sense say that playing cards is a waste of time, but it is never waste of time to amuse oneself; and besides, the day has twenty-four hours and the week seven days, there is always a certain time to be wasted. In passing I may remark that even *they* generally own a greasy pack of cards, and when you come upon them unexpectedly you are just as likely to find them occupied in laying out a patience as in improving their minds with great literature or their souls with reflection. Of course when you ask them how leisure can be better employed they say, in conversation. For they are great talkers. They lament the decay of the art of conversation and ascribe it to the universal passion for bridge. It is obvious that this pastime has deprived many a light prattler of his audience and it is true that there are now few conversationalists in the grand style. I doubt whether the impatience of the present day would suffer their tyranny, for they seem to have indulged much in monologue and they were impatient of interruption. I have a notion that it is pleasanter to read Boswell's record of the conversations than it ever was to listen to Dr Johnson. I have heard that when Mallarmé received his admirers on those Tuesdays which literary gossip has made famous, he stood in front of the fireplace and discoursed on some subject or other amid the silence of the company; and certainly the accounts one hears of the conversation of Anatole France do not lead one to suspect that there was much give and take. I should have thought that sort of thing must have been an interesting experience, and maybe an intellectual treat, but hardly a pleasant relaxation. It can indeed only have been supportable because the listeners were filled with awe of the speaker, and awe, happily, is not a feeling that we, English and

Americans, particularly cherish for men of eminence. On the other hand ordinary conversation, the chit-chat of the drawing-room, is seldom in English-speaking countries witty or profound. Its staple is the foibles of our friends and the affairs of the day. We are shy of speaking in public of our souls, of God and Immortality, and we are rarely so interested in art and literature as to be willing to argue about them. The accompaniment of good music is needed to loosen our tongues. It is not often in a mixed gathering that conversation proceeds long without some of us hankering after the bridge-table, and if there is no sign of it glancing surreptitiously at our watches and wondering how soon we can decently take our leave. It is to meet this situation, I suppose, that in circles where cards are not played the games have been invented that add so much horror to social intercourse, such as Lights, Consequences and Anagrams. There are even people who have brought the torture of their fellows to such a pitch that they force you to invent rhymed couplets upon topics of their suggestion. Such diversions of course point to an abnormal pleasure in the infliction of boredom.

Perhaps the least intolerable of all these methods of passing time is to offer for discussion some point of behaviour. If, for instance, in some disaster you could only save one person and your choice lay between a small boy, a beautiful young woman and an eminent scientist, which would you choose? Another is, if you were going to spend the rest of your life on a desert island and could only take twelve books which would they be? This question occurred to me when I set about choosing the materials for the volume to which this is the introduction. It is of course no test of one's literary inclinations, for in such a case the amount of matter would have to be the first consideration. People very sensibly for the most part mention the Bible and the plays of Shakespeare. I have read the Bible twice through from cover to cover and have no great wish to read it again, but it certainly contains a lot of meat and I suppose would be a good book to take. The same may be said of Shake-speare. There are many of the plays which no one would in ordinary circumstances care to read a second time, but none that if you were pressed for reading matter you could not read at least once or twice a year. After these two the choice becomes more difficult and the answers vary; but the question of quantity is as important as that of quality and the whole of Wordsworth in one volume would evidently be preferred to the whole of Keats. And then you must consider that you will have to read the same thing twenty, fifty or a hundred times. There are a great many books that are worth reading once, a considerable number that are worth reading twice, but not many that are worth reading over and over again. I once knew a man who read *The Pickwick Papers* every year for thirty years, but he eventually died of cirrhosis of the liver.

In the collection of pieces that comprise this book I have not sought to provide a volume for anyone who looks forward to being cast away on a desert island. My object is modest. I have asked myself what I should like to take with me in a single volume of reasonable size if I could have but one book and were travelling from New York to San Francisco by train or across the Atlantic on a tramp steamer. I do not want to tire the reader of this preface with a long account of the reasons for which I have inserted this or that, but I should like him to have patience with me while I tell him exactly what I have been at. I am not a critic or a scholar. Either of these would doubtless have chosen very different things from what I have, but if the publishers of this volume had needed the taste of the one or the learning of the other I should certainly not have been invited to make the selection. I am a professional writer. I have read a great deal, sometimes for instruction and sometimes for pleasure, but never since I was a small boy without an inward eye on the relation between what I was reading and my professional interests. At one time I read omnivorously, but for a good many years I have read little but what immediately concerned me. I am sure that a great deal that was worth reading has thus escaped me. For this reason the reader will doubtless look in vain for much that he would have expected to find here. I am more interested in an author's personality than in the books he writes. I follow him in the attempts he makes to express himself, his experiments in this manner and that; but when he has produced the work in which he has at last said all he has to say about himself, when he has arrived at what perhaps for many years he has only approached, then I read him no longer. At least if I do it is out of politeness, because he has given me his book, or fear, in case he should be affronted if I didn't, and now from inclination. Sometimes I have to read many books by an author before my curiosity about him is satisfied and some-times only his first or second. He may write half a hundred master-pieces after that, but life is short and there is a great deal I urgently want to read, and I am content to leave their enjoyment to others. I dare say some of the authors represented in this volume are not represented by their best things. I dare say they have written since much of greater merit, but I do not happen to have read it. These writers belong roughly to the same period. It is difficult to appreciate any generation but one's own. Few of the writers who were esteemed of importance when I was a young man excite me much now and even then I was doubtless more critical than became me. The young author may be forgiven if he is unfair to his elders. They occupy a place in the sun which he would gladly fill. But it is not only envy that leads him to depreciate them. For they deal with manners and customs that have constrained his youth; they represent an attitude towards life and deliver a philosophy which he is naturally in revolt against. They are realists and he is a romantic or the other way about. He cannot be expected to realize that his attitude and his philosophy will in a little while seem as dull and conventional as those that now outrage his sense of common decency. And it is easy to miss the merits of the writers who are pushing one into the background. I have always a sneaking sympathy with George Crabbe who read the poems of Byron, Walter Scott, Keats and Shelley, and thought them all stuff and nonsense. After all he might have been right. In the case of one of them he was, and perhaps of two. I would offer it as a test that an author can apply to himself; when he can see nothing at all in work that the best critical opinion of the day pronounces good, his hour has struck and nothing remains to him but to shut up shop and like Voltaire's Candide cultivate a garden. It is dangerous for an author to get too set in his own manner and I have always followed, though with circumspection, the productions of my fellow writers in order to see whether in technique or point of view they could teach me something that it behoved me to know. But during the forty years I have been studying my craft I have seen so many writers hailed as masters, enjoy their hour of glory, and sink into an oblivion which is always described as well-merited, that I have become sceptical; and now, when a new genius is discovered I wait a year or two before I concern myself with him. It is astonishing how many books I find there is no need for me to read at all. This volume then does not pretend to be a survey of English literature during the last thirty years or so, but merely a haphazard collection of pieces that I have read and thought I should like to read again. have chosen them from the work of English writers partly because I know current English literature better than current American literature and because it seemed to me that by keeping to the authors of one country I obtained at least an illusion of unity which is the only completeness such a miscellany can hope to have; but also because American literature during the last thirty years is so rich, especially in the short story, a form I am particularly attracted by, and in the light novel, a form not often successfully cultivated in England, that I should have been overwhelmed by the mass of matter. I could never have got into the limits of this book half the things I should have urgently wanted to put in. I have in point of fact read again all that is here offered to the reader and think that it is good. When I was gathering the materials I made a list of a number of things that I thought I should like to include, but when I came to tackle them found that many of them did not bear a second reading. I made some unforeseen discoveries. Stories that I had thought profound now seemed to me pretentious and others that I had thought humorous, silly; verses that had moved me left me cold and essays I had found suggestive I now found trivial. I have thrown many old friends into the dustbin; but not without a sigh. Lest the kindly reader should think me heartless I hasten to add that I speak metaphorically; I have in fact put them in a large packing-case and sent them to the local hospital.

The ablest editor I know is accustomed to say: I am the average American and what interests me will interest my readers; the event has proved him right. Now I have most of my life been miserably conscious that I am not the average Englishman. Let no one think I say this with self-satisfaction, for I think that there is nothing better than to be like everybody else. It is the only way to be happy, and it is with but a wry face that one tells oneself that happiness is not everything. The best writers have been ordinary men and it is because they felt all the emotions of ordinary men that (with genius to help) they have been able to represent human beings with truth and sympathy. It is impossible to draw a complete picture of men unless you can think with their heads and feel with their hearts. There have of course been many excellent writers who in one way or another were abnormal and they have produced works that have a tang and an originality that make them sometimes more readable than the work of the greater writers, but I do not think they can be said ever to have reached those wonderful heights on which the Olympians dwell. I find *Wuthering Heights* more interesting than *David Copperfield*, but I have no doubt which is the greater novel. The accident of my birth in France, which enabled me to learn French and English simultaneously and thus instilled into me two modes of life, two liberties, two points of view, has prevented me

from ever identifying myself completely with the instincts and
prejudices of one people or the other, and it is in instinct and
prejudice that sympathy is most deeply rooted; the accident of a
physical infirmity, with its attendant nervousness, separated me to a
greater extent than would be thought likely from the common life
of others. In my communications with my fellows I have generally
felt 'out of it'; in that uprush of emotion that sometimes seizes a
crowd so that their hearts throb as one I have been lamentably
aware that my own keeps its accustomed and normal rhythm.
When 'Everybody suddenly burst out singing' as Siegfried Sassoon
says in one of the most moving of the poems I have been allowed to
reprint in this book, I have always felt exceedingly embarrassed.
And when on New Year's Eve people join hands and swinging
them up and down to the music, like a nurse rocking the baby, sing
lustily *Should Auld Acquaintance be Forgot*, my shivering nerves
whisper, yes, please. I cannot then offer this book as the choice of
the average man and I cannot say that because these things please
me they will please you. If you like me they will please you, and if
you don't they won't. Though I do not share many of the prejudices that many people have, I naturally have prejudices of my
own, and they will be obvious to anyone who reads this book
through. I am a writer and I look at these things from my professional standpoint. This is the difference between the writer and
the critic, that the critic, the good one, can look upon production
from the vantage-ground of the absolute and putting himself in the
author's shoes can judge of the success of his efforts without the
hindrance of predisposition. I do not think that many writers can do
this. However good a book may be we can difficultly find merit
in it if it is not the sort of thing we do, or think we can do ourselves.
Mr E. M. Forster not very long ago wrote a book called *Aspects of
the Novel*. In a novel of mine I ventured on a little gibe at his
expense, but Mr Forster is a man of great disinterestedness, generous
of soul, and with a delicate sense of humour; I think he forgave me

my jest for he was good enough to write and tell me that he liked my book. His, nevertheless, is a good one, interesting not only to the novelist but also to the novel-reader; but I speak of it now to suggest that an acute reader could certainly divine from it what sort of novels Mr Forster would write. He makes much of just those characteristics in which no one now writing is richer than himself, but holds cheap that element of the novel, the story, in which, I venture to think, his own weakness lies. My private opinion is that if Mr Forster, with his gift for beautiful English, his power of creating significant, interesting and living persons, his emotion and humour, his poetic feeling, could or would submit himself to the indignity of devising a good story he would write a novel that would make his eminent talent manifest to the whole world. But my opinion is neither here nor there. In this volume there is nothing that I would not have been glad to write myself. Of course I know that there is a great deal that I have not the gift to write. When I was young in moments of passion I used to beat my fists on the writing table and cry, but God, I wish I had more brains; but now, resigned though far from content, I am prepared to make do with what I have. Just as there are painters' pictures, there are writers' books. There are also readers' books. These are books that a reader enjoys but a writer, knowing the trick, finds intolerable. They are written to a formula. The author has set himself too easy a task. It is as if you expected a juggler to be amused by a child bouncing a ball. But they are sometimes very well done. They are often painstaking and sincere. When I start on a novel in which there is an elderly man, generally in the lower ranks of life, married to a young wife, and an adolescent, his son or a farmhand in the offing, my heart sinks. The course of the story, with its powerful scenes, is obvious to me. This kind of book is much praised for its 'strength'. But there may be as much 'strength' in a woman offering another a cup of tea as in a man kicking his wife to death with hob-nailed boots. The action is but a symbol. Dialect is the last straw. I do not like yokels who exchange wise cracks. Any workaday novelist knows that that sort of thing can be turned out by the yard and he laughs up his sleeve at the simplicity of the reading public that can find amusement in a form of humour so mechanical. Another kind that comes for me under the head of readers' books is the whimsical. These are much written by the literary sort of critics who think they will take a rest from serious work. They are often cultured and written with distinction. They have what is generally described as a charming fantasy. The formula here is simple. A middle-aged literary man takes a holiday in the country and on his walks meets a leprechaun and exchanges pleasantly philosophical remarks with him; or a young poet seeks lodgings in a London suburb where the maid-of-all-work is of an astonishing beauty; she converses with an ingenuousness that brings a lump to your throat, and there is certainly another lodger, a middle-aged literary man, who makes pleasantly philosophical remarks. Generally somebody dies in the end and it makes a very pathetic scene. There are very delicate descriptions of scenery. The reader will find nothing of the kind in these pages. He will find humour and he will find pathos. He will not find the namby-pamby.

Nor will he find the didactic. Of late years the novel as everyone knows has widened its scope; it has become a platform for the exposition of the author's ideas. Novelists have become politicians, economists, social reformers and what not. They have used the novel to advocate this cause and that. They have been deeply concerned with the vital problems of the day. For this, I think, we may hold the Russians responsible. The Russian novelists brought something new to fiction, but by the circumstances of their civilization they were inclined to subordinate art to social questions. Chekhov, as we know, was much blamed for his indifference to them and his defenders were at pains to rebut the charge. They did not come out into the open and claim that he was an artist and that was enough, but sought chapter and verse to prove that his aim in describing the Russian peasant, for instance, was purely humanitarian. But the novelists who concern themselves with such things run a double danger. The first is that their views are unlikely to be sound (if they had the scientific instinct they would not be novelists) and the second is that the problems they deal with have seldom more than a temporary interest. What are you to say of a novel that becomes unreadable when an act of Parliament has changed a law? I forget what critic it was that said that the subject of great poetry was the common vicissitudes of humanity, birth and death, love and hatred, youth and old age. I venture to think that these are also the subjects of great fiction. I know it is out of fashion just now to think that the object of art is to entertain. I cannot help it. When I want instruction I go to philosophers, men of science and historians; I do not ask the novelist to give me anything but amusement. I am not in bad company, for Corneille (after Aristotle) thought that the pleasure of his audience was the poet's only aim, and the tender and perfect Racine contended, even with acrimony, that the first rule of the drama was to please and all the others were devised merely to achieve that end. And did not the philosophic Coleridge say that the object of poetry was delight? The unfortunate remark made by Terence in a play that few have read has had a disastrous effect on novelists. Of course it is very well that their sympathies should be universal, but that does not prove that their opinions are valuable. My uncle, a clergyman, told one of his curates who had a discordant voice and insisted on singing in church that it would be to the greater glory of God if he praised him only in his heart. I wonder if the writers of fiction who are so determined to teach us and improve us noticed that the other day a racing motorist who had driven a car faster than anyone else in the world was brought up on to a public platform to tell the free-born electors of a great constituency how they should vote on a question concerning the relations between the British Empire and India. There is a certain vulgarity in setting yourself up as an authority in matters on which your knowledge can be but superficial. I do not see why the story-teller should not be content to be a story-teller. He can be an artist and is that so little?

I read in the papers that rhetoric is coming into fashion again; and an eminent anthologist (but a less eminent novelist) is, I hear, bringing out a collection entirely devoted to purple passages. I shall not read it. In poetry, which is the happy avocation of youth, I do not mind, in moderation, a little rhetoric, but I do not like it in prose at all. I think the reader will find little in the following pages that is not written with simplicity. In my youth, influenced by the fashion of the day, I did my best to write in the grand manner. I studied the Bible, I sought phrases in the venerable Hooker and copied out passages of Jeremy Taylor. I ransacked the dictionary for unusual epithets. I went to the British Museum and made lists of the names of precious stones. But I had no bent that way and, resigning myself to writing not as I should have liked but as I could, I returned to the study of Swift. In passing I should like to suggest that the Bible has not had an altogether happy influence on English style. No one would deny that it is a great monument of the language, but after all it is a translation and its grandiloquent imagery is alien to our natures. For long I thought that Swift was the best model on which the modern English writer could form his style, and I still think there is something intoxicating in the order in which he places his words. But now I find in him a certain dryness and a dead level which is somewhat tiring. He is like a man who, whatever his emotion and however emphatic his words, never raises his voice. It is a little sinister. I think if I were starting over again I should devote myself to the study of Dryden. It was he who first gave English prose its form. He released the language from the ponderous eloquence that had overwhelmed it and made it the lovely supple instrument which at its best it is. He had the straightforwardness and the limpidity of Swift; but a melodious variety and a conversational ease that Swift never attained. He had a happy charm of which the Dean was incapable. Swift's English flows like the water in a canal shaded by neat poplars, but Dryden's like a great river under the open sky. I know none more delightful. Of course a living language changes and it would be absurd for anyone to try to write like Dryden now. But his excellencies are still the excellencies of English prose. English is a very difficult language to write. Its grammar is so complicated that even the best writers often make gross mistakes. The various influences to which it has been subjected have made it a difficult medium to handle. Pedants have burdened it with pomposities. Clowns have jumped with it through paper hoops and juggled with its beauties as though they were the properties of the circus ring. Rhetoricians have floundered in the richness of its vocabulary. But its excellencies remain un-impaired. It is with joy and pride that I can point to them in many of the authors who grace this collection by their works.

Teller of Tales

'INTRODUCTION'

(1939)

I

WHEN I set about gathering material for this anthology it was with the ambitious aim of showing how the short story had developed since the beginning of the nineteenth century. My notion was to trace its evolution as the evolution of the horse may be traced from the tiny creature with five toes that ran about the forests of the Neocene period to the noble beast that, notwithstanding the mechanization of the age, still provides a decent living for bookmakers and tipsters. It is natural for men to tell tales, and I suppose the short story began in the night of time when the hunter, to beguile the leisure of his fellows when they had eaten and drunk their fill, narrated by the cavern fire some marvellous incident of which he had heard. In cities of the East you can to this day see the story-teller sitting in the market place, surrounded by a circle of eager listeners, and hear him tell the tales that he has inherited from an immemorial past. But I chose to start with the nineteenth century because it was then that the short story acquired a character and a currency that it had not had before. Of course short stories had been written: there were the religious stories of Greek origin, there were the edifying narratives popular in the Middle Ages, and there were the immortal stories of *The Thousand and One Nights*; throughout the Renaissance, in Italy and Spain, in

France and England, there was a great vogue for brief narrative. The *Decameron* of Boccaccio and the *Exemplary Tales* of Cervantes are its unperished monuments. But with the rise of the novel the vogue dwindled. The booksellers would no longer pay good money for a collection of short tales, and the authors soon came to look askance on a form of fiction that brought them neither profit nor renown. When from time to time, conceiving a theme that they could adequately treat in a little space, they wrote a short story, they did not quite know what to do with it; and so, unwilling to waste it, they inserted it, sometimes, one must admit, very clumsily, into the body of their novels.

But at the beginning of the nineteenth century a new form of publication was put before the reading public which very soon acquired an immense popularity. The result shows that the authors welcomed with delight the chance thus offered to them for disposing to advantage of the brief pieces which for one reason or another they had occasion to write. This was the annual. It seems to have started in Germany. It was a miscellany of prose and verse; and in its native land offered its readers substantial fare, for we are told that Schiller's *Maid of Orleans* and Goethe's *Hermann and Dorothea* first appeared in periodicals of this character. But when their success led English publishers to imitate them they relied chiefly on short stories to attract a sufficiency of readers. The annual soon found its way to America and gave American authors an opportunity they had long been looking for.

II

Now I must interrupt myself to tell the reader something about literary composition of which, so far as I know, the critics, whose duty it is doubtless to guide and instruct him, have neglected to apprise him. The writer has in him the desire to create, but he has also the desire to place before readers the result of his labour and the desire (a harmless one with which the reader is not concerned) to earn his bread and butter. On the whole he finds it possible to direct his creative gifts into the channels that will enable him to satisfy these desires. At the risk of shocking the reader who thinks the writer's inspiration should be uninfluenced by practical con- siderations. I must further tell him that writers quite naturally find themselves impelled to write the sort of things for which there is a demand. When plays in verse might bring an author fame and fortune it would probably have been difficult to find a young man of literary bent who had not among his papers a tragedy in five acts. I think it would occur to few young men to write one now. Today they write plays in prose, novels and short stories. The possibility of publication, the exigencies of editors, that is to say their notion of what their readers want, have a great influence on the kind of work that at a particular time is produced. So, when magazines flourish which have room for stories of considerable length, stories of that length are written; when on the other hand newspapers publish fiction, but can give it no more than a small space, stories to fill that space are supplied. There is nothing dis- graceful in this. The competent author can write a story in a couple of thousand words as easily as he can write one in ten thousand. But he chooses a different story or treats it in a different way. Guy de Maupassant wrote one of his most celebrated tales, *The Legacy*, twice over, once in a few hundred words for a newspaper and the second time in several thousand for a magazine; both are published in the collected edition of his works, and I think no one can read the two versions without admitting that in the first there is not a word too little and in the second not a word too much. The point I want to make is this: the nature of the vehicle whereby the writer approaches his public is one of the conventions he has to accept, and on the whole he finds that he can do this without any violence to his own inclinations.

Now at the beginning of the nineteenth century the annuals and keepsakes offered writers a means of introducing themselves to the public by way of the short story, and so short stories, serving a better purpose than merely to give a fillip to the reader's interest in the course of a long novel, began to be written in greater numbers than ever before. More especially was this the case in America where the lack of a copyright law made it difficult for American authors to find a publisher to publish their novels. English novels were pirated and the competition was too severe for the American author to meet; he was almost forced to write short stories, and fortunately for him, the public, which was content to read of foreign people and foreign scenes in novels, insisted in briefer narratives on native themes and native authors. Many hard things have been said of the annual and the lady's book, and harder things still of the magazine which succeeded them in the public favour; but it can scarcely be denied that the rich abundance of short stories that were produced in the nineteenth century was directly occasioned by the opportunity which these periodicals afforded. In America they gave rise to a school of writers so brilliant and so fertile that some persons, unacquainted with the history of literature, have claimed that the short story is an American invention. That is not so; but it may very well be admitted that in none of the countries of Europe has this form of fiction been so assiduously cultivated as it has been in the United States; nor have its methods, technique and possibilities been elsewhere more attentively studied. The *North American Review* in 1829 looked upon the brief narrative as a literary toy and encouraged it only because it would prepare American authors 'for nobler and greater exertions'. But the event has proved that it could be an end in itself. Many writers have found in it so adequate a means of expression that they have been content to write nothing else. Nor need it be forgotten that the American short story has on more than one occasion profoundly influenced the practice of short-story writers in other countries.

III

It did not seem unreasonable then, when I set out to show the development of the short story, to start with the nineteenth century. The first piece I chose was Sir Walter Scott's *The Two Drovers*, because it began my anthology with a great name and it had several qualities that I thought a good story should possess. But when I embarked upon the serious reading that my aim involved I made a most inconvenient discovery. I began with Washington Irving whose tales I had not read since I was a boy. He wrote them in a style which is now old-fashioned, and he had the mannerisms of his period; he did not attach importance, as have later authors, to the dramatic value of his theme, and he was inclined to talk, though very pleasantly, about his characters, rather than let them by dialogue and action disclose themselves; but when you have made allowances for all that, when you take them as stories apart from the telling, you can hardly fail to see how modern they really are. Of course Chekhov, if he had written *Rip Van Winkle*, would have written it very differently, but it is a story he might quite well have penned. The most astonishing thing in it is that the hero's strange experience has so little effect either on him or on the people of the village to which after his long sleep he returns. The incident is queer and affords a topic for the village gossip, but that is all. I think the truth and humour of this would have greatly pleased the Russian writer. And *The Stout Gentleman*, the second of Irving's tales that I have chosen for this collection, is as modern as it can be. Katherine Mansfield might easily have written it. I could not escape the conclusion that the short story which was written at the beginning of my period was as finished, well constructed, sophisticated and accomplished as any that were written during the last ten years.

When the nineteenth century was young, men had fewer ways

of amusing their leisure than they have now and were not displeased if their fiction moved at a deliberate pace; they accepted
without reluctance a dilatory exposition and a sauntering
digressiveness. Writers still under the influence of the prose of
Queen Anne wrote with greater elaboration than is now esteemed.
Now everyone reads newspapers every day, one or more, and the
reading public has grown to demand succinctness and a graphic
way of putting things; the authors of short stories, newspaper
readers themselves and often writers for the newspapers, have
adopted the style that is in the air; and the elegant period of
Washington Irving, the stately phrase of Hawthorne, are time-
worn. But idiom changes; fashions come and go. The modern
short story with its lack of ornament may well seem bare to a
succeeding generation, and the colloquial manner which is the
mode of the day may easily give way to a more formal style. The
more I read the more was it forced upon my notice that in essentials
the short story has changed little; what was a good story at the
beginning of the nineteenth century is a good story today. I could
not in face of this continue with the instructive intention with
which I had started. I was obliged to relinquish my aim of showing
the same sort of development in the brief narration as the biologist
can show you in the development of the horse. It has been a disappointment to me. Notwithstanding, in the course of reading a
vast number of stories written during the last century I have learnt
a good deal about the form. It is this, and no more, that I can
impart to the reader if he will have the patience to follow me
through the remainder of this introduction.

IV

I have had to abandon some of the notions I held before. The
first of these concerns the nature of the short story. Now I should
warn the reader at once that a writer treating of the art he pursues is

biassed. He very naturally thinks his own practice best. He writes as he can, and as he must, because he is a certain sort of man; he has his own parts, and his own idiosyncrasy, so that he sees things in a manner peculiar to himself, and he gives his vision the form that is forced upon him by his nature. He requires a singular vigour of mind to sympathize with work that is antagonistic to all his instincts. One should be on one's guard when one reads a novelist' criticisms of other people's novels. He is apt to find that excellent which he is aiming at himself and he is likely to see little merit in qualities that he does not himself possess. One of the best books on the novel that has been published in recent years is by an admirable writer who has never in his life been able to devise a plausible story. I was not surprised to find that he held in small esteem the novelists whose great gift is that they can lend a thrilling verisimilitude to the events they relate. I do not blame him for this. Tolerance is a very good quality in a man: if it were commoner, the world of today would be a more agreeable place to live in than it is; but I am not so sure that it is so good in a writer. For what in the long run has the writer to give you? Himself. It is well that he should have breadth of vision, for life in all its extent is his province; but he must see it not only with his own eyes, he must apprehend it with his own nerves, his own heart and his own bowels; his knowledge is partial, of course, but it is distinct, because he is himself and not somebody else. His attitude is definite and characteristic. If he really feels that any other point of view is as valid as his own, he will hardly hold his own with energy and is unlikely to present it with force. It is commendable that a man should see that there are two sides to a question; but the writer face to face with the art he practises (and his view of life is of course part of his art) can only attain this standpoint by an effort of ratiocination: in his blood and his bones he feels that it is not six of one and half a dozen of the other, but twelve on his side and on the other zero. This unreasonableness would be most unfortunate if writers were few, or

if the influence of one were so great as to compel the rest to conformity; but there are thousands of us. Each one of us has his little
communication to make, a restricted one, and from all these
communications the readers can choose, according to their own
inclinations and their own experience of life, what suits them.

I have said all this to clear the ground. I like best the sort of story
I can myself write. This is the sort of story that many people have
written well, but no one more admirably than Maupassant, so I
cannot do better, to show exactly what its nature is, than to discuss
one of his most famous productions, *The Necklace*. At the base of it
is an anecdote. It relates an incident which is curious, striking and
original. But of course it is much more than an anecdote, for when
you know this you can read the story with as much interest as
before. The scene is set before you with brevity, as the medium
requires, but with clearness; and the persons concerned, the kind of
life they lead and their deterioration, are shown you with just the
amount of detail that is needed to make the circumstances of the
case plain. You are told everything that you should know about
them. From this appears the second excellence of this sort of story;
when you have read it to find out what happens you can read it
again for the cleverness of the telling. *The Necklace* is not from its
own standpoint perfect, for this kind of narrative should have a
beginning, a middle and an end; and when the end is reached the
whole story should have been told and you should neither wish nor
need to ask a further question. Your crossword is filled up. But in
this case Maupassant satisfied himself with an end that was ironic
and effective. The practical reader can hardly fail to ask himself,
what next? It is true that the unfortunate couple had lost their
youth and most of what makes life pleasant in the dreary years they
had passed saving money to pay for the lost necklace; but when
they discovered that it was worthless they might very well have
claimed the real one with which they had replaced it and then
found themselves in possession of a small fortune. In the aridity of

spirit to which their sacrifices had brought them, it might very well have seemed a satisfactory compensation. It is a tribute to Maupassant's skill that few readers remain so self-possessed that the objection occurs to them. This brings me to the third characteristic of this kind of story. The author does not copy life; he arranges it in order the better to interest, excite, and surprise. He demands from you a willing suspension of disbelief.

This has caused the sort of narrative with which I am now dealing to fall of late years into some discredit. People say that in real life things do not happen with this neatness; real life is an affair of broken threads and loose ends; to arrange them into a pattern falsifies. Such an author as Maupassant does not mind; he is not aiming at a transcription of life, but at a dramatization of it. He is willing to sacrifice plausibility to effect, and the test is whether he can get away with it: if he has so shaped the incidents he describes and the persons concerned in them that you are conscious of the violence he has put on them, he has failed. But that he sometimes fails is no argument against the method. I am disposed to think that the desire to tell stories and to listen to them is inherent in the human race. At some periods readers exact a close adherence to the facts of life as they know them—it is then that realism is in fashion; at others, indifferent to this, they ask for the strange, the unusual, the marvellous—these are periods that historians of literature call romantic; and then, so long as they are held, readers are willing to accept pretty well anything. They are willing to accept *Sinbad the Sailor* and *Monsieur Beaucaire*. In fiction probability changes with the inclinations of the time; it is what you can get your readers to swallow. No one has stated the canons of the kind of story which I am now discussing with more precision than Edgar Allan Poe. But for its length I would quote in full his review of Hawthorne's *Twice-Told Tales*; it says everything that is to be said on the matter. It is, however, so well known that I can content myself with a short extract.

A skilful literary artist has constructed a tale. If wise, he has not fashioned his thoughts to accommodate his incidents: but having conceived, with deliberate care, a certain unique or single effect to be brought out, he then invents such incidents—he then combines such effects as may best aid him in establishing this pre-conceived effect. If his very initial sentence tend not to the out-bringing of this effect, then he has failed in his first step. In the whole composition there should be no word written, of which the tendency, direct or indirect, is not to the pre-established design. And by such means, with such care and skill, a picture is at length painted which leaves in the mind of him who contemplates it with a kindred art, a sense of the fullest satisfaction. The idea of the tale has been presented unblemished, because undisturbed....

With this declaration to help one I think it is possible to frame a definition of what Poe meant by a good short story: it is a piece of fiction, dealing with a single incident, material or spiritual, that can be read at a sitting; it is original, it must sparkle, excite or impress; and it must have unity of effect or impression. It should move in an even line from its exposition to its close.

V

But as I continued to read, I could not but grow conscious of the fact that there are a great many excellent stories which by these canons would have to be condemned. Now the critic does not prescribe laws for the artist; he takes note of his common practice and from this deduces rules; but when an original talent breaks them, the critic, though he may jib like the devil, in the end is forced to change his rules to accommodate the novelty. It is evident that there are other ways than Poe's of writing a good story.

People grow tired even of good things. They want change. To take an example from another art: domestic architecture during the Georgian era reached a rare perfection; the houses that were built then were good to look at and comfortable to live in. The rooms were spacious, airy and well proportioned. You would have thought people would be content with such houses for ever. But no. The romantic era approached; they wanted the quaint, the fanciful and the picturesque; and the architects, not unwilling, built them what they wanted. It is hard to invent such a story as Poe wrote and, as we know, even he, in his small output, more than once repeated himself. There is a good deal of trickiness in a narrative of this kind, and when, with the appearance and immediate popularity of the monthly magazine, the demand for such narratives became great, authors were not slow to learn the tricks. Craftsmen rather than artists, in order to make their stories effective they forced upon them a conventional design and presently deviated so far from plausibility in their delineation of life that their readers rebelled. They grew weary of stories written to a pattern they knew only too well. They demanded greater realism. Now to copy life has never been the artist's business. If you look at the painting and sculpture of the past you cannot but be surprised to see how little the great artists have occupied themselves with an exact rendering of what they saw before them. We are apt to think that the distortions of the plastic artists have imposed upon their materials, best illustrated in the cubists of yesterday, are an invention of our own times. That is not so. From the beginnings of Western painting artists have sacrificed verisimilitude to the effects they sought. If El Greco gave an extravagant length to the figures he painted, it was surely not because he thought human beings, even though saintly, looked like that, but because he wanted to get on canvas an idea in his mind's eye. It is the same with fiction. Not to go far back, take Poe; it is incredible that he should have thought human beings spoke in the way he made his characters speak: if he put into their mouths dialogue that seems to us so unreal, it must be because he thought it suited the kind of story he was telling and helped him to achieve the deliberate purpose which we know he had in view. Artists have only affected naturalism when it was borne in upon them that they had gone so far from life that a return was necessary, and then they have set themselves to copy it as exactly as they could, not as an end in itself, but as a salutary discipline.

In the short story naturalism in the nineteenth century came into fashion in reaction to a romanticism that had become tedious. One after the other writers attempted to portray life with unflinching veracity. 'I have never truckled,' said Frank Norris, 'I never took off the hat to fashion and held it out for pennies. By God! I told them the Truth. They liked it or they didn't like it. What had that to do with me? I told them the Truth, I knew it for the Truth then, and I know it for the Truth now.' (These are brave words. But it is hard to tell what the truth is; it is not necessarily the opposite of what you know to be a lie.) Writers of this school looked upon life with less partial eyes than those of the generation that had preceded them; they were less sugary and less optimistic, more violent and more direct; their dialogue was more natural and they chose their characters from a world that since the days of Defoe writers of fiction had somewhat neglected; but they made no innovations in technique. So far as the essentials of the short story are concerned they were content with the old models. The effects they pursued were still those that had been pursued by Poe; they used the formula he had laid down. Their merit proves its value; their artificiality exposes its weakness.

But there was a country in which the formula had little prevailed. In Russia they had been writing for a couple of generations stories of quite another order; and when the fact forced itself upon the attention both of readers and of authors that the kind of story that had so long found favour was grown tediously mechanical, it was discovered that in that country there was a body of writers who had made of the short story something new and vital. I would not offer it as a dogmatic statement but merely as a suggestion that the inventor of the Russian story as we know it was Tolstoy. In *The*

Death of Iván Ilých, which the reader will find in this volume, there is a great deal more than the germ of all the Russian stories that have been written since. It comprehends all the merits and all the defects of the Russian story.

It is singular that it took so long for this variety of the brief narrative, not to reach the Western world, for the stories of Turgenev were read in French translations when the Goncourts were writing their *Journal,* but to have any effect on it. About 1905 I was in Paris, where Arnold Bennett was then living. He was widely read in modern literature and was always alert for anything new within the field of his interests. He knew the work of Tolstoy and Turgenev, and his admiration for it, though discriminating, was great; but I do not think that he found in it anything that was personally important to him as a writer. It was another matter when he read Chekhov; in him he found something that very definitely affected him. A writer of short stories himself, he saw in the Russian's impressive achievement new life for an exhausted form. Since then the prestige of the Russian writers in general and of Chekhov in particular, has been immense. It has to a large extent transformed the composition and the appreciation of short stories. Critical readers turn away with indifference from the story which is technically known as well made, and the writers who produce it still, for the delectation of the great mass of the public, are little considered. The stories that Maupassant wrote in France, Rudyard Kipling in England, and Bret Harte in America have come to be regarded with some disdain.

VI

To write a story in accordance with the principles laid down by Edgar Allan Poe is not so easy as some think. It requires intelligence, not perhaps of a very high order, but of a special kind; it requires a sense of form and no small power of invention. But it is plain that this manner of story no longer carries conviction. The modern story fulfils a spiritual need in the modern reader which the old story cannot satisfy. The technique and the outlook of the writers of today differ a good deal from those of the masters of the nineteenth century; but before I go into this I must mention a circumstance that has forced itself upon my attention and that has caused me a certain perplexity; this is that so many of these stories might have been written by the same hand. It looks as though there were something in the method of the modern short story that submerges the personality of the author. The stories of Henry James, of Maupassant and of Chekhov could only have been written by themselves. You may not like the personality of these authors, but there it is, manifest to the grossest sense, in their every page. For my part I have always thought that just this, the personality of the creator, was what gave a work of art its lasting interest; it does not matter if it is a slightly absurd one, as with Henry James, a somewhat vulgar one, as with Maupassant, or a grey, melancholic one, as with Chekhov: so long as he can present it, distinct and idiosyncratic, his work has life. The short-story writers of our time seem to lack this curious power. Violent though they often are, hard, ruthless and devoid of sentimentality, they seldom manage to impress their special individuality upon their work. They are communal writers. They remind one of the decorative painters in the eighteenth century who painted flower pieces to put over doors or let into panels above the chimneypiece; it is a pleasant art, but its merit owes more to a period than to a personal gift.

The writers of the present time, unless I am mistaken, are more interested in social circumstances, in the injustice of modern conditions, in the relation of persons to their environment, in short, than in their relations to one another. The result of this is that they are likely to suffer from a certain shortage of material. If you know all about a sawmill, for instance, if you have yourself worked in one, you can probably write a very good story about it, even two or three; but you cannot go on writing stories about sawmills indefinitely; presently you will have said all you can on the subject, and then you are obliged to look for some other environment. You are lucky if you can find one about which you can learn to write with first-hand knowledge. It is a grave handicap that these specialist writers, of which there are so many nowadays, labour under; they exhaust their subjects, and, as we know, either go on writing the same old story to the weariness of their readers, or lapse into silence. The only subject that is inexhaustible is man. You can go on writing all your life and touch no more than the fringe of it. The difficulty of the writer who eschews a plot—and a plot, I should add, is no more than the pattern that is imposed upon the conduct of the various persons with whom you are dealing—in favour of a narration of the circumstances offered by a certain environment is that, getting nearer and nearer to life as we know it is lived, avoiding surprise, thrill, unexpected yet logical accident, which are the essential characteristics of the formal story, he has nothing to offer the reader that the narrator of actual facts cannot give him with greater force. He has ceased to be a writer of fiction; he has become a reporter. To prove this point I have printed at the end of this anthology a piece from a collection of true accounts of events written by the persons who took part in them. They are so good, so complete, so vivid that the candid reader can hardly fail to admit that they are as well worth reading as many short stories. And the fact that he knows they are true gives them an added point.

It is the death of the short story if it can be beaten at its own game by the naked truth. If the short story is to be a work of art it must be more than that. It will not do to say that the story-teller selects. The writers of this volume of true stories (it is called *Life in the United States* and is published by Scribners) have also selected: from the mass of their experience they have taken occasions that seemed to them significant and their attitude towards life has influenced their choice. They too have had an emotional reaction to the circumstances they describe. It happens to be a different one from those that chiefly affect modern writers, but I cannot bring myself to think it less admirable. It is fortitude. Modern writers are mostly moved by pity and anger; indeed pity is the fashionable literary emotion of our day. It is that for which a novelist is most praised. Critics have even found it in Chekhov, though the readers of his own time often complained that his objectivity was such that you could not tell from his stories where his sympathies lay. Now everyone knows that the world is in a bad way, liberty is dead or dying, poverty, relentless exploitation of labour, cruelty, injustice are everywhere. There is good cause for anger and pity; but they are unprofitable emotions unless they lead you to some effort. They are despicable when, satisfied that you have the generosity to feel them, you will not get busy to change the conditions that have aroused them. It is not for nothing that the tender Spinoza called pity womanish. In our small contemporary world of writers and readers it is too often a balm we apply to our wounded souls in order that we may spare ourselves the inconvenience of action. The writer's business is not to pity, nor to rage, but to understand.

VII

At the beginning of this introduction I called the reader's attention to the fact that writers are more likely to write stories when they can get a public for them. The great flowering of the art during the nineteenth century is due to the popularity of the magazines. As we know, they began to prosper round about the forties and their success finally killed the decaying annuals and keepsakes which at an earlier period had given writers their only opportunity. I suppose that this success reached its culmination during the first third of the present century. Never was there a greater demand for short stories, never were higher prices paid for them, and never was there a larger number of writers to write them.

But the vogue of the magazine, I suspect, is waning. People spend an increasing part of their leisure in athletic exercises, they golf, play tennis, motor and swim; they have the cinema to go to and the gramophone to listen to; they have the radio. Cheaper and cheaper books, of a size convenient for the pocket, offer reading matter that more satisfactorily supplies present needs. One can hardly suppose that the magazines will be displaced by some other form of periodical as the magazines displaced the annuals that once flourished so luxuriantly, but it is at least not unlikely that the magazines will change their character and so cease to offer an outlet to the writer of short stories. Already editors, disturbed by their falling circulations and thinking that in the distressed condition of the world their readers demand more solid fare than fiction, are giving more space to articles of an informative character. But I cannot believe that people will lose their desire to listen to stories. As I said before, that seems to me a desire inherent in the human race. It is not my business to prophesy, the world is sufficiently full of prophets, mostly, I am afraid, of evil; but it is at least not absurd to suggest that this need may well be satisfied by the radio. It may be that listeners will take the place of readers and that those who want the entertainment of the short story will be content to hear it over the air. Then the art will have gone full circle. The short story started with the tale told by the hunter round the fire in the cave which was the dwelling of primitive man, and, having run its long long course, will then return to its origins. The teller of tales, sitting before his microphone, will narrate his story to an immense crowd of unseen listeners.

But if this happens it is hard to believe that he will have an attentive audience if he tells stories that depend on atmosphere, if he tells stories that are sketchy or digressive, stories of implication, or stories whose meaning is obscure. One can but suppose that his stories will have to be direct, gripping, surprising and dramatic. They will have to move swiftly in one unbroken line from the beginning that arouses interest to the end that satisfies the curiosity that has been excited. They will in a word have to resemble more closely the stories of Maupassant than the stories of Chekhov. But that is not yet. Tolstoy, Chekhov and many another writer either influenced by them or, like Sherwood Anderson, arriving at a similar form by native idiosyncrasy, have enriched literature with a number of pieces the merit of which is great; and if these compositions will not fit into the definition of a short story which may be deduced from the formula so well stated by Poe, then the definition must be changed to include them. I would now offer a very simple one. I should define a short story as a piece of fiction that has unity of impression and that can be read at a single sitting. I should be inclined to say that the only test of its excellence is that it interests. It is with this principle in mind that I have chosen the stories in this volume.

VIII

There is a certain amount of fiction that it becomes every well-bred man to have read; it belongs to the culture of the world, and so far as culture is a part of knowledge it must be regarded as essential to everyone's education. But there is not much of it. I think a bookcase that held twenty books would be large enough to contain all the works of fiction that it would leave a man spiritually poorer not to have read. This bookcase would contain *Don Quixote, Wilhelm Meister, Pride and Prejudice, Le Rouge et le Noir, Le Père Goriot, Madam Bovary, War and Peace, David Copperfield, The Brothers Karamazov* and *À la Recherche du Temps Perdu;* but I am not sure that it would contain any short stories. For the short story is a minor art, and it must content itself with moving, exciting and amusing the reader. There are a hundred stories in this book, and I do not think there is a single one that will fail to do at least one of these things, but also I do not think that there is any that will give the reader that thrill, that rapture, that fruitful energy which great art can produce. The most important short-story writers of the nineteenth century were not men who had it in them to achieve such effects. They had talent and they were artists; but Maupassant had some commonness in his nature, and Henry James, who took his calling with such an admirable seriousness, was defeated by a peculiar triviality of soul; Chekhov was neither trivial nor common, but as is evident when on occasion he indulges in general reflection, his mental capacity was mediocre. None of these writers impresses you by the power and fullness of his personality as you are impressed when you read Balzac or Tolstoy.

It is wise then to read short stories for the entertainment they provide. It is unreasonable to ask of them more than they can give you. But it would be foolish to despise them on that account.

IX

But entertainment is a personal thing. Just as there is no obligation to read fiction there is no obligation to like it. The critics often try to browbeat us plain men by telling us that we ought to like this, that and the other, and they call us hard names if we will not do as they bid. There is no ought in the matter. The critic can point out the exellences he sees, and since they may have escaped your attention, in this he does you a service; but when he condemns you because you do not care for the work he admires he is foolish. The history of criticism shows that critics are often mistaken. The only thing that really matters to you is what a work of art says to you. Even if the consensus of educated opinion is against you, you should be unperturbed. However great a work is commonly agreed to be, if it bores you, to read it is futile; it must entertain *you*, or so far as you are concerned it is valueless.

It is on this principle that I have chosen the stories in this volume. I have been influenced neither by the reputation nor by the common opinion that ascribed them merit. These stories are stories

I like. I cannot hope that all my readers will like them all. To do so they would have had to have my particular experience of life and to share my prejudices and my interests. I do not claim that they are the best stories that have been written during the last century; they are the stories amongst all those that I have read that have interested me most.

When my reading forced me to broaden my definition of a short story so that it included almost anything approaching fiction that was not of excessive length, I was able to insert a number of pieces that, if I had adhered to Poe's canon, I should have felt bound to omit. I was able to put in Flaubert's *A Simple Heart*, which he himself called a short story, but which is really a short novel. Such unity of impression as it has depends only on the fact that the interest is concentrated on a single person. But it is only as short as it is and no longer, because in comparatively few pages Flaubert was able to say all there was to say about the straightforward, limited character he set out to describe. It is a moving tale, and it is somewhat important in the history of fiction because it has given rise to numberless studies, sometimes in the form of the short story, sometimes in that of the novel, of women of the servant class. It is besides a story which, I think, no one can read without gaining a sympathetic understanding of the French nature, with its great virtues and pardonable failings; for all France is there. This looseness of definition has also made it possible for me to put in Joseph Conrad's excellent *Typhoon* rather than one of his briefer pieces. Conrad rarely wrote anything but short stories, though, being a writer of an exuberant verbosity, he often made them as long as most novels. He needed sea-room. He had little sense of concision. A theme with him was like the stem of a cauliflower; it great and grew under his active pen until, all its branches headed with succulent flowers, it became a very fine but somewhat monstrous plant. *Typhoon* shows all his power and none of his weakness. It is a tale of the sea, which he knew better than he knew the land, and it is concerned with men, whom he knew better than he knew women. These sailor chaps are a little simpler than most of us now think human beings really are, but they live. *Typhoon* narrates an incident, which was a thing Conrad could do with mastery, and the subject gives him opportunity for his wonderful and vivid descriptions of the phenomena of nature. My final definition has even allowed me to adorn my pages with E. M. Forster's *Mr and Mrs Abbey's Difficulties*, which is a little bit of literary history written in the guise of fiction; it has a surprise ending that would have delighted the mind of O. Henry. It is a moving and exquisite piece, written in such admirable English that it might well find a place in any manual for teaching the language.

X

When I abandoned my ambitious project of showing the development of the short story from the beginning of the nineteenth century, I was able to do something that caused me a considerable measure of relief. I was able, to wit, to omit a number of stories that under my original scheme I should have had to insert. There are few works of art that preserve their vitality from age to age. Even they have their ups and downs. For long periods they lie comatose like hibernating animals, and then, as a new generation finds something in them to satisfy its new wants, they take on a new lease of life. Thus, the archaic sculpture of Greece, the paintings of the school of Siena, after being neglected for a long period, in our own day, with its relish for the primitive, its taste for suggestion rather than for downright statement, have been found to possess a troubling beauty that corresponds to our high-strung needs as does neither the resolute achievement of Phidias nor the opulent splendour of Titian. And in literature when romanticism, fired by the discovery of the Middle Ages, rejected the measure and reason of the eighteenth century, when the sensitiveness of the human soul first recoiled from the mechanization of life, writers found inspiration and readers refreshment in books like Malory's *Morte d'Arthur* and Froissart's *Chronicles*.

But there are many works of art that live their lives and die. They have had something to say to the generation that saw their birth, but with the passing of that generation lose their import. They may still have an interest for the student or the historian, but they are no longer works of art. They can no longer give its specific thrill. They have had a long and honourable career, and there is no cause for their authors to turn uneasily in their graves; they have fulfilled their purpose and may now rest in peace. But I have not wished any of the stories in this collection to be looked upon as museum pieces. I have inserted nothing that does not seem to me to have a living interest. That is why I have chosen mostly stories that are contemporary, or almost so. I dare say that in fifty years many of them will seem as old-fashioned as the stories of fifty years ago that I have discarded. That is not my affair. Now they have the merit of actuality. It is this merit that enables us to compete with the great authors of the past. Otherwise who would read us? The bad, the mediocre, have long since been forgotten and only the best has remained. Who would bother to read a modern novel if *Roxana*, *Tom Jones* and *Middlemarch* had just that appeal that we can give to our works because we can dress our characters in the clothes of today and make them speak the language of our time?

I hesitated a good deal when I considered the tales of Nathaniel Hawthorne. He was a distinguished and important writer of short stories, and he had a considerable influence both on his contemporaries and on his successors. I read him and reread him. It seemed to me that his stories had lost the life they once assuredly had. In order to find an interest in them now, one has to bethink oneself of the circumstances of his life, the period he lived in and the effect on him of the romantic revival which at the time swept Europe like a tidal wave. Historians of literature claim that *Rappucini's Daughter* is a masterpiece. To me it seems stuff and nonsense. I am only too willing to suspend my disbelief, but that is a mouthful that I really cannot swallow. I think the story of Hawthorne's that has most life in it today is *The Artist of the Beautiful*, for that is the story of every creator in relation to his creation and to the world without; it is universal, but alas, so diffuse and so repetitive that its power is sadly diminished. To my mind Hawthorne's best story is the story of his own life, and that you may read in that enchanting book, *The Flowering of New England*, by Van Wyck Brooks. It is on account of this that I could not bring myself to omit Hawthorne from this anthology, and so I have chosen *The Gray Champion*. It has thrill and is informed with a noble patriotism which you will have to hunt far and wide to find represented in the short story. Now that liberty in so many quarters of the world is immured and fettered, it is more than ever necessary to cherish an expression of its beauty.

I had no such hesitations when I came to read the stories that depended for their interest on local colour and dialect. Their vogue started in the seventies and lasted for many years. The manner reached its greatest excellence in the work of Mary Wilkins Freeman. She had grace, feeling and sincerity. I am sure her stories were very good in their day, but their day is past; the sun has faded their delicate tints and they are now somewhat namby-pamby. It is the namby-pamby which till quite recently has been the bane of the English short story. This failing has made it difficult for me to find any stories written in the last third of the century in England that seemed to me to have merit. The writers of that period were gentle, urbane and sentimental. They closed their eyes to such aspects of life as they did not wish to see. English writers on the whole have not taken kindly to the art of the short story. They have felt the novel more congenial to their idiosyncrasy, for the English, though in conversation often tongue-tied, when they take a pen in their hands are inclined to prolixity. They have no natural instinct for succinctness, which is indispensable to the short story, nor a sense of form, which is essential to its significance. So the diffuseness of the national temper has found its most satisfactory literary expression in the long, unwieldy, shapeless novels of the Victorian Era which still remain the country's outstanding contribution to the world's fiction. English writers find it difficult to be brief without being trivial, and for the most part they have looked upon the short story as a thing of no great matter to be thrown off in their spare time in order to earn a few useful guineas without much expenditure of effort. I know only two English writers who have taken the short story as seriously as it must be taken if excellence is to be achieved, Rudyard Kipling, namely, and Katherine Mansfield. Miss Mansfield had a small, derivative, but exquisite talent; and her shorter pieces—for she had insufficient power to deal with a theme that demanded a solid gift of construction—are admirable. Rudyard Kipling stands in a different category. He alone among English writers of the short story can bear comparison with the masters of France and Russia.

Though Rudyard Kipling captured the attention of the public when first he began to write, and has retained a firm hold on it ever since, there was a time when educated opinion was somewhat disdainful of him. He was identified with an imperialism which events made obnoxious to many sensible persons. Certain characteristics of his style, which at first had seemed fresh and amusing, became irksome to readers of fastidious taste. But that time is past. I think there would be few now to deny that he was a wonderful, varied and original teller of tales. He had a fertile invention and to a supreme degree the gift of narrating incident in a surprising and dramatic fashion. His influence for a while was great on his fellow-writers, but perhaps greater on his fellow-men, who led in one way or another the sort of life he dealt with. When one travelled in the East it was astonishing how often one came across men who had modelled themselves on the creatures of his fancy. Critics say that Balzac's characters were more true of the generation that followed him than of that which he purported to describe; I know from my own experience that twenty years after Kipling wrote his first important stories there were men scattered about the outlying parts of the world who would never have been just what they were if he had not written them. He not only created characters, he created men. Rudyard Kipling is generally supposed to have rendered the British people conscious of their Empire, but that is a political achievement with which I have not here to deal; what is significant to my present standpoint is that in his discovery of the exotic story he opened a new and fruitful field to writers. This is the story, the scene of which is set in some country little known to the majority of readers, and which deals with the reactions upon the white man of his sojourn in an alien land and the effect which contact with peoples of another race has upon him. Subsequent writers have treated this subject in their different ways, but Rudyard Kipling was the first to blaze the trail through this new-found country, and no one has invested it with a more romantic glamour, no one has made it more exciting and no one has presented it so vividly and with such a wealth of colour. He wrote many stories of other kinds, but none in my opinion which surpassed these. He had, like every writer that ever lived, his short-comings, but remains notwithstanding the best short-story writer that England can boast of.

XI

Now I wish to speak of Henry James. Greatness is a quality which is loosely ascribed to writers, and it is well to be cautious in one's use of the word, but I think no one will quarrel with me when I say that Henry James is the most distinguished literary figure that America has produced. He was a voluminous writer of short stories. Though he lived so long in England, and indeed in the end was naturalized, he remained an American to the last. I cannot feel that he ever knew the English as an Englishman instinctively knows them, and for that reason I have chosen for this book an American, rather than an English, story. The characters ring more true to life; his English people are more Jamesian than English.

It is impossible, I imagine, for anyone who knew Henry James in the flesh to read his stories dispassionately. He got the sound of his voice into every line he wrote, and you accept the convoluted style of his later work, his long-windedness and his mannerisms, because they are part and parcel of the charm, benignity and amusing pomposity of the man you remember. He was, if not a great, a remarkable man, so the reader will perhaps forgive me if in what follows I do not confine myself precisely to the consideration of his stories, which in this introduction is my only concern. The number of persons who knew him is growing smaller year by year, and such recollections of him as they have must be worth preservation. I do not foresee that I shall ever have a more suitable occasion than this to put my own on record. I knew Henry James for many years, but I was never more than an acquaintance of his. I am not sure that he was fortunate in his friends. They were disposed to be possessive, and they regarded one author's claim to be in the inner circle of his confidence with no conspicuous amiability. Like a dog with a bone, each was inclined to growl when another showed an inclination to dispute his exclusive right to the precious object of his admiration. The reverence with which they treated him was of no great service to him. They seemed to me, indeed, sometimes a trifle silly: they whispered to one another with delighted giggles that Henry James privately stated that the article in *The Ambassador* the nature of which he had left in polite obscurity and on whose manufacture the fortune of the widow Newsome was founded, was in fact a chamber pot. I did not find this so amusing as they did. But I must admit I was often doubtful of the quality of Henry James's humour. When someone transplants himself from his own country to another he is more likely to assimilate the defects of its inhabitants than their virtues. The England in which Henry James lived was excessively class-conscious and I think it is to this that must be ascribed the somewhat disconcerting attitude that he adopted in his writings to those who were so unfortunate as to be of humble origin. Unless he were an artist, by choice a writer, it seemed to him more than a little ridiculous that anyone should be under the necessity of earning his living. The death of a member of the lower classes could be trusted to give him a good chuckle. I think this attitude was emphasized by the fact that, himself of exalted lineage, he could not have dwelt long in England without becoming aware that to the English one American was very like another. He saw compatriots, on the strength of a fortune acquired in Michigan or Ohio, received with as great cordiality as though they belonged to the eminent families of Boston and New York; and in self-defence somewhat exaggerated his native fastidiousness in social relations. I think it should be added that perhaps in England his more intimate associations were with persons who were not, to use the vulgar phrase, out of the top drawer; but out of a drawer just below. Their own position was not so secure that they could ignore it.

Two of my meetings with Henry James stand out in my memory. One was in London at a performance of a Russian play by the Stage Society. I think it must have been *The Cherry Orchard*, but after so many years I cannot be certain. It was very badly acted. I found myself sitting with Henry James and Mrs Clifford, the widow of a celebrated mathematician and herself a well-known novelist; and we could none of us make head or tail of it. The intervals were long, and there was ample opportunity for conversation. The play disconcerted Henry James, and he set out to explain to us how antagonistic to his French sympathies was this Russian incoherence. Lumbering through his tortuous phrases, he hesitated now and again in search of the exact word to express his dismay; but Mrs Clifford had a quick and agile mind, she knew the word he was looking for and every time he paused immediately supplied it. But this was the last thing he wanted. He was too well mannered to protest, but an almost imperceptible expression on his face betrayed his irritation, and obstinately refusing the word she offered, he laboriously sought another. The climax came when they began to discuss the actress who was playing the leading part. Henry James wanted to know to what class she belonged, and both Mrs Clifford and I knew exactly what in plain terms he wished to say. But that, he thought, would be tasteless, and so he wrapped up his meaning in an increasingly embarrassed flow of circumlocution till at last Mrs Clifford could bear it no longer and blurted out: 'Do you mean, is she a lady?' A look of real suffering crossed his face. Put so, the question had a vulgarity that outraged him. He pretended not to hear. He made a little gesture of desperation and said: 'Is she, *enfin*, what you'd call, if you were asked point-blank, if you were put with your back to the wall, is she a *femme du monde*?'

The second occasion I remember is when Henry James, his brother William having recently died, was staying at Cambridge, Massachusetts, with his sister-in-law. I happened to be in Boston, and Mrs James asked me to dinner. There were but the three of us; I can remember nothing of the conversation at table, but it seemed to me that Henry James was troubled in spirit; after dinner the widow left us alone in the dining room, and he told me that he had promised his brother to stay at Cambridge for, I think, six months after his death, so that if he found himself able to make a communication from beyond the grave there would be two sympathetic witnesses on the spot ready to receive it. I could not but reflect that Henry James was in such a state of nervousness that it would be difficult to place implicit confidence in any report he might make. His sensibility was so exasperated that he was capable of imagining anything. But hitherto no message had come, and the six months were drawing to their end.

When it was time for me to go, Henry James insisted on accompanying me to the corner where I could take the streetcar back to Boston. I protested that I was perfectly capable of getting there by myself, but he would not hear of it; this not only on account of the kindness and the great courtesy that were natural to him, but also because America seemed to him a strange and terrifying labyrinth in which without his guidance I was bound to get hopelessly lost. When we were on the way, by ourselves, he told me what his good manners had prevented him from saying before Mrs James, that he was counting the days that must elapse before, having fulfilled his promise, he could sail for the blessed shores of England. He yearned for it. There in Cambridge he felt himself forlorn. He was determined never again to set foot on the bewildering and unknown country that America was to him. It was then that he uttered the phrase which seemed to me so fantastic that I have always remembered it. 'I wander about those great empty streets of Boston,' he said, 'and I never see a living creature. I could not be more alone in the Sahara.' The streetcar hove in sight and Henry James was seized with agitation. He began waving frantically when it was still a quarter of a mile away. He was afraid it wouldn't stop, and he besought me to jump on with the greatest agility of which I was capable, for it would not pause for more than an instant, and if I were not very careful I might be dragged along, and if not killed, at least mangled and dismembered. I assured him that I was quite accustomed to getting on streetcars. Not American streetcars, he told me; they were of a savagery, an inhumanity, a ruthlessness beyond any conception. I was so infected by his anxiety that when the car pulled up and I leapt on, I had almost the sensation that I had had a miraculous escape from a fearful death. I saw him standing on his short legs in the middle of the road, looking after the car, and I felt that he was trembling still at my narrow shave.

When for this book I read, yet once again, the short stories of Henry James, I was troubled by the contrast offered by the triviality of so many of his themes and the elaboration of his treatment. He seems to have had no inkling that his subject might be too slight to justify so intricate a method. This is a fault that lessens one's enjoyment of some of his most famous tales. A world that has gone through the great war, that has lived through the troubled years that have followed it, can hardly fail to be impatient with events, persons and subtleties that seem so remote from life. Henry James had discernment, a generous heart and artistic integrity; but he applied his gifts to matters of no great import. He was like a man who should provide himself with all the impedimenta necessary to ascend Mount Everest in order to climb Primrose Hill. Let us not forget that here was a novelist who had to his hand one of the most stupendous subjects that any writer ever had the chance of dealing with, the rise of the United States from the small, provincial country that he knew in his youth to the vast and powerful commonwealth that it has become; and he turned his back on it to write about tea parties in Mayfair and country-house visits in the home shires. The great novelists, even in seclusion, have lived life passionately; Henry James was content to observe it from a window. But you cannot describe life unless you have partaken of it; nor, should your object be different, can you fantasticate upon it (as Balzac and Dickens did) unless you know it first. Something escapes you unless you have been an actor in the tragicomedy. Henry James was shy of the elementals of human nature. His heart was an organ subject to no serious agitation, and his interests were confined to persons of his own class. He failed of being a very great writer because his experience was inadequate and his sympathies were imperfect.

XII

Now I have little more to say. I have limited myself in this anthology to five countries, France, Germany, Russia, England and the United States. Scandinavia, Denmark especially, has produced stories of uncommon merit, and Italy, too, has several writers who should find a place in any anthology; but if I had inserted them, there seemed no reason why I should leave out Spain, Hungary, and half a dozen more. It would have made this book unwieldy. None of these countries, moreover, has produced the immense body of work that has been produced in the five countries from which I have chosen; nor has any of them (with the exception of Denmark with Hans Andersen) produced anything that could not be paralleled in them. At one time I used to buy modern pictures, and Rosenberg, the dealer, said to me: don't bother with any but the *chefs d'école*; their followers may have merits, but in the long run it is only the leaders that count. So far as short stories are concerned the *chefs d'école* are to be found in the countries whose works are represented in this volume.

The reader who glances at the table of contents will notice that I have chosen more stories from England and America than from France and Russia and Germany. This is not because I think they are better, but because the book is designed for American and English readers, and to them stories of their own writers will, I imagine, prove more interesting. Besides, however well a story is translated, it loses something in the process; it can never have the flavour it had and so it is not quite so good as it was in its own language. I have arranged the stories roughly in chronological order, but not so strictly as to prevent me from putting them in the order in which I thought they could be most agreeably read. I have sought to balance matter and manner, the serious and the gay, the short and the long, so that the reader should be led from story to story without tedium. I have mixed up the various countries in such a manner as I have thought would help me in this. The exception I have made is in the case of Russia. Russian stories are so singular, they have on the whole so slender a connection with occidental culture, that I feel they must be taken by themselves. One has to shift one's outlook on life, one's feelings on all manner of things, on to another plane, as it were, in order to get into a suitable relation with their authors. I have chosen those printed in this volume because there was in them at least some glimmering of form; but more particularly because they give a picture of an experiment in civilization to which none of us who have to live for some little time yet on this earth can be indifferent. Their authors are Soviet authors, now living in Russia; the lack of skill shown by most of them gives their stories a convincing character which, if they had known their business, might not have been so apparent. To my mind they show very strikingly how men and women have been living together in Russia in the recent past and how the conditions of existence have affected their attitude towards the elemental things of life and love and death which are the essential materials not only of poetry but of fiction. I should like to point out that in the humorous story called *The Knives*, the reader will find one that might have been written in any country in the world. It is foolish to generalize on a single instance, but this suggests to me that humour has a universal quality, so that it is at least possible that if it were more generally exercised among the nations there is a chance that the differences dividing us, and the discords that afflict us, might be in some measure mitigated.

Now I have but one more thing to say. I have left out stories by certain living writers who hold an honourable position in the world of letters. I have done so because I do not myself happen to like them. Their authors, should they chance to glance over this book, would be wrong to be offended with me. We can none of us expect to be liked by everybody, and when we realize that somebody has no fancy for us, we may be curious to know why but we have no right to be angry. There are doubtless excellent stories by writers of perhaps considerable talent that do not chance to please me. That does not in the least affect their merit. I would never claim that my taste is perfect; all I can claim is that in making such a selection as this the anthologist's taste is the only standard.

A Choice of Kipling's Prose

'INTRODUCTION'

(1952)

IN this essay it is my business to deal only with Rudyard Kipling's short stories. I am not concerned with his verse nor, except in so far as they sometimes directly affected his stories, with his political opinions.

In making a selection of them I have had to decide whether I should choose only those I most liked. In that case I should have chosen nearly all the Indian stories. For in them to my mind he was at his best. When he wrote stories about Indians and about the

British in India he felt himself at home and he wrote with an ease, a freedom, a variety of invention which gave them a quality which in stories in which the subject matter was different he did not always attain. Even the slightest of them are readable. They give you the tang of the East, the smell of the bazaars, the torpor of the rains, the heat of the sun-scorched earth, the rough life of the barracks in which the occupying troops were quartered, and the other life, so English and yet so alien to the English way, led by the officers, the Indian Civilians and the swarm of minor officials who combined to administer that vast territory.

A great many years ago, when Kipling was still at the height of his popularity, I used sometimes to meet Indian Civilians and professors at Indian universities who spoke of him with something very like contempt. That was partly due to an ignoble but natural jealousy. They resented it that this obscure journalist, of no social consequence, should have achieved world-wide renown. They protested that he did not know India. Which of them did? India is not a country, it is a continent. It is true that Kipling seems to have been intimately acquainted only with the North-West. Like any other sensible writer he placed the scene of his stories in the region he knew best. His Anglo-Indian critics blamed him because he had not dealt with this and that subject which they thought important. His sympathies lay with the Muslims rather than with the Hindus. He took but a very casual interest in Hinduism and the religion which has so deep-rooted an influence on the great mass of the teeming populations of India. There were qualities in the Muslims that aroused his admiration: he seldom spoke of the Hindus with appreciation. It never seems to have occurred to him that there were among them men of erudition, distinguished scientists and able philosophers. The Bengali, for instance, to him was a coward, a muddler, a braggart, who lost his head in an emergency and shirked responsibility. This is a pity, but it was Kipling's right, as it is of every author, to deal with the subjects that appealed to him.

But I felt that if in this volume I confined myself to Kipling's Indian stories I should not give the reader a fair impression of his varied talent. I have therefore included a few stories with an English setting which have been very widely admired.

It is not to my purpose to give more biographical details of Kipling's life than seem to me useful in my consideration of his short stories. He was born in 1865 at Bombay, where his father was Professor of Architectural Sculpture. When a little more than five his parents took him with his younger sister back to England and placed the two of them in a family where, owing to the unkindness and stupidity of the woman who looked after them, they were miserably unhappy. The wretched little boy was nagged, bullied and beaten. When his mother, after some years, once more came home she was deeply shocked by what she discovered and took the two children away. At the age of twelve Kipling was sent to a school at Westward Ho! It was called the United Services College and had been recently founded to provide education at a small cost for the sons of officers who were to be prepared to go into the army. There were about two hundred boys and they were herded together in a row of lodging-houses. Now, what the school was really like has nothing to do with me; I am only concerned with the picture Kipling has drawn of it in the work of fiction to which he gave the title *Stalky & Co*. A more odious picture of school life can seldom have been drawn. With the exception of the headmaster and the chaplain the masters are represented as savage, brutal, narrow-minded and incompetent. The boys, supposedly the sons of gentlemen, were devoid of any decent instincts. To the three lads with whom these stories deal Kipling gave the names of Stalky, Turkey and Beetle. Stalky was the ringleader. He remained Kipling's ideal of the gallant, resourceful, adventurous, high-spirited soldier and gentleman. Beetle was Kipling's portrait of himself. The three of them exercised their humour in practical jokes of a singular nastiness. Kipling has narrated them with immense gusto and it is only just to say that the stories are so brilliantly told that though it may give you gooseflesh to read them, when you have once begun you will read them to the end. I should not have dwelt on them at all if it were not plain to me that the influence Kipling was exposed to during the four years he spent at what he called 'the Coll' gained a hold on him which throughout his career he never outgrew. He was never quite able to rid himself of the impressions, the prejudices, the spiritual posture he then acquired. Indeed there is no sign that he wanted to. He retained to the end his relish for the rough and tumble, the ragging, the brutal horseplay of fourth-form schoolboys and their delight in practical jokes. It never seems to have occurred to him that the school was third-rate and the boys a rotten lot. In fact after visiting it many years later he wrote a charming account of it, in which he paid a glowing tribute to that harsh disciplinarian, his old headmaster, and expressed his gratitude for the great benefits he had received during the period he had spent under his care.

When Kipling was a little less than seventeen, his father, who was then curator of the museum at Lahore, got him a job as assistant editor of the English paper, *The Civil and Military Gazette*, which was published in that city, and he left school to return to India. This was in 1882. The world he entered was very different from the world we live in now. Great Britain was at the height of her power. A map showed in pink vast stretches of the earth's surface under the sovereignty of Queen Victoria. The mother country was immensely rich. The British were the world's bankers. British commerce sent its products to the uttermost parts of the earth, and their quality was generally acknowledged to be higher than those manufactured by any other nation. Peace reigned except for small punitive expeditions here and there. The army, though small, was confident (notwithstanding the reverse on Majuba Hill) that it could hold its own against any force that was likely to be brought against it. The British navy was the greatest in

389

the world. In sport the British were supreme. None could compete with them in the games they played, and in the classic races it was almost unheard-of that a horse from abroad should win. It looked as though nothing could ever change this happy state of things. The inhabitants of these islands of ours trusted in God, and God, they were assured, had taken the British Empire under his particular protection. It is true that the Irish were making a nuisance of themselves. It is true that the factory workers were underpaid and overworked. But that seemed an inevitable consequence of the industrialization of the country and there was nothing to do about it. The reformers who tried to improve their lot were regarded as mischievous troublemakers. It is true that the agricultural labourers lived in miserable hovels and earned a pitiful wage, but the Ladies Bountiful of the landowners were kind to them. Many of them occupied themselves with their moral welfare, sent them beef tea and calves-foot jelly when they were ill and often clothes for their children. People said there always had been rich and poor in the world and always would be, and that seemed to settle the matter.

The British travelled a great deal on the Continent. They crowded the health resorts, Spa, Vichy, Homburg, Aix-les-Bains and Baden-Baden. In winter they went to the Riviera. They built themselves sumptuous villas at Cannes and Monte Carlo. Vast hotels were erected to accommodate them. They had plenty of money and they spent it freely. They felt that they were a race apart and no sooner had they landed at Calais than it was borne in upon them that they were now among natives, not of course natives as were the Indians or the Chinese, but—natives. They alone washed, and the baths that they frequently travelled with were a tangible proof that they were not as others. They were healthy, athletic, sensible, and in every way superior. Because they enjoyed their sojourn among the natives whose habits were so curiously un-English, because, though they thought them frivolous (the French), lazy (the Italians), stupid but funny (the Germans), with the kindness of heart natural to them, they liked them. And they in turn thought that these foreigners liked them. It never entered their heads that the courtesy which they received, the bows, the smiles, the desire to please were owing to their lavish spending, and that behind their backs the 'natives' mocked them for their uncouth dress, their gawkiness, their bad manners, their insolence, their silliness in letting themselves be consistently overcharged, their patronizing tolerance; and it required disastrous wars for it to dawn upon them how greatly they had been mistaken. The Anglo-Indian society into which Kipling was introduced when he joined his parents at Lahore shared to the full the prepossessions and the self-complacency of their fellow-subjects in Britain.

Since his short sight prevented him from playing games, Kipling had had the leisure at school to read a great deal and to write. The headmaster seems to have been impressed by the promise he showed and had the good sense to give him the run of his own library. He wrote the stories which he afterwards published in book form as *Plain Tales from the Hills* during such leisure as his duties as sub-editor of *The Civil and Military Gazette* allowed him. To me their chief interest is in the picture they give of the society with which he was dealing. It is a devastating one. There is no sign that any of the persons he wrote about took any interest in art, literature or music. The notion seems to have been prevalent that there was something fishy about a man who took pains to learn about things Indian. Of one character Kipling wrote: 'he knew as much about Indians as it is good for a man to know.' A man who was absorbed in his work appears to have been regarded with misgiving; at best he was eccentric, at worst a bore. The life described was empty and frivolous. The self-sufficiency of these people is fearful to contemplate. And what sort of people were they? They were ordinary middle-class people, who came from modest homes in England, sons and daughters of retired government servants and of parsons, doctors and lawyers. The men were empty-headed;

such of them as were in the army or had been to universities had acquired a certain polish; but the women were shallow, provincial and genteel. They spent their time in idle flirtation and their chief amusement seems to have been to get some man away from another woman. Perhaps because Kipling wrote in a prudish period which made him afraid of shocking his readers, perhaps from an innate disinclination to treat of sex, though in these stories there is a great deal of philandering, it very rarely led to sexual intercourse. Whatever encouragement these women gave the men whom they attracted, when it came to a showdown they drew back. They were, in short, what is described in English by a coarse hyphenated word, and in France, more elegantly, by *allumeuses*.

It is surprising that Kipling, with his quick mind and wonderful power of observation, with his wide reading, should have taken these people at their face value. He was, of course, very young. *Plain Tales from the Hills* was published when he was only twenty-two. It is perhaps natural that, coming straight from the brutalities of Westward Ho! to the unpretentious establishment of the curator of the Lahore museum, he should have been dazzled on his first acquaintance with a society that to his inexperienced eyes had glamour. So was the little bourgeois Marcel dazzled when he first gained admittance to the exclusive circle of Madame de Guermantes. Mrs Hauksbee was neither so brilliant nor so witty as Kipling would have us think. He reveals her essential drabness when he makes her compare a woman's voice to the grinding brakes of an underground train coming into Earl's Court station. We are asked to believe that she was a woman of fashion. If she had been she would never have gone to Earl's Court except to see an old nurse and then not by underground, but in a hansom cab.

But *Plain Tales from the Hills* is not only concerned with Anglo-Indian society. The volume contains stories of Indian life and stories of the soldiery. When you consider that they were written when their author was still in his teens or only just out of them they show an astonishing competence. Kipling said that the best of them were provided for him by his father. I think we may ascribe this statement to filial piety. I believe it to be very seldom that an author can make use of a story given to him ready made, as seldom indeed as a person in real life can be transferred to fiction just as he is and maintain an air of verisimilitude. Of course the author gets his ideas from somewhere, they don't spring out of his head like Pallas-Athene from the head of her sire in perfect panoply, ready to be written down. But it is curious how small a hint, how vague a suggestion, will be enough to give the author's invention the material to work upon and enable him in due course to construct a properly disposed story. Take, for instance, the later story, *The Tomb of his Ancestors*. It may very well have needed no more than such a casual remark from one of the officers Kipling had known at Lahore as: 'Funny chaps these natives are. There was a feller called So-and-So who was stationed up country among the Bhils, whose grandfather had kept them in order for donkeys' years and was buried there, and they got it into their thick heads that he was a reincarnation of the old man, and he could do anything he liked with them.' That would have been quite enough to set Kipling's vivid imagination to work upon what turned out to be an amusing and delightful tale. *Plain Tales from the Hills* is very uneven, as indeed Kipling's work always was. That I believe to be inevitable in a writer of short stories. It is a ticklish thing to write a short story and whether it is good or bad depends on more than the author's conception, power of expression, skill in construction, invention and imagination: it depends also on luck. So the clever Japanese, taking from his little pile of seed pearls, all to his eyes indistinguishable from one another, the first that comes to hand and inserting it into the oyster, cannot tell whether it will turn into a perfect, rounded pearl or a misshapen object neither of beauty nor of value. Nor is the author a good judge of his own work. Kipling had a high opinion of *The Phantom 'Rickshaw*. I think if he had been more sophisticated when he wrote it, it might have occurred to him that there was more to be said in extentuation of the man's behaviour than he apprehended. It is very unfortunate that you should fall out of love with a married woman with whom you have had an affair and fall in love with someone else and want to marry her. But such things happen. And when the woman won't accept the situation, but pursues you and waylays you and pesters you with tears and supplications it is not unnatural that at last you should grow impatient and lose your temper. Mrs Keith-Wessington is the most persistent *crampon* in fiction, for even after her death she continued to harry the wretched man in her phantom 'rickshaw. Jack Pansay deserves our sympathy rather than our censure. Because a story has been difficult to write an author may well think better of it than of a story that has seemed to write itself, sometimes there is a psychological error at the basis of it which he has not noticed, and sometimes he sees in the finished story what he saw in his mind's eye when he conceived it rather than what he has presented to the reader. But we should not be surprised that Kipling sometimes wrote stories which were poor, unconvincing or trivial; we should wonder rather that he wrote so many of such excellence. He was wonderfully various.

In the essay Mr T. S. Eliot wrote to preface his selection of Kipling's verse he seems to suggest that variety is not a laudable quality in a poet. I would not venture to dispute any opinion of Mr Eliot's on a question in which poetry is concerned, but though variety may not be a merit in a poet, it surely is in a writer of fiction. The good writer of fiction has the peculiarity, shared to a degree by all men, but in him more abundant, that he has not only one self, but is a queer mixture of several, or, if that seems an extravagant way of putting it, that there are several, often discordant aspects of his personality. The critics could not understand how the same man could write '*Brugglesmith*' and *Recessional*, and so accused him of insincerity. They were unjust. It was the self called Beetle who wrote *'Brugglesmith'* and the self called Yardley-Orde who wrote *Recessional*. When most of us look back on ourselves we can sometimes find consolation in believing that a self in us which we can only deplore has, generally through no merit of ours, perished. The strange thing about Kipling is that the self called Beetle which one would have thought increasing age and the experience of life would have caused to disintegrate, remained alive in all its strength almost to his dying day.

As a child at Bombay Kipling had spoken Hindustani with his ayah and the servants as his native language and in *Something of Myself* he has told that when he was taken to see his parents he translated what he had to say into broken English. It may be supposed that on his return to India he quickly recovered his old knowledge of the language. In the same book he has related in terms that couldn't be bettered how at Lahore he got the material which so soon afterwards he was to make effective use of. As a reporter 'I described openings of big bridges and such-like, which meant a night to two with the engineers; floods on railways—more nights in the wet with wretched heads of repair gangs; village festivals and consequent outbreaks of cholera or smallpox; communal riots under the shadow of the Mosque of Wazir Khan, where the patient waiting troops lay in timber-yards or side-alleys till the order came to go in and hit the crowds on the feet with the gunbutt, and the growling, flaring, creed-drunk city would be brought to hand without effusion of blood' . . . Often at night 'I would wander till dawn in all manner of odd places—liquor-shops, gambling- and opium-dens, which are not a bit mysterious, wayside entertainments such as puppet-shows, native dances; or in and about the narrow gullies under the Mosque of Wazir Khan for the sheer sake of looking . . . And there were "wet" nights too at the Club or one Mess, when a tableful of boys, half crazed with discomfort, but with just sense enough to stick to beer and bones which seldom betray, tried to rejoice and somehow succeeded . . .

I got to meet the soldiery of those days in visits to Fort Lahore and, in a less degree, at Mian Mir Cantonments. . . . Having no position to consider, and my trade enforcing it, I could move at will in the fourth dimension. I came to realize the bare horrors of the private's life, and the unnecessary torments he endured on account of the Christian doctrine that lays it down that "the wages of sin is death." '

I have included in this selection two stories in which figure the three privates, Mulvaney, Learoyd and Ortheris. They have been immensely popular. I think they have the disadvantage for most readers that they are written in the peculiar dialect of the speakers. It is no easy matter to decide how far an author should go in this direction. Manifestly it would be absurd to make men like Mulvaney and Ortheris deliver themselves in the cultured language of a don at King's, but to make them speak consistently in dialect may well make a narrative tedious. Perhaps the best plan is to use the turns of phrase, the grammar and the vocabulary of the persons concerned, but to reproduce peculiarities of pronunciation so sparingly as not to incommode the reader. That was not, however, Kipling's way. He reproduced the accents of his three soldiers phonetically. No one has found fault with Learoyd's Yorkshire, which was corrected by Kipling's father, himself a Yorkshireman; but critics have claimed that neither Mulvaney's Irish nor Ortheris's cockney was real. Kipling was a master of description and could relate incident brilliantly, but it does not seem to me that his dialogue was always plausible. He put into the mouth of Ortheris expressions he could never have used and one may well ask oneself how on earth he came by a quotation from Macaulay's *Lays of Ancient Rome*. I cannot believe that a well-bred woman such as the Brushwood Boy's mother is supposed to be would speak to him of his father as 'the pater'. Sometimes the language used by the officers and officials in India is unconvincingly hearty. To my mind Kipling's dialogue is only beyond reproach when he is translating into measured, dignified English the speech of Indians. The reader will remember that as a child talking with his parents he had to translate what he had to say from Hindustani into English: it may be that that was the form of speech that came most naturally to him.

In 1887 Kipling, after five years as sub-editor of *The Civil and Military Gazette*, was sent to Allahabad, several hundred miles to the south, to work on the much more important sister-paper, *The Pioneer*. The proprietors were starting a weekly edition for home, and he was given the editorship. An entire page was devoted to fiction. The *Plain Tales from the Hills* had been restricted to twelve hundred words, but now he was allotted sufficient space to write stories up to five thousand. He wrote 'soldier tales, Indian tales, and tales of the opposite sex'. Among them were such powerful but gruesome stories as *The Mark of the Beast* and *The Return of Imray*.

The stories Kipling wrote during this period were published in six paper-covered volumes in Wheeler's Indian Railway Library, and with the money he thus earned and a commission to write travel sketches he left India for England 'by way of the Far East and the United States'. This was in 1889. He had spent seven years in India. His stories had become known in England and when he arrived in London, still a very young man, he found editors eager to accept whatever he wrote. He settled down in Villiers Street, Strand. The stories he produced there are of the highest quality, a quality which later he often achieved but never surpassed. Among them are *On Greenhow Hill*, *The Courting of Dinah Shadd*, *The Man Who Was*, *Without Benefit of Clergy* and *At the End of the Passage*. It looks as though the new surroundings in which he found himself brought into greater vividness his recollections of India. That is a likely enough thing to happen. When an author is living in the scene of his story, perhaps among the people who have suggested the characters of his invention, he may well find himself bewildered by the mass of his impressions. He cannot see the wood for the trees.

But absence will erase from his memory redundant details and inessential facts. He will get then a bird's-eye view, as it were, of his subject and so, with less material to embarrass him, can get the form into his story which completes it.

It was then too that he wrote the tale which he called '*The Finest Story in the World.*' It is interesting because he dealt in it, for the first time, I think, with metempsychosis. It was natural that the theme should interest him, for the belief in it is ingrained in the Hindu sensibility. It is as little a matter of doubt to the people of India as were the Virgin Birth of Christ and the Resurrection to the Christians of the thirteenth century. No one can have travelled in India without discovering how deep-rooted the belief is not only among the uneducated, but among men of culture and of experience in world affairs. One hears in conversation, or reads in the papers, of men who claim to remember something of their past lives. In this story Kipling has dealt with it with great imaginative power. He returned to it in a story which is less well-known called '*Wireless.*' In this he made effective use of what was then a new toy for the scientifically minded amateur to persuade the reader of the possibility that the chemist's assistant of his tale, dying of tuberculosis, might under the effect of a drug recall that past life of his in which he was John Keats. To anyone who has stood in the little room in Rome overlooking the steps that lead down to the Piazza di Spagna and seen the drawing Joseph Severn made of the emaciated, beautiful head of the dead poet, Kipling's story is wonderfully pathetic. It is thrilling to watch the dying chemist's assistant, in love too, worrying out in a trancelike state, lines that Keats wrote in *The Eve of St Agnes*. It is a lovely story admirably told.

Six years later Kipling, in the entrancing tale *The Tomb of his Ancestors*, to which I have already referred, took up once more the theme of metempsychosis, and this time in such a way as not to outrage probability. It is the Bhils, the mountain tribes among whom the story is set, who believe that the young subaltern, its hero, is a reincarnation of his grandfather who spent many years in their midst and whose memory they still revere. Kipling never succeeded better in creating that indefinable quality which for want of a better word we call atmosphere.

After spending two years in London, years of hard work, Kipling's health broke down, and he very sensibly decided to take the rest of a long journey. He returned to England to be married and with his bride started off on a tour of the world, but financial difficulties obliged him to cut it short, and he settled down in Vermont where his wife's family had long been established. This was in the summer of 1892. He stayed there off and on till 1896. During those four years he wrote a number of stories many of which were of a quality which only he could reach. It was then that he wrote *In the Rukh* in which Mowgli makes his first appearance. It was a propitious inspiration; for from it sprang the two *Jungle Books* in which, to my mind, his great and varied gifts found their most brilliant expression. They show his wonderful talent for telling a story, they have a delicate humour and they are romantic and plausible. The device of making animals talk is as old as Aesop's fables, and for all I know much older, and La Fontaine, as we know, employed it with charm and wit, but I think no one has performed the difficult feat of persuading the reader that it is as natural for animals to speak as for human beings more triumphantly than Kipling has done in *The Jungle Books*. He had used the same device in the story called *A Walking Delegate* in which horses indulge in political discussion, but there is in the story an obviously didactic element which prevents it from being successful.

It was during these fertile years that Kipling wrote *The Brush-wood Boy*, a story which has deeply impressed so many people that, though it is not one of my favourites, I have thought it well to print it in this selection. He availed himself in this of a notion which has attracted writers of fiction both before and after him, the notion, namely, of two persons systematically dreaming the same dreams.

The difficulty of it lies in making the dreams interesting. We listen restlessly when someone at the breakfast table insists on telling us of the dream he had during the night, and a dream described on paper is apt to arouse in us the same impatience. Kipling had before done the same sort of thing, though on a smaller scale, in *The Bridge-Builders*. There I think he made a mistake. He had a good story to tell. It is about a flood that suddenly rushes down on a bridge over the Ganges which, after three years of strenuous labour, is on the point of completion. There is doubt in the minds of the two white men in charge of the operations whether three of the spans, still unfinished, will stand the strain, and they fear that if the stone-boats go adrift the girders will be damaged. They have received by telegram warning that the flood is on the way, and with their army of workmen spend an agonized night doing what they can to strengthen the weak places. All this is described with force and the telling detail of which Kipling was a master. The bridge stands the strain and all is well. That is all. It may be that Kipling thought it wasn't enough. Findlayson, the chief engineer, has been too anxious and too fully occupied to bother about eating anything and by the second night is all in. His lascar aide persuades him to swallow some opium pills. Then news comes that a wire hawser has snapped and the stone-boats are loose. Findlayson and the lascar rush down to the bank and get into one of the stone-boats in the hope of preventing them from doing irreparable injury. The pair are swept down the river and landed half-drowned on an island. Exhausted and doped they fall asleep and dream the same dream in which they see the Hindu Gods in animal form, Ganesh the elephant, Hanuman the ape and finally Krishna himself, and hear them talk. When the two wake in the morning they are rescued. But the double dream is needless and because the conversation of the Gods is needless too it is tedious.

In *The Brushwood Boy* the identical dreams are an essential element in the story. It is here for the reader to read and I hope he will agree with me that Kipling has described these dreams with felicity. They are strange, romantic, frightening and mysterious. The long series of dreams which these two people have shared from their childhood seems, though you don't quite know why, so significant of something of high import that it is somewhat of a disappointment that such amazing occurences should result in no more than 'boy meets girl'. It is of course the same difficulty that confronts the reader of the first part of Goethe's *Faust*. It seems hardly worth while for Faust to have bartered his soul to see Mephistopheles do conjuring tricks in a wine-cellar and to effect the seduction of a lowly maid. I find it difficult to look upon *The Brushwood Boy* as one of Kipling's best stories. The persons concerned in it are really too good to be true. The Brushwood Boy is heir to a fine estate. He is idolized by his parents, by the keeper who taught him to shoot, by the servants, by the tenants. He is a good shot, a good rider, a hard worker, a brave soldier adored by his men, and after a battle on the North-West Frontier is awarded a D.S.O. and becomes the youngest major in the British army. He is clever, sober and chaste. He is perfect and incredible. But though I carp I cannot deny that it remains a good and moving story admirably told. One must look upon it not as a tale that has any relation to real life, but as much of a fairy story as *The Sleeping Beauty* or *Cinderella*.

It was on his short periods of leave that Kipling came to know that Anglo-Indian society which he wrote about in *Plain Tales from the Hills*, but his experiences as a reporter, so well set forth in the passage I quoted earlier in this essay, surely made it plain to him that in those little stories he had described but one aspect of Anglo-Indian life. What he saw on his various assignments deeply impressed him. I have already spoken of *The Bridge-Builders* with its fine account of those men who on little pay, with small chance of recognition, gave their youth, their strength, their health to do to the best of their ability the job it was their business to do. In the unfortunately named *William the Conqueror* Kipling has written a tale in which he shows how two or three ordinary, rather commonplace men, and a woman, the William of the story, fought a disastrous famine all through the hot weather and saved a horde of children from dying of starvation. It is a tale of selffless, stubborn tenacity soberly narrated. In these two stories and in several more, Kipling has told of the obscure men and women who devoted their lives to the service of India. They made many mistakes, for they were but human. Many were stupid. Many were hidebound with prejudice. Many were unimaginative. They kept the peace. They administered justice. They built the roads, the bridges, the railways. They fought famine, flood and pestilence. They treated the sick. It remains to be seen whether those who have succeeded them, not in high place, but in those modest situations in the hands of whose occupants the lot of the common man depends will make as good a job of it as they did.

William the Conqueror is not only the story of a famine; it is a love story as well. I have mentioned the fact that Kipling seems to have shied away, like an unbroken colt, from any treatment of sex. In the Mulvaney stories he makes casual reference to the amours of the soldiery and in *Something of Myself* he has an indignant passage in which he remarks on the stupid and criminal folly of the authorities who counted it impious 'that bazaar prostitutes should be inspected; or that the men should be taught elementary precautions in their dealings with them. This official virtue cost our army of India nine thousand expensive white men a year always laid up from venereal disease.' But he is concerned then not with love, but with an instinct of normal man that demands its satisfaction. I can only remember two stories in which Kipling has attempted (successfully) to represent passion. One is *'Love-o' Women'*, which for this reason I have inserted in this book. It is a terrible, perhaps brutal story, but it is finely and vigorously told, and the end, mysterious and left unexplained though it be, is powerful. Critics have found fault with this end. Matisse once showed a picture of his to a visitor who exclaimed: 'I've never seen a woman like that', to which he replied: 'It isn't a woman, madam, it's a picture.' If the painter is permitted certain distortions to achieve the effect he is aiming at, there can be no reason why the writer of fiction should not accord himself the same freedom. Probability is not something settled once for all; it is what you can get your readers to accept as such. Kipling was not writing an official report, he was writing a story. It was his right to make it dramatically effective, if that is what he wanted to do, and if the gentleman-ranker of the story might not have said in real life to the woman he had seduced and ruined the words Kipling has put into his mouth, that is no matter. It is plausible and the reader is moved, as Kipling intended him to be.

The other story in which Kipling has depicted genuine passion is *Without Benefit of Clergy*. It is a beautiful and pathetic tale. If I had to choose for an anthology the best story Kipling ever wrote, this I believe is the one I would choose. Other stories are more characteristic, *The Head of the District*, for instance, but in this one he has come as near as the medium allows to what the story-teller aims at, but can hardly hope to achieve – perfection.

I have been led to write the above on account of the love scene which gives *William the Conqueror* its happy ending. It is strangely embarrassing. The two persons concerned are in love with one another; that is made clear; but there is nothing of ecstasy in their love, it is a rather humdrum affair, with already a kind of domestic quality about it. They are two very nice sensible people who will make a good job of married life. The love scene is adolescent. You would expect a schoolboy home for the holidays to talk like that with the local doctor's young daughter, not two grown, efficient persons who have just gone through a harrowing and dangerous experience.

As a rough generalization I would suggest that an author reaches the height of his powers when he is between thirty-five and forty.

It takes him till then to learn what Kipling made a point of calling his trade. Till then his work is immature, tentative and experimental. By profiting by past mistakes, by the mere process of living, which brings him experience and a knowledge of human nature, by discovering his own limitations and learning what subjects he is competent to deal with and how best to deal with them, he acquires command over his medium. He is in possession of such talent as he has. He will produce the best work he is capable of for perhaps fifteen years, for twenty if he is lucky, and then his powers gradually dwindle. He loses the vigour of imagination which he had in his prime. He has given all he had to give. He will go on writing, for writing is a habit easy to contract, but hard to break, but what he writes will be only an increasingly pale reminder of what he wrote at his prime.

It was different with Kipling. He was immensely precocious. He was in full possession of his powers almost from the very beginning. Some of the stories in *Plain Tales from the Hills* are so trivial that later in life he would probably not have thought them worth writing, but they are told clearly, vividly and effectively. Technically there is no fault to find with them. Such faults as they have are owing to the callowness of his youth and not to his want of skill. And when, only just out of his teens, he was transferred to Allahabad and was able to express himself at greater length he wrote a series of tales which can justly be described as masterly. On his first arrival in London, the editor of *Macmillan's Magazine*, whom he had gone to see, asked him how old he was. It is no wonder that when Kipling told him that in a few months he would be twenty-four, he cried 'My God!' His accomplishment by then was truly amazing.

But all things have to be paid for in this world. By the end of the century, that is by the time Kipling was thirty-five, he had written his best stories. I do not mean that after that he wrote bad stories, he couldn't have done that if he'd tried, they were well enough in their way, but they lacked the magic with which the early Indian stories had been infused. It was only when, returning in fancy to the scene of his early life in India, he wrote *Kim*, that he regained it. *Kim* is his masterpiece. It must seem strange at first that Kipling after leaving Allahabad never went back to India except for a short visit to his parents at Lahore. After all it was his Indian stories that had brought him his immense fame. He himself called it notoriety, but it was fame. I can only suppose that he felt India had given him all the subjects he could deal with. Once, after he had spent a period in the West Indies he sent me a message to say that I should do well to go there, for there were plenty of stories to be written about the people of the islands, but they were not the sort of stories he could write. He must have felt that there were plenty of stories in India besides those he had written, but that they too were not the sort of stories he could write. For him the vein was worked out.

The Boer War came to pass and Kipling went to South Africa. In India he had conceived a boyish, touching if rather absurd admiration for the officers with whom he was brought in contact. But these gallant gentlemen who cut so fine a figure on the polo field, at gymkhanas, dances and picnics, showed a horrifying incapacity when it came to waging a war very different from the punitive expeditions they had conducted on the North-West Frontier. Officers and men were as brave as he had always thought them, but they were ill led. He surveyed the muddle of that unhappy war with consternation. Did he see that this was the first rent in that great fabric, the British Empire, which was his pride and to the awareness of which he had done so much, in verse and prose, to awaken his fellow-subjects? He wrote two stories, *The Captive* and *The Way that He Took*, in which he attacked the inefficiency of the authorities at home and the incompetence of the officers in command. They are good stories, and if I have not given them a place in this volume it is because of the strong element of propaganda in them and because like all stories that have a topical interest the passage of time has deprived them of significance.

I should warn the reader that my opinion that Kipling's best stories are those of which the scene is laid in India is by no means shared by eminent critics. They think those Kipling wrote in what they call his third period show a depth, an insight and a compassion of which they deplore the lack in his Indian tales. For them the height of his achievement is to be found in such stories as *An Habitation Enforced*, *A Madonna of the Trenches*, *The Wish House* and *Friendly Brook*. *An Habitation Enforced* is a charming story, but surely rather obvious; and though the other three are good enough they do not seem to me remarkable. It did not need an author of Kipling's great gifts to write them. *Just So Stories*, *Puck of Pook's Hill* and *Rewards and Fairies* are children's books and their worth must be judged by the pleasure they afforded children. This *Just So Stories* must have done. One can almost hear the squeals of laughter with which they listened to the story of how the elephant got his trunk. In the two other books Puck appears to a little boy and a little girl and produces for their instruction various characters by means of whom they may gain an elementary and romantic acquaintance with English history. I don't think this was a happy device. The stories are of course well contrived; I like best *On the Great Wall*, in which Parnesius, the Roman legionary, appears, but I should have liked it better if it had been a straightforward reconstruction of an episode in the Roman occupation of Britain.

The only story Kipling wrote after he settled down in England that I would on no account leave out of this selection is '*They*'. (In reading it you must keep in mind that his use of the House Beautiful for the country house in which the events he relates take place, reminding one of Ye Olde Tea-Shoppe and horrors of the same sort, had not been made obnoxious by the vulgar purveyors of whimsy and the pretty-pretty.) '*They*' is a fine and deeply moving effort of the imagination. In 1899 Kipling went with his wife and children to New York, and he and his elder daughter caught colds which turned into pneumonia. Those of us who are old enough can remember the world-wide concern when the cables told us that Kipling lay at death's door. He recovered, but his daughter died. It cannot be doubted that 'They' was inspired by his enduring grief at her loss. Heine said: 'Out of my great griefs I make these little songs.' Kipling wrote an exquisite story. Some people have found it obscure and others sentimental. One of the hazards that confront the writer of fiction is the danger of slipping from sentiment into sentimentality. The distinction between the two is fine. It may be that sentimentality is merely sentiment that you don't happen to like. Kipling had the gift of drawing tears, but sometimes, in his stories not for children, but about children, they are tears you resent, for the emotion that draws them is mawkish. There is nothing obscure in 'They' and to my mind nothing sentimental.

Kipling was deeply interested in the invention and discoveries which were then transforming our civilization. The reader will remember what effective use he made of wireless in the story of that name. He was fascinated by machines and when he was fascinated by a subject he wrote stories about it. He took a great deal of trouble to get his facts right, and if sometimes he made mistakes, as all authors do, the facts were so unfamiliar to most readers that they did not know. He indulged in technical details for their own sake, not to show off, since though argumentative and self-opinionated as a man, he was modest and unassuming as an author, but for the fun of it. He was like a concert pianist rejoicing in the brilliant ease of his execution who chooses a piece not because of its musical value, but because it gives him an opportunity to exercise his special gift. In one of his stories Kipling says that he had to interrupt the narrator over and over again to ask him to explain his technical terms. The reader of these stories, and he wrote a number of them, unable to do this, remains perplexed.

They would be more readable if their author had been less meticulous. In '*Their Lawful Occasions*', for instance, I surmise that only a naval officer could fully understand what goes on, and I am quite prepared to believe that *he* would find it a jolly good yarn. *.007* is a story about a locomotive, *The Ship that Found Herself*, a story about an ocean tramp; I think you would have to be respectively an engine-driver and a ship-builder to read them with comprehension. In *The Jungle Books*, and indeed in *The Maltese Cat*, Kipling made the various animals concerned talk in a highly convincing manner; he used the same device in the locomotive numbered *.007* and in the ship named *Dimbula*. I do not think with advantage. I cannot believe that the ordinary reader knows (or cares) what a garboard strake is, or a bilge-stringer, a high-pressure cylinder or a web-frame.

These stories show another side of Kipling's varied talent, but I have not thought it necessary to include any of them in this selection. The object of fiction (from the reader's standpoint from which the author's may often be very different) is entertainment; and as such to my mind their value is small.

I have been more doubtful about those stories concerned with practical joking, ragging, and drunkenness which he wrote from time to time. There was a Rabelaisian streak in him which the hypocrisy of the times, with its deliberate turning away from what are known as the facts of life, constrained him to express in the description of horseplay and inebriation. In *Something of Myself* he tells how he showed a story about the 'opposite sex' to his mother, who 'abolished it' and wrote to him: 'Never you do that again.' From the context one may conclude that it dealt with adultery. Whether you find drunkenness amusing depends, I suppose, on your personal idiosyncrasies. It has been my ill-fortune to live much among drunkards, and for my part I have found them boring at their best and disgusting at their worst. But it is evident that this feeling of mine is rare. That stories dealing

with drunkards have a strong allure is shown by the popularity of
Brugglesmith, a crapulous ruffian, and of Pyecroft, a sottish petty
officer, who amused Kipling so much that he wrote several tales
about him. Practical joking, till the very recent past, seems to have
had an appeal that was universal. Spanish literature of the Golden
Age is full of it and everyone remembers the cruel practical jokes
that were played on Don Quixote. In the Victorian Age it was
still thought funny and from a recently published book we may
learn that it was practised with delight in the highest circles. Here
again it depends on your temperament whether it amuses you or
whether it doesn't. I must confess that I read Kipling's stories which
deal with this subject with discomfort. And the hilarity which
overcomes the perpetrators of the exploit grates upon me; they
are not content with laughing at the humiliation of their victim;
they lean against one another helpless with laughter, they roll
off their chairs, they collapse shrieking, they claw the carpet; and
in one story the narrator takes a room at an inn so that he may have
his laugh out. There is only one of these tales that I have found frankly
amusing and since I thought it only right to give the reader at
least one example of this kind of story I have printed it in this
volume. It is called *The Village that Voted the Earth Was Flat*. Here
the comedy is rich, the victim deserves his punishment, and his
punishment is severe without being brutal.

I have in this essay only referred casually to Kipling's success.
It was enormous. Nothing like it had been seen since Dickens took
the reading world by storm with *The Pickwick Papers*. Nor did he
have to wait for it. Already in 1890 Henry James was writing to
Stevenson that Kipling, 'the star of the hour', was Stevenson's
nearest rival and Stevenson was writing to Henry James that
Kipling was 'too clever to live'. It looks as though they were both
a trifle taken aback by the appearance of this 'infant monster' as
James called him. They acknowledged his brilliant parts, but with
reservations. 'He amazes me by his precocity and various endow-

ment,' wrote Stevenson. 'But he alarms me by his copiousness and haste.... I was never capable of – and surely never guilty of –such a debauch of production ... I look on, I admire, I rejoice for myself; but in a kind of ambition we all have for our tongue and literature I am wounded.... Certainly Kipling has gifts; the fairy godmothers were all tipsy at his christening: what will he do with them?'

But copiousness is not a defect in a writer; it is a merit. All the greatest authors have had it. Of course not all their production is of value; only the mediocre can sustain a constant level. It is because the great authors wrote a great deal that now and then they produced great works. Kipling was no exception. I don't believe any writer is a good judge of the writing of his contemporaries, for he naturally likes best the sort of thing he does himself. It is difficult for him to appreciate merits that he does not possess. Stevenson and James were not ungenerous men and they recognized Kipling's great abilities, but from what we know of them we can guess how disconcerted they were by the boisterous exuberance and the sentimentality of some of his tales and the brutality and grimness of others.

Of course Kipling had his detractors. The plodding writers who after years of labour had achieved but a modest place in the literary world found it hard to bear that this young man, coming from nowhere, without any of the social graces, should win, apparently with little effort, so spectacular a success; and as we know, they consoled themselves by prophesying (as once before they had of Dickens) that as he had come up like a rocket he would go down like the stick. It was objected to Kipling that he put too much of himself into his stories. But when you come down to brass tacks what else has an author to give you but himself? Sometimes, like Sterne for instance, or Charles Lamb, he gives you himself with a beguiling frankness, it is both the inspiration and the mainstay of his creativity; but even though he tries his best to be objective what he writes is inevitably infused with his ego. You cannot read a dozen pages of *Madame Bovary* without receiving a strong impression of Flaubert's irascible, pessimistic, morbid and self-centred personality. Kipling's critics were wrong to blame him for introducing his personality into his stories. What they meant of course was that they did not like the personality he presented to them; and that is understandable. In his early work he exhibited characteristics which were offensive. You received the impression of a bumptious, arrogant young man, extravagantly cock-sure and knowing; and this necessarily excited the antagonism of his critics. For such an assumption of superiority as these rather unamiable traits indicate affronts one's self-esteem.

Kipling was widely accused of vulgarity: so were Balzac and Dickens; I think only because they dealt with aspects of life that offended persons of refinement. We are tougher now: when we call someone refined we do not think we are paying him a compliment. But one of the most absurd charges brought against him was that his stories were anecdotes, which the critics who made it thought was to condemn him (as they sometimes still do); but if they had troubled to consult the Oxford Dictionary they would have seen that a meaning it gives to the word is: 'The narration of a detached incident, or of a single event, told as being in itself interesting or striking.' That is a perfect definition of a short story. The story of Ruth, the story of the Matron of Ephesus, Boccaccio's story of Federigo degli Alberighi and his falcon are all anecdotes. So are *Boule de Suif*, *La Parure* and *L'Héritage*. An anecdote is the bony structure of a story which gives it form and coherence and which the author clothes with flesh, blood and nerves. No one is obliged to read stories, and if you don't like them unless there is something in them more than a story, there is nothing to do about it. You may not like oysters, no one can blame you for that, but it is unreasonable to condemn them because they don't possess the emotional quality of a beefsteak and kidney pudding. It is equally unreasonable to find fault with a story because it is only a story.

411

That is just what some of Kipling's detractors have done. He was a very talented man, but not a profound thinker – indeed I cannot think of any great novelist who was; he had a consummate gift for telling a certain kind of story and he enjoyed telling it. He was wise enough for the most part to do what he could do best. As he was a sensible man, he was no doubt pleased when people liked his stories and took it with a shrug of the shoulders when they didn't.

Another fault found with him was that he had little power of characterization. I don't think the critics who did this quite understood the place of characterization in a short story. Of course you can write a story with the intention of displaying a character. Flaubert did it in *Un Coeur Simple* and Chekhov in *The Darling*, which Tolstoy thought so well of; though a purist might object that they are not short stories, but potted novels. Kipling was concerned with incident. In a tale so concerned you need only tell enough about the persons who take part in it to bring them to life; you show them at the moment you are occupied with; they are inevitably static. To show the development of character an author needs the passage of time and the elbow-room of a novel. Perhaps the most remarkable character in fiction is Julien Sorel, but how could Stendhal have shown the development of his complicated character in a short story? Now, I suggest that Kipling drew his characters quite firmly enough for his purpose. There is a distinction to be made between 'characters' and character. Mulvaney, Ortheris and Learoyd are 'characters'. It is easy enough to create them. Findlayson in *The Bridge-Builders*, and Scott and William in *William the Conqueror* have character; and to delineate that is much more difficult. It is true that they are very ordinary, commonplace people, but that gives point to the narrative, and surely Kipling was well aware of it. The father and mother of the Brushwood Boy are not, as Kipling thought, 'County', landed gentry living on an ancestral estate, but a nice, worthy couple from Arnold Bennett's *Five Towns* who, after amassing a competence, had settled down in the country. Though lightly sketched, they are alive, recognizable human beings. Mrs Hauksbee was not the fashionable and distinguished creature he thought her, she was a rather second-rate little woman with a very good opinion of herself, but she is far from a lay-figure. We have all met her. Yardley-Orde in *The Head of the District* dies four pages after the story opens, but so sufficiently has Kipling characterized him that anyone could write his life-history, after the pattern of one of Aubrey's *Lives*, with a very fair chance that it would be accurate. I hurry on so that I may not yield to the temptation of writing it here and now to show how easily it could be done.

A distinguished author not long ago told me that he disliked Kipling's style so much that he could not read him. The critics of his own day seem to have found it abrupt, jerky and mannered. One of them said that 'it must be insisted that slang is not strength, nor does the abuse of the full stop ensure crispness.' True. An author uses slang to reproduce conversation accurately and in the course of his narrative to give his prose a conversational air. The chief objection to it is that its vogue is transitory and in a few years it is dated and may even be incomprehensible. Sometimes of course it passes into the language and then gains a literary validity so that not even a purist can object to its use. Kipling wrote in shorter sentences than were at that time usual. That can no longer surprise us, and since the lexicographers tell us that a sentence is a series of words, forming the grammatically complete expression of a single thought, there seems no reason why, when an author has done just this, he should not point the fact with a full stop. He is indeed right to do so. George Moore, no lenient critic of his contemporaries, admired Kipling's style for its sonority and its rhythm. 'Others have written more beautifully, but no one that I can call to mind has written so copiously. . . . He writes with the whole language, with the language of the Bible, and with the language of the street.' Kipling's vocabulary was rich. He chose his words, often very unexpected words, for their colour, their precision, their cadence. He knew what he wanted to say and said it incisively. His prose, with which alone I am concerned, had pace and vigour. Like every other author he had his mannerisms. Some, like his unseemly addiction to biblical phrases, he quickly discarded; others he retained. He continued throughout his life to begin a sentence with a relative. Which was a pity. He continued to make deplorable use of the poetic *ere* when it would have been more natural to say *before*. Once at least he wrote *e'en* for *even*. These are minor points. Kipling has so made his style his own that I don't suppose anyone to-day would care to write like him, even if he could, but I don't see how one can deny that the instrument he constructed was admirably suited to the purpose to which he put it. He seldom indulged in long descriptions, but with his seeing eye and quick perception he was able by means of this instrument to put before the reader with extreme vividness the crowded Indian scene in all its fantastic variety.

If in this essay I have not hesitated to point out what seemed to me Kipling's defects, I hope I have made it plain how great I think were his merits. The short story is not a form of fiction in which the English have on the whole excelled. The English, as their novels show, are inclined to diffuseness. They have never been much interested in form. Succinctness goes against their grain. But the short story demands form. It demands succinctness. Diffuseness kills it. It depends on construction. It does not admit of loose ends. It must be complete in itself. All these qualities you will find in Kipling's stories when he was at his magnificent best, and this, happily for us, he was in story after story. Rudyard Kipling is the only writer of short stories our country has produced who can stand comparison with Guy de Maupassant and Chekhov. He is our greatest story writer. I can't believe he will ever be equalled. I am sure he can never be excelled.

APPENDIX

Traveller's Library

Lady into Fox – David Garnett
Louise – Saki (H. H. Munro)
Tobermory – Saki (H. H. Munro)
Esmé – Saki (H. H. Munro)

POEMS

The Making of a Poet – Roy Campbell
The Serf – Roy Campbell
Horses on Camargue – Roy Campbell
On Some South African Novelists – Roy Campbell
'Blighters' – Siegfried Sassoon
Base Details – Siegfried Sassoon
Idyll – Siegfried Sassoon
Vision – Siegfried Sassoon
Everyone Sang – Siegfried Sassoon
Tarantella – Hilaire Belloc
Lines to a Don – Hilaire Belloc
The Statue – Hilaire Belloc
On a Dead Hostess – Hilaire Belloc
On a Great Election – Hilaire Belloc
Partly from the Greek – Hilaire Belloc
Autumn Evening – Frances Cornford
To a Lady Seen from the Train – Frances Cornford
In the Caves of Auvergne – W. J. Turner
The Bull – Ralph Hodgson
The Mystery – Ralph Hodgson
Leisure – William H. Davies
Sea-Fever – John Masefield
I See His Blood upon the Rose – Joseph Plunkett
The Rio Grande – Sacheverell Sitwell
A Passer-by – Robert Bridges
On a Dead Child – Robert Bridges
Nightingales – Robert Bridges
Renouncement – Alice Meynell
The Hound of Heaven – Francis Thompson
The Kingdom of God (In No Strange Land) – Francis Thompson
The Soldier – Rupert Brooke
The Hill – Rupert Brooke

The Old Vicarage, Granchester – Rupert Brooke
Heaven – Rupert Brooke
An Epitaph – Walter de la Mare
The Three Strangers – Walter de la Mare
The Little Salamander – Walter de la Mare
Arabia – Walter de la Mare
The Listeners – Walter de la Mare
The Golden Journey to Samarkand: Prologue—
    James Elroy Flecker
War Songs of the Saracens – James Elroy Flecker
The Old Ships – James Elroy Flecker
Brumana – James Elroy Flecker
Hyali – James Elroy Flecker
Down by the Salley Gardens – William Butler Yeats
The Lake Isle of Innisfree – William Butler Yeats
When You Are Old – William Butler Yeats
To a Friend Whose Work Has Come to Nothing –
    William Butler Yeats
That the Night Come – William Butler Yeats

NOVELS

The Old Wives' Tale – Arnold Bennett
Trent's Last Case – E. C. Bentley
The Two Drovers – Sir Walter Scott
Rip Van Winkle – Washington Irving
The Stout Gentleman – Washington Irving
La Grande Bretêche – Honoré de Balzac
The Gray Champion – Nathaniel Hawthorne
The Crimson Curtain – Jules Barbey d'Aurevilly
The Gold-Bug – Edgar Allan Poe
A Simple Heart – Gustave Flaubert
Krambambuli – Marie von Ebner-Eschenbach
The Outcasts of Poker Flat – Francis Bret Harte
Olympe and Henriette – Villiers de l'Isle Adam
The Three Strangers – Thomas Hardy
The Jolly Corner – Henry James
The Procurator of Judaea – Anatole France
Youth – Karl Emil Franzos

Markheim – Robert Louis Stevenson
The Necklace – Guy de Maupassant
The Legacy – Guy de Maupassant
Useless Mouths – Octave Mirbeau
The Happy Prince – Oscar Wilde
The Adventure of the Bruce-Partington Plans –
   A. Conan Doyle
Typhoon – Joseph Conrad
The Fate of the Baron – Arthur Schnitzler
The Whirligig of Life – O. Henry
Without Visible Means – Arthur Morrison
The Stricken Doe – Pierre Mille
The Monkey's Paw – W. W. Jacobs
The Coach – Violet Hunt
The Last Visit – Tristan Bernard
The Man Who Would Be King – Rudyard Kipling
Without Benefit of Clergy – Rudyard Kipling
Papago Wedding – Mary Austin
Uncle Franz – Ludwig Thoma
The Door in the Wall – H. G. Wells
An Experiment in Misery – Stephen Crane
Tobermory – Saki
To Build a Fire – Jack London
The Death of Iván Ilých – Leo Tolstoy
The Toupee Artist – Nicolai Lyeskov
Mouzhiks – Anton Chekhov
Twenty-Six and One – Maxim Gorky
Sunstroke – Ivan Bunin
Captain Ribnikov – Alexander Kuprin
Hydromel – Vassili Iretsky
Without Cherry Blossom – Pantaleimon Romanof
In the Town of Berdichev – Vassili Grossman
Hunger – Alexander Neweroff
Romance – Vera Inber
Earth on the Hands – Boris Pilnjak
A Letter – Isaac Babel
The Child – Vsevolod Ivanov
The Customer – Georgy Peskov

The Knives – Valentine Katayev
Pippo Spano – Heinrich Mann
Old Rogaum and His Theresa – Theodore Dreiser
A. V. Laider – Max Beerbohm
The Amulet – Jacob Wasserman
Cavalry Patrol – Hugo von Hofmannsthal
Seeds – Sherwood Anderson
The Other Woman – Sherwood Anderson
Early Sorrow – Thomas Mann
Mr and Mrs Abbey's Difficulties – E. M. Forster
The Invisible Collection – Stefan Zweig
Uncle Fred Flits By – P. G. Wodehouse
In the Last Coach – Leonhard Frank
Counterparts – James Joyce
The Tragedy of Goupil – Louis Pergaud
Odour of the Chrysanthemums – D. H. Lawrence
The Chink – Alexander Arnoux
Haircut – Ring Lardner
Champion – Ring Lardner
A Balaam – Arnold Zweig
Old Man Minick – Edna Ferber
The Golden Beetle – Bruno Frank
The Catalan Night – Paul Morand
Silent Snow, Secret Snow – Conrad Aiken
The Lovely Day – Jacques de Lacretelle
On the Farm – Hans Friedrich Blunck
The Killers – Ernest Hemingway
The Stranger – Katherine Mansfield
The House of Mourning – Franz Werfel
A Start in Life – Ruth Suckow
The Desert Islander – Stella Benson
Big Blonde – Dorothy Parker
Orphant Annie – Thyra Samter Winslow
Nuns at Luncheon – Aldous Huxley
The Rich Boy – F. Scott Fitzgerald
The Imposition – L. A. G. Strong
Turn About – William Faulkner
The Doll – J. Kessel

419

APPENDIX

Reduced – Elizabeth Bowen
María Concepción – Katherine Anne Porter
The Cherry Feast – Ernst Glaeser
No More Trouble for Jedwick – Louis Paul
If You Can't Be Good, Be Cautious – T. O. Beachcroft
The Ball – Irène Némirovsky
Kneel to the Rising Sun – Erskine Caldwell
The Nowaks – Christopher Isherwood
Convalescence – Kay Boyle
The Station – H. E. Bates
Oklahoma Race Riot – Frances W. Prentice

This book, designed by
William B. Taylor
is a production of
Edito-Service S.A., Geneva

Printed in Switzerland